The Limits of

PURE
DEMOCRACY

For Dr. David Smith,
Visionary President
and Friend !
with much respect !
H Lee Cheek
16 August 2007

The Limits of

PURE DEMOCRACY

W. H. Mallock

With a new introduction by
H. Lee Cheek, Jr.

Transaction Publishers
New Brunswick (U.S.A.) and London (U.K.)

Library of Congress Catalog Number: 2007024212
ISBN: 978-0-7658-0846-2
Printed in the United States of America

Library of Congress Cataloging-in-Publication Data

Mallock, W. H. (William Hurrell), 1849-1923.
   The limits of pure democracy / W. H. Mallock.
       p. cm.
   Includes bibliographical references and index.
   ISBN 978-0-7658-0846-2 (acid-free paper)
     1. Democracy. 2. Economic history. 3. Socialism. I. Title.

JC423.M3 2007
321.8—dc22
                                                2007024212

CONTENTS

BOOK I

POLITICAL DEMOCRACY

CHAPTER I

The violation of thought by the use of inaccurate language, as exemplified by Rousseau's fantastic conception of freedom (1–4). Its analogue in current conceptions of democracy (4). Modern definitions of political democracy analysed (4–6). Pure democracy as government by the spontaneous and identical wills of the units of the average mass (6–10). Except, as to certain questions, no spontaneous identity of average wills exists. Classification of political questions with regard to which a pure democratic will is possible and impossible (10–19).

CHAPTER II

A pure democratic will possible as to very simple questions, but as to those only (20–21). As to the composite or complex questions which arise in great and complex states, a general will requires the formative influence of the few (21–22). Examples from English history, Electoral reform, Free Trade, the Right to Work, Scientific implements of war (22–25). The part played by oligarchy in the formation of general wills as to such questions (25–29).

CHAPTER III

The devising of definite measures by the few, which the many are induced to ratify (30–31). The methods by which, in the absence of bribery, the necessary ratification is obtainable (31–32). Concerted agitation, advertisement and concerted exposition. The object of these and the object of bribery the same (33–35). The Referendum as an implement of oligarchy (35–37).

CONTENTS

CHAPTER IV

Every man an oligarch, whatever his rank, who intentionally influences the vote of any other man. Oligarchs of the
tap-room (39–40). Conversation as an implement of oligarchy (39–41). Pure democracy would suppress the public
meeting and all oratory (42). With regard to simple and
fundamental questions, such methods, as a fact, are not resorted to (42–43). The fact that they *are* resorted to, with
regard to complex questions, shows that oligarchic methods
are necessary (43–45).

CHAPTER V

Oligarchy in Trade Union and Labour Parties (46–47).
These parties at first purely democratic, but oligarchy has
inevitably developed in them (46–48). Socialist and Trade
Union leaders inevitably become oligarchs—that is to say,
more than mere employees (48–49). Experience has shown
certain special gifts to be necessary in these leaders. When
once in power, it is difficult to dismiss them (48–49). A
" gregarious inertia " characteristic of the majority in all
revolutionary parties, the energy necessary for leadership
being found in small minorities only (50). The ambitions
of rival oligarchs (51). Causes which solidify the position
of leaders actually in office : examples from Germany and
Italy (51–52). The oligarchs of "The International,"
Marx and Engels (53). Lassalle and Proudhon admit that
purely democratic wills must be merged in those of the
leaders (55–56). Recent admission by socialists to the same
effect (57). Syndicalist oligarchs, such as Labriola (58–59).
Open repudiation of pure democracy by modern revolutionaries (59–61).

CHAPTER VI

Means and a general objective. Impotence of any purely
democratic will to prescribe complex means (62–64). The
conception of a will which is purely democratic as to objectives, though not as to means (64–65). Confusion in this
conception between *will* and *wish* (66). A general wish for
welfare through governmental action (66–67). This is totally
different from a will as to complex means (68). Welfare,
as subserved by government, is a plexus of definite means
to a generally wished-for end (69). The average man wholly
incompetent to define this plexus of means for himself, or

CONTENTS

BOOK II

DEMOCRACY AND TECHNICAL PRODUCTION

CHAPTER I

The conception of Industrial Democracy as a means by which the masses will appropriate all incomes now derived from mere " possession " (78–79). This conception based on a loose idea of what industry is (79). Industry is a technical process affecting material substances (80). Trade Unions and Labour Parties, as such, have nothing to do with the details of this process (81). Industry is simply the application of hand-work, knowledge, and other mental forces to the fashioning and movement of material substances which are given to man by Nature (81–82).

CHAPTER II

Pure democracy in industry means hand-work directed solely by the knowledge and mental powers common to all average men, and excludes all authority or guidance exercised by the exceptional few (83). This doctrine reduced to a quasi-scientific form by Marx (84–85). Summary of the Marxian doctrine that manual labourers are the sole and equal producers of all wealth (85–87). This doctrine true of production in its earlier stages (75–88). But if this be the whole truth, how has production ever increased in efficiency ? (88–89). Attempts made by Marx to answer this question (89–91). Actual, but limited progress of purely democratic hand-work (91). The four causes to which this limited progress has been due (92–96). From the decline of Roman slavery to the end of the eighteenth century, the productivity per head of industrial workers stationary (97). Extraordinary progress since that time. To what has this progress been due ? (97–98).

CONTENTS

CONTENTS

CHAPTER II

CHAPTER III

CONTENTS

CHAPTER IV

CONTENTS

BOOK IV

DISTRIBUTION BY DEMOCRATIC SENTIMENT

CHAPTER I

An interesting and typical exposition of the reasoned content of socialism has been given by Mr. Bernard Shaw (188–189). Analysis of Mr. Shaw's Exposition. Industrial collectivism (which is merely the American Trust-system nationalised) is demanded by, but is not in itself, socialism (189–190). Collectivism (as the Trust-system shows) involves inequality of effort, but socialism differs from the Trust-system in demanding equality of payment, this demand being based on an imperious moral sentiment (190–191). If all are to be paid alike irrespective of what they produce, how will work be secured from the idle ? Mr. Shaw answers : By quasi-military discipline (191). But most men, according to him, will naturally work their hardest for the sake of "being precious to humanity" (191–192). All the highest work, he says, is done without thought of "payment," and thus in a socialist polity, though the idle would be whipped like slaves, the mass of the citizens would perform industrial work with voluntary fervour, and would not require whipping (192–194). Extraordinary confusions of thought involved in this contention shown : firstly, as to the nature of "work" (194–195) ; secondly, as to the nature of "income" (195–197). Other absurdities involved in Mr. Shaw's typical programme (197–200).

CHAPTER II

Reluctance of socialists to test their industrial programme by experiment (201–202). A large number of experiments have nevertheless been made (202). Seven typical examples here reviewed—Religious experiments—Their complete but limited success (202–203). Five of the secularist experiments which lasted for more than five years (203–204). Socialism by solidarity of average sentiment (204–205). Failure of such sentiment apart from eclectic religion (205–207). Owen's experiment, and its final collapse (207–210). Brook Farm (210–211). The Wisconsin and Phalanx (211–213). The North American Phalanx (213–216). Lane's experiment, "New Australia" (217–225) Its collapse, Lane's second experiment, and his utter disappointment (225–226). His emphatic recognition that the requisite sentiment was wanting in even his most devoted followers (227).

CONTENTS

CONTENTS

CHAPTER II

CHAPTER III

CONTENTS

as though he were merely so much "labour" (271–273). Just respect of wage-earners for employers (273). Exaggerated attempts at conciliation which disregard hard facts (274–276). Men, if justly treated in respect of real equalities, do not naturally demand any absolute and fictitious equality (276–277). This is shown by actual popular demands in respect of the Right to Rise (278).

CHAPTER IV

The Right. to Rise, or Equality of Opportunity, one of the main demands of Revolutionary France (279–280). This was due to artificial restrictions of opportunity (280). Equal opportunity the Magna Charta of unequal achievement (280–282). The wages of exceptional skill (282–283). "Democratic education" as a means of getting to "the top of the tree" (283–288). Demands for absolute equality mere protests against artificial inequality (288–289). The elements of truth and justice which have been here set forth as latent in the demands of socialism (289–290).

BOOK VI

THE DATA OF CONTENT

CHAPTER I

Three stages of socialist thought. Modern reversion to sentiment as the basis of a socialist policy, instead of the facts of production, which were the basis of the Marxian doctrine (291–293). This adoption of a psychological, instead of a purely industrial basis, involves an inverted psychology (293). It involves the assumption that interest in others stands first in the scale of motive, whereas it is really derived from an antecedent interest in self (294). No one desires equality, as a fact external to himself, for its own sake (295). When such equality is really desired, it is desired for the sake of certain accidental results, as happens at times in cases of extreme want or danger; otherwise it appeals only to the idle and the jealous (295–297). Even so, it appeals only to individuals, as secretly dissociating themselves from the mass (297). Pure socialist sentiment is a mere psychological mare's nest (297–298). The minimum wage with its adjuncts (as described in the foregoing chapters) is rational, as contrasted

CONTENTS

with socialist demands, because it is based primarily on the self-interest of all (298–301). Summary of conditions here described as the objects of sane reform (302–303). How nearly are these attainable? Certain difficulties in the way of their complete attainment must be considered (303–304).

CHAPTER II

The objective difficulties most apparent in relation to the minimum wage (305). The ideal minimum wage, as here described, is essentially contingent on work (306). Unearned income possible for a few only. No conceivable polity could satisfy all the idle (306). Security of work completely attainable in some countries, but not in others (306–310). Causes which rendered unqualified security of occupation impossible in certain countries (310–311). But even in such countries a reasonable security may be approached (311–312). Yet apart from objective difficulties in the way of ideal conditions there are other difficulties which are subjective (312).

CHAPTER III

Popular discontent often due to ideas as distinct from experienced facts (313). A just minimum must not only be just; the recipients must know it to be so (314). Further, even should the recipients know that a certain minimum is the amplest possible, the imagination of each might present it to him as insufficient for himself (314–315). The indiscriminate encouragement of personal ambition as a stimulus to discontent with even the best conditions possible for any large number of men (316). Two kinds of education necessary to correct discontent which is due to mere ideas (316–317). One is a dissemination of knowledge as to broad statistical facts, the other is a training of the imagination (316–317). Statistical education, its scope (317–318). Immense effect of false statistics, e.g. those of Marx and Henry George. What false statistics can do, substantially correct statistics will tend to undo (318–323). The imagination as a disturbing and protesting influence (323–324). If not artificially inflamed, the imagination tends to accommodate itself to possibilities (324). The inflammatory effect of a falsification of general standards of living: examples (325–326). Striking example of agitators reverting to a natural standard in the case of the Highland peasantry (326–327). A training of the imagination with regard to life taken as a whole (328–329).

CONTENTS

BOOK VII

DEMOCRACY AND THE FINAL LIFE-PROCESS

CHAPTER I

Government, war and industry alike subserve the drama of individual life, or social intercourse (330–331). In all highly civilised states these three subservient activities are oligarchic ; but the final end, namely social intercourse, is democratic (332). Social intercourse for the individual is not a national process, but a group-process, each group being numerically small (332–334). Within the limits of each group social intercourse is democratic (334–335). The inner democratic lives of these social groups are a democracy imposing orders on the oligarchies of subservient effort, and notably on the industrial oligarchy (334–335). The influence of the social democracies on architecture (335–336). The influence of social democracies on the production of all superfluous goods, or "riches" (336). The real substance of income not money but goods, which are bought mainly at shops (337). Difference between Needs and Tastes (337–338). Riches as distinct from bare sufficiencies are goods that minister to Tastes, Tastes indefinitely various (338–339). Democracy in shopping analysed (339–340). Demand in shopping imposes purely democratic orders on the oligarchy of production (340–341). Such democracy much more complete than any democracy possible in complex politics (341). Each customer determines the substance of his real income (342). Examples of how the same wage-income is converted into different real incomes, of which some mean affluence, others poverty (342–344). The real income is the man, so far as material things are concerned (345).

CHAPTER II

Just as politics and industry subserve real income, so does real income subserve mental and moral culture (346–347). The Life of Knowledge, the Life of Art, the Life of Religion (346–347). These lives oligarchic in origin on one side, but essentially democratic on another (348–349). This is specially clear in the case of religion (349–350). Democracy in one sense the final process, but the higher forms of democratic life are only achieved through oligarchy (351). Current ideas which militate against content under the best possible conditions re-examined (352).

CONTENTS

CHAPTER III

Any lot which man can reasonably covet must, by implication, be for himself possible (353). The exceptional man
may reasonably covet more than the man of ordinary
capacity (353–354). If the average reward does not content the ordinary man, his discontent must be due not to
reason, but mere mood or temper (354–355). Striking examples of mere Mood versus Reason (355–356). Methods
by which socialist thinkers endeavour to insinuate moods
which they cannot defend by direct reasoning (356–357).
These methods evade the direct facts of economics. Two
great examples. Practicability of exposing them. False
conception of the State. False interpretation of history
(357–358). Ludicrously false analogy between the State
and an animal organism (358–361). Partial analogy between the two, which is fatal to all socialist suggestion.
The State has no common sensorium (362). The socialist
mood as insinuated by an absurd misinterpretation of history (362–363). Analysis of this misinterpretation which
was formulated by Marx (362–365). The peculiar power
of the few, operative in all civilisations (e. g. those of the
Incas and the Aztecs (365–367). Origin of this paradoxical
power everywhere exercised by the few (367–369). Socialist history represents this power as due everywhere to
accidents. Such a theory absolutely false. It excludes
the main fact which renders history intelligible (367–369).
Nevertheless in socialist history there is one element of
truth (369). In past times the few (mainly representing
military force) have lived on abstractions from national
wealth, not on additions to it (369–370). Difference between the modern industrial oligarchy and other forms of
oligarchy which preceded it (370–371). The wealth of the
scientific employer comes from additions, in which the
employed participate. The participation of the employed
the foundation of stability (371). Participation involves
obedience (371). The root of impracticable discontent is
comprised in the formula of pure democracy, which represents civilisation as a result of the co-operation of equals.
Experience will teach this, if the teaching of reason is
neglected (371–372).

CHAPTER IV

The few being necessary agents in all complex government, in efficient production and in culture, from what is
the power of the few derived ? (373). According to modern

CONTENTS

INTRODUCTION TO THE
TRANSACTION EDITION

To challenge the prevailing social and political orthodoxies of one's time and place often encourages recrimination and eventual neglect. Such has been the fate of William Hurrell Mallock (1849-1923), a seminal thinker of the late Victorian period and a figure who is deserving of greater scholarly attention. Mallock's increasing concern for the diminishing influence of personal restraint and ethical discrimination was at odds with Western society's ennobling of plebiscitary democracy and state control of the means of production. For Mallock, a steady concentration of political and economic power in national governments, increasing social and regional hostilities resulting from the quest for control, and the debasement of democratic rule, were ominous signs of the future that awaited the West.

MALLOCK: HIS LIFE AND TIMES

Born into a privileged family at Cheriton Bishop in Devonshire, England, Mallock was the oldest child of the Reverend William and Margaret Mallock. Both sides of Mallock's family included personages of great influence and intellect, and most of his immediate family were members of the agrarian gentry who were Tories in politics and ultra-High Anglicans as churchmen. In his *Memoirs of Life and Literature*, written in 1920, Mallock gives the only account of his upbringing, contained within a larger study of the social and political world he had inherited.[1] In almost every regard, Mallock accepted and affirmed the aristocratic view of social and political life, and this influence would permeate all of his writings.

Mallock's education began at home, under the private tutelage of the Reverend W. B. Philpot, a student of Matthew Arnold and a close friend of Tennyson. While under Philpot's pedagogical care, Mallock began to question his teacher's bent towards radicalism and innovation, themes the young student would continue to critique for the remainder of his life. In 1869, following in his father's footsteps, he entered Balliol College, Oxford, where he distinguished himself as a writer of some ability. From most accounts, he was not an accomplished student, preferring to write verse and occasionally meet with prominent literary figures, including Swinburne and Browning. Indeed, his writing was his salvation, and his diligent work bore fruit: in 1871, at Oxford, he won the Newdigate Prize for a poem he composed on the Isthmus of Suez.

During this period, Mallock began to create a series of outlines that would eventually become his most famous work, *The New Republic*, which, upon publication in 1877, brought great acclaim to the young writer.[2] A satirical novel, *The New Republic* was Mallock's first attempt to expunge the "disease" of liberalism and religious skepticism from civil discourse.[3] The publication of *The New Republic* provided Mallock with a literary reputation as a critic, and this work would remain his most popular novel, although many more novels would follow. The emphases of *The New Republic*, especially the problem of faith and the nature of truth, would form the first part of Mallock's literary corpus. He would spend the second part of his career as a man of letters addressing the prevailing social and political issues of his age, and *The Limits of Pure Democracy* serves as his last major—and most important—political critique.[4]

Mallock continued to write for various publications, composing a wide variety of works, including poetry, novels, theological works, and political treatises. He was a prolific author who produced over forty books and as many articles during his long career. As a result of his commentaries and the ardent nature of his own beliefs, Mallock also had many detractors, including George Bernard Shaw, J. A. Hobson, and T. H. Huxley. As he advanced in years, the appeal of Roman Catholicism for Mallock became profound, but he never became a convert. He died on April 2, 1923, in Wincanton, Somerset.

MALLOCK ON HUMAN NATURE AND THE MODERN PREDICAMENT

Over time, Mallock became apprehensive about what he perceived to be the decadence of modernity. The very nature of social and political life was being transformed by the perversion of democratic and socialist thought. Mallock feared the tradition that he had inherited was being replaced by a radically different view of human nature that included new, malleable institutional entailments as well. In describing the human predicament in this fashion, Mallock affirmed the Hebraic-Christian conception of human nature, viewing humanity as divided between the higher and lower ethical possibilities, and in need of personal and societal restraint as protection against the impulse of the moment. Mallock's theory of human nature also rejected social contractarian typologies devoted to promoting humankind's inert strength and virtue or ability to survive amidst isolation. Mallock contended that humankind's primary obligations lie in his community and an aristocratic ordering of society. Self-discipline and love of neighbor begin with the individual, and spread to the community, and then to society as a whole. In other words, human nature serves to define the limitations of society and politics for Mallock on one hand, while on the other it presupposes and defends the necessity of a properly constituted community for securing the moral and ethical results concomitant to society's perpetuation.

Mallock's view of society and politics affirmed humanity's situation between the earthly and the transcendent. The implicit role of the transcendent undergirds all of his writing, although his writings do not attempt to affirm a particular Christian worldview. If the fundamental religious tenets of Christianity were accepted, namely, immortality and the necessary vitality of belief, human freedom could be nourished and defended.[5]

Continuing to approach the fundamental questions of the human condition, Mallock undertook a comprehensive and demanding process of examination. Against the prevailing attitudes of most defenders of tradition during this period, Mallock refused to rely upon tradition alone; the practicality of everyday life for Mallock often coincided with the need for contemplation and reflection. Mallock assumed an empirical approach to politics, amassing data of various types, and basing his critiques upon the evidence collected. Amidst a long life, Mallock acknowledged the need for a serious study of the great principles of politics and the moral life. Mallock was a lifelong defender of tradition, claiming that he "unconsciously assumed in effect, if not in so many words, that any revolt or protest against the established order was indeed an impertinence, but was otherwise of not great importance."[6]

MALLOCK AS CRITIC

The Limits of Pure Democracy is a defense of aristocratic political, social, and economic theory and practice. Mallock endorsed a properly constituted notion of popular rule, but the excesses of modern democratic thought were of great concern to him. The limitations of vague language pervaded most discussions about politics and economics, and Mallock feared such a lack of precision would undermine the political and economic order.[7] Without considering the diversity within the community itself, most theories of democracy assessed overall electoral outcome as the only indicator of preference, Mallock argued. Simple majorities were based upon electoral whims—Whitman's "divine average"—a radical majoritarian understanding of participation that eschews all considerations besides the act of voting itself.[8] Such a concept of popular government requires a unitary vision of politics and the state, and Mallock believed J. J. Rousseau and Abraham Lincoln—especially—Lincoln's "barren platitudes" found in his public addresses—were the most dangerous examples of such thinking.[9] Mass or "pure" democracy "reduces the units of influence [people] to their lowest common denominator."[10] In addition, Mallock rejected the argument made by advocates of pure or plebiscitarian democracy, that the apparatus of voting can resolve all conflict, even profound crises where no consensus of opinion exists. Mallock believed the "mechanical" limits of pure democracy were always present, and that simplification of voting procedures or enlarging the franchise did not lead to salutary ends. To truly understand the stronger interests or combinations of interests, and to assume this to be the sense of the community, the aristocratic element within the political order must be integrated with the regime.[11] Resulting from its simplicity and facility of construction, pure democracy possessed a troubling propensity for reporting cumulative electoral outcomes without regard for the natural divisions of authority.

The leveling influence of pure democracy in politics and industry presumes that humankind can participate in governing and decision-making *en masse*, at every available opportunity, and with the necessary leverage to undertake any possible action. Mallock's fundamental criticism of such an understanding of democracy suggests that attaining a true majority under any circumstances is illusory at best, a "phantom objective," and utopian at worst.[12] The simple majority can only function effectively in a political world devoid of geographical and economic divisions and without competing claims upon authority. In fact, Mallock argued that this pure democracy could not sustain authentic popular rule, and was incompatible with a comprehensive appreciation of the concept. Secondly, if popular rule is predicated upon providing the citizenry with an expedient option to initiate whatever they desire, then popular rule itself must no longer be claimed as the primary achievement of modern political life. Individual and communal assertion and preference, after all, are often prominently associated with other political systems, especially modern authoritarian and totalitarian regimes that discourage true popular rule in any concrete form while professing to represent the actual sentiments of an oftentimes amorphous populace. As the twenty-first century commences, Mallock's insights provide a guide for understanding and responding to the crisis of a postmodern internationalism in politics and economics that promotes a vulgarized model of popular rule and corporate decision-making that merely consists of the collection of individual wills and sentiments without regard to the substantial and historical limitations of humankind.

Mallock further argued that the electoral and participatory attributes of genuine popular rule suffer as the result of pure democracy's tendency to identify the majority as whomever votes in a particular election while disregarding the range of responses necessary to adequately canvass the citizenry. Moreover, the leveling theories of political socialism associated with Karl Marx, the Webbs, and George Bernard Shaw, only denigrated the genius of enduring, aristocratic influence on the body politic, weakening the infrastructure in terms of its ability to govern.[13] Finally, Mallock noted, if the spirit of restraint that is so essential to the English constitutional and political tradition suffers a devaluation, the future prospects for the regime are diminished.

Restraint—societal and personal—encourages a tenor of resiliency within the political and economic order by imposing some limitations upon a temporally elected majority's ability to assert sovereign authority. Imbued with societal and personal restraint, this type of government and political economy also guards against the impulse of the moment controlling its decision-making, while developing political and economic institutions that mirror those qualities premised upon restraint. It is precisely the inculcation of these habits into social, political, and economic structures that exemplified Mallock's worldview.

ENDURING LESSONS

In *The Limits of Pure Democracy*, Mallock successfully developed a science of conservatism based upon an affirmation of personal restraint, aristocratic rule, and market economics.[14] He attracted a wide array of critics and supporters from diverse perspectives. The epigones of his detractors remain consistent in their criticisms.[15] The defenders of Mallock's work have also recently experienced a resurgence of scholarly activity, which proves the continuing relevance of his perceptive insights for contemporary situations.[16]

For Mallock, pure democracy was a practical and theoretical impossibility. To resolve the dilemmas facing the West, he urged systematic research and the rejection of simplistic responses, such as the "crude puerilities" proposed by Marx and others.[17] Published in the assumed heyday of plebiscitarian democracy in 1918, at the end of World War I, combined with Britain's approval of the Representation Act that enfranchised women, it is possible to dismiss the profound insights offered by Mallock in *The Limits of Pure Democracy*. But to neglect Mallock's vital re-articulation of popular rule, and his stress on the need for ethical-political restraint in all its modes, is to also diminish the prospect of recovering a humane social order in an age of increased social fragmentation. To the end, Mallock remained hopeful for a regeneration of the spirit and character of authentic democratic life.

H. Lee Cheek, Jr.

NOTES

1.   W. H. Mallock, *Memoirs of Life and Literature* (New York and London: Harper and Brothers, 1920). For studies of Mallock's early life, see Douglas P. Brown's "The Formation of the Thought of a Young English Conservative: W. H. Mallock and the Contest for Cultural and

Socio-Economic Authority, 1849-1884 (Ph.D. dissertation, University of Missouri, 2004); Russell R. Gartner, "William Hurrell Mallock: An Intellectual Biography" (Ph.D. dissertation, City University of New York, 1979); Russell Kirk, The *Conservative Mind: From Burke to Eliot* (Washington, D.C.: Regnery, 1995); William O. Reichert, "The Conservative Mind of William Hurrell Mallock" (Ph.D. dissertation, University of Minnesota, 1956); and J. N. Peters, "William Hurrell Mallock," in H. C. G. Matthew and Brian Harrison, eds., *Oxford Dictionary of National Biography*, Vol. 36 (Oxford: Oxford University Press, 2004), pp. 337-338.

2.   W. H. Mallock, *The New Republic: Culture, Faith, and Philosophy in a English Country House*, intro. John Lucas (Leicester: Leicester University Press, 1975).

3.   *Memoirs*, Ibid., p. 89.

4.   Mallock's other seminal work of political analysis is his *A Critical Examination of Socialism* (New York and London: Harper and Brothers, 1907; reprint, Transaction Publishers, 1989).

5.   See Gartner, Ibid., pp. 70-71.

6.   *Memoirs*, Ibid., 251-251.

7.   W. H. Mallock, *The Limits of Pure Democracy* (New Brunswick and London: Transaction Publishers, 2007), p. 1 [hereafter cited as *Limits*].

8.   *Limits*, Ibid., pp. 10-11.

9.   *Limits*, Ibid., p. 7.

10.   *Limits*, Ibid., p. 10.

11.   *Limits*, Ibid., p. 59.

12.   *Limits*, Ibid., p. 72.

13.   *Limits*, Ibid, p. 108.

14.   *Limits*, Ibid., p. 286-287.

15.   For a thoughtful example of the recent reawakening of interest in the debates between Mallock and those he criticized, with special attention to Henry George, see Roy Douglas, "Mallock and the 'Most Elaborate Answer,'" *American Journal of Economics and Sociology*, Volume 62, Number 5 (November 2003), pp. 117-136. Mallock was also interpreted on occasion as complementing social and political causes that may not have been in accord with his own views. The efforts of Alan Ian Percy, the eighth Duke of Northumberland, in republishing an abridged version of *The Limits of Democracy* after Mallock's death (*Democracy* [Chapman and Hall, 1924]), should be viewed in this light.

16.   See Brown, Ibid., and J. N. Peters, "Anti-Socialism in British Politics, 1900-1922 (D.Phil. dissertation, University of Oxford, 2002). In terms of Mallock's more sustained criticism of plebiscitarian democracy,

see Claes G. Ryn, *Democracy and the Ethical Life: A Philosophy of Politics and Community*, Second Edition, Expanded (Washington, D.C.: The Catholic University of America Press, 1990); Ryn, *The New Jacobinism: Can Democracy Survive?* (Washington, D.C.: National Humanities Institute, 1991); Ryn, *America the Virtuous: The Crisis of Democracy and the Quest for Empire* (New Brunswick, N.J.: Transaction Publishers, 2003); and H. Lee Cheek, Jr., *Calhoun and Popular Rule* (Columbia and London: University of Missouri Press, 2001 and 2004).

17.   *Limits*, Ibid., p. 179.

PREFACE

THIS work was planned, and the opening chapters were written, in the earlier months of the year 1914, when the outbreak of a great war was only a remote contingency. Since then, and more especially during the last twelve months, the subject here discussed—namely, the nature and the limits of the power of pure democracy—has acquired day by day a more immediate importance. Indeed, all practical controversies may be said now to turn on it. It thus has happened that the principles here laid down in general terms have, whilst the work was in progress, been illustrated by a series of extraordinarily apt examples. References to many of these have been added in brief footnotes. Four-fifths of the work were, however, substantially complete before the world was astonished by the revolution in Russia; and, though it has been possible to add a few footnotes relating to that movement, such notes are necessarily inadequate to the magnitude and significance of the occasion. The author has therefore thought it desirable to rewrite the concluding pages, and substitute a more detailed mention of recent events in Russia and other countries also, for a final discussion of various general facts and problems, such as the genesis and functions of a leisured class, the possible equalising of certain industrial faculties by education on the one hand, and the probably increasing difference between the highest and the lowest on the other, the increasing pressure of the world-population against the means of subsistence, and the increasing importance of mere mental efficiencies in combating this pressure, etc. The publication of these discussions (growing as they do out of the questions here dealt with) is deferred.

The author desires to record his obligations to the singularly interesting work on oligarchy in revolutionary parties, by Professor Michels of Basle, which was published in England in the year 1915 (see Book I, Chap. I); to Mr. Stewart Graham's account, published some years ago by Mr. Murray, of the socialist experiment in Paraguay known as New Australia (see Book IV, Chap. III); and also to *The Daily Mail*, for the letters published by it from a socialist correspondent in Russia.

Further, the author regrets that it has been impossible to include any reference to certain articles on "Industrial Revolution or Ferment," which were published in *The Times* in October, 1917, and attracted wide attention. The whole of the present work was by that time in the printer's hands.

November, 1917.

THE

LIMITS OF PURE DEMOCRACY

BOOK I

POLITICAL DEMOCRACY

CHAPTER I

THE CONCEPTION OF A GENERAL WILL

ATTENTION has often been called to the astonishing extent to which the thoughts, the passions and the actions of vast multitudes of men have been vitiated or misdirected by the use of ambiguous language. A signal example of this fact may be found in the doctrines of a writer who, more perhaps than any other, was instrumental in inflaming the passions which gave force to the first French Revolution.

"Man is born free, and is everywhere in chains." Such are the opening words of the most celebrated work of Rousseau; and though the philosophy of Rousseau himself is by this time largely obsolete, these words to-day are significant in a sense far deeper, though quite other, than that which their author and his disciples imputed to them. To Rousseau they seemed, and to multitudes they have seemed also, the condensed expression of some liberating and momentous truth. Indeed even to-day, if repeated to audiences of a certain kind, they would doubtless be received with acclamation. But anybody who takes them to pieces in the daylight of common intelligence, will now discover that they either mean nothing at all, or else that they mean something which, even if true, is absolutely without importance. It will be interesting here to submit them to a short but a close analysis.

If there is anything really important in what they profess to enunciate, this obviously is comprised in the first four of them—"Man is born free" : the assertion that he is "everywhere," as an actual fact, "in chains" being nothing more than a rhetorical way of saying that the actions of the human unit are, under existing conditions, artificially hampered by the actions of units other than himself. Hence, when the man who is " free " and the man who is in " chains " are contrasted, the former is understood to differ from the latter in the fact that his way of life and his actions are determined by himself only—by his temperament, his desires, and the extent of his personal faculties—and are not controlled by others in opposition to his own bent.

Such, then, being here the meaning of the word " free," what, let us ask next, is the meaning of the word "man"? Since here it is plainly synonymous with "the individual human being," its meaning may at first sight seem to be clear enough. But this is not so; for, even when defined thus far, it may mean either the human being at any stage of its existence, or it may mean the human adult as distinguished from the child or baby. There is also an ambiguity which attaches itself to the words "is born." If these are taken literally, the only human beings that are born at all are babies; and to say that "man is born free" must mean, and can mean only, that babies are born free; and this again must mean, if it means anything, that so long as they are utterly helpless their condition and actions are determined by no desires, by no intelligence, and by no judgments but their own. The mothers of the human race will hardly endorse this proposition as accurate, nor will anybody claim much value for it as a contribution to social science.

Let us, however, suppose that when "man" is stated to be "born free," the statement is not to be taken in its strict obstetrical sense, but means that, though doubtless born in a natural condition of dependence, he naturally comes to be free by a process of post-natal development. This meaning is at all events less absurd than the other; but let us consider if it is true. If it is true at all, it must be true of actual human beings, either as they exist to-day or as they existed once on the surface of the earth somewhere. That is to say, in the lifetime of every average individual a period normally arrives, or normally did so in the past, when his actions cease or ceased to be " chained," controlled or limited by the actions and existence of anybody except himself; for if no such freedom is exemplified in the history of human nature it would be nonsense to represent such freedom as natural, and it would similarly be nonsense to represent the so-called " chains " as artificial.

Is it, then, possible to discover any portion of the earth's surface where either now or formerly such freedom either is, or ever has been, achieved by the inhabitants as a natural incident of their maturity, and enjoyed by them in peace thenceforwards without any " chains " to limit it ? The answer is that, with a few chance exceptions, a freedom of this kind is altogether imaginary. Just as every baby is bound to have two parents, most adults are bound to mate and to have babies, for unless they did so the human race would end; and as soon as a man sets himself to woo, and keep on terms with a mate, and as soon as children are born for whom he must provide food, his actions begin through the operations not of artifice, but of Nature, to be so " chained " by the existence and the demands of others that they differ inevitably from what they would be if he lived alone. To say that a man is naturally free as soon as he achieves maturity is no truer than to say that he is born free as a baby. Here and there, there may be a free baby; here and there, there may be a free adult; but the only kind of baby that is free is the baby that is left to die, and the only kind of free adult is the solitary on a desert island.

Here, then, in this insane proposition that "man is born free," and in the wide effects produced by it on the thoughts and temper of multitudes, we have a signal example of the condition of moral and mental chaos to which language used ambiguously is able to reduce mankind, causing their demands and arguments to resemble the cries of animals vaguely conscious of anger, disease, or wounds, rather than a rational diagnosis of what is really the matter with them. From this prefatory example we will now pass on to another, for ourselves far more important—namely, the chaos of thought and sentiment, of which the nucleus is the word "Democracy" as used at the present time.

"Democracy" is a word which, whatever it may mean otherwise, is now, with equal frequency, used in several senses, the epithet "political" being used to indicate the one, the epithets "industrial" and "social" being used to indicate the others. The first is of great antiquity, the second and third are modern, and between the first and the latter two, even popular thought draws a fairly clear distinction. The principles, indeed, of industrial and social democracy, by those who project and look forward to their triumph in the near future, are consciously regarded as novel extensions of a principle the action of which is already familiar in the sphere of political government. Hence political democracy is regarded by all parties as democracy in the basic form with which all argument as to its nature and the extent of its application starts; and political government, in respect of its current functions and limitations, means for all parties substantially the same thing. Its objects, whether achieved by restriction, adjudication, or command, are understood to be limited to the maintenance and improvement of such general conditions as will for each citizen, in respect of his private life, guarantee the utmost freedom which consists with the freedom of others, and which the scope of his own talents enables him to utilise for himself.

This general conception of the functions of political governments being assumed, the word "Democracy," if ambiguous in its political sense, is not ambiguous for want of attempts to define it. Professed democrats are constantly addressing themselves to the task of describing Democracy as a peculiar system of government, and defining its peculiar features with an ostentatious semblance of precision; but, the moment their definitions are analysed, all of them, as we shall see presently, fall to pieces, leaving no idea behind them which has any counterpart in the world of actual or of possible fact.

This assertion must not be taken to mean that such persons are attempting to define a nothing. On the contrary, they have all of them at the back of their minds a something so profoundly real that, although it is operative in very various degrees, it is never absent from the government of any human society; and if we want to understand what this something really is, we must set ourselves to consider exactly how far, and why, it differs from those conceptions of it which all current definitions popularise.

Of these current definitions, which naturally exhibit much verbal variety, we will accordingly take three versions, which everybody will recognise as signally, and also as favourably, representative.

Our first shall be the most famous of all—still unrivalled as a talisman for eliciting instant cheers—namely, the definition of a great American statesman : " Democracy means government *of* the people, *for* the people, *by* the people."

Our second shall be that of a more recent authority—an American likewise and a very distinguished publicist, according to whom democracy is a special system of government which ensures that "every man, in virtue of his manhood alone, shall have an equal voice in the affairs of the common country."

Our third definition shall be taken from a contemporary English writer, Mr. Cecil Chesterton, whose style has a ring of homely common sense like Cobbett's, and who, in a volume entitled *The Great State*,[1] has joined certain other reformers in a very temperate attempt to harmonise the dreams of revolutionaries with the bald actualities of life. The definition which Mr. Chesterton contributes to this volume, being given at some length and not in the form of an aphorism, may be briefly summed up thus. Democracy in its essence is government which, by whatever means, is actually in accordance with the general will of the governed; and ideally this result might be realised by an ideal despot. Practically, however, ideal despotisms are impossible; and no less impossible, except in microscopic communities,

[1] A Collection of Essays by English writers of Socialist or semi-Socialist Sympathies, edited by Mr. H. G. Wells.

is government by the extreme alternative—namely, the
voice of all the citizens assembled under the same tree.
The only device, therefore, which is practicable in the
great States of to-day is the election by the many of a
small number of delegates, to whom the mass of the
citizens specify what " the general will " is and whose
sole business is to execute it in accordance with the
terms specified. True democracy exists, so this writer
proceeds, in proportion, and only in proportion, as the
correspondence between the action of the delegates and
the general will is complete.

Let us now consider what these definitions come to,
beginning with the first and most famous of them.

This definition consists of three separate statements :
firstly, that Democracy is government *of* the people;
secondly, that it is government *for* the people; and,
thirdly, that it is government *by* the people. It is
obvious that the first purports to enunciate something
which, however profound, can at once be grasped by
everybody; whilst the second adds something more profound and distinctive still, and that both lead up to the
cumulative profundity of the last. Let us ask, then,
what intelligible meaning can be possibly read into each.

To begin, then, with the first—" government *of* the
people " is a phrase which, with equal verbal propriety,
may be taken as meaning either of two opposite things.
It may mean government exercised over the people by
some power external to them—a meaning like that of
the preacher when he speaks about the government of the
passions; or it may mean government which the people
themselves exercise. It cannot, however, bear the latter
of these two meanings here; for this, without any ambiguity, is reserved for the final statement that democracy
is government *by* the people, which either means this or
nothing. Unless, therefore, it is an instance of pure
tautology, government *of* the people must mean government which is somehow exercised over them; and it
must, in so far as it is realised in any concrete case, mean
government exercised over the people of some particular
country. As to the second statement, its meaning is as
plain as that of the last. Government *for* the people
must mean, in any concrete case, government carried on

in the interest of the people of a particular country, and not in the interest of the people of any other. What, then, is the meaning of the three statements in combination? Its three clauses being combined, this world-famous definition of democracy reduces itself to the following propositions: that Democracy in any concrete case—let us say in the case of France—is government which is exercised over the French people, and not (for example) over the German; that it is exercised by the people of France, not by the people of Germany; and that it is exercised by the people of France with a view to their own advantage.

Now what, with all its solemn crescendo of emphasis, does this definition convey to the mind of any human being which was not in his mind already before he began to listen to it? What is it more than a sequence of superlatively barren platitudes? And yet after all it must, as addressed to millions, be the vehicle of something vital: or it would never be quoted as a watchword, and call forth plaudits, as a spark sets fire to gunpowder. In what part of it, then, does its vital meaning reside? Its vital meaning, its sole distinctive meaning, resides in nothing that the words say by way of an informative proposition. It resides in some sense, altogether unstated, which is presupposed to be already attached to one of them; and that word is the word "people." This presupposed sense is like the skin of a drum, and the so-called definition is nothing but a drum-stick beating a tattoo on it.

This drum-beating, however, does us one service at all events. Though answering no question itself, it loudly calls attention to the question which requires to be answered. What, in detail, for persons calling themselves "democrats," does this one word "people" mean, thereby for them acquiring its peculiar resonance? The "people" of any country cannot, in this connection, be merely a synonym for the inhabitants taken as a whole, as it would be were we classifying peoples according to their racial colours. It must carry with it some implication of a narrower and more incisive kind. It must mean, and it obviously does mean, one or other of two things—either some particular section of the inhabitants, which governs or ought to govern, to the specific *exclusion* of some other section; or else the whole of the inhabitants, regarded as a governing body, to the specific *inclusion* of some section which is, under certain forms of government, excluded.

Now there are doubtless many agitators who, animated by passion or prejudice, would maintain that the former of these two meanings is the correct one, and that government by the people means the specific, and indeed the vindictive, exclusion of all individuals from power who are in any way sufficiently eminent to be distinguishable as a separate class. But no democrats of to-day, who claim to be serious thinkers, commit themselves intentionally to any position such as this. On the contrary, as Mill points out, they profess altogether to repudiate it. The essence of " pure democracy " according to modern conceptions of it is, says Mill, " government by the people as a whole," no individuals being excluded, whether high or low, and none of them having less power, though none may have more, than any others. This conception is expressed with unmistakable clearness in the second of those definitions of Democracy which have here been chosen for examination, and to which we will now turn.

The essence of political democracy, according to this definition of it, is " that every man shall have an equal voice in the affairs of the common country," and that he shall have this equal voice " in virtue of his manhood alone." Here again we have a formula the ultimate purport of which must be looked for in what it implies rather than in what it enunciates; but what it does enunciate is so precise that its full implications can be reached by a use of the simplest logic; and in realising what these are the author himself aids us. The formula in question does not, he says with the utmost emphasis, imply that all men are equal, or even approximately equal in all respects. On the contrary, " the differences between men and men in their capacities for rendering honest service to society are," he says, " immense and incalculable," as may be seen in the spheres of art, philosophic thought, and more particularly the scientific control of industry. In the general business of life, this writer freely admits, it is the influence of exceptional men that makes the world move onwards; but in the sphere of political government—and here we come to what his formula really means—it is the essence of democracy to render all such influence inoperative. The doctrine that the right of each citizen to "an equal voice," or to one vote and only one, "in the government of the common country " is a right which belongs to him "in virtue of his manhood alone," means this, and it cannot mean anything else. It means that the ground on which a citizen is entitled to vote is simply and solely his possession of those residual characteristics which enable an anthropologist to distinguish a man from an erect monkey. It is these residual characteristics that each vote represents, and it is because these characteristics are equal that each vote should have an equal value. Hence, if this definition of political democracy be correct, true democracy must be government determined by faculties which, however unequal actually, have for this special purpose been reduced artificially to their lowest common denominator. It might recognise in a Newton a master of all mathematical science, but it would not allow him, in examining the business books of the nation, to impose on his fellows any conclusions with regard to them which his washerwoman could not arrive at just as well as he by use of the simple arithmetic required for adding up her bills.

Such would be the result, in strict or abstract logic, if democracy means government by all as units of equal influence. But practically, though not in the abstract, the principles of even the strictest doctrinaires lead to a conclusion which is much more moderate than this. All such persons recognise when they talk of equality the existence of some men so low in the scale of intelligence, or by temperament so perverse or slothful, that no State which consisted solely of men like these could thrive. Indeed, Socialists often admit that in dealing with such a residuum a Socialist polity would have to resort to measures not less but more severe than any which are applied to-day. They certainly would never contend that men who, possessing nothing, refuse to produce anything, or that idiots or obstinate drunkards, should be able to influence legislation in accordance with their own ideas. The extremest democrats, however, may without practical inconsistency maintain that such men should have votes nevertheless, for such men being necessarily a small minority, the cumulative power of their votes would, if it stood for anything mischievous, be nullified by the votes of a normally sane majority. Thus the abstract theorem that under a true democracy the power of all citizens would be equal in virtue of their manhood alone is modified by the theorem that the power of each would in practice be contingent on his manhood being of an average or a normal kind. And here we reach what to all intents and purposes is the working conception of democracy which is at the present day implied in the formulæ of doctrinaires, and which floats in the minds of multitudes. It is a conception of a government determined solely by the mass of inconspicuous men—by what Whitman, the poet of democracy, celebrates as "the divine average."

Now, apart from certain facts which will claim our attention presently, this conception is very far from fantastic. For what is it that ideally the average man represents? He represents common honesty, common sense, common neighbourly goodwill, and the common family affections. He is moreover so far from being an abstraction that, if average men in this sense did not form the majority of mankind, no social life of a tolerable kind would be possible. The most towering genius in respect of his household conduct must reason, feel, and comport himself like nine men out of every ten, or else there will be no dealing with him. Why, then, it may be asked, should not political government be determined by men acting as equal units through an exercise of those faculties only in respect of which all average men are equal? Is there anything in the nature of the case to make such a régime impossible?

The answer is that there are two things, the first of which is as follows : We have seen that the most obvious difficulty which, in strict or abstract logic, the theory of democracy suggests—namely, that it reduces the units of influence to their lowest common denominator—is solved by the fact that persons of appreciably subnormal character would have in practice no influence at all. But, though in this way the difficulty which comes from below is eliminated, the corresponding difficulty which comes from above remains. For just as, if the influence of every unit is equal, the judgments of ninety average men would nullify those of any ten men who were subnormal, so likewise would the judgments of the average ninety nullify those of any ten men their superiors in so far as these, by the exercise of superior talents, reached any conclusions which anybody not notably imbecile could not entirely understand, and was not on the point of reaching by his own unaided faculties. Else, if the ninety voters allowed the ten to guide them, ten men would have the votes of ninety other men in their pockets, and the primary principle of pure democracy would be violated.

Here is one of the difficulties involved in the very plausible conception of democracy as government determined by the people alone, the word "people" being taken as meaning the units of the average mass. But below this difficulty lies another of a yet more fundamental kind; and in order to gain a clear idea of what this difficulty is we will now pass on to the third of the three definitions of democracy which have here been cited as typical, and consider it more minutely. All theories of democracy as government by the will of the people involve an assumption, which we have not as yet noted, that if we only exclude the upper and lower minorities the remainder of any population, or the units of the average mass, are certain, with regard to all political questions, to think, feel, and judge in substantially the same way; and this aspect of the question Mr. Chesterton's definition brings into full prominence.

Mr. Chesterton, as we have seen already, sets out with observing that democracy, if conceived in terms of its ultimate object, is simply an absolute harmony, no matter how ensured, between the acts of the executive government and "the general will" of the governed; but he adds that, in practice, so far as large States are concerned, it can be realised only through the agency of elected representatives, to whom the general will is communicated by those electing them, and whose sole busi-

ness is to obey it with abject accuracy.   He admits,
however, that the realisation of such a government is a
feat less simple than it seems.   Elections, he says, may
rest on the widest possible suffrage, and the result may,
as ample experience shows, be not democracy, but a
kind of degraded oligarchy.   For example, he says, " Sir
Josiah Gudge is elected to represent the radical borough
of Slocum," but does Sir Josiah, he asks, represent this
borough in reality ?   Sir Josiah, as a member of Parliament, must, he says, do one of two things or the other.
"He must vote in accordance with the will of the
inhabitants of Slocum, or against it.   If he does the
former, he is acting as a faithful representative.   If he
does the latter, he is not a representative at all, but an
oligarch."   How far, then, is the official conduct of the
typical Sir Josiah of to-day really determined by any
instructions which the inhabitants of Slocum have dictated to him ?   The inhabitants, says Mr. Chesterton,
will really have dictated nothing.   Sir Josiah will have
come to them with a programme of measures already
formulated ; his opponent will have come to them with
another ; and all that the inhabitants will have had any
chance of doing will have been that of making through
the ballot-box a Hobson's choice between them.   Such
a method of government is certainly not democratic ;
and yet, says Mr. Chesterton, it is the method which, as
modern experience shows, has thus far emerged invariably from the most elaborately democratic institutions.
What, then, is the explanation of this practical paradox ?
The explanation, says Mr. Chesterton, is as follows :
Both the primary essentials of pure democracy are
present—the general will, like a great toothed driving-
wheel on the one hand, and the executive body, like a
small wheel, on the other ; but in all democratic constitu-
tions which have thus far been elaborated, the mechanism connecting the two has always been defective in some
way which prevents the former, except on rare occasions,
from imposing its own movements on the latter, thus
leaving those of the former for the most part quite
inoperative.   Hence the only difficulty in the way of
rendering democracy complete is, says Mr. Chesterton,
altogether mechanical.   It has no connection with the

nature of the democratic principle itself; and the task of surmounting it, though not altogether simple, needs only a few experiments and a little ingenuity for its accomplishment.

Mr. Chesterton's explanation of a difficulty thus emphasised by himself is interesting because, by its candour, it exhibits him as looking for it in every place but the right one. The fundamental difficulty does not lie in the fact that the present machinery for realising the general will is defective. It lies in the fact that any general will, which does or which can exist, is something widely different from Mr. Chesterton's own conception of it, and from that which all modern theories of pure democracy postulate. That such is the case will be obvious if we only take the trouble to analyse this conception carefully.

There are three points, then, as to which all democrats are agreed. One is that any will which can be called general is the sum of the judgments of the units of the average mass. The second is that the judgments of each unit shall be represented by a single vote, and thus be of equal influence. The third is that the judgments of each unit shall, as represented by his vote, be freely formed by himself, and shall not, for governmental purposes, have been warped into conformity with the judgments of any other person or group of persons, whether by bribery, intimidation, or any other device of any kind.

This last point deserves special attention; for if large numbers of men, though their votes are recorded by themselves, are really expressing by them the dictated judgments of others, these others will, as has been said already, have, not their own votes only, but to all intents and purposes an indefinite number added to them. That such is the case when the judgments which votes express are changed from what they otherwise would be by brutal and direct bribery, is a fact on which democrats themselves are the first persons to insist; but results essentially similar are, as presently we shall see in greater detail, producible by other methods. An Iago might revenge himself on a faithful Desdemona who had repulsed him, by the simple process of bribing an assassin to murder her; but he might compass the same end by persuading an Othello that she was faithless, and thus inciting the husband to do the deed on his own account. What money would do in the former case, statement would do in the latter. It would enable one man to determine the conduct of a second, or—to put the matter in terms of political life—to transfer the control of the second man's vote to himself; and in political life, under a system of universal suffrage, the promulgation of statements which are made with the deliberate object of swaying the judgment in some special direction is one of the most powerful means by which one man may master the votes of many, and virtually multiply his own. This is not true, it must be noted, of the publication of bare facts, if these be stated in their integrity; but whenever, with a view to the effect of it on the public mind, news is coloured by comment, or a calculated distribution of emphasis, those responsible for such procedure are, in so far as they are successful, transferring the control of the votes of other men to themselves. Inconvenient electors were, in the days of Pickwick, kept from the polling-booth, and so deprived of their votes, by "hocussing their whisky," and leaving them drunk in a barn. Hocussing the facts is a method of the same character; and in proportion to its success is no less incompatible with the principles of pure democracy.

No one could admit this more fully than democrats themselves, as the violent outcries raised by them in Great Britain and Germany against official manipulations of news in time of war have testified. But let us suppose that full purity of voting, in the sense here indicated, were achieved. Would the difficulties involved in the postulates of pure democracy be ended? We shall, on the contrary, be simply brought at last to the ultimate difficulty out of which all the others spring.

This ultimate difficulty resides in the obvious fact, which we have not as yet considered, that if the judgment of the people, or the units of the average mass, are to be so united as to acquire a force that is cumulative, and thus constitute a will which deserves to be called "general," it is necessary that these judgments shall be, in all important respects, identical. The question, therefore, is whether or how far, with regard to governmental matters, all average men are, if left to themselves, certain or even likely to judge, and therefore to will, in the same way, simply because none of them are distinguished by conspicuous incapacity on the one hand, or even by the rudiments of conspicuous talent on the other. To answer this question in a few words is impossible. The matters with which governments have to deal are various; and, as we shall see, it is only with regard to certain of them that any general will of a spontaneous kind is possible.

Let us begin with taking two simple examples of governmental action, with regard to one of which all men do, as a fact, spontaneously judge alike; whilst, with regard to the other, the spontaneous judgments of most men—even men of considerable capacity—are a blank. Our first example shall relate to protection from murder; our second to the question of bi-metallism.

All men, even murderers themselves, so long as they are left at large, desire that the Government, by laws and the maintenance of an adequate police, should minimise the risks which any citizen runs of being stuck in the ribs when he is asleep or enjoying an evening stroll. No prompting, no agitation, no bribery is needed to bring even the stupidest citizen to this way of thinking.

But let us suppose that the question with regard to which the will of the average mass is consulted is the question of whether the system of mono-metallism, as at present established, shall be maintained or shall be modified by what is called "the remonetisation of silver." Here is a question the answer to which, according as it was yes or no, might very appreciably affect the well-being of everybody; but if it were put by any member of Parliament to each of the voters who elected him, the answer of all but a few of them, if they spoke their minds, would be this: "The question of the respective merits of mono-metallism and bi-metallism is a remarkably difficult and, we may add, a remarkably dry one. We know nothing about it ourselves, and the most eminent experts disagree. You, however, though you only muddle us when you talk about it, presumably know more than we do, or else you are not worth your salt. So do not worry us about *our* judgments. Make the best use you can of your own." Mr. Chesterton lays it down with an air of blunt finality that a representative must always do one or other of two things—"that he must vote either in accordance with the will of his constituents or against it." It does not occur to this often very sensible writer that there is yet a third alternative —which is, with regard to many questions, the only one ever realised—that the constituents may have no definite will at all.

These two illustrations show clearly enough what, if considered broadly, the state of the case is. They show us that a will of the kind which pure democracy postulates is, with regard to certain questions, a permanent, a familiar, and a completely realised fact; while they show that, in contrast to such questions, others exist also with regard to which such a will is so completely a myth that it has in the world of realities no possible counterpart. It is evident, therefore, that the postulate of a general will in politics can, if we are to accept it as more than an idle and academic dream, be so accepted only with important and specific limitations. Let us now take a bird's-eye view of governmental questions as a whole, dividing them into groups, according to the degree of completeness, or of incompleteness down to the point of nullity, in which such a general will as pure democracy postulates either does exist, or can possibly exist, with regard to them.

We shall find that, roughly and for the purposes of the present discussion, political questions are divisible into four groups as follows:

(1) Fundamental, simple and unaltering questions;
(2) Momentary and simple questions;
(3) Temperamental questions;
(4) Composite questions, or questions which, though not momentary, are constantly presenting themselves in practically new forms, and which, though varying in complexity, are all of them far from simple, whilst certain of them constitute a sub-group meriting the designation of Abstruse.

Of these four groups of questions the first and fourth—the Fundamental and the Composite—are normally the most important. We will, therefore, begin with disposing of the intermediate two, before turning to the others, which will be the main subject of our discussion.

Of Momentary questions, the most striking example is one which relates to war. It has nothing to do with the conduct of war itself or the kinds of preparation and action on which its success depends. It has to do solely with the question of whether war on a given occasion shall be undertaken or no. On certain occasions the inhabitants of some one country become so exasperated by the behaviour and the menaces of another that all conflicting judgments as to the complex facts of the situation give place to a common passion, and there is thus developed a cumulative will to fight the force of which is a multiple of individual wills formed by the citizens severally "in virtue of their manhood alone." But a general will of this kind, however vast its effects on the course of human history, is in itself short-lived, not outlasting the crisis which called it forth; and, as such crises are happily rare, it is exceptional. It is not a characteristic of the normal life of nations.[1]

As examples of the questions here called Temperamental, we may take those relating to the consumption of alcoholic liquors and those into which a religious element enters. Such questions, so far as the possibility of any general will is concerned, not only differ from those involved in any momentary crisis but are essentially and diametrically opposed to them. With regard to Temperamental questions, the units of the average mass not only fail to arrive at judgments which even approach identity, but they form and maintain judgments which are intentionally and even violently conflicting. Who can contend that all average men, simply because they are neither illustrious thinkers nor fools, will feel and judge alike as to the drinking of beer or

---

[1] Amongst Momentary questions may be included the abolition of a monarchy. In many cases the dethronement of monarchs has been the work of intrigue; but regarded merely as a single act, a spontaneous general will may quite conceivably sanction it. But to abolish one kind of government is a very different thing from governing.

spirits ? Some of them will be for free drinking, some
of them for regulated drinking, some of them for pro-
hibiting the drinking of alcoholic liquors altogether.
They will judge and feel differently, not because their
intellects are unequal, but because their temperaments
and prepossessions are diverse. The same observation
holds good of the judgments of average men as to questions connected with religion. Many Socialists are at
great pains to explain that a man's religion, in any
reasonable polity, has no more to do with government
than the colour of his hair or trousers; and so far as
religion is merely an inward conviction this is no doubt
true. But if in any country, whilst masses of men are
atheists, others are sincere Christians, and if the religion
of the latter has any effect on their lives, there are two
sets of questions at all events in which religion is closely
implicated, and which Government must deal with in
one way or another. These are questions relating to
education and marriage; and it is obvious that, as to
any legislation by which these two questions are affected,
any million of convinced Christians will spontaneously
differ in opinion from any million of similarly capable
atheists. In the case, then, of all those questions here
called Temperamental the postulate of pure democracy,
that all men of average intelligence will, as to questions
of government, come to the same conclusions, is so absolutely contradicted by fact that it would not be worth
while to discuss it, if it were not one of the implications
of much popular argument.[1]

Thus, if we set aside Momentary questions because
with regard to these, though a general will is possible,
it is possible only on signally rare occasions; and if we
set aside Temperamental questions because, with regard
to these, average men, as such, have no natural pro-
clivity to will in the same way, or join together in

---

[1] Amongst Temperamental questions must be included those into
which the racial element enters, such as those involved in the relation
of Ireland to the United Kingdom, and Ulster to the rest of Ireland.
Even in Ulster itself there is a Catholic will and a Protestant. Of
divergencies in popular opinion which are due to racial temperament,
examples on a still larger scale have been provided by the United States
in connection with the European war.

developing any general will at all, it is with the Fundamental questions and the Composite questions that we
are here mainly concerned; and we shall see that, if
regarded as the subjects of a general will of any kind,
the difference between these last, though mainly one of
degree, is practically so profound that, whilst a purely
democratic will is a reality with regard to the former it
is, from the nature of things, with regard to the latter
impossible.

CHAPTER II

OF Fundamental questions an example has been given already—namely that of protection from murder; and to this may be added the protection of chattels from theft, the protection of the home from intrusion, and the fulfilment of contracts in accordance with terms specified. Such questions are Fundamental because they relate to the maintenance of certain primary conditions in the absence of which no society could exist.

Now, with regard to questions such as these, little reflection is necessary to show us that in all societies a general will is present the correspondence of which to the requirements of pure democracy is complete. Every will which is capable of being translated into action is related to two things—a desired end, and the means or machinery by which this end may be realised; and in both respects, so far as Fundamental questions are concerned, the completeness of the general will is an obvious and universal fact. In the first place as to ends, the individual judgments of which such a will is the sum are the same for the simple reason that all men, as to ends like these, naturally feel or think in precisely the same way. No man, however stupid, requires to be persuaded by a neighbour, or an oligarchy of superior persons, that the Government should protect him from the chances of being murdered any night in his bed, or of having his teaspoons stolen before he comes down to breakfast. In the second place, the means by which ends of this kind are to be achieved are, in their main features, as familiar as the ends themselves. They consist of some system of police, law-courts, and penalties, with which, though its minor details vary with place and circumstance, all men, in respect of its essentials, have been acquainted

20

since the dawn of history. Here, therefore, there is a general will as to means which is no less spontaneous and unanimous, and hardly less specific, than the general will with regard to ends which accompanies it.

That such is the case is sufficiently obvious from the fact that, whenever Governments are too weak to accomplish these ends efficiently, every man seeks to accomplish them as best he can for himself. Thus on a well-known occasion a prominent English Socialist was attacked by a man in Paris who attempted to steal his watch. No police being present, the Socialist very rightly knocked his assailant down. If the then Government of France had but given effect to the general will completely, it would merely with the arm of the law have done what the alien democrat did instinctively with his own.

Let us now pass on to the questions here called Composite, which comprise in normal times the whole of the subject-matter of political government in so far as political government has any history at all, or suggests any controversy as to the will, democratic or otherwise, by which its actions are, or by which they ought to be, determined.

Composite questions differ from Fundamental questions in the fact that they are far more complex, and at the same time are always changing. With regard to Fundamental questions, the will of the units governed, except when it takes the form of a protest against inefficient administration, is simply a standing demand, not requiring to be reaffirmed, for the effective maintenance of a routine already established. As to composite questions, the case is essentially otherwise. Composite questions have their root in Fundamental questions, and up to a point coincide with them; but they represent such questions as multiplied, complicated, combined, and recombined, by the evolution of new circumstances, such as new industrial methods, increases in wealth and population, and the growth of commercial relationships between one country and another. Thus, whereas in societies which are small, isolated, and stationary Fundamental questions of government are practically the only questions, the questions as to which alone in the great

States of to-day the Government requires any positive guidance, either from the brains of the governed or from those of the executive itself, are questions in respect of which the ends to be achieved are novel, whilst the means present themselves in the form of many untried alternatives, each of which requires to be very carefully devised, for and against each of which there are many things to be said, and from which it is impossible for anybody to select the best except by the use of a keen and balanced intellect, corroborated by vigour of character, and acting on wide knowledge.

Of the growth, as just described, of Fundamental questions into Composite, we may take from English history the following four examples :—The question of the distribution of Parliamentary seats prior to the first Reform Bill; the question of Free Trade versus Protection; the question of the Right to Work; and a fourth, which shall be specified presently.

To all who acquiesce in the system of government by elected legislators it is obvious that, whatever be the qualifications on which the right to a vote depends, there must logically at all events be some approach to equality in the number of voters or citizens for whom each representative speaks; and if the number and distribution of a population always remained the same, the question of "the distribution of seats," if settled satisfactorily once, would be settled for all time. Now, when George III succeeded to the throne of England, the then distribution of seats, if not ideally perfect, was not obtrusively at variance with the size and distribution of the constituencies. Hence, if number and distribution of the population of England had never since then changed, a distribution of seats which satisfied the men of the eighteenth century would have satisfied the men of the next century also. As a matter of fact, however, between the accession of George III and his death the population of England had not only so increased, but its distribution also had altered in so rapid and extraordinary a way that, whilst huge towns in the north were represented by no member at all, there were two members in the south for three men and a hay-stack. Here is one case in which it is easy to understand how an old question, taken for a time as settled, may become a new one, and one, as we shall see presently, which required a solution involving many new complexities.

The question of Free Trade versus Protection, as it finally shaped itself in England at the beginning of the Victorian epoch, will be readily recognised as one of similar character. The main issue involved related to national food supply—more especially to the supply of bread, and came to be known as the question of "the big and the little loaf." Here we have a question as old as the days of Jacob. But in Georgian England it was absent till the close of the eighteenth century, for England till then, so far as corn was concerned, was not an importing—on the contrary she was an exporting—country, and there was no staple food on which a protective tax could fall. Owing to the subsequent growth of the population, coupled with other changes, this question which till then meant nothing for the public consciousness, formed fifty years later the subject of the bitterest non-military conflict which had ever agitated the nation in the whole course of its history.

The question commonly indicated by the phrase "The Right to Work" is one which has always been latent in all coherent polities; but in primitive times it was simple, and carried with it its own solution. In the case of populations which were stationary, and drew most of their wealth from agriculture or from pasture, or from both, it did not emerge into a practical form at all; for a territory which had provided each man out of a thousand with enough for his wants in one age would continue to do so in another. Or, again, in primitive times, when the earth was sparsely occupied, if a given population increased, it had merely to enlarge its borders, or else, like the Scythian nomads, move in a body from one territory to another. And, indeed, in countries such as Canada and Australia such a solution is theoretically adequate to-day. But the question as it presents itself in modern, especially in Western Europe, and has already begun to present itself in the United States, is novel and far more complex, and it is so for two main reasons. In the first place, in some of these countries the whole of the fruitful area is by this time occupied already, whilst

in others the unoccupied portion is very rapidly con-
tracting. In the second place, work itself, which was
primitively of a few kinds only, is now divided into
kinds so numerous and so diverse in character that different men, in demanding that work should be found for
them, are not demanding productive work of any kind,
but each is demanding some special kind out of many.

Let us now take our fourth example. This shall be
the question of providing a kind of gun by which German
airships may be destroyed on their way to London. Here
we have a question which, in respect of its general character, was present and vital in the first cluster of huts
which was ever threatened by the ferocity of any hostile
tribe. Like all practical questions, it is a question of
ends and means. With regard to ends, to-day as in
the earliest times, we have a general will of an absolutely
democratic character; for all men are equally anxious
"in virtue of their manhood alone" that the roofs and
the walls that shelter them shall not be burnt or shat-
tered; and in primitive times, when men had no other
weapons than stones, sticks, firebrands, and their naked
fists, there was a will equally democratic with regard
to the means also. In other words, the will of a tribe
to protect itself comprised a similar will in respect of the
weapons to be used. But, as weapons of war became
gradually more complex and various the will as to means
and the will as to ends became separated. So far as ends
are concerned, the average Londoner of to-day, in willing
that his home shall be guarded from German aircraft,
wills precisely what the savage wills in some primeval
kraal; but the question of the means by which aircraft
may be driven off or destroyed calls, as we shall see
presently, for a will profoundly different from that by
which the average savage is actuated when, equipped
only with the familiar arms of his ancestors, he cracks
the skull of another with a club or with a slung pebble.

These four illustrations are sufficiently indicative of
the manner in which questions, in themselves Fundamental and permanent, exfoliate under new circumstances into Composite questions which are new, and
each of which, as it arises, must be the subject-matter
of a new will. Let us, then, consider how far a will of

that purely democratic kind, which is with regard to Fundamental questions an actually existing fact, is capable of reproducing itself in relation to Composite questions likewise.

Stated in a general way, what we shall see is this, that in all countries possessing what is commonly called a Constitution the action of the Government must reflect a general will of some kind : and that this will is the sum of a multitude of judgments which are all in substance identical; but that their identity is due to the fact that, even if they are spontaneously recorded, they are, in respect of Composite questions, not spontaneously formed.

Let us turn again to the question of the distribution of Parliamentary seats in England as it forced itself on public attention at the beginning of the nineteenth century. The scheme of distribution which that century had inherited from the past was already so widely at variance with the logical object of all representative government that its anomalies were patent to the least intelligent man who was sufficiently interested in the subject to consider it worth a thought. Long before the first Reform Bill, though numbers remained apathetic, an opinion was widely prevalent which, as a vague criticism of abuses and a vague demand for their abolition, was, so far as it went, of a genuinely democratic character. But if each of the units by whom this opinion was held had been invited to explain in writing what representation, if proportional in any true sense, would be, most of them could have formulated no series of intelligible answers at all; and their answers taken together would certainly have resulted in nothing which a statesman could construe into a series of specific and practicable orders.

The history of the popular will in England, in so far as it reflected itself in the passing of the first Reform Bill, is the history of a judgment which was in its first stage the sum of individual judgments spontaneously formed and identical, but at the same time vague, and for practical purposes futile, and which was gradually by the influence of certain super-energetic minorities endowed with a force and unity of which it was itself incapable. This process was of a double nature. It was, firstly, a process of raising a vague opinion from a temperature of lukewarm protest to a temperature at which, like scraps of lead in a ladle, individual opinions are fused into a common passion. It was, secondly, a process of forcing this fluid mass to run itself into various moulds which minorities of active men had deliberately prepared for its reception. Both these processes, whose spectacular aspects are familiar to readers of history, took the form of resolutions passed at meetings, of quasi-military marches or riots, and of monster petitions weighted with miles of signatures. But though each of these phenomena seemed to be purely popular, each as its active principle always had some one man, or small cluster of men, exceptional in point of energy, exceptional in powers of persuasion, and exceptional for the most part in mental alertness also, by submitting themselves to whom (and by this means only) the masses acquired a unity and a temporary precision of thought, without which they would have been powerless for any definite purpose. Indeed, the meetings and the marches and the riots were, if considered psychologically, monster petitions changed into other forms— petitions of which the definite substance was the work of a leading few, whilst the miles of signatures were the mere Amens of the multitude. If the substance had been withdrawn, the meaning of the signatures would have disappeared, as a Reform meeting in London melted away at once when Hunt, the principal orator, was frightened from his platform by a bullet through his celebrated white hat.

The question of Free Trade versus Protection, and the triumph in Great Britain of the former over the latter, which was one of the main events of the middle of the nineteenth century, constitute a case whose essentials are precisely similar. Here again the principle involved is one of extreme simplicity—that a Government ought, so far as a Government can affect the matter, to secure for the masses the largest and cheapest supply which under given conditions is possible of food, and more particularly of bread. The question, moreover, at that particular time had been simplified to an unusual degree by a long experience of the evils of very ill-devised corn-laws. And yet it required the tireless and protracted efforts of a specially gifted minority, which had Bright and Cobden for its heroes, their organising powers, their powers of argument and presentation, and their sanguine prophecies, many of which were totally falsified by events, to fashion out of a vague opinion, however spontaneous in itself, a cumulative will sufficiently precise and vehement to overbear all obstacles and accomplish the end desired.

Let us now turn to the question of the Right to Work. If in great modern States this were really as simple to-day as many foolish persons imagine it, and as in primitive times it was, everybody would will that the general right to work should be admitted by the Government, and secured by means as simple as those by which it secures each citizen's right to live. "For if," said Louis Blanc, "a Government is bound to protect life, it is bound to secure the means by which men can be kept alive." But, as Mill observes, this principle, though simple enough in the abstract, presents itself in modern States as one of extreme complexity; for, if a Government is bound to find work for all the units of a given population, it can do so only on condition that it is empowered to control their numbers. Would such control be possible? If possible, are there any means by which it would be rendered tolerable? Here we have a host of difficulties emerging from the very roots of life, like wasps from a disturbed nest, and provoking most men merely to beat them off, or else to upset one another in trying to run away from them. But Mill, in reviewing this matter, sees one of its difficulties only. The very idea of the right to work is in itself ambiguous. It may mean the right of every man to have work found for him by which he can gain a living, either within the limits of a certain geographical area, or else to have it found for him on the surface of the earth somewhere. Early in the nineteenth century the inhabitants of the Tyree—one of the Hebridean islands—were largely maintained by the manufacture of certain chemicals obtained by burning a peculiar kind of seaweed. This industry was destroyed by the triumph of Free Trade principles,

and the consequent admission to Great Britain of these
chemicals from abroad; some three-fourths of the
islanders being in this way deprived of their main
means of sustenance. Had these persons claimed from
the Government the right to have work found for
them, what would this claim have meant?—that such
work was to be found for them within the coastline of
their native islet, or that it was to be found for them
somewhere within the limits of the British Empire?
Had the principle involved in it borne the former meaning, it would have plainly been as great an absurdity
as the principle that a farmer, on a limited number
of acres, is bound to provide grazing for a limitless
number of cows. Had it meant, on the other hand,
that the Government was bound to provide work for
them somewhere, it would have meant that the Government should be empowered to determine where; and
this could only have meant that the Government should
be empowered to transport them to any spot—whether
in Canada, Jamaica, Australia, or the recesses of British
Africa—which Parliament or a State Department might
see fit to select. Here, then, we have again a question
with regard to which any number of answers is possible.
If any Government attempted to answer it practically
by asking each citizen for guidance "in virtue of his
manhood alone," it would elicit nothing but a babel of
conflicting voices, which individually meant little, and
which cumulatively meant nothing. If any practical
advance towards a general and systematic solution of the
question of the right to work is ever to be made—and it
never has been made yet—it will be made by an exceptional few imposing their own schemes on the many, not
by the many imposing the scraps of abortive thought,
as shaped spontaneously in their own minds, on the few.

Of our four typical questions, it remains for us to
review the last—namely the question which first arose
during the great European war, of how the British
Islands should protect themselves from attack by in-
vading air-craft. No question, in respect of the end
involved in it, could evoke a will—a general will—more
purely democratic than this. The will of any one unit
is spontaneously the same as the will of every other. It

presents itself to the imagination of each in precisely the same picture—an airship in ignominious flight, or an airship falling down in flames. But a will as to ends, let it be never so general, is, if we think of it as a power which can definitely guide a Government, nothing unless it carries with it a will as to specific means; and in this most illuminating case it is sufficiently clear from events that the purely democratic will is a hopeless and helpless blank. In a case like this, all that the units of the average mass can do is to cry out for somebody whose talents exceed the average, and who, presenting them with some plan or mechanism by which the end in view may be accomplished, ask them to say "Yes" to the proposal that this mechanism shall be adopted. This particular case is no doubt an extreme one; but all political questions of the kind here called Composite— that is to say, all questions of government which are possible subjects of controversy, and require that any action of a novel kind shall be taken, conform to this type of case in a greater or less degree. In respect of such questions the many have wills of some kind, but they are vague, incomplete, and, taken as a whole, they are powerless, until the talents and energies of the few present them with specific materials, on which, whether by way of selection, of acceptance, or of rejection, they can act. But even when matters have reached this point, the necessary functions of the few are so far from being ended that they merely enter on a new career of activity. What the nature of that activity is we will consider in the following chapter.

CHAPTER III

THE ARTS OF OLIGARCHY

As an approach to the fresh question which has just now been indicated, let us continue for a moment longer the use of our last illustration—namely that of a general will with regard to an anti-aircraft gun. The Many, in merely willing the use of some gun or mechanism by which hostile aircraft may be driven off or destroyed, but the nature of which they themselves are quite incompetent to suggest, are like passengers trying in a boat to be sick on an empty stomach; but we have assumed that when once a contrivance sufficient for this end was presented to them, they would with one consent all will the adoption of it. This assumption, however, if we apply it to actual life, is by no means so simple as it seems. A contrivance of the kind in question would, from the nature of the case, be novel, and, however perfect it might be, only experts of very special capacity could form, before it was tried, any independent judgment with regard to its merits whatsoever. Indeed, even Boards of experts have often rejected contrivances, subsequently shown to possess the highest value, as not being worth the cost of so much as a systematic trial. And this difficulty is increased when, as usually happens, not one contrivance only is submitted to their judgment, but several. Now it is true that of contrivances such as an anti-aircraft gun, the cost of which is individually not enormous, several might be tried simultaneously or in rapid succession before the occasion for the use of them had altogether passed away; and the Government might invite the masses to record a general will that the type of gun should be adopted which experiment had shown to be the best. This is a part in the drama which the masses, as a pure democracy, would be fully competent to play, just as a crowd at Epsom is competent to acclaim the Derby winner when it has won. But the questions to which experiments of kinds like these are applicable form but a small part of those Composite Questions with which Governments have to deal. A dozen different guns devised for the destruction of Zeppelins might be tested by practice at so many floating targets, in a dozen consecutive days, or even in a single morning; but schemes of electoral reform, or of Protection or of Free Trade, can be tested by no such preliminary means as these. Of any electoral or fiscal schemes that are possible, it is impossible at the same time to experiment with more than one; and the one which happens to be adopted must be kept in operation for years before, as an experiment, it is able to teach us anything. Its adoption must, therefore, be determined by psychological processes whose action precedes the event, not by the results which follow it.

All Composite questions, then, as related to the will of the many, resemble the question of defences against hostile aircraft in the fact, which this example so signally illustrates, that before the many can collectively will anything about them at all, two distinct tasks must be carried out by the few. In the first place the question at issue must be invested by the few with the form of some definite scheme or schemes, for otherwise the judgments of the many will have nothing to act on. In the second place, if these judgments are to be so precise on the one hand, and so absolutely unified on the other, as to constitute an injunction that some one scheme shall be adopted, the devisers of this scheme must so present it to the mass of average men that a judgment in favour of its adoption shall, somehow or other, develop itself in the mind of each. Further, it is evident that, if such a consensus of judgment cannot be elicited beforehand by short and sharp experiment—a feat which is possible in exceptional cases only—it must be elicited by the arts of deliberate and systematic persuasion.

It is in the practice of such arts, which are essentially the arts of an oligarchy, that at least one half of the activity of any Constitutional Government, actual or possible, consists; and the more nearly a Constitution conforms in outward semblance to the principles which the theory of pure democracy postulates, the more necessary does the practice of such arts become, and the more industriously do statesmen who call themselves democrats practise them. Let us consider this fact further in the light of well-known examples.

The object of such arts may be briefly restated thus. Owing to changed social conditions some Composite question arises, such as that of providing some new military weapon or some new fiscal system. Before the many can play any part in the matter, some new weapon or some new fiscal system—or, as generally happens, several—complete in respect at least of their main details, must be devised. The devising of this or of these requires special abilities, and is necessarily the work of the few. The many can, as a whole, play no part in the matter except that of agreeing to pronounce that some one device, if there be only one, is satisfactory, or, if several be offered, that some one of these is the best. The situation of the many with regard to such devices is very much what it would be with regard to a medicine which nobody had ever tried, and the probable effects of which could not reasonably be anticipated by anybody otherwise than from some knowledge of its chemical composition and the action of chemical substances on the tissues of the human body. The only means by which in each of a countless number of people, most of them certainly not chemical experts, a confidence in the merits of an untried medicine could be elicited would be a system of puffs on the part of the would-be vendor. Now such puffs or advertisements are of various kinds and grades, but they all conform to one or other of two types. They may contain some fragments of vague scientific information which even to the most ignorant man is in a vague way familiar, and suggests to him some judgment which he attributes to his own intelligence; or else they may consist of a number of bare assertions, the efficacy of which depends on the art with which they are emphasised.

Thus, if a man has invented a compound called "Radium Cocoa," he may commend its virtues to the public in either or both of the two following ways.

"Madame Curie, the renowned French scientist, has,"
he may say, "pronounced that one atom of radium is
beyond all doubt an epitome of the self-renewing vitality
of Nature. Those who drink Radium Cocoa are taking
the vitality and undying youth of Nature into their own
systems." Or else, adopting a style which for many is
more insidious, he may say, "What YOU so often suffer
from is that Tired Feeling, that Bored Feeling, a Feeling
that you've had Enough of it. Whenever you feel that
way, just drink a cup of Radium Cocoa. The House of
Lords drinks it. The House of Commons drinks it.
Your Best Girl drinks it, directly after you have been
talking to her. Baby Bubbles, of Paradise Mews, Clac-
ton, drinks it. Here are two pictures, showing Baby
Bubbles before a cup of Radium Cocoa, and after."
But whichever method the advertiser of an untried compound may adopt, the object of his advertisements will
be to create in the minds of all who look at them a
similar will or judgment, which they would not and could
not have formed if left to their own devices. And any
Government which, in respect of any composite or complex questions, requires the definite support of any
general will at all, is bound, so long as it cannot resort
to bribery, to manufacture such a will for itself in
substantially the same ways.

As practised by statesmen, whether actually in office
or struggling for it, the arts of eliciting from each unit
of a miscellaneous mass an identical judgment with
regard to any complex measures, are, as history shows
us, divisible roughly into three. One of these may be
called the Art of Political Incendiarism; another the Art
of Political Stimulation; whilst the third, which alone
gives meaning to either of the two others, is the Art of
Popular Exposition, or the art of placing before the
public in a manner which compels conviction statements
as to fact which have been so chosen and marshalled
that average minds, unconscious of external pressure,
shall naturally tend to draw from them some desired
conclusion.

What is here meant by the art of Political Incendiarism
is the art of kindling in multitudes by loose and popular
rhetoric a belief that they are suffering from some par-

ticular grievance for which some statesman professes to have devised a cure, his object being to achieve or retain power as the social saviour by whom alone the cure can be applied. This art is like that of the quack American doctor, of whom the story is told that, when asked to cure a child of smallpox, he began with giving it a powder, saying to the parents as he did so, "This powder will bring on the convulsions. I'm not much at pustules, but I reckon I'm hell on fits."

The art of Political Stimulation has for its object a mere overcoming of the inertia which disinclines a vast number of persons, even when suffering from conditions really onerous and remediable, not only to think out political remedies for themselves, but even to accept with interest those thought out by others. Except for the fact that one of these arts is fraudulent whilst the other is legitimate and on most occasions necessary, it is impossible to draw any definite line between them. The nature of both is very vividly illustrated by a remark which an English statesman of the extreme radical school is reported to have addressed to a friend, who endowed it with immortality by repeating it. "I have sometimes feared of late that my personal influence was declining. I find, however, that my fears were groundless. Let me only make the people angry, and I can do with them what I please."

Of the last of these three arts—namely that of Popular Exposition, or the art of creating a will in favour of specific measures, not by rhetorical statements calculated to inflame opinion, but by plying the public with facts which, even if accurately stated, are so selected and emphasised that the average mind will draw from them some special conclusion for itself, signal examples have been provided by various governments during the great European war. During the earlier months of that war the German Government spent more than £1,000,000 in America with the object of manufacturing an opinion by this precise method—we may call it a campaign of emphasis. It may have been, as is said, a campaign of falsehoods also; but this, if such were the case, is no more than an accident. It is the art with which statements are selected, whether true in themselves or no, and the concerted emphasis which they thus acquire when presented, that gives them their cumulative effect, and converts them into an instrument for securing the end desired.

Such methods of manipulating the judgments of average men by systematising the supply of facts on which judgments are formed are certainly not what is commonly meant by bribery, though when emissaries are paid to conduct the process these methods very closely resemble it; but they are no less inconsistent than bribery with the pure democratic principle. If a witness by manipulating or merely suppressing facts causes a jury to do what they would not have done otherwise—to acquit a man really innocent, or acquit a man really guilty—he is no less interfering with the natural action of others than he would be had he bought the verdict by slipping a banknote into each juryman's pocket. Whichever were his object—a just result or an unjust—the nature of his conduct would in this respect be the same, namely an influencing of the recorded judgments of men other than himself. For, except in the case here described as that of Political Incendiarism, it must not be supposed that these arts of oligarchic influence are in any way necessarily sinister, nor are they peculiar to one party only. On the contrary, they are compatible though not always associated with the strictest moral integrity. In any constitutional country their employment is inseparable from statesmanship. In so far as it is necessary, with regard to any Composite question, that a government should secure the support of any general will at all—a will possessing any definite content—these arts of manipulation must be practised by all statesmen equally. Neither the will of the governing few nor the will of the governed many could, without such oligarchic arts, become so much as articulate.

These observations are primarily made with reference to the action of persons or parties either actually in power, or competing for it with a reasonable prospect of obtaining it. In all modern countries, however, much of the business of eliciting corporate wills is performed by sectional bodies, or parties in a narrower sense; and in these the arts of the few are not confined to the arts of mere incitation or persuasion, but are to a considerable extent supplemented by those of discipline.   Such sectional bodies as these, which have no general authority, will be dealt with in another chapter.   We are for the moment concerned with national government only; and here we must proceed to note that, in the opinion of many persons, absolutely pure democracy may, despite all difficulties, be realised by a constant use of the Referendum, or plebiscite, this being taken to carry with it the popular right, not only of decision but of personal initiative also.   The opinion is specious, but it is altogether illusory, merely bringing us back to oligarchy under a new disguise.

The device of the Referendum, or plebiscite, though often very effective, is effective only when the questions which form its subject have been previously reduced by the few to the last state of real or seeming simplicity. Those who formulate the questions do not, indeed, give the answers, but they determine within narrow limits what the nature of the answers shall be, and they alone make definite answers possible.   A plebiscite might elicit an answer of the kind required to the question of whether the parish wants a new pump or no; but it certainly could not do so if what each parishioner was asked for were an accurate description or sketch of the pump which he thought most suitable.   If a bride and bridegroom, whose cherished dream was to visit the north of Ireland, had been promised by a tribe of relations the costs of their wedding tour on condition that they asked the relations what the course of their tour should be, it would be idle for them to ask each one of a hundred aunts or cousins, each haunted by personal recollections and preferences, for the route, the hotels, the excursions, which he or she would recommend.   They would if they did this get a hundred answers, which would practically amount to none.   If they wished to get an answer at once distinct and general, they would have to frame their question in a very different way. Instead of saying to each, "Where do you wish us to go?", they might say to all at once, "Shall we go to Hell or Connaught?", and they thus would elicit an answer which was not only clear and general, but was also the precise answer which they themselves desired. When a plebiscite established the dynasty of Victor Emmanuel, the question addressed to each unit of the Italian people was not " What kind of government would you wish to establish if you could? " It was simply "Do you wish that Italy shall remain what it is now— a collection of petty States each afraid of its neighbours, or else that it shall be a great kingdom united under one great king? " If each Italian had been asked for a sketch of whatever government—ducal, royal, papal, federal, republican, or communist—corresponded to his own ideal, the plebiscite would have meant no more than a buzz of quarrelling voices heard through a single telephone, instead of what statesmen were waiting for— a clear business-like message on which business men could act.

Nor would the situation be mended by the popular right of initiative—the right of every citizen " in virtue of his manhood alone " to submit to the Executive any proposal he might please, and to claim that it should— for this is what the matter comes to—have in the last resort a special little plebiscite to itself. Such a right, no doubt, might be possibly exercised with effect by a citizen here and there, and on very rare occasions; but it could not be exercised by all. Were it exercised by all, the life-work of each adult would be mainly taken up with examining the vagaries of all the rest. On the other hand, if it were exercised by a few, and a few only, the principle of oligarchy would be back again without any disguise whatever.

The right of initiative would be meaningless even in theory, except in so far as it enabled the individual who insisted on using it to obtain for his own proposals the support of a considerable number of other men, and cause them to form some judgment which they would not have formed otherwise—a process which is essentially that of imposing his will on theirs. If we ask how one man would be able to do this, we can only say that, if he did not do so by bribery, he would have to do so by practising as a private individual, and for some one isolated purpose, the essentially oligarchic arts which, as we have seen already, are practised by leading statesmen systematically and on a larger stage.

In other words, with regard to Composite questions, the pure will of the many, unless it is unified by the formative influence of the few, is neither a foolish will nor a wise will. It is a will which does not exist. It can only come into action and acquire a definite content when the few have provided it with a subject-matter on which to act. Hence, in all advanced states of society the exceptional influence of a more or less numerous few is absolutely essential to the operation of the democratic principle, and this fact is at the same time fatal to the theory of pure democracy.

CHAPTER IV

INEXPUGNABLE OLIGARCHY

The meaning of the paradoxical fact that, in any complex society, democratic action would be impossible under a régime of pure democracy, will be more clearly appreciated if we consider with more minuteness what the theory of pure democracy, when seriously taken, implies—the theory whose basic principle expresses itself in the common formula of "One man one vote," or of "One man one unit of influence," or in the aphorism of the Abbé Sieyès, who said of the King of France that his rightful influence was to that of his subjects exactly in the ratio of one to thirty millions.

If this theory or principle really means what it affects to mean, it would, were it translated into fact, have one very startling consequence. It would not only mean that a King, if kings were permitted to exist, should have no more influence as a voter than the obscurest man in the street. It would also mean that, if any prestige were left to him, he should not use it, no matter how informally, to influence the votes of any members of his entourage who respected the dignity of his office, or were animated by loyalty to his person. But the application of this principle would not be confined to kings. It would apply with equal strictness to the men in the street themselves. It would mean with regard to the judgments by which votes are determined that no one man, whatever his social status, should, by his decision of character or his reputation for superior knowledge, so sway the mind of even a single companion—whether a worker in the same workshop, or a frequenter of the same eating-house—that the thoughts and votes of two men were determined by the mind of one; and if such a condition were to be realised, what would have

39

to happen would be this.   Every voter would be bound
to form his judgments in an atmosphere artificially
sterilised like that of a sick-room, so that no germs of
suggestion should be able to attack him from without,
and inoculate his thoughts or feelings with those of any
other person.   If this regulation were pushed to its full
logical consequences, it would be necessary to treat all
questions of politics as though they were obscene
subjects which each man might have to confront in the
hermitage of his own mind, but about which no conversation between man and man was to be tolerated.
For let any dozen men begin to discuss politics round the
hearth of any village inn, there will always be one or
more who will, through some special alertness alike of
mind and speech, influence to some extent the judgments
of the larger number; and the first faint breath of
oligarchy will mix itself with the smoke of pipes, and the
odours of the fraternal tap-room.   Oligarchs need not be
men distinguished by wealth or station, or by any of
the advantages possible for a small class only.   The
officials of a trade union, who order a strike or prohibit
it, may be oligarchs just as truly as a senate of hereditary
peers, or any elected chamber packed with aristocratic
landlords.   When, as sometimes happens, a number of
trade unionists refuse to obey the orders which their
leading officials issue, such movements, though often
described as outbursts of democracy pure and simple,
are always found to have, as their cause and nucleus, the
activity of new oligarchs struggling to displace the old,[1]
and in all such cases one main instrument of oligarchy
is some special power of speech—of speech whether
uttered by the mouth or committed to printed paper.
If there were a hundred men who could think and could
understand language, but who could themselves neither
utter a word nor read it, one man who could speak would
necessarily rule the rest.   Only through him, who interpreted each to all, would any concerted action on the
part of the rest be possible.   All men, as a matter of

---

[1] It is hardly necessary to call the reader's attention to the frequency
with which this fact was illustrated by strikes amongst munition
workers on the Clyde, in Sheffield and elsewhere, contrary to the
orders of the official heads of the unions.

fact, are able to talk somehow, and consequently take or attempt concerted action of some sort; but since some men can notoriously talk with much more effect than others, the mere use of unrestricted speech inevitably communicates to a few certain powers inconsistent, no matter whether they are small or large, with the absolute equality of influence which pure democracy postulates.

It is true that no democrats, however rigid their creed, would propose that for this reason all political conversation should be suppressed.[1] They would reject such a plan as absurd, even if it were not impracticable. But this does not show that it is not in strict logic imperatively demanded by the principles of pure democracy. It shows that, with regard to the affairs of any complex policy, these principles are not strictly compatible with the unalterable facts of life.

But let this argument be waived as merely academic or captious. Let us suppose that, if reasonably interpreted, the principles of even the purest democracy would not demand the suppression of such political talk as forms a natural incident of ordinary social intercourse, or of such inequalities of influence as are naturally bound to result from it. Other things remain, however, the suppression of which they *would* demand, and these, in the eyes of democrats, are very much more important. The principles of pure democracy would, if applied with even the roughest semblance of logic, suppress all political discussion which, emerging from the conversational and wholly informal stage, develops into discussion the conditions of which have been deliberately prearranged

---

[1] Since these words were written, the precise conditions there suggested as logical necessity but a practical impossibility, were actually realised by the German Government. In a London Journal (June 9, 1917) it was reported that, with a view to preventing " discouraging statements as to the war," no one " of lower rank than a member of parliament" should be permitted to make any such statement to any other person, and a reward was offered of £150 to anyone who "should bring any violater of this regulation to book." " Police regulations to this effect," the report continued, " adorn the advertisement pillars in the streets. Nobody is safe in even the most confidential conversation." Pure autocracy, in order to suppress any general will or opinion, creates the very conditions which pure democracy logically postulates, and which at the same time prevent the development of any general will at all.

by a few men for the purpose of influencing many in any
special and calculated way. In other words, the principles of pure democracy, which demand before all things
else that no one voter of any kind shall, so far as such
an abuse is preventable, exercise more than one unit of
influence, would suppress everything which partakes of
the nature of oratory, under which heading we may
include all incitation or persuasion which is, with a
political object, accomplished either by voice or literature. Wherever the orator begins pure democracy ends;
for if the aim of the political orator is not to make men
vote as they would not have voted if he had not been
there to move them, the labour of the orator would be
labour thrown away.

Now here again, it may be urged by the doctrinaires
of pure democracy, we have a conclusion which, if it be
true at all, is true only in a cloudland of idle academic
quibbling. It is, they may say, a conclusion which
would, if practically accepted, destroy all such movements as are now called "campaigns," all newspapers
which did not strictly confine themselves to the publication of bare news unaccompanied by explanation or
comment, and—more unthinkable still—it would actually
destroy the great political meeting. These things can,
these things must co-exist, so such persons will say, with
democracy which is pure in the highest degree possible—
in other words, which is pure to all reasonable intents
and purposes; and no truth can be established of any
practical value by comparing it with a democracy in
which all such things were absent, and which could not
exist anywhere except in a fantastic dream. And in
arguing thus, such persons would up to a point be right.
The logic of pure democracy, if applied in the way here
indicated, would make a clean sweep of all those methods
and institutions with which democratic action has thus
far been identified. But should such persons go on to
object that, if these methods and these institutions were
absent, no democracy of any kind, pure or impure,
would be possible, they would be wrong.

It must be remembered that throughout the discussion
in which we are immediately engaged we have been
dealing only with those Composite questions which,

constantly changing their form, always highly complex, and peculiar to the life of great and elaborately civilised States, comprise nearly all the questions which, to any important extent, demand the formation of any novel will by anybody. But let us only turn back to the questions which have here been called Fundamental, and which still persist everywhere, though constantly inter-tangled with others; and we shall find, as has been said already, that with regard to these a pure democratic will, which requires for its formation and maintenance neither campaigns, newspapers, meetings, nor even private discussion, is so far from being an impossible fancy that it is an inexpugnable fact in the life of all societies; and if we compare this will with the only kinds of general will which can, with regard to Composite questions, be induced to form and record themselves, we have a standard by which to measure the difference between these last and the will on which pure democracy, as a political theory, rests.

Let us suppose, then, that a formal reaffirmation was necessary of a general judgment to the effect that robbery and arson were evils of an intolerable kind, and that a police force, with whose efficiency the public was already familiar, should be maintained as a defence against them. What need would there be of meetings all over the country to secure the due expression of such a judgment by everybody? If a meeting were called for this pur-pose, the most powerful orator on the platform could tell the audience nothing which every member of the audi-ence could not tell the orator. A meeting might as well be held for the purpose of expressing a belief in the fact that Queen Anne was dead. Why, then, is it that, when Composite questions are at issue, such as that of Free Trade for England in the middle of the nineteenth century, meetings are, in all constitutional countries, one of the principal expedients to which all parties resort? Why are public buildings packed with excited crowds? Why does a Bright or a Chamberlain strain every nerve in addressing them, often continuing patiently this arduous labour for years? The reason why public meet-ings would be superfluous and ridiculous in connection with Fundamental questions, whilst they are in connection with Composite questions necessary, is this. Whereas in the former case the wills of the many, as freely formed by each, are practically the same in substance and are thus spontaneously united in a cumulative will already, the wills of the many in the latter case are vague, various, and for the most part practical nullities, and cannot acquire any general meaning whatever, until the few, treating them as so much raw material, manufacture such a meaning out of them by intricate processes of their own.

If any one doubts whether this manufacturing process is necessary, conclusive proof that it is so is to be found in the mere fact that, in spite of its immense cost in the way both of money and effort, the task of conducting it is systematically and continually undertaken; just as if proof were required that raw cotton from America is not in itself cotton ready to be stitched into night-shirts, such proof would be found in the mere existence of the spindles and the mills of Lancashire. Here, however, it must be noted is a fact which has a converse side. If the process carried on by the few of manipulating the wills of the many is shown to be necessary by the mere fact of its being undertaken, the intensity of effort involved in it shows something else as well. It shows that the wills of the many, however incapable in their crude and spontaneous forms of determining the actions of a government as to any questions but the simplest, are far from being purely passive and without some bent of their own; for otherwise the process of manipulating them would be far less laborious than it is. There is not only action on the part of the relatively few; there is also reaction on the part of the relatively many. This fact will be fully discussed hereafter in connection with other questions, not merely with those which are commonly called political; but it does not affect the counter-fact with which alone we are concerned at present, that in the political government of any large and complex society, unless some exceptional influence were systematically exercised by the few, there would be on the part of the many no effective action or reaction at all.

Such being the case, then, the result of the preceding

analysis may be summed up by saying that all current definitions of democracy err, even before they are stated, by reason of a false assumption which underlies the formulation of all of them.   They all assume that democracy is a system of government of some kind.   This is precisely what, except in primitive and minute communities, pure democracy is not, nor ever has been, nor ever can be.   It is not and never can be a system of government of any kind.   It is simply one principle out of two, the other being that of oligarchy, which two may indeed be combined in very various proportions, but neither of which alone will produce what is meant by a government, any more than saltpetre or charcoal will itself produce gunpowder.

It has, however, been pointed out already that this general argument has thus far been mainly applied to the government of entire nations, either as carried on by some party actually in possession of power, or to the conduct of some other party which, having possessed it once, has some reasonable prospect of regaining it, and is constantly on the watch to do so.   We will now turn our attention to those sectional parties which are known by such names as Leagues, Associations, Federations or Unions, each of which aims at exercising over public affairs some will which is democratic, at all events so far as its own members are concerned, and consider whether democracy without any oligarchic concomitant is more practicable in the microcosm of the League than it is in the macrocosm of a great and highly civilised nation.   With regard to this question, as will be seen in the following chapter, evidence is available of a signally pertinent kind.

CHAPTER V

REVOLUTIONARY OLIGARCHIES

SHORTLY before the outbreak of the great European war, a distinguished economist, Professor R. Michels, of the Universities of Basle and Turin, issued an elaborate volume devoted to an examination of the democratic principle as operative in those sectional parties whose one avowed aim is to exhibit it in its purest form. These parties, he says, which side by side make their appearance everywhere—a Socialist Party on the one hand, a Labour Party on the other—are still everywhere a minority; but they have for the last half century been increasing with such rapidity that they are now an important minority in most European countries. The former is more comprehensive than the latter, and stands for "the rights of man," whilst the latter stands more particularly for the rights of a man as a labourer. The attitude of both, however, towards existing systems of government—even towards those in which a radical element preponderates—is, says Professor Michels,[1] the same. The object, or at all events the professed object, of both is not to play a permanent part in these systems of government as they are, but rather to establish in their place a system altogether new, in which pure democracy, unadulterated by any alien element, and representing solely the will of equal and equally influential units, shall be a realised fact at last. Hence, says the author, if we wish to see what democracy means in practice, it is in the actual development and working of these two parties, and of the many and various sub-

[1] *Political Parties*, by Robert Michels, Professor of Economics and Statistics in the University of Basle, and Professor of Statistics in the University of Turin. English translation by Eden and Cedar Paul. London. Jarrold and Sons. 1915.

sections of them, that the question can be most easily, if not most comprehensively, studied. It will, therefore, be instructive to consider the nature of the conclusions drawn by him from a mass of detailed and accumulated data, and compare them with the conclusions which have already been elucidated here.

The general conclusion reached is in both cases the same—that, except in the case of communities or organisations which are small, and whose objects are extremely simple, no corporate action which is purely democratic is possible, and that every attempt to eliminate oligarchy is bound to end in a re-creation of it. This conclusion, says Professor Michels, is rendered specially clear by the case of those parties or organisations on which his own attention has been concentrated, for the leaders of these, together with the rank and file, have been clearly conscious from the first of what the primary principle of pure democracy is. They have realised that pure democracy, as represented by any body of men bound together in the pursuance of any united policy means that no unit of this mass shall exercise any influence greater than that which is exercised by any other, and that no one unit shall, on behalf of the rest, do or execute anything which any one of the rest could not have executed as well and with equal ease, and would not have spontaneously executed in substantially the same way. They have not only realised this as a matter of unambiguous theory, but they set out with showing that such was the case by their conduct. Thus, says Professor Michels, in England, which was the cradle of the Trade Union movement, some of the Unions began with choosing their officials by lot or else in alphabetical order, and the agricultural unions of Italy, in their earlier days, went farther. Every proposal of the officials had to be reduced to writing, and before it could be put into execution it had to be sanctioned by the signature of every one of the members. Moreover, the official accounts were open to the inspection of all, so that any member might be able, as soon as his own turn came, to step at a moment's notice into any vacated place. But as time went on, as the membership of the Unions grew, and the duties of the officials assumed a more complex character,

this primitive plan of election or selection at haphazard
was generally found to be more and more inadequate.
It was found that the duties of the officials comprised
some exercise of initiative, and that a leader, if he was
to be worth anything, must in most cases have natural
talents not to be found in everybody—especially the
talents of a stimulating or explanatory speaker—and
also some special equipment in the way of digested knowledge.   Hence the more important of the democratic
organisations of to-day have abandoned choice by lot
from a medley of supposed equals for a method so elaborately different that some of them have established
colleges at which certain students—a carefully picked
minority who promise to be fit for leadership—are hand-
somely paid and put through a course of training, so
that out of these a minority smaller still may be ultimately chosen by their teachers as eligible for posts of
power.   The existence of even a few institutions of this
kind is an index of how far the spirit by which they are
animated differs from that which prompted the pioneers
of the Trade Union movement to leave the selection of
their leaders, so far as was possible, to chance, and deliberately to ignore, rather than deliberately measure,
such differences in public efficiency as exist between man
and man.

It is argued by some, Professor Michels observes, that
the power as exercised by the leaders thus selected represents, not a negation of the democratic principle, but its
triumph, such men being nothing but specially skilled
employees, hired by the average mass to do its difficult
work for it, and liable to curt dismissal if they are not
punctual in obeying their masters' orders.   But to speak
of such persons as nothing more than employees is
merely, he says, to play with words.   Whether we call
them employees or no, the plain fact is that the men by
whom the affairs of the democratic parties are conducted,
though they may perhaps take some orders, give far
more orders than they take; and although, like employees generally, they are as a matter of theory always
liable to be dismissed, it is rarely possible to dismiss
them by purely democratic means.   The reasons why
this is so may, he says, be divided into two groups, the

first consisting of negative reasons which render dismissal difficult, the other of positive reasons, which combine to render tenures of office permanent, and augment in so doing the kinds of power attached to them.

Of the negative reasons, the chief are, according to Professor Michels, these. In the first place, as the influence of any democratic organisation grows, and its points of contact with affairs in general multiply, many of the duties of the leaders become so highly technical that any serious discussion of them is over the heads of laymen, and efficient criticism of the leaders in respect of such duties as these is beyond the competence of the mass of members collectively. In the second place, the efficiency of the leaders in the management of large affairs becomes more and more dependent, not merely on natural gifts whether these be moral or mental, but also on powers of judgment and prompt action, which most men can acquire by experience of office only. Hence any leaders who, having once been chosen, have remained in office for a certain number of years, will be men whom, if their party dismissed them, it would be very difficult to replace. Further, the democratic parties have found out from experience how greatly their external influence and also their internal cohesion depend on their actions possessing a certain substratum of continuity, and are therefore inclined on principle, except in extreme cases, to preserve a continuity of leadership as a thing desirable in itself. All these facts, except in extreme cases (such as that in which an Italian agitator was found to be taking fees from employers for his services in settling strikes), tend to remove the leaders from the category of mere employees, and endow them with powers largely, if not wholly, independent of the source from which they were first derived. Thus, the Amalgamated Association of Operative Cotton-spinners in England have a rule to the effect that the posts of their officials shall be permanent, unless one or all of the staff should provoke universal censure. Similarly, with special reference to a strike of the first magnitude, a resolution, says Professor Michels, was passed by the Italian Federation of Labour, that even if the results of a referendum should be adverse to the views of the leaders then in office, this should not be construed as invalidating the position of the leaders themselves; whilst still more widely significant is the general fact that in Germany the leaders of the Socialist and the Trade Union parties have proved to be practically irremovable except by death or voluntary resignation.

Further, to such difficulties of a mental and tactical kind which render dismissal of the leaders by the action of the mass difficult, there are two more to be added, one of which is purely mechanical, whilst the other, which underlies this, has its roots in human nature itself.

The mechanical difficulty consists of the simple fact that, as soon as a party has become sufficiently numerous to constitute, by pervading a country, a force in national life, it becomes impossible that all, or even most of its members, these being widely diffused, shall meet in their thousands except on very rare occasions, and they would even then be unmanageable for the purposes of detailed criticism. But closely connected with this mechanical result, increase of membership has brought to light another which is in itself of wholly independent origin. Although the parties of revolutionary protest are, in every country where they exist, a minority of the nation as a whole, and are thus presumably permeated by some special democratic fervour, the majority of this minority, with regard to questions of detail, is everywhere found in practice to be apathetic to such a degree that critics have described them as suffering from the malady of "gregarious inertia." Impatient enthusiasts have said of them that these masses of professed democrats are no better than ordinary men, "being far more interested in a road at the bottom of their back gardens " than in any administrative details connected with democratic policy, and that, except when excited by some sensational cry—"A bas la vie chère," for instance—they signify no interest in party affairs whatever. Thus, says Professor Michels, on occasions both in Holland and Italy, when the conduct of the leaders was attacked with regard to the most momentous questions, the number of members who took the trouble to vote varied from one-fifth to one-tenth of the whole. In France, of the members of the General Federation of Labour, only one in fifty is a reader of the party journal. In this case and in that of similar organisations everywhere, the section of the rank and file which alone keeps a watchful eye on the doings of the party leaders is a certain small minority, which, distinguishable from the rest as oil is distinguishable from water, makes a habit, like the habit of inveterate playgoers, of attending party meetings, and fills hall after hall with the same familiar faces. It is from this minority that, except on very rare occasions, all close and effective criticisms of the party leaders emanates, and it has, says Professor Michels, been found that this minority, which alone realises what the difficulties of party leadership are, is for the most part disposed to support, rather than attack, those at present in office who are taking such difficulties on themselves. Amongst the minority in question there are on occasion, doubtless, embittered malcontents, and in the activity of such, not in spontaneous disaffection on the part of the larger number, lies the only adverse influences which the leaders have to fear. But influences of this kind, Professor Michels observes, are not in their origin democratic, nor do they represent any protest against the influence of an oligarchy as such. On the contrary, they originate in men who are anxious to be oligarchs themselves, and who seek to convert the mass into an instrument of their own ambition. Such revolts, when they occur, may be formidable and at times successful, but, says Professor Michels, definite experience has shown that the actual leaders, as a rule, not only are able to hold their own against them, but tend to acquire increased powers in doing so, these indeed being thrust on them by the mass of their respective parties, with a view to preventing the recurrence of paralysing or useless discords. Amongst the new powers thus placed in the leaders' hands is the power, which according to circumstances is more or less fully developed, of choosing, as posts fall vacant, new colleagues or subordinates at their own personal discretion. Thus, in Germany, of the Trade Union officials one in every five is a nominee of the Central Council. By a congress of Trade Unions in Italy, held at Modena in the year 1910, it was not only permitted to the leaders, but enjoined on them as a primary duty, that, exercising their best judgment, they should nominate every member of their official staff themselves; whilst as for the General Federation of Labour in France, which of all labour organisations claims to be most revolutionary, the highest posts in this are, as they fall vacant, filled up by a process which is tantamount to nomination by the chief secretary.

It is idle, the author proceeds, in the face of facts like these, to pretend that the democratic leaders are no more than employees. It is idler still to dismiss the contention that they are oligarchs as though it were a baseless calumny due to conservative prejudice; for this is, on the contrary, the precise contention or accusation which the various democratic groups are constantly levelling at one another. Indeed, the intellectual representatives of certain of them do not altogether repel it, but are, as we shall see presently, coming to admit that some element of oligarchy is inevitable.

The groups, however, which still adhere to the strict teaching of Marx are, Professor Michels observes, singularly tart and vehement in declaring that the charge of oligarchy has no application to themselves—and that they, at all events, still reflect in their organisation the democratic teaching and the democratic mind of their master. It will, therefore, be instructive to consider what, as shown by his conduct, the practical mind of their great master was. The principal life-work of Marx, apart from his theoretical writings, was the founding of the International—a society which was to exhibit his own theories in action. The International was to be a Union of the manual labourers of the world, having for its object to combine them as equal units in pure democratic action against one common foe—the ubiquitous oligarchy of the present employing classes. It was necessary that, like every other organisation, this world-wide democracy should have some central executive. There thus came into existence a supreme General Council, and if this Council was to be an implement of democracy in any sense, it was further necessary that the labourers of every included country should, by some means or other, be represented in it. It was, therefore, not unnaturally proposed that for this purpose the labourers of each country should elect and be represented by a President—a compatriot, a labourer like themselves, and acquainted with their own conditions. This proposal, however, through the influence of Marx was negatived. It was, indeed, resolved that each country should be represented by a Secretary, but this resolution was immediately followed by another, to the effect that these secretaries•need have no connection whatever, by way either of birth or election, with the country which they affected to represent, but should be chosen from amongst its own members by the General Council itself. By this means, so Marx and his friends announced, a glorious event had been accomplished, new to human history. The world-wide democracy of Labour "had at last been provided with a common and purely democratic leadership," which announcement was almost directly followed by the nomination of Engels, the intimate friend of Marx, as acting secretary for four countries at once. Such were the first notes of the overture to the opera of universal democracy—of the overthrow of the few by the many under the guidance of scientific socialism. The active performers were a small circle of men who proposed to make all humanity dance to their own tunes, and out of this small group there was one man whose notes from the very first were heard above all the rest. This one man was Marx, whose influence as time went on asserted itself more and more. Not only did Marx, in pursuance of his own tactical purposes, shift the meeting-place of the Council from London to New York at his pleasure, but he edited most of the documents which the Council issued, revising them on his own authority; and at last he was openly attacked by two indignant colleagues for having dared to make public a Manifesto to which their signatures were not attached. Jealousy matured and spread. He, and Engels along with him, were denounced as presuming upstarts. One after another most of his colleagues deserted him, declaring that he and they could no longer work together; and mainly owing to the quarrels of these few individuals the terrible International came to an early end. Its collapse was not due to the action of democracy rebelling against oligarchy, but of several oligarchs rebelling against the superior power of one. "The larval monarchy of Marx," as Professor Michels calls it, perished, not by the stones of the populace, but by the daggers of his own associates.

When we consider that Marx is still revered by Socialists as the intellectual founder of the modern democratic movement, his practical career as an autocrat has an almost unique significance, as illustrating how inevitably the power, which in theory is that of the multitude, is bound, as the condition of its exercise, to centre itself in the persons of a few, whilst when one of the few has appreciably a stronger will than the rest, it tends to centre itself in the person of one man only.

Cases like that of Marx in his rôle of autocrat are rare, for the kinds of genius are rare which render such cases possible; but whether power be centred in the persons of a small class or of an individual, it is at all events the antithesis of that impossible power which the theory of pure democracy ascribes to the homogeneous mass. It may, says Professor Michels, be urged that the more extreme of the oligarchic characteristics by which certain leaders, such as Marx, have notoriously separated themselves from the people, are due, not to the necessities of the situation, but merely to the fact that human nature is weak, and that some of these men succumb, by a moral accident, to the selfish whispers of insidiously disguised ambition. But, says Professor Michels, in the case of such extreme arrogations of power, mere selfish ambition is not the primary cause, although it may be often present. The most absolutely unselfish enthusiast, who believes that he can accomplish great things for the multitude, is, in proportion to his faith in his own mission, bound to act as an oligarch, often as a barefaced autocrat, no less than the most selfish schemer, for unless he is prepared to do so, he must cease to act at all. Nobody has expressed this fact more clearly and boldly than Lassalle, whose magnetic influence over his followers was greater than that of any other modern revolutionary. Lassalle was no doubt ambitious in the strictly personal sense—ambitious to an extraordinary degree, but his claims to autocracy were made on public grounds, and these, he was able to boast, were understood by his followers no less plainly than by himself. "It is," he said, "well recognised by the masses of the labourers themselves that, if their wills are to be effective they must be forged into a single hammer, and that this hammer must be wielded by the sinews of one strong hand. And this," he added, "which happens in our own organisation already, represents in miniature the coming social order." To the example of Lassalle two others may be added, which are not mentioned by Professor Michels, and to which we shall recur hereafter—namely those of Robert Owen, who attempted to establish a community purely democratic in America, and of William Lane, who attempted a similar feat in Paraguay. Owen, who in some respects was wholly without thought of self, had no sooner settled his adherents in their new homes, than he did what Lassalle did not do. He insisted on divesting himself of every shred of power which was not shared equally by all. Left to themselves, however, and soon threatened with ruin, his adherents implored him to save them by assuming the office of dictator. With great reluctance he did so. Affairs began to mend. Again he resigned his office. Troubles again beginning, he was once more forced to resume it, the moral of these events being ultimately emphasised by the sequel. Lane began as a preacher of the most absolute democratic equality, denouncing every man who aspired to be more influential than his fellows; but even whilst his practical experiment was no more than a project, the question had been forced on him of whether a pure democracy, if it is to have any practical success, must not have at the head of it what he described as "some better Napoleon, with the heart of Christ and the brain of a Jay Gould"; and this question, as we shall see in a future chapter, he answered by attempting the part of all three characters himself.

It is not, however, necessary for the purpose of our immediate argument to lay any special stress on extreme cases such as these. What here concerns us is the fact, not that oligarchy on occasions tends to culminate in autocracy, but that even in the case of those sectional and eclectic parties which have the realisation of democracy as their conscious and primary object, any attempt at democratic action with regard to any complex questions is bound to culminate in the establishment of a more or less numerous oligarchy. This, indeed, in general terms was admitted long ago by the arch-revolutionary, Proudhon. As soon, he said, as any masses of men depute the power latent in their mere numbers to representatives or selected leaders in order that it may be put to any effective use, these men, if they are so to use it, are bound—they cannot help themselves—to consolidate it in their own persons. "All power," he continues, "thus moves in a cycle. Issuing from the People, it ends by raising itself above the People."

It remains for us to consider how experience since the time of Proudhon has affected the theoretical as well as the practical views of the intellectual leaders of the democratic parties of to-day. It will be found that, though for the purpose of playing on popular sentiment the formulæ of pure democracy are as widely used as ever, and are indeed adopted not only by would-be revolutionaries, but also by parties whose views are conservative or conservatively liberal, serious revolutionary thinkers, in so far as they speak seriously, are everywhere modifying the theory which these formulæ express, and investing it with a new import which is widely different from the old. They are seeking to justify in theory those methods of conducting affairs which have been found by their active leaders, whether autocrats or oligarchic groups, to be absolutely inevitable in practice. This fact will be evident to any one who has given any careful attention to their more recent utterances. Professor Michels has collected a number of significant and typical illustrations of it. Of these, for our present purpose, it will be enough to mention the following. They may be divided into two groups, the one relating to the limitations of popular power, the other to its true foundations, or the particular sources from which it really emanates.

Of the various current definitions of absolutely pure democracy, one of the most famous, as has here been observed already, is "Government of the People, for the

People, by the People." This formula, says Professor
Michels, the more serious democratic thinkers, especially
in Germany and England, have now radically revised, or
in other words repudiated. They assert with redoubled
emphasis that everything must be done *for* the People,
but they wholly deny that the People can accomplish
this "everything" by themselves. "If democracy is
to be effective," they say, "democracy must be taken
as including the personal authority ' of leaders.' " "In
all the affairs of management," says one of them, "for
the decision of which there is requisite specialised knowledge, and for the performance of which a certain degree
of authority is essential, a measure of despotism must
be allowed, and thereby a deviation from the principles
of pure democracy. From the democratic point of
view," he continues, "this is perhaps an evil, but it is
a necessary evil." The leader must, says a philosopher
of the English Labour Party, "have a scheme of his
own to which he works, and he must have the power
to make his will prevail." "Apart from his leaders,"
says Bernstein, "the average man has no political competence. . . . Everything which is tactically of importance must of necessity devolve on the leaders;" and it
has been seriously suggested that the party of true
democracy in England would be directed to the best
advantage by a cabinet of "three persons."

The theory, then, being thus discarded that the great
mass of the people, as units of equal influence, can
determine the government of any complex society for
themselves, and the action of some power which is above
the people being thus admitted as necessary, it remains
to be asked from what popular source the power of the
autocrat, the triumvirate, or the leading minority (whatever its number) is to be derived. It is not contended
by any of the new theorists that those who hold this
power shall hold it in right of inheritance. They must,
therefore, have acquired it at some time of their lives
through a popular sanction of some kind, which commits
it to them personally, in personal preference to others.
If, then, the masses as a whole are incompetent to conduct the government of any complex society by themselves, in what sense are they competent to select with

any discretion the particular men best fitted to conduct
it on their behalf ?   How is this question answered by
the new logic of democracy ?

The answer is one which has its basis in a broad
empirical fact, of which mention has been made already,
and which fifty years of experience have taught democratic leaders to recognise and accept as general.   This
is the fact that as soon as any revolutionary party so
far increases its membership as to make it a considerable
force by the mere weight of its numbers, it invariably
tends to divide itself into two well-marked sections—
one being a majority which, absorbed in its own private
affairs, would rather play skittles in a tavern with a
revolutionary name than concern itself with the details
of dry revolutionary tactics, which in mood, though not
in theory, is afflicted with "a gregarious inertia" often
akin to conservatism, and contents itself with shouting
for revolution in moments of rare excitement; the other
being a minority relatively small, which pores over party
journals, which listens with upturned faces to the oratory
of the party platform, and whose party principles are
held with the energy of sincere conviction.   Such being
the case, then, Professor Michels observes, the apathy of
the large majority, which the democratic leaders at first
found disconcerting, has now come to be viewed by them
in a very different light.   Thus, he says, in France active
members of the General Federation of Labour argue that
the apathy of the mass is positively favourable to the
true revolutionary cause, for it eliminates what would
else be opposition to the policy of the more daring few.
Bakunin, who at one time was celebrated for the terrific
announcement that "the chariot of revolution was roll-
ing, and gnashing its teeth as it rolled," had expressed
the same view already in somewhat different language,
maintaining that the manual labourers, who were to
gain most from the movement, should not be allowed
any voting power in its management, and this same view
or admission is reduced to a definite formula by the
Italian revolutionist, Labriola, prominent as a preacher
of Syndicalism, who, having observed "that it is certainly not revolutionary tactics to entrust the sword of
Brennus to any body of men who, like peasant pro-

prietors, are inclined to the sloth of conservatism,"
proceeds to define what democracy in its true sense is.
"In politics," he says, "as in everything else, the last
thing that true democracy means is the influence of all
men acting as units of equal influence, as though right
were always the sum of the largest assortment of like
individual wills. True democracy, on the contrary, is
the concentrating of power in an *élite*, who can best
judge of the interaction of social cause and effect."

Here we have a clear and temperate statement of
what, in the minds of the leaders of modern revolutionary
parties, the working conception of democracy has at last
come to be. This conception, says Professor Michels,
amounts "to a deliberate denunciation of democracy
in any sense of the word." It will, however, be more
accurate to say that it amounts to a conception of democracy founded on a new conception of the Demos. What
it means or implies is that of any given population a
certain minority alone is found to be endowed with
certain peculiar energies—namely those which exhibit
themselves in connection with social and public questions
as the subject-matter of politics; that for political purposes this minority alone constitutes the Demos in any
reasonable sense of the word; and that in virtue of its
susceptibility to suggestion on the part of the leaders—
that is to say, of the men "who have their own schemes
to which they work"—it forms a Prætorian guard on
which the authority of the leaders rests. In other words,
according to the modern theory, revolutionary democracy (whether in the case of a nation or a party) is
primarily government by a considerable but a relatively
small minority, who are not the people but are simply
the most energetic section of them, and ultimately by a
group of persons "working to schemes of their own,"
who are not this considerable minority, but only an
infinitesimal fraction of it. These two oligarchies—the
larger oligarchy and the less—are practically to settle
the conduct of affairs between them, and the mass of the
citizens—some eighty per cent. of the whole—are for
their own good, which they cannot understand themselves, to submit to the two oligarchies with the best
grace they may.

Conceptions of government such as these can hardly be described as amounting to " a deliberate denunciation of democracy in any sense of the word "; but they do amount to a repudiation—and this is all that concerns us here—of democracy in its pure form. They amount to a negation of everything supposed to be represented by the formula of " one man one vote," or of " equal influence for every man in virtue of his manhood alone." They amount to a direct negation of the idea that the people, taken as a whole, and confronting political questions as an aggregation of equal units, possess any common, definite and effective will at all. They amount to a direct affirmation that an oligarchic element is essential, and that no general will could possibly exist without it.

We need not for the moment push this argument farther, but may content ourselves with noting that the experience of those revolutionary parties which aim at realising democracy to the extremest degree which is practicable, has compelled them in practice, and gradually taught them in theory, not only to recognise that in all complex government an element of oligarchy is indispensable, but also to invoke its action in forms as drastic as any which it ever tends to assume, in the wider sphere of national government, or of the State. If, then, even professional revolutionaries, whose war-cry is " the will of the people," have discovered from experience that the people, except as to the simplest questions, have no definite and guiding will at all, unless it forms itself under the influence, and expresses itself through the action of an oligarchy, we have here a very remarkable illustration of the necessary character of the fact that a similar situation reveals itself in the case of national governments, which have to deal with problems of much greater complexity than any presenting themselves to mere parties of protest.

There are, however, certain democratic optimists, by no means revolutionary in the extreme sense of the word, who, though recognising that the pure and independent will of the people is incapable of dictating to an executive all the details of any national policy, still maintain that a popular will exists, which is quite sufficiently definite for the broad practical purpose of turning the Executive into its humble though trusted servant, and is only hindered from doing so by purely accidental impediments. In order to see how far their position is tenable, we will now resume the main line of our argument, which relates to the nation and the accepted national government, rather than the internal discipline peculiar to this or that disaffected and disruptive party.

CHAPTER VI

DISAPPEARING ILLUSIONS

OUR general argument thus far may be briefly restated thus. It starts with insisting on the fact that, in communities small and primitive and isolated, pure democracy, or government determined by the spontaneous wills of all, is not only a possible system, but is practically the system which exists; and, further, that it continues to exist with regard to those fundamental questions which, in all communities, simple or complex, are the same. In its relation, therefore, to questions such as these, we have a working example of what pure democracy is, by which we can measure how far, with regard to others, its only effective action diverges from the pure type. The extent and nature of its divergence may be indicated once again by a series of simple illustrations such as those which have been used already.

Let us suppose that all the voters of England are assembled in some vast hall, and that the executive government is represented in the person of a single minister, who asks for their corporate will as to the three following questions which he puts before them thus.

(1) "Of late, as you all know, there have been constant attempts at incendiarism by the use of matches and kerosene. Is it your will that the government shall still maintain the police-force which, as you all know, has proved itself able to frustrate them?

(2) "Of late, as you all know, a number of conflagrations have been caused, and might any day be caused again, by incendiary bombs dropped from German airships. Is it your will that the government shall produce an anti-aircraft gun which will shoot down airships as easily as a sportsman shoots a pheasant?

(3) "What is the precise construction, or what are the vital peculiarities, of the gun which, for that purpose, you will that the government shall produce?"

The first question would at once be answered by acclamation, and this would tell the minister everything he asked to be told. All the citizens would know what is meant by the word "policeman," and in expressing by a unanimous shout their will that the police-force should be maintained, they would be giving a definite order which could at once be carried into execution.

The second question would probably be answered by acclamation likewise, and this would tell the minister something of what he asked to be told. It would mean that the people spontaneously willed or ordered the production of a gun of some sort.

But a gun of some sort is practically a gun of no sort. If the minister wanted an order which could definitely guide his actions, he would have to go on to the third question; and if he put this to his audience—if he asked for any working instructions as to what sort of gun this particular gun should be—his question would elicit a response of a very different kind. Most of the assembled voters would stare at him in awkward silence. Some of them would giggle, and think that the minister was laughing at them. Then from a miscellaneous minority would come a volley of answers, most of them worthless, whilst those which were not worthless were so conflicting and various that no ingenuity could invest them with any corporate meaning. The unhappy minister would be driven to shout out to his instructors the very familiar adjuration, "Don't all speak at once."

But that everybody should speak at once is the very thing which the theory of pure democracy demands, and the fact that this demand elicits in some cases the precise result desired illustrates by contrast the absurdity of supposing that it would, or ever could, do so in others. Of the three typical questions which we have just now been imagining, the first elicits a will which is spontaneous, which is unanimous, which is complete. The will elicited by the second is spontaneous, it is unanimous, but it is incomplete, stopping far short of the point at which definite orders must begin. It is, therefore, for

purposes of practical guidance, a nullity. The third
question, which demands that this incomplete will shall
complete itself, fails to elicit any general will at all.
Between will and action there must be a further will
which is still missing. This must be the will of the
minister or oligarchy on whose behalf he speaks, and if
the construction of the desired weapon is ever to be
accomplished at all, the only will which can render its
accomplishment possible is not any will which the many
dictate to the few. It is essentially one which the few
dictate to the many, and which the many must somehow
or other be induced to make their own. Or to put the
matter in more general terms, in proportion as political
questions recede from fundamental simplicity, the power
of unalloyed democracy to deal with such questions
evaporates, and, unless it is quasi-chemically changed
by combination with oligarchy, ceases practically to
exist.

Now the general truth of this argument, as we have
seen in the preceding chapter, has come to be admitted
even by the prophets of extreme revolution. In what
sense, then, can it be contended by persons of more
moderate principles that the people as a homogeneous
whole, or the units of the average mass, have, in spite
of all appearances to the contrary, some definite will of
their own, complete in itself, and independent of any
minority whose talents may happen to be necessary for
the transaction of detailed business? The idea which
such persons have at the back of their minds is well
expressed by a writer who has here been quoted already
as able to state bluntly what many other persons mean.
This writer maintains that, with regard to political questions, no matter how complex, a will is naturally imma-
nent in the units of the average mass, which, due to the
likeness of one unsophisticated man to another, deserves
to be called the specific will of the people, in the only
important sense which that phrase is intended to suggest.
That is to say, in complex cases no less than in simple,
the mass of the people, as distinct from special minorities, have a definite will with regard to "the general
objective of government," though they may not in
complex cases be able to prescribe the means.

There is enough of truth in this argument, and also of very common error, to render it worth attention.

Both the truth and the error are connected with a confusion of thought which, at once fostered and hidden by an inaccurate use of language, makes the term " will " interchangeable with the term " wish." The most careless thinker, if he only gives his mind to the matter, is bound to recognise that, although he constantly confuses them, they stand for two different things, and that though a will must always include a wish, and the two in practice may thus often coincide, a wish in itself is very far from constituting a will. Thus a man may wish, what is probably wished by most men, that he had not perpetrated in his youth a number of foolish actions; but nobody can will, and nobody would say that he wills, not to have done something which twenty years ago he did. He may wish that he could get to Mars, and have a look at the supposed canals. He may wish to get from London to York, and have a look at the Minster. But his wish that he could get to Mars must remain a wish, or an idle emotion only. Why? Because no means exist which he can possibly employ for getting there. His wish to get from London to York may be any day matured into a will. Why? Because means of getting there exist, such as trains or his own legs, by choosing and employing which his wish any day may be accomplished. In other words, a wish is no more than a feeling of desire for a mentally imaged something which, whether possible or absolutely impossible, the imagination presents to the consciousness of the wisher as desirable. A will is a feeling of desire for a mentally imaged something which the person so desiring it knows or believes to be possible by the use of specific means; and only becomes a will when it causes him to adopt, or do his best to adopt them.

These observations as to the difference between wish and will have a special bearing on the question of a general will in politics. When the writer to whom we are here referring claims that in the sphere of political government there is always a general will with regard to the governmental objective, though except in very simple cases there is no such will as to means, what he obviously intends to say—and the nature of his argument shows this—is that, with regard to the objective, there is not a general will, but only some general wish. In the statement, as thus amended, there is doubtless a certain truth. Let us consider how much it comes to.

Governments and their actions are not ends in themselves. Free Trade is not an end in itself. Even the legal administration of justice is not an end in itself. Each is valued only as conducing to some end or objective ulterior to it. The objective in the former case is some kind of prosperity. In the latter it is justice itself, not the means of administering it. Every voluntary action which man is capable of performing is performed, says Aristotle, for the sake of some immediate end; but all such ends, except one, are one after another subsidiary to some end which is beyond themselves; and the ultimate end or objective which alone is desired for its own sake, and which has often been identified with pleasure, is best described, says Aristotle, as "eudaimonia," or happiness. What Aristotle says of human action in general is, with one qualification, true of the actions performed by governments. The objective of governmental action is not happiness itself, but it is the next thing to it. It is best described as Welfare, or the conditions out of which Happiness is most likely to arise, in so far as regulation by an external power can produce them.

The statement must, therefore, in a certain sense be true, that, with regard to the governmental objective, all the units of the average mass, and those indeed of exceptional classes also, do spontaneously wish for one and the same thing; for any one man may be trusted, "in virtue of his manhood alone," to wish for his own welfare just as devoutly as any other man. But a wish of this kind, in so far as it has any relation to the detailed possibilities of life or the possible action of any government whatsoever, is general and unanimous so long only as it is vague. Thus if each citizen, as one out of so many millions, were asked to describe in detail his own conception of the conditions which would constitute welfare for himself, the first condition which they all would agree in naming would no doubt be an income of at least some hundreds a year. Most people, while they were about it, would probably say some thousands.[1] Here, in one sense, would be a very happy unanimity, and it is quite possible that a government might so act (whether by granting monopolies, by creating new posts, or otherwise) as to realise this wish in the case of a citizen here and there. But since there is no country under the sun whose resources could provide even half of such an income for everybody, it is obvious that so many millions of individual wishes, of which only a few thousands or a few hundreds could be gratified, would not, if considered as a guide to governmental actions, be a general wish at all. It would, on the contrary, be a general conflict of wishes, like the wishes of persons pushing for the best seats in a theatre; for every man would be wishing for himself a something which, if obtained by him, would render the fulfilment of other men's wishes impossible.

Let us suppose, however, that the citizens perceive this, and that their wishes for welfare are sobered down to wishes for such conditions only as governmental action of any kind is competent to secure for all; and let us consider how far in detail their wishes are likely to coincide, and thus coalesce into any general will which, to a government waiting for orders, would be clear or even approximately intelligible.

In a simple society, or one relatively simple, which has just emerged from the hunting stage into the agricultural, welfare is spontaneously identified in the minds of most of the citizens with the tenure by each of a sufficient quantity of land, which tenure shall be so secured to him by law that his sole means of earning a livelihood shall never be taken away from him. All such men, therefore, in wishing for their own welfare, wish for the enactment or maintenance of some particular land-law, the essential content of which can be grasped and expressed by everybody; and the expression

---

[1] Amongst the early incidents of the Russian revolution, the strike was announced by a mass of workmen at Rostoff, who demanded wages at the rate of £90 a month, or more than £1000 a year. The total income of Russia did not come to as much as £13 per head of the population.

of it, as addressed to the government, transforms a
general wish into a true general will. It must, however,
be observed that, simple though this case is, there is
one element in it which is not at first sight apparent.
If a government in obedience to such a will is to render
each man's right to a given plot of land inalienable, it
can do so only by depriving him of the right to quit it;
and so long as a society consists mainly of cultivators
this deprivation will be hardly so much as noticed, for
no one would wish to run away from his sole means of
subsistence. But if trade and manufactures begin, as
they did in mediæval England, to offer the cultivator
chances of greater gain than any which he can hope for
whilst he is tethered to the clods of a few acres, his idea
of welfare (as happened in mediæval England) begins
to be complicated by the intrusion of a new element.
To the wish for security is added a wish for freedom.
Hence a further wish arises in a growing number of
minds that a law, which can only secure the means of
subsistence for a man by chaining the man to one means
of subsistence, shall be superseded by a law which will
render this connection dissoluble, and allow him to
choose, if he can find it, a means of subsistence for himself. At the same time, the new law, although it would
have its advantages, would obviously deprive him of
those secured by the old; and every interested person,
before his wish could mature itself into a will that the
new law should be enacted, would have to balance
against its promised advantages the advantages it would
take away—to calculate which alternative would yield
him a net gain : and different minds would be certain
to work out such a sum differently.

This case is typical. In any complex society, out of
all the many wishes which, in the mind of every average
man, vaguely make up the general idea of welfare, there
are few which, if fulfilled completely, would not be found
inconsistent with the complete fulfilment of others.[1]

[1] Here, again, is a fact which has been strikingly illustrated by
incidents of the Russian revolution. The dockers at Archangel refused
to work for more than six hours a day or for more than three days a
week. The docks were blocked with cargoes of coal and other necessaries, which could not be unloaded. By the strikers themselves fuel

The wished-for objective is not a single condition, but a plexus of many, each of which must be limited by the co-existence of others, in order that all together may produce the result, welfare. If the people, then, in respect of their several complete objectives are to have any common will which they are able to impose on the government, this will must be a highly complex thing; and if it is to be expressed in a manner which any government can understand, the expression of it must be equivalent to a picture representing welfare divided into its component parts, the position, dimensions and configuration of each being indicated with such precision that the government may be able to shape its conduct accordingly. Further, if a picture of this kind, with all its complex details, is really to represent the will of the average mass, all the units of the mass must, spontaneously and without prompting, draw it—each for himself—in precisely the same way. But there are two reasons why such a result is impossible. In the first place, a picture of this elaborate kind would have to be drawn from a conception no less elaborate, which the person drawing it had already thought out and matured; and the train of thought required for this purpose would be not only so intricate, but would also deal with quantities so incapable of exact measurement, that the conception thus formed of welfare by any one mind would rarely coincide, even in its main details, with that formed by any other. In the second place, whatever the conception of welfare in a man's own mind may be, it would in most cases bear very little resemblance to the only definite picture by means of which he would be able to communicate it to a government or to anybody else. Such a picture, as drawn by most men, would be like a drawing of its mother by a child, who,

---

was hardly obtainable. The workmen in one great factory insisted on an increase of wages in the ratio of 1 to 5. The value of the total product, out of which alone their wages could come, had presently sunk in the ratio of 200 to 15. Unskilled girls demanded and managed to secure £3 10s. a week. They presently found that their boots cost them £10 a pair. Peasants, who demanded communism in land, were aghast when grain was demanded of them for certain other workers and the army.

being lost in a crowd, should hand it to a policeman in order that he might be able to find her.   If the policeman appeared at the door of the child's nursery afterwards with a creature whose features and proportions were like those of the child's drawing—a creature with legs like sticks, with one eye in its forehead, and another eye in its cheek—the child would certainly exclaim that this was not its mother, but the devil.   The truth of the matter is that for any man to analyse accurately his own conception of the welfare for which he himself wishes, and express it in terms intelligible to any other human being, is a task requiring talents of an exceedingly rare order.   The task of inducing millions of men to unify, for governmental purposes, their various conceptions of what they wish for, by adopting a single conception which is not identical with any of these, is a task requiring talent of a rarer order still; and it is only when this latter task has been accomplished with something like substantial success that a multitude of wishes, previously vague, unlike in their content, and ineffectual, can be converted into a demand for a single set of conditions, all of them absolutely specific, and thus be made to constitute a cumulative and effective will.

Those, then, who claim that the units of the average mass, though they cannot dictate means to the government or the executive oligarchy, have nevertheless, with regard to the governmental objective, some corporate will of their own which a government could be ordered to execute, absolutely ignore the essential point at issue. It is true, and has been said already, that just as will must always precede voluntary action, so must wish always precede will.   The very idea of government, the very idea of a people to be governed, presupposes on the part of the people one common wish at all events—that is to say, the wish to live; and the wish to live, owing to the constitution of the human body, is primarily identified with, and is indistinguishable from, the wish for food.   Now if all men were congregated on an absolutely barren rock, the wish for food would be a wish and a wish only.   No action could follow it, and the human race would die.   Nature, however, has taught men for countless thousands of years that this wish can be satisfied by the immemorial practice of agriculture; but the wish for food is not agriculture itself, although there would be no agriculture without the wish for food. Agriculture is a wish for food-stuffs which has translated itself into a will to produce them by certain means, such as ploughing, sowing, draining, selection of seeds, rotation of crops, and so forth. Similarly, the wish for welfare in a highly civilised State is not political government, though there would be no political government if nobody wished for welfare. Welfare, in so far as political action can secure it, is in any complex society a plexus of intricate and interconnected means, each of which must represent some will as definite as itself; and if each of these means is to represent a will of the people generally, each must represent an indefinite number of wills, all so exactly unified that they practically amount to one. For, just as the same pig can be killed in one way only, so this plexus of means which, so far as government can affect the matter, constitutes welfare in its only possible form, cannot in any one country and at any given moment be, even in the smallest detail, other than the thing it is.

If, then, in order that any particular plexus may be definitely willed by the people to the exclusion of all others, it is necessary (as most serious democrats are now coming to admit) that the means comprised in this plexus, or at all events the larger part of them, shall be first devised by the few, and the people in some way or other induced to will the adoption of them, we are brought by a new route back to the old conclusion. The people, except with regard to simple and fundamental questions, have, apart from an oligarchy, no place in the arena of political life whatever. The contention, in short, that the people, without any oligarchy to guide them, have a definite will of their own as to a highly complex objective, though they have, apart from an oligarchy, no such will as to the means, is a contradiction in terms. It is a contradiction which is disguised by, and due to, a confusion of wish with will; for in the world of political government, as in the world of action generally, the bald truth is this—that a wish which is not identified with a will as to definite means is not a will at all.

Nobody in his senses can deny that such is the case with regard to certain governmental means or objectives when these are taken individually—such, for example, as safety and an anti-aircraft gun. Welfare as a general objective is not only no exception to this rule, but it is, on the contrary, the crowning and the all-comprehensive illustration of it.

The theory, however, of a phantom objective, the realisation of which can be definitely willed by the people though they cannot dictate the means by which such a result may be accomplished, is not the less interesting because it is altogether illusory. On the contrary, it is more so; for it is simply the condensed expression of a vague idea or feeling which the theory of pure democracy tends to develop in the consciousness of the average man. That theory means for each average man who accepts it that there is no individual in the world whose wishes are more important than his own, and no individual who, if all men had their rights, would have greater power than he to impose his own wishes on the government. It thus engenders in him the feeling (which is far more intimate and less open to regulation than the thought) that welfare, as wished for by himself, he being secretly the hero of it, is the special kind of welfare which the government ought to realise.

A homely illustration of this general fact may be found in a letter which was addressed to an American journal by a workman—an immigrant from Austria—after some prolonged experience of affairs in the great Republic. "I was brought up," he said, "in the most aristocratic country in the world, and I have come here to the most democratic. But what good has all this democracy done me? I am no more up to the top of the tree than I ever was." This man's ingenuous complaint was an expression of what millions of other men more or less vaguely feel. Each of these others, animated by the democratic idea that he has no superior either in rights or power, wishes to be at or near the top of the tree somehow. He expects the government somehow or other to put him there; and since the top of the tree, from the nature of things, can be occupied by a few men only, each member of the majority, let the government do what it may, will feel that he is defrauded by it of his own democratic due.   The more democratic a government may be in semblance, and the more profuse, as a consequence, it is in its popular promises, the greater is the discrepancy between its promises and the utmost it is able to perform.   The more widely amongst the governed does a sense of grievance diffuse itself— a mood of unrest and suspicion—which makes it increasingly difficult for any executive oligarchy to secure a democratic assent to such limited measures as alone can, when the time for action comes, be put before the people by any statesmen as practicable.   In a word, the broad result of the theory of pure governmental democracy, especially with reference to the general governmental objective, is to render the people restive by popularising impossible expectations.

That such is the case is shown clearly enough by the course of modern and comparatively modern history. If we take it roughly that the ideas at the root of modern political democracy first became widely effective towards the close of the eighteenth century, we may say that such a mood of restiveness has from the very first, in one country or another, accompanied all attempts at translating the conception of pure democracy into practice.   The true content of such moods, however, has been not precisely what it may seem to have been. It has not amounted, and it does not amount, to a mere uneasy protest that this or that particular government (such as those which formed and dissolved themselves during the course of the French Revolution) was not governmental democracy in its pure and proper form. It comprised from the first the germs of a wider judgment, to the effect that no democracy, the scope of which is purely political, can do anything to secure the conditions which the idea of democracy suggests.   The Austrian immigrant in America who attacked political democracy at the beginning of the twentieth century because it had not enabled him to reach the " top of the tree," did but express a feeling which had developed itself, as we shall see hereafter, when the French Revolution was merely a maturing dream. Before the more immediate effects of that movement had spent themselves Babeuf had boldly declared that no purely political revolutions could have for the masses of the people any meaning whatever, and lost his head in consequence for conspiring against the French Republic. During the earlier years of the nineteenth century, to mention a few names only, (George Rapp, a German; St. Simon and Fourrier, Frenchmen; and Robert Owen, an Englishman,) whilst political democracy was by a large majority still regarded as the key to a near millennium, each in their several ways, and supported by numerous followers, denounced it as wholly incapable of fulfilling its own promises. What these men and others said in effect was this : "The great thing the people want, and the only thing about which they really care, is not to vote equally, but to live equally; and equal living is a thing which political democracy by itself does not give, and does not even tend to give them."

From the middle of the nineteenth century onwards this kind of criticism has continued to increase in volume, and to seek for justification in an increasing number of illustrations. Thus, in France, those who had hoped most from democracy in political government, complain to-day that it has, as a working system, replaced a noblesse by a bourgeoisie far more oppressive; whilst in America, where political democracy has been attempted on the largest scale, conditions are more unequal than in any other country in the world.

But the judgments and the mood of mind which such criticism expresses have been far from taking the turn which at first sight might have seemed likely. Though directed against democracy as a principle which vainly attempts to realise itself so long as it is applied to problems of mere political government, they have not been directed against the principle of pure democracy as such. Their actual meaning has gradually developed into one, which is merely the meaning foreshadowed by men like Babeuf and Owen—that the democratic principle has failed to accomplish its promises hitherto, because it has sought to display itself in too narrow a field. It has followed men to their doorsteps, but has

left them when they went inside. Its action has stopped
short just where it ought to begin. If democracy is
ever to result in a scheme of equal living, it must mainly
be realised in connection with the affairs of private life,
such as industrial production, the distribution of industrial products, and the social interests and intercourse
to which such distribution ministers.

The word "Democracy," when used in this extended
sense, is, as has been said already, commonly distinguished by the epithet "industrial" or "social," or by
both, these being taken to indicate two substantially
different, though closely associated things. Each of
these will here be considered in its proper order. Meanwhile, as to democracy in the sphere of political government, the results of our analysis may be recapitulated
thus.

Pure political democracy, or government in which
every citizen plays really an equal part, is not in itself,
or under all circumstances, impossible. On the contrary,
it is the type of government which in certain communities actually tends to exist. These are communities
which are minute, primitively simple in their conditions,
and isolated. In such communities pure democracy is
possible, and indeed inevitable, because all the questions
are simple which the government has to settle, and
everybody tends to think about them in virtually the
same way. Thus, according to Cæsar, the Gallic tribes
of his day were democracies in times of peace, and
oligarchies in times of war; for in times of war alone
was there any scope or need for the leadership of men
more sagacious and more courageous than the rest.
Further, since in all communities, no matter what their
character, certain simple questions persist as the basis
of associated life, there is an element of pure democracy
in all governments alike. In proportion, however, as
communities increase in size, advance in civilisation, and
come to have chronic dealings with communities other
than themselves, the problems of government multiply,
and most of them become more complex. With regard
to most of them there is room for endless differences of
opinion. The mere task of considering them carefully
is congenial only to men whose mental energy is some-

what above the average, whilst the task of solving them successfully calls for talents and knowledge of special and unusual kinds. For these reasons, two results are inevitable. In the first place, the business of dealing actively with political problems at all tends, from the mere fact of its being laborious, to pass into the hands of the more energetic minority, this body being thus a sort of oligarchic nebula. In the second place, since the solution of these complex problems is not only laborious but difficult, out of this large and nebular oligarchy smaller oligarchies nucleate themselves, which represent, not energy only, but energy combined with various unusual talents, until at last some group is reached (or on critical occasions some one individual) under whose will the wills of the nebular oligarchy range themselves, and are transmitted by oratory or by other means to the mass.

Such is the process which, in every highly civilised country possessing a popular constitution, is taking place under our very eyes. This persistence of oligarchic action is not, as some thinkers contend, due to any defect in the details of mere constitutional mechanism. On the contrary, it becomes more and more pervasive in proportion as such details conform in outer semblance to the democratic ideal. It reveals itself, as we have seen, in the internal organisation of even those sectional parties whose avowed aim is to raise popular power to a maximum. It is due to the permanent facts of human nature on the one hand, and the inevitably complex character of all civilised societies on the other. The case, indeed, may be summed up thus. Nobody would contend, in dealing with the affairs of any great country or empire, whether in times of peace or war, that all exceptional intellect, all exceptional knowledge, all exceptional sagacity and strength of character were superfluous. If talents like these, then, are not absolutely superfluous, it follows that oligarchy of some kind is a necessity; for talent as applied to government can exert itself in one way only—namely that of an influence exercised by a few men over many. The most talented man in the world might be a Cæsar, a Napoleon or a Lincoln within the limits of his own bedroom; but, if he could influence nobody besides himself, his talents would be paralysed if he sat as the chairman of a parish council.

The paralysis of oligarchy would be, therefore, the paralysis of talent. It must, however, be clearly recognised—for here we have a complementary fact which is no less important—that the activity of oligarchy is not the paralysis of democracy. It leaves democracy, in relation to simple and fundamental questions, untouched; whilst with regard to the composite questions which civilisation adds to these, it provides the only means by which, in any definite form, it is practically possible for the principle of democracy to express itself.

We will now extend our inquiry, and consider whether the expulsion of oligarchy and the establishment of pure democracy are projects more practicable in the spheres of industrial and social life than they are in the sphere of politics, as the word "politics" is still commonly understood.

BOOK II

DEMOCRACY AND TECHNICAL PRODUCTION

CHAPTER I

THE DEFINITION OF INDUSTRY

THE idea of extending the application of the democratic principle beyond the scope of such government as is commonly called political is in itself no novelty. The speeches which Aristophanes in his play, *Women in Parliament*, puts into the mouths of his agitators male and female correspond almost word for word with countless actual speeches which are made on socialist platforms and at street corners to-day. This idea, however, in the forms with which the world is now familiar is distinctively modern in respect of its theoretical details, and also of the extent to which it has become prevalent. Democracy to-day, in the extended sense of the word, is, as we have seen already, commonly described as "Industrial" Democracy, or "Social." These two epithets are often used interchangeably; but implications of the latter, as we shall see more fully hereafter, differ from those of the former in the fact that they are more comprehensive, and less easy to define. It will be necessary, therefore, to consider Industrial Democracy first, and rigidly exclude, in doing so, all reference to activities which do not pertain to the process of actual industry itself. How important precision with regard to this point is, will be seen from the following statement made by a well-known socialist, which we may take here as our text.

"Every day," says Mr. Sidney Webb, "there is a growing consensus of opinion that the inevitable outcome of democracy is the control of the main instruments of production by the people themselves, and the consequent recovery of what John Stuart Mill calls ' the enormous share which the possessors of industry ' are able to take of ' the total produce.' " Now, this short statement, which seems simple enough, is in reality a combination of three.

The first is to the effect that, though the actual process of production is carried on mainly by a body called " the people themselves," they get at present only a part of what they produce, the remainder being appropriated by persons who are mere " possessors " of the materials on which, and the great mechanisms and appliances by which, the actual producers operate.

The second is to the effect that if the democratic principle were really applied to industry, the present privileges of these mere " possessors " would cease, and " the people themselves " would be able, in accordance with their several efficiencies, to secure that " share " of their products which is now unjustly withheld from them.

The third is to the effect that this share is " enormous."

Now it is obvious that, even if all these statements were correct, there would be no integral connection between the first two and the third. Whether the " share " alleged to be withheld is so great as to merit the name " enormous " or no, is a question which can be determined by statistical inquiry only, and it might conceivably be answered in one way or another without the first statement or the second being in point of principle affected. But the difference between the first and the second is even more fundamental. As Mr. Webb puts these, they are indeed united by the implication that production and distribution should in justice go hand in hand, and that no man should get more than he produces, and no man should get less. But the fact that these two processes are in their nature separable, is shown by the socialists themselves, whose chief complaint is that under the existing system the facts of individual production and the principles of distribution are separated.

When Mr. Webb starts with saying that the inevitable

outcome of democracy is the transference of the control of industry or production to the people, and that this transference is to be accomplished by putting the people in possession of the great modern instruments, which must include the raw materials, of production, he shows clearly enough what industry is understood to be. Industry is the fashioning by men of the crude gifts of nature into finished goods with the aid of appropriate implements, and the transport of these goods to the shops or other places where they pass at length into the hands of the final user or consumer. But the process which determines what share of the goods, when they are finished, shall pass into the hands of one class of consumer or another has no effect on the processes by which goods of any given kind are produced. The income, or, as Mill calls it, "the total produce" of a nation may be compared to a great plum-pudding of specified weight and quality. Now, if nobody was going to eat it or get any share of it at all, it is perfectly true that the pudding would never have been made; but the fact that it is there, and ready to be eaten by somebody, is the primary fact that Mr. Webb's statement presupposes. Such being the case, then, the processes involved in the production of it will have consisted of a number of operations, such as the getting together of certain given materials—flour, suet, sugar, spice, raisins and so forth—the mixing of them in given quantities, and the boiling of them for a given time; which operations performed by human hands might be accurately recorded in a series of photographic diagrams; and these operations, which are a type of what is meant by industry, would, if the pudding were to be produced at all, be in themselves the same, no matter whether this man or that man should eat more or less than the rest.

This is what the doctrinaires of Industrial Democracy forget, and the origin of their error is not far to seek. Assuming as they do that a few men, under existing conditions, tend to swallow up most of the national income between them, they fix their attention on the fact that great masses of men engaged in industrial work are already able, by forming themselves into Trade

Unions, to secure in the form of wages a larger share of what Mill calls "the total produce" than the "possessors" or the employers would have conceded to them had compulsion of this kind been absent. Hence, to such thinkers it seems that we here have a living example of industrial democracy beginning to come into its own. Now such thinkers may be perfectly right in claiming for the Unionist movement a democratic character of some sort, but the error which they commit is this. They assume that because the action of Unions as a means of augmenting wages is the action of men who happen to be engaged in industry, it must of necessity be in itself industrial. They might just as well argue that if some important fortress had been captured by the gallantry of a regiment made up wholly of post-impressionist painters, the feat was a triumph of the principles of a particular school of painting. Let us suppose that the English dyeing industry, having suffered for years from the scientific competition of Germany, suddenly gets the better of its rival through the discovery and perfecting of some secret and hitherto undreamed-of process. The wage-earners employed in an industry thus resuscitated might conceivably manage by strikes or other concerted action to raise their collective wages from (let us say) half the total gains of the business to two-thirds, three-quarters, four-fifths or even a larger fraction. But such action on their part would not have the least effect on any one of those novel actions, elaborately prescribed and timed, which their hands would have to execute in order to render that total gain possible out of which their wages, whether large or small, would come. What they did as members of a Union would have been democratic action of some sort, but it would not have been action of the sort which alone is industrially productive. It would have belonged, not to the province of industrial democracy, but to that wider province of democratic action which must, as we shall see in greater detail hereafter, be comprehended under the term "social." We will, therefore, in discussing Industrial Democracy, use the word "industrial" here in its sole legitimate sense—the sense indicated by Mill, when he says that every action which

is commonly called "industrial" or "productive"
resolves itself ultimately into one species of operation—
namely the transference by human hands of material
substances from one position to another. Mill ought to
have included the action of the human intelligence in
determining what the substances selected for transference should be, and how and in what order the various
rearrangements should be made; but the fact remains
that no action is industrial which does not subserve or
culminate in the re-arrangement of material substances
in such a way as to convert them into material or
economic goods, or which does not consist of such
services as may be requisite for the final enjoyment of
them.

The scope of our present inquiry having been, then,
thus delimited, we may now go on to consider what,
according to current conceptions of it, the principle of
pure democracy as applied to industry means.

CHAPTER II

PURE DEMOCRATIC INDUSTRY

WHAT, according to current conceptions of it, democracy means in the sphere of political life has been shown by reference to the words of the American writer, who describes it as a system of government which ensures that "every citizen shall, ' in virtue of his manhood alone,' exert an equal influence ' over the affairs of the common country.' " In the same way, when extended to the sphere of industry, the idea of pure democracy means that every worker, not indeed because he is a man, but because, and in so far as, he is a man who works industrially, shall play an equal part in the technical process of production; or that production, as Mr. Webb and others say in more general language, "shall be controlled by the people themselves."

Now, the first point emphasised in our argument with regard to political government was that the word "people," as used by the doctrinaires of democracy, must, if it has any distinctive meaning at all, mean the units of the average mass to the exclusion of any minority whose talents and energies are above the average standard, and whose judgments, in so far as they differed from those of the great majority, would, if allowed to prevail, make the average mass subject to them. The units of this minority would, under such a system, not indeed be in theory disfranchised; but the majority could always outvote them, and in this way would necessarily render their exceptional judgments nugatory.

Here, as we have seen already, is one of the most obvious difficulties which besets the idea of democracy as applied to political government; but in the sphere of technical production it is practically much more for-

midable. A rudimentary example of it may be seen in
the Trade Union policy which forbids a bricklayer,
specially alert and dexterous, to lay more bricks in a
day than can be laid with ease by the great mass of his
fellows. This is a policy which experience shows to be
practicable, but the principle involved in it has its
obvious limits. Not even the extremest advocate of
democratic or Trade Union principles would forbid a
very skilful surgeon to mend a man's broken leg, on the
ground that most surgeons could do nothing better than
amputate it. Indeed, in view of modern applications
of abstruse science to industry, the most careless thinker
will experience a difficulty in contending that production
could have reached or could maintain its present
efficiency if no judgments or faculties took any part in
controlling it except such as are formed and exercised
by ninety-nine men of every hundred. And that here
we have a difficulty which at all events requires attention is shown by the fact that the doctrinaires of Industrial Democracy have of late years spent much of their
ingenuity in attempts at explaining it away. The
nature and the value of these attempts we shall have
occasion to discuss presently. For the moment it is
enough to observe that, whatever their value may be,
they must, for a time at all events, have seemed satisfactory to a large number of enthusiasts; for they have
enabled even thinkers who claim to be taken seriously
to go on repeating, without any admitted qualification,
that Industrial Democracy is the goal of all human
progress, and that Industrial Democracy, according "to
a growing consensus of opinion," means the control or
the entire direction of industry by the units of the
"people themselves," which can only mean the units
of the average mass to the exclusion of all those whose
talents are above the average.

If we wish, then, to arrive at any conclusion as to how
far the conception of pure industrial democracy is in any
way consonant with the facts or the possibilities of life,
let us consider it as reduced to a strict and ostensibly
scientific theory by the thinker to whom, however widely
they may have come to differ from him in detail, the
industrial democrats of to-day all owe their inspiration.

That thinker is Marx; and he has this merit, at all
events, that he provides us with a doctrine which, if we
can accept it as true, invests the idea of production as
a purely democratic process with a clear-cut and intelligible meaning, and also connects this meaning with
daily-experienced fact.

The primary propositions of Marx may be briefly
summed up thus. If we take at starting the raw gifts
of nature for granted, all economic wealth is the product
of manual labour, or the impact of hands on matter;
and further, if allowance be made for cases of abnormal
weakness, the amount of wealth which every labourer
produces by working with normal diligence for a given
time is equal. Marx was careful to add that, when
labour is thus spoken of, it must not be taken to consist of mere manual efforts as such, but includes in the
case of each individual labourer those mental activities
by which his manual efforts are directed, and which form
an essential part of his indivisible manhood. But this
careful enlargement of the meaning of the term
"labour" is so far from enlarging the sense of the
original formula that it does but accentuate what were
intended by Marx to be its limitations. The essence of
his meaning is that, though mental effort of some sort
must always direct manual, this mental effort in the case
of each labouring unit must be taken as directing the
movements of his own hands only, and not as dictating,
controlling, or exercising a mastery over the technical
movements of the hands of an aggregate of other men.

That such is his general meaning when he lays down
the proposition that the wealth-product of all labourers,
hour for hour, is equal, will be seen more clearly if we
consider his argument in detail. Labour in all civilised,
and even in semi-civilised countries, is, he says, so far
divided that different labourers devote themselves to
different trades. Each of them, wholly or mainly, lives
by producing one class of goods only, of which he himself
will consume little, or perhaps nothing. Hence, the
results of his labour, in so far as they are wealth for
himself, will not consist of the things which he has
fabricated with his own hands, but of other and various
things which have been fabricated by the hands of

others, and which, by parting with his own products, he is able to get in exchange for them. Hence, whenever an exchange is made, the first thing necessary is a common standard of some kind, by which the value of unlike goods may be estimated; and, according to Marx, wealth-value is determined by one thing only—namely the amount of manual labour which, as measured by time, is commonly required for the production of whatever goods may be in question. Thus, if each of a hundred labourers labouring for a hundred hours produces so many finished commodities, no matter what their character, whether they consist of mince-pies, watches, pints of blacking, delicate carvings, jewels, or flints broken into fragments for the purpose of mending roads, the total product [1] of each man will purchase as much of the products of any number of the others as requires, if they are taken together, a hundred hours to produce them. Hence, Marx and his followers have contended that the proper medium of exchange would be, not money in its ordinary form, but "labour-checks," each of which would be a certificate that the holder had worked with his hands for so many hours or minutes, and was therefore entitled to so much of any commodities as any other worker could produce in the same time.

Now, if this theory of wealth-production be at once correct and complete, it not only provides a logically coherent meaning for the conception of industrial democracy in its most unqualified form, as a multitude of processes conducted by absolutely equal units, but it also gives us a picture of industrial democracy in action —in action not only as a possibility, but as a hard contemporary fact. Indeed, to call it a theory at all, as is often done, is misleading. When Marx said that manual

---

[1] The total product of each labourer is to be understood as the value which his own labour adds to the raw material on which he works. Thus the value of an ounce of gold represents the labour necessary, on an average for finding it, and presenting it to other labourers in a workable form. According to Marx every goldsmith who spends a week in fashioning an ounce of gold into a spoon adds an equal value to the metal, no matter what may be the artistic quality of his work. An artist adds no more to the value of an ounce of gold in a week than a stone-breaker adds to the value of a heap of stones, or than a pastry-cook adds to the value of so much flour and butter.

labour is the sole human agency involved in the production of wealth, he did not mean that it would be so
under such and such changed conditions. He meant
that it is so now, that it always has been and will be,
and that no productive agent other than the man who
works with his hands is possible. Similarly, when he
said that every manual labourer produces in a given
time goods of an equal value, he meant that everywhere,
in the actual markets of the world, goods do exchange
in proportion to the labour-time required for their production, the kind and quality of the labour being matters
of complete indifference. And if anybody should ask
why, in the minds of Marx and his followers, industrial
democracy—a thing already established—should be
associated with revolutionary change, the answer is that
the kind of change they contemplated had nothing to
do with the industrial process as such. It related solely
to the fact that the implements which the equal labourers
use (such as factory plant and means of transport) have,
owing to political or social accidents, been nefariously
appropriated by men who, so far as production is concerned, have nothing to do with the industrial process
at all. Marx was never weary of insisting that the
modern "possessors of industry"—the employing or
capitalist classes—owe their present positions to historical accidents solely, which enable them to appropriate most of what the industrial democracy produces,
whilst they themselves—to use a phrase frequent in
Marxian oratory—"do but sit in their chairs watching
the machine go." Let these mere parasites be eliminated either by the social pressure of Trade Unions, or
politically by the pressure of legislation, or if needs be
by armed rebellion, and industry itself—so the argument
of Marx proceeds—will not be hampered or dislocated
by any technical change. Remaining what it always
has been and must be, namely a purely democratic
process, it will still be as efficient as before; but the
fact that it will operate under changed social conditions
will render that vast fraction of the product which the
parasites now appropriate available for distribution
amongst the manual labourers alone, whose hands and
brains have alone played any part in producing it.

Here we have the outlines of that classical doctrine of production on which all the earlier conceptions of industrial democracy based themselves, and which the industrial democrats of to-day, whilst repudiating many of its details, have endeavoured to re-establish in the form of revised versions. But, before considering what these revised versions come to, let us consider the doctrine in the form in which Marx left it, with its two salient propositions—that wealth is produced by manual labour only, and that all manual labourers as productive agents are equal; and let us ask whether there is or ever has been any state of society to which these propositions are applicable. The answer to this question will probably be a surprise, not only to critics who regard Marx with contempt, but even to the more discerning of those who, being in sympathy with his temper and his objects, are naturally inclined to agree with him so far as they reasonably can.

Without indulging in any non-historical fancies, such as those which constituted the stock-in-trade of Rousseau, it is possible to look back to stages of primitive life in which the process of production actually did conform, with substantial exactness, to the terms of the Marxian doctrine. In those societies which preceded the organisation of slavery all the little wealth that existed was produced by manual labourers, each using his hands under the direction of his own intelligence. Further, we may assume that as producers they were all of them fairly equal, and that their products, in so far as there was any occasion to exchange them, exchanged in proportion to the time that was necessary for the production of each.

But, however completely primitive conditions such as these may have realised the Marxian conception of the industrial process in some respects, there is one respect in which they differ notoriously from that process as it exists to-day. Relatively to the time consumed, and to the number of individuals engaged in it, the volume of products in which that process results to-day is incomparably greater than it was, not only in the primitive, but even in a recent past. If, then, manual labour directed solely by the minds of the labourers themselves remains always and under all conditions the sole productive agency as it was when the world began, and if no one labourer working for a given time produces appreciably more wealth than another, the question arises of how the output of labour as a whole can ever be greater in one age than in another.

The pertinence of this question was recognised by Marx himself, but in the sole answers which he himself could suggest he merely evaded the difficulty by translating it into another form. Manual labour, he said, has in the modern world acquired an efficiency never known before, because "the implements of production have been concentrated," whereas prior to the development of capitalism on a large scale they were "scattered." Thus, for a thousand hand-looms once scattered amongst a hundred villages is now substituted the mechanism of a single gigantic mill; and a thousand weavers, previously working in isolation, cluster round this one mill for a common productive purpose. By such means, says Marx, two results have been accomplished. Manual labour, within the limits of each industry, has been enabled to divide itself to an extent never before possible; and through the employment of great unitary mechanisms, each actuated by a single monstrous engine, "society" has acquired "a new control over the productive forces of nature."

Now, all this may be true enough, but it leaves the question at issue altogether untouched. Certain changes, such as those which Marx roughly indicates, have no doubt occurred. So much we may take for granted. But these changes must have been due, and their maintenance must be due also, to the actions of human beings—mental actions or manual, or mental and manual combined. The question is, by whom were these actions performed? Were they all planned and performed by average manual labourers, directed by no knowledge and no intelligence but their own? Did no other class play any part in the matter? Does no other class play any part in it to-day? Marx himself admits—he not only admits, he asseverates—that one of the changes in question, namely "the concentration of the implements," was the work of "infamous persons" who never did a stroke of manual labour in their lives, and who concentrated the implements merely by getting possession of them, thus causing the labourers to "concentrate themselves" in the same way. But since the men—the modern capitalists—by whom the implements came to be possessed, had, according to Marx, no other object than that of extracting a toll from the labourers whom they allowed to use them, these capitalists certainly, if the argument of Marx is correct, can have done nothing personally to make labour more productive. The crucial questions still unanswered are these. Did the labourers, their concentration being once accomplished, proceed to divide their individual labour-tasks for themselves? Did they, and do they, as units of equal influence, accomplish for themselves the intricate task of coordinating them? And finally, to come to the point on which everything else turns, is it solely to the equal talents of average manual labourers, cogitating in their spare time, that we owe that "new control over the productive forces of nature" by which the modern system of production is distinguished from all others?

It will be observed that, in speaking of the triumphs of industrial science, Marx shrinks from the naked proposition that nobody but manual labourers played any part in achieving them. He takes refuge in saying that they have somehow been achieved by "society." But since, according to his own reiterated statements, "society" is composed of two classes only—namely labourers who produce everything, and idlers who produce nothing—he cannot mean that the most important additions ever made to the productive efficiency of mankind are due to the latter—that the latter, the mere idlers, have had anything whatever to do with them. He must mean that they are due to the labourers, and due to them only—men no one of whom, in point of productive efficiency, is, according to him, superior to any other. Further, he must mean precisely the same thing with regard to that other process which he notes as no less peculiar to production in modern times—that is to say, the new subdivision of labour-tasks, and the elaborate organisation of the multitudes performing them in scientific concert. He must mean that this subdivision and organisation are devised, determined and carried out by the manual labourers themselves, all of them acting together as units of equal influence, and unaided by any intelligence superior to or other than their own. He must mean that industry in its most elaborate, most scientific and most productive forms, is a process no less purely democratic to-day than it was in the days when the homes of men were caves, when their clothes were skins or loin-cloths, and their implements were sticks and stones. He must mean, in short, that in any human society the labour of the average units, if we begin with taking it in its rudest and most primitive stage, contains or has contained in itself the potency of indefinitely great developments, solely through the exercise of those mental and manual faculties in respect of which no one unit is appreciably superior to the rest. Is this the case? Does the history of mankind offer any evidence to show that mere average labour, uninfluenced by any oligarchic authority, becomes able to produce in one age an output of material wealth appreciably larger than it previously had been in another? And the answer is that, up to a certain point, a purely democratic progress of this kind is indubitable, the implications of the Marxian doctrine being up to that point justified.

The explanation of this progress is to be found in the following historical causes, none of which, so far as the technique of production is concerned, involve the exertion of any mental or manual faculties beyond such as are possessed by the vast majority of the units of whatever race may be in question. These causes are four in number :—

Firstly, the early localisation of industries, which, as Herbert Spencer points out, has been the first distinctive feature of every community when emerging from the primitive or sub-primitive stage ;—

Secondly, a gradual division of task-work within the limits of each industry itself ;—

Thirdly, certain very simple inventions, such as the plough, the hand-loom, the potter's wheel, and the small boat ; together with the discovery, due to common experience or to chance, of the qualities of various substances (such as flints or metals), and of various very simple processes :—

Fourthly, a certain coercion of the labourers which, though exercised over them by men other than themselves, is not necessarily connected with labour in respect of its technical details, but which merely causes it to be more intense and continuous.

All these causes consist either of the action of experience and circumstance on average minds and hands, or of the average reaction of such minds and hands to these.

Thus, the early localisation of industries was, as Herbert Spencer explains, due to the unequal manner in which the gifts of nature are distributed, cultivable land, potter's clay, and fish, for example, being severally most plentiful in so many different neighbourhoods, and the occupants of each neighbourhood, in accordance with this distribution, devoting themselves severally to tillage, the making of pots, and fishing.[1] By dividing their industries thus, so that each is confined to the places where it can be practised to the best advantage, men have increased the efficiency of their otherwise unchanged labour, without the exercise of any mental faculties beyond those by which all men alike are distinguished from the higher animals.

The division of labour-tasks within the limits of each industry itself is, up to a certain point, a spontaneous process likewise. In the case of any commodity the production of which requires more than one kind of operation, any one labourer can discover just as easily as any other that if he confines himself to a few operations only he acquires a quickness of hand which would else be beyond his reach. A group of labourers may thus become more productive without invoking the aid of any faculties but their own.

The same thing may be said of those basic inventions and discoveries which have become, one after another, almost co-extensive with mankind. They have been the results of diffused experience, or a multitude of sporadic accidents, each of them speaking plainly to the average

---

[1] Thus in Fiji the coastal inhabitants produce salt. The inhabitants of an inland district, who have never seen the sea, produce sails.

human brain, and telling nothing to any one man which could not be grasped by all.

The fourth of the four causes here in question—that is to say, the institution of slavery—by enabling (as Mill says) a permanently leisured class to devote its faculties to the accumulation of systematic knowledge, gradually resulted in the application of such knowledge to industry. In the great empires of antiquity the genius of the scientific architect and the abstruse lore of the astronomer were stamped on the labours of the mason. The genius of Archimedes was operative in the ship-yards of ancient Syracuse. This aspect of the matter, however, does not concern us here. In the present connection the sole fact to be noted is that, quite apart from any technical guidance of the labour of slaves by slave-owners, the coercion of the former by the latter made the labour of the former more pro-ductive by merely rendering more intense and continuous a number of industrial actions, such as those involved in agriculture, which the labourers, with less assiduity, had already carried out by themselves.

We may therefore concede to Marx and the earlier socialists that, not only in primitive and sub-primitive times, but even under the ancient slave-systems such as those of Rome and Egypt, the industrial process was, to a very great extent, a process carried on by manual labourers only, who were subject to orders so far as results were concerned, but who, in respect of their methods, operated as a true democracy. Since, then, the wealth of the world in primitive times was small, and since, owing to the technical actions of manual labourers alone it has increased notoriously up to a certain point, the question is what, as a matter of history, are the utmost limits which this increase has reached, and to what extent, and to the presence of what new causes, has the industrial process as a whole made a further advance since then?

If we take as our standard of efficiency production as it is to-day, we shall find that the progress thus exhibited by the manual labourers themselves, striking as its results have been, does not carry us far. The mere localisation of industries, important though it is as a starting-point, is a process, if taken by itself, the results of which are soon exhausted, as is plain from the fact that it is extant in many communities whose condition is still one of semi-primitive poverty. Of those basic inventions and discoveries, examples of which have just been given, and also of the increased dexterity due to divisions of task-work in its earlier and simpler forms, the effects on the efficiency of the manual labourers as a whole have limits which are susceptible of more accurate measurement. That the great basic inventions such as the loom and plough were the products of industrial democracy when still in its earlier stages, is a fact frequently emphasised by industrial democrats to-day; and the inference which they draw from it is that all inventions and discoveries—those of to-day no less than those of yesterday—are attributable to the mass of average labourers likewise. They could hardly have hit on an argument of a less fortunate kind. It is one which proves nothing but the narrowness of its own application; for in all countries where labour is still to be found operating solely or mainly under the direction of the manual labourers themselves, the inventions and processes in use at the present day still remain what they were thousands of years ago. These primitive inventions of democracy having once been made, democracy in its pure state has subsequently made no others. Mere dexterity has, as a productive agent, shown itself capable of a more protracted progress; but this, too, reached its limits before any of the extant civilisations of the western world began. The brick-makers, the masons, the carpenters, and other craftsmen of to-day, if left to perform their tasks under the guidance of their own brains only, would in a given time produce nothing more or nothing better than their predecessors did in Rome at the dawn of the Christian era.

It remains for us to consider the extent to which the product per head of a given number of labourers working under their own direction may be increased by mere coercion. The increased continuity of effort which was imposed on the labourers from without by the slave-systems of the ancient world, and (we may add) by the *corvée* system of the Middle Ages also, has had effects which spectacularly were very much more conspicuous than any which have resulted from the other causes here in question. But these effects have had their narrow limits likewise. Of all these four causes, indeed, the mere coercion of labour from without is really the one whose influence is least expansive; for its effects are determined, not by the potentialities of the average man's brain, or of his hands as mere instruments of skill, but by something much less elastic—namely the maximum of muscular effort of which, within a given time, a man's organism is, as a whole, capable. Thus, if so many primitive labourers, working (let us say) for twelve hours a day, would have produced a product per head which was expressible by the number 6, it is conceivable that through division of task-work, simple inventions and so forth, they might, without more physical effort, have come to produce in a labour-day of the same length a product per head expressible by the number 12. But it is obvious that their product could not, by any mere prolongation of their labour-hours, be raised in the proportion of 12 to 24, for no slave-owner could extort from the strongest slave a regular labour-day of twice twelve hours' duration. It is true that the splendours of Rome, imperial, public and private, could never have come into existence if the manual labour of multitudes had not been intensified by pressure on the part of the ruling few; but mere pressure as thus applied to a mass of manual labourers, though an essential element of the case, was far from being its sole peculiarity. An accessory feature, in many ways more important, was the fact that the slave-owning classes, besides intensifying to the utmost the labour of the democracy which worked for them, were to a degree far greater able to increase its numbers. The wealthy classes of antiquity, when their wealth had reached a certain point, may be compared to a single individual who, starting with a patrimony (let us say) of five hundred slaves, lets them out to a mine-owner—a case of this precise kind is mentioned by Athenæus—receiving for each a rent of £10 a year, ends with raising his income from £5,000 to £10,000, not by making five hundred slaves work either harder or better, but simply by getting possession of five hundred more. The income of the slave-owner is doubled, but the product of each slave separately is no greater than it was before.

Thus, a labouring population being given, which is in a technical sense a self-directing democracy, the extent to which its output can be increased by mere coercive pressure, is, though considerable, nothing like so great as at first sight it may seem; and without attempting to fix an exact date, we may say that it reached its maximum under the earlier Roman emperors. It is needless to enlarge on the fact—for no one is likely to dispute it—that the societies of Mediæval Europe were not richer than the society for which Pompeii was a third-rate watering-place, and Antioch, Alexandria and Corinth, with its four-hundred-thousand slaves, were no more than provincial towns. The movement called the Renaissance was, in industry as in other things, an attempt to recover ground which since the days of the Cæsars had been lost; and it may be said with confidence that, up to the end of the eighteenth century, there was not a country in the world in which self-directed manual labour produced, relatively to the number of persons engaged in it, more than it did in the days of Nero or Hadrian.

If, then, we concede to Marx and his followers—as for purposes of argument we may do, though with many actual reservations [1]—that even up to a time so recent as the close of the eighteenth or the beginning of the nineteenth century manual labour as directed by the minds of the labourers themselves was the sole producer of wealth no less truly than it is amongst primitive savages to-day, the history of labour so far, as a productive agent, will be as follows. The productivity of labour having been at the beginning of things not more than sufficient to provide the human animal with the bare necessaries of existence, such as leaves to sleep on and scraps of skin for clothing, the labourers gradually in the course of untold ages, through the simple interaction of experience and common human intelligence,

---

[1] Sombart has dealt with examples of capitalist or oligarchic enterprise in the Middle Ages, and in the 16th and 17th centuries. We are dealing here not with existencies, but with predominancies.

found themselves able to fashion an increasing number of commodities—such as huts adroitly thatched, lake-dwellings of morticed wood-work, gracefully-shaped utensils, hideous nose-rings, and patterned textile fabrics. They thus raised their manner of life to the lower levels of civilisation, and the personal faculties acquired by them were, as Herbert Spencer explains, raised to a higher power when certain warlike races, cradled in barren regions, enslaved the less virile inhabitants of regions exceptionally fertile, and compelled them to exert these faculties with a new and more sustained intensity. Under this stimulation the powers of manual labour rose and fell in one region after another, until, having reached their maximum prior to the days of Diocletian, they declined or came to a standstill for more than fifteen hundred years. Then in a manner so rapid that history may regard it as sudden, a change took place the like of which had never been seen before. First in England, and subsequently throughout most of the western world, the industrial process as a whole acquired some new vitality; and the volume and variety of its products, relatively to the number of human beings engaged in it, made a greater advance in the course of a single century than it had done during all the millenniums of human life preceding it.

· With this general account of the matter Marx himself would have been in entire agreement. Indeed, the recent unparalleled increase in the productive efficiencies of mankind is a phenomenon which he and his followers have inclined to caricature rather than to underestimate. Further, they admit, as we have seen, that in order to produce such a change in the industrial result, there must have been commensurate changes in the technical details of the industrial process likewise—changes which, as Marx says, developed themselves first in England, and which, though far from sudden in the strict sense of the word, became first assured and conspicuous at a date which was not much earlier than that of the battle of Waterloo. How the nature of these changes is explained by Marx himself has just now been briefly stated; but, as has been said already, the only explanations which he suggests must have some other explanation at the back of them, and one which his own do not even so much as hint at. We will now go on to consider what this ultimate explanation is. We shall find that it lies in none of the facts which Marx contents himself with enumerating—not in the mere growth of knowledge, not in the mere development of scientific ma- chinery, not in the mere concentration of the labourers, or in any new subdivision of their labour tasks. All these causes, however real, are secondary, and require themselves to be explained. The basic explanation is to be found in a fact which lies deeper than any of them.

CHAPTER III

THE SECRET OF MODERN PROGRESS

LET us summarise once again the explanation which Marx gives of the vast productive powers of industry in the modern world. These novel and unparalleled powers are due, he says, to three causes;—

Firstly, a "concentration" of the implements of pro-duction which in former times were "scattered," and used more or less in isolation by the individual labourers owning them;—

Secondly, the new subdivision and more intelligent co-ordination of labour tasks which in each business becomes possible by the massing together of all the labourers concerned in it;—

And, thirdly, the new stores of practical scientific knowledge which "Society" has acquired whilst these changes were in progress, and which, embodied in new mechanisms and processes, have given man a "new control over the productive forces of nature."

Now, the first of these three causes—namely the con-centration of implements—vast as have been its indus-trial effects, was, according to Marx, not in itself an industrial process at all. It consisted in the buying up by men otherwise idle of all the little implements pre-viously owned by the users of them, and the stacking of these implements together in so many walled enclo-sures, to which the labourers had to flock if they wished to produce anything. It was simply the triumphant generalisation of a practice actually rife in England in the middle of the sixteenth century. This was a practice inaugurated by "the great clothiers," and called "the engrossing of looms" (which meant the acquisition of the implements of production in the weaving trade) and "the letting them out to poor artificers at a rent." Its object and its result were, according to Marx, simply to affect distribution by enabling the "engrossers" to appropriate the larger part of the product; but it had nothing to do with the details of the productive process at all. These were still determined by the manual labourers themselves. The causes, therefore, to which modern industry owes those vastly increased efficiencies which are still the wonder of the world, are, according to the Marxian logic, not three, but two—namely the acquisition of " a new control over the productive forces of nature," and a new subdivision and a more elaborate co-ordination of the tasks performed directly by the labourer's own hands.

Now, this explanation of the first cause—namely the acquisition and concentration of the implements by a personally non-productive class—might have at all events some superficial plausibility, if applied to conditions as they were up to the middle of the eighteenth century. In Hogarth's series of pictures, "The Industrious and the Idle Apprentice," there are two representing the interior of the business premises of a rich cloth-weaver; and what we see is one room after another in which a number of hand-looms are being worked, each by a single operative. The implements are practically the same as they had been in the Middle Ages. They have undergone no change whatever, except for the fact that they have been congregated under a single roof. But between an establishment such as this, which was typical of the eighteenth century, and the kind of establishment which was typical of the century following there is one profound difference of which Marx was fully aware, but of which, when he speaks of concentration, he takes no account whatever. This difference consists in the fact that, whereas in the middle of the eighteenth century the implements of earlier periods had been changed only by being concentrated, they were, from the beginning of the nineteenth century onwards, not concentrated only, but reconstructed, unified and entirely metamorphosed also. That metamorphosis accompanied concentration—that the two processes rapidly came to be inseparable—was as plain to Marx as to anybody, as his own language shows; for it was only the metamorphosis of hundreds of puny appliances into vast unitary mechanisms actuated by huge engines that gave to the human worker what he calls "a new control over the productive forces of nature." But as to how the metamorphosis was accomplished, the theory of Marx is silent, and he hides its silence under a veil of inept tautology. The metamorphosis, he says, is attributable to the modern growth of knowledge. That, no doubt, is true; but of knowledge acquired, and knowledge applied, by whom? What he aims at proving is that, apart from the concentration of the various implements of production, in respect of their ownership and their locality, by a purely possessive and industrially idle class, the entire progress of industry was accomplished by the labourers alone. If such was the case, then, the manual labourers generally must, from the beginning of the nineteenth century onwards, have not only reorganised for themselves the whole of the various tasks performed by their own hands, readjusting and re-devising them in the light of new and abstruse knowledge, but the whole of this new knowledge must have been acquired by themselves also. They must themselves have translated it into that new order of mechanisms without which their new accomplishments in the way of self-organisation would be nugatory.

Is there, then, any reason for supposing, or is it even remotely conceivable, that the labourers, unguided by any brains but their own, accomplished by democratic agreement both these processes, or either of them? The knowledge involved in the metamorphosis of a collection of old hand-looms into the plant of a modern cotton-mill, or of a yardful of old stage-coaches into motor-cars or express trains, was of a very elaborate kind. Did it spring up in the brains of all the labourers spontaneously, as a sense of sin springs up at a revival meeting? Did it even originate in the brains of Trade Union delegates, from whose speeches their constituents imbibed it, assenting to it by a show of hands? On the contrary, in the process of acquiring the multitudinous knowledge in question, and translating it by means of machinery into "a new control over the productive forces of nature," the labourers as a class have played

no part whatever except one which is purely negative—
namely that of suspicious and occasionally of violent
opposition. As history shows us with minute biographi-
cal detail, this process has in all its main particulars
been the work of individuals, or small groups of individuals, who were distinguished from their fellows by
doing what the mass of their fellows did *not* do—what
few of them had the enterprise to attempt, fewer still
the genius to accomplish, and what most of them had
not the capacity or even the wish to understand. It
must, moreover, be noted that these exceptional men,
though many of them had at one time been manual
labourers themselves, did not increase the efficiency of
manual work generally by any unusual skill in the
performance of such work on their own part, or indeed
by the performance of any manual tasks at all. A man
like Watt added to the productive forces of the world,
not by means of any engines which his own hands had
fabricated, but by the influence which, through his
models and instructions, he exercised over the hands
of others.   And all inventors who by means of novel
mechanisms—"wrought (as Herbert Spencer says they
are) from the very substance of the inventors' brains "—
have given men "a new control over the productive
forces of nature," have done so as powerful thinkers,
and not as dextrous craftsmen.

The same considerations are no less pertinent as
applied, not to such mechanisms themselves, but to the
reflex action of these on the conduct of the labourers
using them—a reflex action resulting in that new subdivision and new co-ordination of labour-tasks by which,
Marx rightly says, the efficiency of each pair of hands,
as distinct from the mechanisms, has been increased.
The argument of Marx implies that both of these new
developments are due to some exercise of faculties resident in the labourers themselves, but previously latent
because there was no scope for them. Let us, however,
consider in detail what this new subdivision and co-
ordination of labour-tasks mean.

When the labour-tasks involved in the production of
any one finished article are divided, and different
labourers are set to fashion different parts of it, each

part must be shaped in accordance with a settled pattern, so that all the parts shall ultimately fit together.   Now, when the parts are few, when the finished article is of a simple and unchanging kind, and the labourers are a small group at work in the same shed, the allocation of these tasks, and the precise nature of each, can be settled by the labourers themselves.   But when the number of parts into which an article is for purposes of manufacture divided rises, let us say, from four or five to a hundred; when the number of labourers rises from ten or twelve to a thousand; when the principles on which the tasks are divided cease to be merely empirical, and involve an elaborate knowledge of mathematics, mechanics and chemistry; when the character of the finished article itself has constantly to be improved or modified in order to meet new demands, and when the specification of each task in particular requires an alert ingenuity of the highest practical order; this constant re-devising and subdividing of tasks becomes, from the nature of the case, a separate task in itself, which cannot be included in the category of labour as Marx defines it.

And the same thing is true with regard to the organisation of the labourers, as distinct from the mere devising of the various tasks prescribed to them.   Organisation comprises the allotment of different tasks to the most suitable persons; an accurate timing of their movements in relation to one another, so that no labour may be lost by preventable pauses on the one hand or preventable overstrain on the other; and also an alert inspection of the work of each individual, so that errors may be seen and rectified before any appreciable dislocation of the general process has been caused by them.   Here, again, when the labourers are few, and when their different tasks are few, and when the interconnection of these can be seen at a glance by all, the business in question is easy, and the labourers can accomplish it by talking together as they hold their tools.   But when the labourers are numbered by thousands, and their different tasks by hundreds, the business of organising the execution of these last changes like the business of devising them, and changes for like reasons.   Whoever may be the persons by whom this business is performed, it is one which engages their entire time and attention; and it cannot be performed by labourers whose efficiency in manual task-work, according to the argument of Marx himself, depends on the fact that each of them gives his time, his attention and his hands to manual task-work, and one kind of task-work only.

With regard, then, to the several arguments by which Marx seeks to exhibit the unapproached efficiency of the modern industrial process as due to capacities which, in the course of a single century, have come to life in the persons of the manual labourers themselves, and in all of them to an equal extent, what we have seen thus far has been this : Firstly, that "man's new control over the productive forces of nature " which is embodied and concentrated in mechanisms such as those of the modern factory, instead of being due in any sense to the manual labourers generally, is due to the activities of a small minority of individuals—activities which are not in the nature of manual labour at all. Secondly, we have seen that, though the use of each great mechanism by a large number of labourers has resulted in a new subdivision and a new organisation of labour which has enabled the labourers personally to operate with increased effect, the actual business of subdividing and organising no more belongs to the category of labour, as Marx defines it, than the solitary ferments of knowledge and constructive imagination which take place only in the brain of the practical genius, and to which the world owes the steam-engine, the telephone and the electric light. In other words, whatever increased efficiency may in modern times have been acquired by the hands of the labourers themselves through new organisations of their hand-work, is primarily due to men who may never have touched a tool.

And here we are brought at last to the heart of our present question. Human beings, as they come into the world to-day, are very much the same as they were in any previous century; and, whatever the activities may be to which the increased industrial efficiency of the modern world is due, they were always in a potential form, as plentiful as they are now. How, then, is it that from the close of the eighteenth century onwards they have produced, and are still producing, effects on industry which they never produced before? What new condition of things is everywhere at the bottom of this unexampled change?

This is the crucial question; and Marx himself, though he completely misses the answer, and could indeed not have admitted it without destroying the whole fabric of his economic doctrines, approaches it very nearly. He takes every step necessary to reach it except the last.

Having assumed that, through the possession of new mechanisms of production, labour has gained a new control over the productive forces of nature, the one other cardinal fact, on which he insists as explaining the increased efficiency of ordinary or average hand-work, is, as we have seen, a new subdivision of labour-tasks into ever simpler parts, so that the work of each man's hands becomes more rapid and easier. Now, in order to understand what his full meaning is we must remember his emphatic assertion that actual labour, as performed by a living man, is in itself a process not single, but dual. Even the simplest manual operation, such as that of sorting nails according to their different sizes, involves the activity, not of a man's hands only, but also of his mind by which the action of his hands is directed. Hence, in pointing to a subdivision of labour-tasks as a cause of increased productivity on the part of the individual labourer, Marx means that when a labourer devotes himself to one kind of task alone, not his hands only, but his directing intelligence also, acquires a quickness and certitude not otherwise possible.

But here the argument of Marx, so far as it relates to the division of task-work, stops. It stops short just where it ought to begin. He is right in asserting that the efficiency of the modern system of production is closely associated with the principle of division somehow; but the kinds of division with which alone he concerns himself are secondary phenomena only. They are the consequences of another division which is very much more profound. This, which, in respect of the extent to which it has been carried out, is the root-

peculiarity of the modern system of production, is not
a subdivision of one manual task into several or a large
number; it is a division of that composite activity
which the execution of all manual tasks involves into
its two component parts—the manual part and the
mental—so that these are no longer performed by the
same persons. A limited control over the operations
of his own hands is, of course, necessarily left to the
manual labourer himself; but all intellectual direction of
the higher and more comprehensive kinds is transferred
to a new, a separate and a numerically small class, whose
sole connection with labour consists in the business of
directing it.

This fission of industrial effort into the manual and
the purely mental, like the fission of a single cell, first
shows itself in a very rudimentary form. Whenever
more than a score of manual labourers are gathered
together in a shed, or (as Adam Smith calls it) a single
"workhouse," for the purpose of making and putting
together four or five separate parts of any simple product
such as a pin, some record has to be kept of the output
of each group, so that the multiplication of no one part
shall be more rapid or less rapid than the multiplication
of the others. When the total output is small, these
simple arithmetical records can be made by the labourers
themselves; but as soon as the business expands, these
records, though arithmetically they will be no less simple
than before, will be such that a man or a boy must give
his entire time to them. The work of the manual
labourers must be supplemented by that of the clerk.
Here at once we have a fission of industrial work into
manual work and mental; but it is a fission which is
embryonic only, and gives no hint of the effects which
are peculiar to it when it is carried farther. The work
of the clerk who counts what the labourers do is no more
difficult than theirs. All we can say is that the two
kinds of work are different, and are naturally assigned to
two classes of men. The effects of this fission, which are
peculiar to it as a cause of increased production, do not
begin to be apparent till the action of the mental workers
no longer merely records the various operations of the
manual, but begins at the same time to alter and dictate

their details, and whilst rendering these last individually more simple, becomes in itself more complex.

This fact may be illustrated by an example which has already been used as illustrating by way of analogy the problem involved in complex political government. All the higher applications of mental activity to manual may be typified by one which, as Herbert Spencer says, is actually amongst the most important of them. That is to say, the application to industry, not of a simple arithmetic which counts the pieces of matter affected by the labourers' hands, but of the higher mathematics, by which application the movements of the labourers' hands in dealing with matter are modified. In proportion, then, as the mathematical knowledge is abstruse on which the joint efficiency of any group of labourers depends, the number of persons diminishes by whom the requisite knowledge is possessed, or who have even the capacity for acquiring it. High mathematical genius, as everybody knows, is rare. The union of it with practical genius is notoriously rarer still. And of all the other purely mental activities by which industrial production is affected the same thing holds good. In proportion to the extent of their influence in augmenting the output of industry generally, the number of persons in whom they are to be found is small.

Let us suppose, then, that some particular industry is prosecuted, as it might have been in the days of Adam Smith, in a hundred "workhouses" by a hundred groups of labourers, each group consisting of twenty men; and let us suppose, further, that in one of these separate groups one labourer out of the twenty happens to develop a genius like that of a Watt or an Edison, and quadruples the output of this particular group by ceasing to operate with his own hands himself, and merely showing each of the nineteen others how his hands from moment to moment may be used to the best advantage. In that case the rest of the labour-groups will find themselves in a condition, not of absolute, but of relative helplessness, and their natural tendency will be to unite with the group in which a man of genius is present, so that the benefit of his guidance may be extended to all alike.

Here we have the true underlying cause of the modern clustering of the manual labourers in large groups instead of remaining in small ones, or instead of working singly. The centres round which they cluster are not what Marx or the ordinary socialist supposes. These primarily are not great mechanisms, but the mental efficiencies of exceptionally able individuals, to which the mechanisms themselves are due, and to which are due also the new organisation of the labourers, and the new subdivisions of their tasks. By means of such a clustering, exceptional individuals such as these are enabled to do the thinking for thousands and tens of thousands of average men, so that each of these last— even the most incapable of them—is in turn enabled to execute his own special piece of hand-work precisely as it would have been executed had he been himself one of the máster intellects of the world.

Never has this fact been more dramatically illustrated than it has been during the course of the great European war. In every belligerent country the objects at which industry aims have been largely changed from commodities for private use and enjoyment into commodities or goods essential to the preservation of national life, such as aeroplanes and anti-aircraft guns; and in order that such weapons might be produced, the first step necessary has been this—to place the labour required for their construction under the control of those picked intellects who are able to devise the best. In industry for normal, just as much as for military purposes, this fission of productive effort into its two component parts, so that the highest intellects may control the largest number of hands, has been the primary cause of all that increased efficiency by which the modern system of production is so sharply distinguished from all that have gone before it. It alone has rendered possible that application of intellect to industrial effort generally which has gained for man, and which still continues to gain for man, "a new control over the productive forces of nature." In other words, the increased efficiency of industry in the modern world is due primarily (though, as we shall see hereafter, not exclusively) to a development, not of the democratic principle, but of the oligarchic.

Let us now go on to consider what kind of reply will be made to this statement of the case by thinkers who have, since the days of Marx, endeavoured to maintain that industry, as a technical process, can conserve, and indeed increase its present productive powers, and yet remain or become what it was in earlier times—a process which is exclusively, or even preponderantly democratic.

CHAPTER IV

THE PRODUCTIVITY OF THE FEW

IF the foregoing argument be correct, one thing is at once evident—namely that the essence of industrial efficiency is the rule of the Many by the Few, or that the modern system of production is more efficient than its predecessors precisely because it has lost the characteristics of a pure democracy. And, curiously enough, in the writings of Marx himself there are passages which show that even he, in moments of transitory insight, perceived that this conclusion had some elements of truth in it. Thus, on one occasion he compares the labourers of the modern world to a company of instrumentalists performing some great oratorio, and adds that no performance of this kind would be possible unless some great composer had dictated to each performer the notes which he had to play. In his case, however, admissions of this kind are merely like isolated boulders, brought down by an intellectual glacier from some distant region of thought, and deposited here and there on a plain with which otherwise they have no connection.

But what Marx recognised only by fits and starts, later industrial democrats have come to perceive more clearly. Thus, *Vorwärts*—the leading organ of the industrial democrats of Germany—has described the Marxian doctrine that all wealth is produced by manual labourers as comparable to the doctrine of Thales that the universe is nothing but different forms of water. The intellectual socialists of America repudiate the vulgar idea that the industrial functions of the purely mental worker are less apparent to them than to any other sane men. The need of the oligarch in the technical conduct of industry has been clearly recognised by labour-leaders in Italy; but of all comprehensive

110

statements sufficiently brief for quotation, that which illustrates this change of attitude best has been provided by Mr. Sidney Webb. Now, Mr. Webb, as we have seen already, identifies industrial democracy with the "control" of industry by what he calls "the people themselves"; and this control they will, according to him, acquire by appropriating those implements of production which are at present owned by capitalists, and which indeed constitute the bulk of the industrial capital of to-day. But, so he proceeds, democrats must remember one thing—namely, that if, in their capacity of mere possessors, the private monopolists of capital were all dispossessed to-morrow, yet, though one monopoly would be gone, another would still remain, and one of a kind which, so far as we can see, is ineradicable. This, says Mr. Webb, is "a natural monopoly of industrial or business ability"—or "a natural energy with which some men are born," and with which the masses of mankind are not born; "and to dream," he says, "of a complicated industrial state" from which the influence of such men is eliminated, and "in which the workman is free to work just as he likes, without strict subordination, and without obedience to orders, is to dream, not of socialism, but of anarchism." Hence, according to him, the business of those thinkers who would, under modern conditions, place the theory of industrial democracy on a practically defensible basis, is not to ignore these facts, but to show that their real significance is quite other than what it seems to be, and that the principle of industrial democracy in spite of them remains intact. And that Mr. Webb is merely describing a view which he shares with his brother intellectuals in this and in other countries is shown by the fact that socialists all over the world have, since the days of Marx, employed much of their speculative ingenuity in endeavours to get over the difficulties which Mr. Webb's language indicates, and which none of them any longer ignore.

We will now briefly consider the nature and the value of the arguments by which the accomplishment of this feat has been attempted. These arguments, though expressed in a great variety of forms, are in substance reducible to five, each of which can be summarised in a few words. Two of them only are deserving of any serious consideration. The other three, though when stated on a platform they may have some popular effect, will be found when considered soberly to be no better than claptrap. We will first dispose of these.

One of these arguments is as follows. However completely we may admit that the efficiency of modern production depends on a submission by the great mass of the workers to the intellect and technical guidance of the specially gifted Few, yet if this submission is an act of free consent, the Many in the very surrender of their own judgments are exercising them, and the system which requires the surrender thus expresses the will of an industrial democracy after all. Of this argument it is enough here to observe that it does but emphasise what nobody in his senses will deny—namely the action of the democratic principle as one element of the situation; but it does not disprove—on the contrary, it implicitly admits—the active operation of the principle of oligarchy as its counterpart. The harmonious working of any system, whether democratic or otherwise, requires the willing consent of all parties engaged in it; but the fact that the Many consent to be guided by the Few would no more prove that oligarchy was pure democracy in disguise than the fact that a patient chooses his own doctor proves that the patient is the author of his own prescriptions. If the two things were the same thing, all doctors would be superfluous.

A second argument, which may be dismissed with equal brevity, is this. However important the fact that in modern production a few persons must direct the technical operations of the many, this does not mean that the few, considered as human beings, are in any way more capable than the great mass of their fellows. It merely means that they have, by some chance or other, been chosen to exercise what are necessarily exceptional functions. The great directors of labour, whatever the talents may be which appear to distinguish them from the mass, resemble a watcher on a hill, who signals to an army on one side of it the movements of an army on the other. The signals of this one man may influence the actions of thousands; but any unit of these thousands, if placed in that man's position, could signal with equal effect, and be no less influential than he. In other words, in the school of industrial life men are not at the bottom of the class because they have no conspicuous abilities, but they exercise no conspicuous abilities because they are at the bottom of the class. This argument does indeed deserve to be noticed, for it forms one of the modern flavourings of the lowest popular oratory; but no serious thinker, whatever his democratic zeal, either affects to believe it himself, or addresses it to a thoughtful audience.

A third argument is this. It is idle to pretend that the great directors of industry are not what they seem to be—namely men who in point of talent are indefinitely superior to the mass. Indeed, the influence of men like these is, in a certain sense, the motive-power of all modern progress. This influence, however, operates only as the initiator of new departures, in the way of inventions and methods, and the industrial application of new knowledge generally. As soon as each new movement has been started, its special connection with its author or initiator ceases. All knowledge, when once it has been achieved and applied to industrial purposes, becomes thenceforth common property. Any one can apply it who pleases, and in practice become equal to the initiator; and if it were not for patents and other legal devices, which secure for the initiators some interest in the results of their own inventions, whatever these men contribute to the fund of human efficiency would at once diffuse itself through the whole industrial mass, no trace being left of its origin in any special nucleus. Now, to a very limited extent this argument is true, but to a limited extent only. It is true in proportion as the knowledge and its industrial applications are simple, and the latter are on a small scale. What is commonly called knowledge—namely, knowledge of general principles—is mainly perpetuated and mainly diffused by books; but it only becomes common to all men in proportion as they are able to assimilate it. Any child can assimilate the contents of a child's book of arithmetic; but a hundred men might live with the works of Newton before them, and only one man out of

ɪ

the hundred be able to grasp their meaning. Any schoolboy to-day, after reading a page of instructions, can make a pound of gunpowder which is better than Roger Bacon's, or a model steam-engine which in principle is more perfect than the engines of Newcomen. But when from the world of pastime we pass to that of practical modern life, in which the object of industry is to multiply as well as to make commodities, in which steam-engines are as big as houses, and steamships are as long as streets, problems arise which in the world of pastime are absent; and these demand for their solution, not only a knowledge which few can completely master, though books may contain it which any dunce can buy. They demand a knowledge of a different kind also, which is not transmissible by books, or even by living example, and which those who possess it owe to the favour of nature only. This is the knowledge of how to manage men, and this, in the world of industry, no more becomes common property because certain individuals have already possessed and exhibited it, than the powers of a great general transmit themselves to any nervous book-worm who puzzles himself over Cæsar's Commentaries. The argument, then, that the powers of an industrial oligarchy are, as fast as they are successfully exercised, converted into the powers of a democracy, is, in so far as it is true, so limited in its range of application that the question here at issue is not even appreciably affected by it.

Contrasted with these three arguments, and altogether rejecting them, are two others, of quite different kinds, each of which in a sense is true, and would, were it only relevant, be doubtless of great importance.

The first of these is an argument which, though specially applied to industry by the doctrinaires of industrial democracy, is applied by others to human action of all kinds. It begins with admitting that if men are in reality what to vulgar observation they seem to be—namely, so many separate units whose faculties are self-existent—what seems to be industrial oligarchy is precisely the thing it seems, and the idea of industrial democracy must be given up as a delusion. If, however, under the searchlight of sociological science we

look below the surface of things and see them as they
really are, we shall see that the individuals who present
themselves as the Few and the Many are not self-existent
or independent entities at all. In any given society the
great men and the average men alike are what they are,
and are able to do what they do, only because, like
variously-tempered puppies who have come into the
world together, they are all products of a common corporate past. Hence, if a certain minority of them
happen to have derived from their ancestors a larger
share of industrial ability than the rest, this share is the
result of an age-long social struggle, to which the strong
and the weak were both necessary parties. It does not
belong properly to the present possessors of it themselves, but is merely a temporary deposit drawn from a
common store. So far as the possessors are concerned,
it is, says Mr. Sidney Webb, "nothing more than a
species of unearned increment," and, herein resembling
"the unearned increment of rent," it belongs not to
them, but to society, or the community as a democratic
whole.

Now, of this argument it is sufficient to say here that
it is merely an application to industry of a wider philosophic conception which is as old as human thought—
namely, the conception of the All or the One as the
reality which is behind the Many. According to this
conception of things, which appears in various forms as
Pantheism, Determinism, and mental or material Monism, the existence of the separate personality is altogether a delusion. There is no question of whether one
individual does or produces more or less than another.
The indivisible Whole, whether God or the Universe, or
(as Herbert Spencer called it) the Unknowable, does
and produces everything. The individual, as a separate
entity, does or produces nothing. Now, as a matter of
speculative logic, this doctrine may be impregnable;
but as Kant, Hume, St. Augustine, and (we may add)
common sense point out, the moment we attempt to
apply it to practical life philosophers and ordinary men
reject it alike as nonsense. If Socrates quarrels with
his wife he is quarrelling with Xantippe; he is not
quarrelling with the Universe. If a murder has been

committed we look for the individual murderer, on the
ground that he is the criminal and other people are
innocent. If we want a great picture painted we look
for an individual artist, on the ground that he can paint
it and most individuals cannot. That is to say, we
assume, for all practical purposes, that individuals
really do what they seem to do; and unless we assumed
this there would be no dealing with anybody. The
application of these criticisms to the industrial process
is obvious. The "monopolists of business ability," as
a matter of practical experience, are as radically different
from the average units directed by them as a man who
murders his mother in order to steal her savings is different from a mother next door who is teaching her child
its prayers. They are able to do things, and they do
things, which are not done and which cannot be done
by others; and unless these differences were recognised,
no complex business of any kind would be possible. The
philosophy of industrial Monism, by which these differences are obscured, may amuse the philosopher in his
study; but if preached in a factory or a shipyard it
would be the maundering of a strayed lunatic.

The last of the arguments which are urged with the
object of showing that industrial democracy combined
with unambiguous oligarchy is nothing but a mode of
pure democracy after all, still remains to be considered.
It is in many respects a great improvement on the preceding. Moreover, the credit is due to it of having, for
the benefit of the practical agitator, replaced the doctrine of Marx that all wealth is the product of manual
labour only, by another, equally popular in its suggestions, but less open to criticism on the part of common
intelligence. This is the argument that wealth is the
product, not of labour, but of society. It is an argument which in certain ways is a great improvement on
the preceding, because instead of being an exercise in
the logic of remote speculation, it addresses itself frankly
to the world of concrete fact. It admits that men must
be treated as separate entities varying greatly in the
scope of their industrial powers, some men directing
and others submitting to direction; and yet aims at
establishing the industrial equality of all, not by eluding

or transcending these facts, but by facing them. It is, therefore, as a weapon of popular agitation, very much more in vogue than any of the four others. It may be summed up thus. However unequal may be the efforts of individual producers otherwise, such as those of the genius and those of the average labourer, they are practically equal in the fact that they are all equally necessary. Necessity has no laws; it also has no degrees.

The contention that all industrial factors in production are in a practical sense equal if they are equally necessary for the production of a given result, was first formulated by Mill, in connection with the business of agriculture. Some thinkers, he observes, referring to the French physiocrats, have debated whether, of a given agricultural product—such, for example, as twenty bushels of corn—land or labour produces the larger part. All such questions as this, however, he declares to be void of meaning; and he explains this statement by laying down the following principle. Whenever two causes, however different otherwise, are both so necessary to the production of what he calls "the effect" that this (which in the present case is agricultural produce) could, if either were wanting, not be produced at all, it is idle to say that most of it is produced by one or the other, for the absence of either would make the difference between the production of a given effect or none. Thus, he adds by way of illustration, it is idle to ask whether, if 2 be multiplied by 10, the 2 or the 10 does most in producing the number 20; for if either the 10 or the 2—no matter which—were altered, the production of the 20 would be equally out of the question. This argument which Mill applies to land and labour is that which is now applied by the theorists of industrial democracy to average manual labourers and "the monopolists of ability" who direct them.

Now, if we make certain suppositions, the argument of Mill is correct. One of these is that land is a constant quantity, the other is that "the effect" is a constant quantity also. Thus, if there were only one acre of land in the world, and if the effect were always twenty bushels of corn or nothing, it would doubtless be impossible to say that the land produced more bushels than the

labourer or the labourer more bushels than the land.
But in the actual world of agriculture there is not one
acre only; there are many—which acres vary greatly in
quality. Further, the joint produce of an acre of land
and a labourer is not a given number of bushels or
nothing. The whole question of produce is a question
of less or more; and if the same labourer were transferred from a bad acre to a better one, and if thereupon
"the effect" rose from twenty bushels to thirty, we
should at once be able to say that, in a very practical
sense, the extra ten bushels were the product, not of the
labourer, but of the land. Indeed, Mill elsewhere insists
on this very fact himself; for in one of his own chapters
he explains with great lucidity that an extra product of
this kind is distinguishable as economic rent, and goes
to the recipient solely because the land is his. On the
same principle, the matter may be put conversely. If
the same acre of land is tilled successively by two different labourers, and if when it is tilled by the one there
is a product of twenty bushels, and when it is tilled by
the other there is a product of thirty, we are able to say
that, in a strictly practical sense, the extra product is
produced by the superior efficiency of the second.

And the same argument applies to the industrial process generally in respect of the parts now played by the
manual workers on the one hand and the mental directorate on the other. If the producers of any commodity
—let us say, for example, boots—were always one small
group of nineteen manual labourers, whilst a twentieth
man directed them; and if "the effect" of their joint
efforts were always the same likewise—say, forty pairs
of boots in a week; and if, moreover, unless the tale of
forty pairs of boots were completed, the whole output
would be worthless or would vanish into thin air; it
would then be impossible to say that the director produces more boots than any one of his workers or fewer.
But if the director absented himself for a year, and his
place was taken by a labourer no better and no worse
than the rest, and if thereupon the weekly product fell
from forty pairs of boots, not to none, but to twenty
pairs; and if, when the director returned and resumed
his duties, the product forthwith rose from twenty pairs

of boots to forty; we should then be able to say that, in a very practical sense, that twenty pairs of boots were the product of the director alone. In other words, any mental director of a group of co-operating workers produces so much of the joint output as would cease to be produced if his mental functions were suspended, and would be produced again when the exercise of these functions was renewed.

Those, however, whose object is to evade this conclusion will endeavour to do so by the method of a *reductio ad absurdum* thus. If it is true, they will say, that the mental director of labour produces so much of a product as the labourers whom he directs could not have produced without him—let us say one-half of it—it must be equally true that the labourers produce the whole, because in the absence of the labourers the director could have produced nothing. This argument, though absolutely worthless, is interesting and demands attention; for its worthlessness is due to a fact which is not superficially apparent. Its worthlessness lies in the fact that it is false to the essential principle on which all reasoning of a practical kind rests. All reasoning which precedes and determines action is in its very nature hypothetical, and reduces itself to the following formula : "If I do this or that particular thing it will be the cause of this or that result." Thus a man, if he puts a match to shavings, reasons that if he does so he will cause them to catch fire. When a man, seeing a fire, throws a bucket of water over it, he reasons that if he does so he will cause the fire to cease. But there is another kind of reasoning—namely, that of the thinker whose province is not action, but speculation; and for him neither the match nor the water will have been *the* cause of the results in question. They will each of them have been but one cause out of countless causes all equally necessary, such as those which have caused water and trees to exist, the action of gravity, and the existence and composition of the atmosphere. But with causes such as these the practical reason has no concern whatever. The man who applies the match and the man who applies the water do not ask what would happen if the law of gravitation were suspended, or if water, wood, and air became things other than they are. Out of a countless number of hypotheses they concern themselves with two only. On what principle, then, is this selection made? The answer is that the hypotheses with which practical reason concerns itself relate to such acts alone as on any given occasion may either be performed or not be performed, according as the practical reason of human beings determines.

Let us now apply this principle to the two special hypotheses with which we are here concerned—namely, those relating to labour and a purely mental directorate. We shall see that, in computing the product of any director of labour as so much of the total as would not be produced on the hypothesis that he ceased to direct, we are arguing in accordance with the laws of practical reason; but if we argue on the counter-hypothesis, that the labourers ceased to labour, we are indulging in a speculation which practically has no meaning at all; for the first hypothesis represents a practical possibility, the second does not. The labourers as a whole can never cease to labour, except for very brief periods, for if they ceased to labour they would die, and nothing would be left to reason about; but the direction of labour by the Mind of a non-labouring class is in its present form a purely modern phenomena. Mankind existed for thousands of years without it, and if it disappeared to-morrow mankind would exist still.

Hence, to say that all wealth is produced by Society —that is, by the labour and the mental director jointly— is no doubt true enough; but, except for one special purpose, with which we will deal presently, it is a truth that tells us nothing. What we want to know is, not how much these agents produce jointly, but how much the second adds to the product of the first. To say that all wealth is a social product is like saying that malaria is a local product. Malaria prevails in some countries, it does not prevail in others. All countries are, in many respects, alike. All must possess, for example, soil, air, and sunshine. Were any of these absent malaria would be absent also; therefore, all these things in a sense are its joint causes. But since malaria prevails in certain localities only, some cause must be present there which is not present elsewhere; and if malaria is an evil which men desire to extirpate, they must concern themselves with the identification of this exceptional cause alone. That cause, it has now been discovered, is a fly. If the fly is extirpated, malaria disappears along with it. If the fly returns, malaria reappears also. Thus the practical reason concerns itself with this cause alone, for it is the only cause in respect of which human beings can take action. They can get rid of the fly, but they cannot get rid of earth, air, and sunshine. If we substitute for malaria, as a product which we desire to abolish, an increased output of wealth, as a product which we desire to retain, the case is just the same. We may compare the directors of labour to so many malarial flies. Wherever one settles the industrial output is increased; and just as the fly is practically the one cause of malaria, so is the director practically the one cause of the increment—not of the total product, but of just so much of the total as may happen to appear and to disappear along with him.

The application of this argument is, however, as was just now observed, limited by one exception. When it is said that all wealth is produced by society, the word "society," if it stands for more than a mere abstraction, must be used to designate some society or societies in particular, such, for example, as the English, French, or German. Now if, as happens in war time, one society has, either as an ally or an enemy, to consider the efficiency of another from the standpoint of an outside observer, then to say that the latter society, as a whole, produces so much is a really informative statement. It is so for this reason—that the great practical question for such an observer is, not how this total is produced, but the mere fact of its production. But for each society, in respect of its own internal forces—and in times of war this is specially obvious—the practical question is what are the agents of production when these are considered separately, and what, when so considered, is the nature of their interaction; for it is only when matters are considered in this way that the conditions which will result in a maximum product are discoverable.

For those, then, who desire to understand what,

within any given society, different men, different classes
of men, or different kinds of productive effort, contribute
severally to the product of the society as a whole, to
answer that the product as a whole is produced by
society as a whole, is not to throw any light on the workings of these different parts, but simply to hide them
from observation under the tarpaulin of a barren
platitude.

The proposition that the wealth of a society is produced by that society itself comes, if not absolutely
barren, to no more than this—that modern production
requires co-operation of some kind, or that wealth as the
world now knows it cannot be produced by a solitary.
Here we have a principle which is applicable, not to
industry alone, but to nine-tenths of all possible human
conduct. If a man lives absolutely alone, he cannot
commit murder, for no one exists into whom he can
stick a knife. It is equally obvious that he cannot
commit perjury, for nobody exists to whom he can tell
a lie. He cannot exhibit the virtue of unselfishness, for
the only person in whose interests he can act is himself.
Such being the case, it is obviously true, in a sense, that
murder is a social product, that perjury is a social
product, and that heroic self-sacrifice is a social product
likewise. But would this mean that if, out of so many
thousand men, three excite horror by murder or false
swearing, or public admiration by acts of unusual
heroism, all are equally criminals and equally moral
heroes? If this were true, a murdered man should be
hanged along with his murderer, for the latter could not
have killed him if he had not been there to kill. A
government which made such an assumption would be
a government fit for Bedlam.

And what is true of moral action is equally true of
industrial. In the estimation of industrial forces, as
in the administration of legal justice, that which has
to be dealt with is the voluntary actions, and the results
of the actions, of individuals. If a society of workers
in which one man directs the many produces more than
a society in which the many direct themselves, it is idle
to say that society is as truly the producer of the larger
product as of the less. The sole question is, what pro-

duces the excess of the one product over the other? And here we are brought to the answer already given. The excess is produced by one man—namely, the director, the presence or the absence of whose activities is the only element which differentiates one society from the other. The extra output is produced by that one man as truly as malaria is produced by the presence of the malarial fly.

This method of reasoning is no mere exercise in the logic of remote speculation, like that of the Industrial Monists. It is the instinctive and inevitable reasoning of all practical men. This fact has been brought into prominence by the great European war, as though it were lit up by successive flashes of lightning. War, to an extent never before paralleled, has become a war of intellectual industries as well as a war of armies. In every belligerent country it has made ceaseless demands on industrial intellect in both of its two main forms— the intellect which shows itself in scientific invention, and the intellect which shows itself in the scientific organisation of men; and the demand for each, wherever it has found utterance, has always couched itself in the same inevitable terms. The cry of all parties alike has not been a cry addressing itself to "society," to "the people themselves," or to the mass of average men. It has been a cry for individuals who stand out from the mass, and are able to do what the average man cannot do. With regard to the mechanisms of war, such as (to quote an example which has here been used already) an anti-aircraft gun, what England has cried out for has been, in the common-sense words of a prominent London journal, "a new inventive brain, capable of large generalisations, and capable of applying them in detail." With regard to the organisation of the mass of average workers, these being already in existence, and equipped with their normal faculties, the demand has been for exceptional brains likewise, which shall organise these men anew in accordance with new requirements. When the food-problem in Germany first threatened to become urgent, this demand found clearer and more instant expression nowhere than it did in the leading journal of the Social Democrats themselves.

" What Germany wants," said *Vorwärts*, "in the present internal crisis is one man of large knowledge and supreme business ability." And what do such demands mean—demands which the stress of circumstance has purged of fantastic theory, and restored to that common sense by which all men are naturally guided whether they recognise the fact or no? Such demands mean, when translated into terms of their implications, that, if Society is to act efficiently, the mass of average workers, of which society is mainly composed, must group themselves for industrial purposes, not primarily (as Marx said) round this or round that great mechanism, but round certain centres of control which are the intellects and localised influence of exceptionally able men.

Let us suppose, then, that some exceptional man devises a mechanism or weapon of such power and precision that the course of a war is altered in favour of the country using it. Would any one say that the part played by a man like this was not distinguishable and not greater than that which was played by others who could merely cry out for his appearance, or who helped to construct this weapen in accordance with the inventor's orders? The refutation of such an opinion is embedded in the very language in which ordinary thought expresses itself. Everybody would instinctively say, with regard to the fortunes of war, that the appearance of a man like this "had made all the difference." If the case were one, not of a change in the fortunes of war, but of an addition to the national output of common comforts and luxuries, everybody would say precisely the same thing, with the alteration of one word only. Everybody would say that this man had not " made " all the difference, but had " produced " it— the difference being the difference between a larger output and a less.

Such being the case, then, it must always be borne in mind that in every industrial system which yields a return sufficient to keep the workers alive, the democratic principle, as embodied in the hands of the self-directed workers themselves, and producing a certain minimum, must always be assumed as a starting-point, and is necessarily always present. The sole point here insisted on is, that all modern additions to this minimum, which itself is approximately constant, are contingent on the direction of the labourers by a purely intellectual class, or (as Mr. Webb calls them) "the natural monopolists of the best business ability." In other words, Industrial Democracy is not an impossible system of production, but it is an inefficient system. It is the system of the world in its babyhood. Industry, after a certain early stage of progress has been reached, grows in efficiency in proportion as it ceases to be purely democratic, and becomes a system in which two distinguishable principles—the democratic and the oligarchic—the average intelligences of mankind, and the exceptional intelligences—interact. It is true that, even if the labourers worked solely under their own direction, none of them issuing any orders to others, a certain minority of them would be appreciably more productive than the rest. But the larger products of individuals such as these would be merely like so many molehills which, though lifting themselves here and there, did nothing to alter the general level of a field. "Society," or "the people themselves," may, in their capacity of producers, be compared to a regiment of soldiers ordered to move across country to a given spot by night, and possessing in its ranks one man who can see by night as well as he can by day. If such a man directs his own movements only, he may reach the spot in question with the utmost ease and promptitude; but unless he is able by his orders to direct the movements of the rest, the mass will be left helpless to flounder or drown in ditches. The same is the case in industry. If a thousand men of average vision are to derive any benefit whatever from the presence amongst them of one man of exceptional vision, one man must issue orders to a thousand, and the thousand must obey one man; and if this is not oligarchy as definitely distinct from democracy, there is not, and never has been, such a thing as oligarchy in the world.

That such are really the essential facts of the situation is now being admitted, as Professor Michels shows, by various revolutionary writers without any attempt to disguise the matter. The Italian syndicalist, Labriola, insists, as we have seen already, that political progress can never be the work of the multitude, but can be accomplished only by "an *élite* who alone can judge of the interaction of social cause and effect"; and what this writer says with regard to political government, other revolutionary writers are now saying with regard to industry. Thus Kautsky, who in some respects is a professed follower of Marx, dismisses as impossible the application of the democratic principle to commerce. Commerce, or commercial distribution (which is production in its final stage) is, he says, "outside the competence of the rank and file." We may talk, he proceeds, of this or that commercial business as "co-operative"; but in the cases to which this name is applied, the conduct of affairs is really in the hands of a few managers, unless, indeed, "the customer can be said to co-operate with the shopman" whenever a bit of ribbon changes hands over the counter. Another socialist critic, speaking of a business at Ghent, which claims to be a great example of successful co-operation or democracy, declares that "it bears in every detail the imprint of the strong will that has created it. The one man who is its master issues his orders in the brusque and imperious tone of a bourgeois captain of industry; and this is what he practically is." It has, says Professor Michels, been claimed that in societies for co-operative manufacture, true co-operation is theoretically far more practicable than in commerce. He goes on, however, to observe—herein agreeing absolutely with the argument of the present work—that this claim is valid for groups of workers only, whose numbers are small, and whose methods are of the simplest kind— such, for example, as ten or twelve village cobblers cutting and stitching leather at the back of a small shop. But as soon as such an industry increases, and endeavours by the aid of science to secure a larger output per head of the workers engaged in it, the case entirely changes. Technical subordination begins, and equal co-operation ends. Thus, he says, one of the foremost leaders of the labour movement in Italy has expressed himself to the following effect: "We have learned by prolonged experience that those businesses only can survive which are headed by a good organiser. Categories of the most various trades, found in the most diverse environments, have been unable to secure organisation and to live through crises, except in so far as they have been able to find first-class men to manage their affairs."

Now, all this is substantially what is said by Mr. Webb himself. "In any complex system of industry" such as that which prevails to-day, the efficiency of the workers as a whole is the average efficiencies of the Many multiplied by the efficiencies of the Few—the Few whom he describes as "the natural monopolists" of ability, and whose function is to issue orders, whilst that of the Many is to execute them with "strict obedience."

Why, then, do he and other democratic reformers endeavour to hide this fact by declaring that, "according to a growing consensus of opinion," the inevitable outcome of democracy" is the "control" of production by "Society," or "the people themselves"? If "the people themselves" include the directing few, production is controlled by the people themselves already. If the people themselves are the masses, as distinct from the few and excluding them, then, according to Mr. Webb's own opinion, and a growing consensus of revolutionary opinion generally, no efficient production by "the people themselves" is possible. For what conceivable reason, then, can men not deficient in intelligence, who have seen with very fair clearness what the nature of the situation is, have betaken themselves to reasonings and formulæ such as those which we have just examined, and which are practically useless except for the purpose of obscuring it? The answer to this question will be indicated in the following chapter, and it will carry us on directly to inquiries of a new order.

BOOK III

DEMOCRATIC DISTRIBUTION AS RELATED TO THE FACTS OF PRODUCTION

CHAPTER I

DISTRIBUTION IN ENGLAND

THE explanation of the curious fact that the democratic doctrinaires of to-day, having come to admit that an efficient system of production involves at all events a large element of oligarchy, should endeavour to obscure this truth under a veil of pseudo-philosophic or wholly irrelevant platitudes, is not to be found in any mental defect on their part which renders them liable to oscillate between sound reasoning and unsound. It is to be found in the ultimate object which they practically have in view. Their object is not to establish any theory of production, however true, for its own sake. Their object is to provide, as an instrument of popular agitation, some basis in principle for a certain popular demand—a demand which relates, not to the process of production, but to the manner in which the products are, and the manner in which they ought to be, distributed.

The content of this demand, which in all countries is the same, is plainly expressed in the latter of the two clauses which make up Mr. Webb's account of "the inevitable outcome of democracy." Having said that the immediate outcome is the control of production by what he calls "the people themselves," he goes on to explain that the ultimate end in view is the "recovery by the people themselves" of a certain share of the product which is, under the existing system, appropriated by mere "possessors."

128

The demand thus indicated will, as has been said already, be found to derive all its significance from certain propositions as to fact which are contained in it by way of implication. These implied propositions are as follows :—

(1) In all the civilised countries of the modern world, a few men, commonly called " the rich," over and above any income which they may produce by their own abilities and enterprise, appropriate a secondary income, in the production of which they have played no part whatever.

(2) The whole of this secondary income is produced by " the people themselves "—by the efforts present or past of the units of the average mass; and as soon as the people come to own the means of production they will " recover " it.

(3) This secondary income, regarded as a " share of the total produce," is so " enormous " that the " recovery " of it by " the people " is, " according to a growing consensus of opinion," the sole objective of Democracy throughout the modern world, and will, when accomplished, metamorphose the whole character of social life.

The core of these propositions is obviously contained in the last, which asserts the immense magnitude of the " share " awaiting recovery, and the extent to which the people must have hitherto been underpaid. Everybody knows that in all civilised countries some share of the national produce goes to persons who are mere " possessors," for otherwise nothing in the nature of a leisured class could exist. The practical question is the quantitative question of " What share ? " Neither Mill, nor Mr. Webb, nor any of the thinkers who agree with them, assert, as Marx did, that the Many produce everything and the exceptional Few nothing, or that any man who is rich must be *ipso facto* a thief. On the contrary, they admit that " the Rich," or at all events the active section of them, produce or earn a " share " which, relatively to their numbers, is considerable—a share which Mill describes as " the wages of the employers' superintendence," which Mr. Webb and others describe as " the rent of their ability," and which American statisticians and economists describe as " gains from the effort of the entrepreneur." The essence of the democratic contention is that, whatever the amount of this earned share may be, the few Rich in any case get a great deal more than their earnings, and the People get a great deal less; and the practical object of the exponents of the democratic idea is to persuade the People that the "share" of which they are thus defrauded is something so vast that it is well worth their while to do and to dare everything in order to gain possession of it. Since, however, as we have seen, it is no longer possible to deny in serious argument the exceptional productivity of the Few, and their consequent rights to an exceptional "share" of some sort, the doctrinaires of Democracy have betaken themselves to every possible device by which the exceptional productivity of the Few, though it cannot be denied, may be obscured, as being a fact which, if too clearly recognised, would lower the temperature of the passions to which the doctrinaires make appeal.

Here, then, we have the origin of those ludicrous or platitudinous theories which aim at representing the productivity of unequal men as equal on the ground that all of them are creatures of a common biological process, or are all alike parts of some national aggregate. These are theories which, as applied to practical life, are so absolutely insane and futile, except for the one purpose of fomenting popular passion, that not even the most rabid of democrats would dream of applying them for a day to his dealings with his own household, in respect even of such trivial matters as the choice of a wife or cook, or the bringing up of his children. Indeed, as we shall see presently, such methods of argument are now being rapidly abandoned by the doctrinaires of democracy themselves for others which, though similar in their practical purport, are deduced intellectually and morally from a wholly different principle. Meanwhile there is one proposition to which, in some form or other, they adhere with unabated tenacity. This is the proposition, relating not to principle but to fact, that of "the total produce" or income of every modern country the share appropriated by the "Rich," over and above what certain of them may earn by their own ability, is of such a magnitude that no revolution would be too hazardous which promised the mass of the workers even a remote prospect of "recovering it."

Now this proposition, whatever be its exact sense, may quite imaginably be true. It is impossible to say *a priori* that the great mass of the producers in any one country or in all are not defrauded of some share of their products, or whether, if they are so defrauded, this share deserves the name "enormous" or no. We can reach a conclusion only by an examination of concrete facts; and if we find that, under such conditions as are now prevalent, the products are, as a fact, systematically and not merely by accident, mal-distributed in the way described, we shall have to consider by what principles the systematic mal-distribution is determined, and in what way and how far democratic action can alter them. But the broad facts of the case are what we must deal with first, and we can deal with them only as embodied in some typical instance or instances. The best instance to begin with will be naturally that of the country in which the modern industrial system has been on trial for the longest time, and of which, moreover, the statistical records are sufficiently comprehensive and precise. It has been commonly admitted by socialists of all nations that no country could be chosen which fulfils these conditions more signally than the United Kingdom. Let us take, then, the case of the United Kingdom as (to speak roughly) it was about the year 1907, this year being the central year of a quinquennium with regard to which statistics are available of an exceptionally ample kind.

Two methods of investigation, each independent of the other,[1] united to show that the net income of the

---

[1] Prior to the year 1907 the national income was computed, firstly on the basis of wage-rates recorded as current amongst various classes of workers, and the number of workers comprehended in each class; and secondly on the basis of the records relating to income-tax, which deal mainly, though not entirely, with incomes exceeding £160 a year. About the year 1905 statisticians had come to the conclusion that the then income of the United Kingdom was somewhat in excess of 2000 million pounds. In the year 1907 a novel inquiry was instituted—that is to say, a "Census of Production"—which took no cognisance of individual incomes at all, but dealt only with the net selling value of

United Kingdom in the year 1907 amounted approximately to 2100 million pounds, of which it is ascertainable from the records relating to income-tax that 790 (or, let us say 800) million was made up of net incomes in excess of £160, whilst 1300 million was the sum of incomes below that figure.

Now all the individual receipts which made up this grand total were derived by the recipients either from the mere possession of property, or from personal effort of some kind, or in part from one of these sources, and in part, also, from the other.   Let us deal with the total derived from personal effort—or, as it is commonly called, " earned income "—first.

The kinds of effort by which, in a modern society, incomes are earned may be broadly reduced to five.

Firstly, the effort of manual workers, most of whom work for wages.[1]

Secondly, the effort of mental workers, such as school-teachers, government functionaries, and business clerks or managers, who work for wages commonly called salaries.

Thirdly, the effort of independent professional men who, as to the details of their work, are practically their own masters.

Fourthly, the effort of the very small employers who not only direct their employees (very few in number), but also share their work.

Fifthly, the effort of the larger employers, who alone are typical of the modern industrial system, and whose sole connection with their employees consists in the task, purely mental, of directing them.

Let us begin with the income derived from ordinary manual and from salaried mental effort.   This may be

---

the products of each of the industries and gainful services of the country, and arrived at the total income by putting all these values together. These values yielded about 2100 million pounds as the net national income ; thus confirming the result of those independent methods according to which the total, a few years before, had been between 2000 and 2100 million pounds.

[1] In this class are comprised certain independent workers, such as the village blacksmith, and small farmers who rarely use hired labour, but normally cultivate their holdings with the aid of their own families. The class comprises domestic servants also.

taken as comprising the aggregate — namely, 1300 million pounds—of incomes not exceeding £160 a year, to which must be added about 150 million, ear-marked and analysed by the Commissioners of Inland Revenue, as the salaries of those mental workers whose total incomes range from £160 upwards. Thus wages, in the wider sense of the word, amounted in all to about 1450 million pounds, or 70 per cent. of the entire produce of the nation. To this sum must be added the earnings of professional men, and those of the smaller employers. The aggregate of professional earnings was, according to a common estimate, something like 60 million, and the net gains of the partners in the smaller business firms—gains which averaged less than £300 per partner— were in the aggregate something like 50 million. It is impossible to distinguish between these two categories with exactitude, but together they made up a total of about 110 million; and if this sum be added to wages and salaries, we have an income identifiable as earned which did not amount to less than 1560 million,[1] or 75 per cent. of what is described by Mill as "the total produce" of the nation.

To this sum must be added the profits of the larger businesses, in so far as these are the result of the active ability of the principal and controlling partners, and are not mere interest on capital as held by the outside public. Such businesses are here taken as including all whose gross profits exceeded £1000. Nearly all of them were constituted in the form of firms or companies.

---

[1] Those who desire to work out these figures for themselves should consult the analytical reports of the Commissioners of Inland Revenue for the years 1905–10, especially the Synopses of Incomes, Schedules D and E. It should be noted that what are called "the gross amounts reviewed" include about 200 million pounds which form no part of net incomes exceeding £160, but are made up of outgoings and small incomes not subject to tax. In the case of business' incomes (Schedule D) these deductions must be carefully distributed, as some of them (e. g. allowances for wear and tear of machinery) are applicable only to businesses of a certain kind. The 60 million pounds, given in the text as the estimated earnings of some 200,000 professional men, are taken as being included in incomes classified as being earned by "Persons," the purely business profits being mainly, though not wholly, comprised in profits recorded as those of "Private Firms" and "Companies."

Their aggregate profits at the period here in question amounted, in round figures, to 300 million pounds; and of this sum, as will be shown in detail presently, about half was interest on capital, and the other half, or 150 million, was the product directly resulting from the ability of the controlling partners. Thus, to the income already specified as earned, this further sum of 150 million must be added, the total earned by direct and daily renewed effort being thereby raised to 1710, or (in round figures) to 1700 million pounds out of an entire national income of 2100 million.

Of the remaining 400 million [1] (so we may roughly call it, although in reality it was less) which was proximately derived by its recipients from the mere possession of property, about 240 million consisted of the rents of buildings, building sites, agricultural land with its improvements, and interest on certain stocks, mainly foreign, which was paid by governments, or agents acting on their behalf, whilst the residue—about 150 million, as has just now been said—represented the interest on shares held by the general public in the larger businesses of the kingdom.

The nature, the composition and the magnitude of this proximately unearned income have, however, been the subject of so many popular misconceptions that the figures here given, and their significance, must be examined in greater detail.

Of these misconceptions the most obvious and familiar is the following, which largely accounts for the overestimates often made of the magnitude of the unearned total. It relates to the notorious fact that business enterprises for the most part are, under modern conditions, organised in the form of companies, and largely worked with capital provided by mere investors. Now, the doctrine which is popular on democratic platforms to-day is that, when businesses were mostly small, and the capital was owned by the person, or two or three

---

[1] The above total of nearly 400 million of income from possession is exclusive of about 50 million ear-marked in the official returns as going to persons whose total incomes do not exceed £160. This sum being distributed already amongst "the workers," it cannot form part of any sum which democracy can aim at "recovering" from them.

persons who administered it, the profits might be fairly
attributed to the efforts of such persons themselves; but
that ever since the rise of the modern company system
the whole situation has in this respect been changed. In
the case of any large company—so the argument runs—
the employer who controls the business in his capacity
of predominant partner is altogether eliminated; his
services are relegated to a manager whose salary figures
in the wage-bill, and the total profits are interest pure
and simple, going to a body of shareholders who know
nothing about the business whatsoever, except in so
far as it yields them a larger or smaller dividend. Should
this argument be correct, the proximately unearned total
would be raised from 400 million to 550. Now, as
applied to certain companies, of which railways are the
chief example, it is doubtless correct enough; but if
applied to companies generally it is nothing better than
nonsense. Can any one suppose that all the novel inventions and conveniences which have been placed at
the disposal of mankind by the enterprise of modern
companies have been simply due to the entrusting by
idle and inexpert persons of so much money to the hands
of wage-paid managers, who forthwith proceed to use
it in any manner they please? If things stood really
thus, the growth of wealth would be a charmingly simple
process. Any section of the investing public, having
deposited its sovereigns in a bank, would merely have
to issue an advertisement to some such effect as this:
"A Company having been formed with a capital of a
million pounds for the production of something new,
useful and marvellous, a Manager is wanted to settle
what this something shall be, and to supervise its production. Salary £5000 a year. As the shareholders
know nothing about any kind of business themselves,
and are quite incapable of judging between man and
man, the first applicant will be accepted."
Such an idea is ludicrous. Nevertheless, the fact
remains that the growth of the company system has
given rise to a question which is really of extreme importance, and is practically novel on account of its novel
magnitude. This is the question of what, in the profits
of the larger companies, is the average proportion borne

by interest on mere investment to the earning or products of the ability of the active and controlling partners.
An answer to this question was attempted by the German
economist Wagon, which was based on the business
records of a number of selected companies, so far as
these records were accessible to the inquiry of a private
person.   He found, as might be expected, that the ratio
of the product of the activity of the controlling partners
to what he described as "company gain," or interest,
varied greatly in different cases, and he does not appear
to have arrived at any general average.   Evidence,
however, of a very much ampler kind—namely, that
provided by the official statistics of America—was
tabulated in the year 1914 by Dr. W. S. King, Professor
of Statistics in the University of Wisconsin.   In Dr.
King's tables the gains of all businesses are divided
into three portions, described respectively as Rent, or
"the value-product attributable to sites and buildings ";
"Interest, or the value-product attributable to plant or
mechanical equipment "; and "Profits," which term
is defined as "the value-product attributable to the
efforts of entrepreneurs."   Thus, "Rent" and "Interest " together correspond to what Wagon calls "Company gains," or income from mere possession; whilst
"Profits " are the product of the ability of the active
and controlling employers, or (to use Mill's language)
"the wages of the employers' superintendence."   Such
being the case, the total gains of all the industrial and
commercial undertakings in the United States, in the
year 1910, were, according to these fables, about 1900
million pounds, of which 850 million consisted of rent
and interest, and 1050 million consisted of the product
of "the efforts of the entrepreneurs."   In the year 1900,
though the figures were much lower, the proportion was
substantially the same.   It would thus seem, from the
results of a scientific analysis of the greatest mass of
contemporary data in the world, that of the total gains
of businesses, industrial and commercial of to-day, the
collective product [1] of the efforts of the active employers

---

[1] How greatly the proportions which yield this general average vary
in particular cases may be seen from the following examples.   The proportion of the total gain attributable to the "efforts of the entrepre-

is about 55 per cent., and those of the investing public 45 per cent.

We shall, therefore, probably be under the mark rather than over it if we assume, as we have done here, that, in the United Kingdom at the period here in question, of the total net gains of the larger firms and companies— that is to say, 300 million pounds—as much as half was the product of the efforts of the employers, and that not more than a half went as interest to the mere investor.

But it is not only in respect of the profits of Companies that popular thought as to unearned income errs. Another error is prevalent which relates to the conception of unearned income generally. It is no doubt true, as popular thought assumes, that all income not earned or produced by direct effort is necessarily income from possession; but all income from possession is not necessarily unearned. There are many kinds of effort, such as efforts devoted to the perfecting of some great invention, which, until they are ended, produce practically nothing. Not till an invention is so complete in design that it is fit to be multiplied by manufacture and put into general use does it come into being as a something which adds to the world's wealth, or can bring to the inventor any reward whatever. When it is completed, he sells the right of producing it, we may so suppose, to a company, which pays him in shares to the value (let us say) of £30,000, and he thenceforth enjoys an income of £1500 a year without the necessity on his part for any further effort of any kind. Such income would take the form of income from mere possession; but anybody who maintained that it was not truly earned could do so only by committing himself to the impossible principle that no effort, however long and laborious, which results in the production of any permanent utility, can possibly produce, or possibly earn, anything.

---

neur" was, in the case of Railways, 10 per cent.; of Mines, 12 per cent.; of Electric Power and Light, 33 per cent.; of Manufactures, 54 per cent.; of Commerce, 66 per cent.; and of Transportation by Water, 69 per cent. The small percentage representing "rent and interest" in this last case would appear to be due to the fact that no rent is payable for the permanent way—namely the sea.

The same argument applies to the rent of buildings. Brown and Jones are, let us say, two clerks, each of them earning a salary of £400 a year, out of which, by living with care, each of them could save £300. Brown, however, spends his surplus in getting men and women to dance, sing and dress up for his pleasure at music-halls. Jones pays it to builders who year by year in return for it build him a model dwelling fit for a workman's family. At the end of ten years a row of such dwellings is owned by him, for which he receives a rental of £150. His total income is now £550, whereas that of Brown is still £400 only. The extra income of the house-owner would be commonly called unearned, its immediate origin being possession, and not, like that of his salary, the performance of daily duties. But, as any one can see, who takes the trouble to think, it is just as truly earned—as truly the result of work—as the annual salary itself out of which the houses were created. If the salary is the equivalent of effort, the houses are the equivalent of the saved portion of his salary. They are so much salary converted into a permanent instead of a perishable form, and endowed with a lasting utility which recoins itself in an annual rent. This rent, indeed, is not only earned but is super-earned; for the salary out of which the houses were created represented the product of technical efforts only, but the rent is the product of these efforts with foresight and will added to them. If, however, Jones when dying should bequeath his houses to his companion, the rental, as received by Brown, would immediately change its character. Instead of being earned, it would be unearned, for its new recipient would have played no part in creating it.

Here we see what the really essential difference between earned income and unearned income is. Earned income is income which, whether its proximate source be the possession of property or no, has its ultimate origin in efforts made by the recipient himself at some time of his life, be that time what it may.[1] Unearned

[1] The practical bearings of this fact is illustrated by an article on "Income-tax Hardship" in a popular London Journal (Sept. 1914). "The hardship," it says, "of the present system is illustrated by the case of a retired professional man, who for the forty years of his work-

income is income which, coming as it always must do from permanent property of some kind, comes from property created by the efforts of persons other than the present recipients themselves. That is to say, apart from gifts of property *inter vivos* or of property acquired by marriage or some form of gambling, all income from property is earned which comes from property produced by the efforts of the living. The only kind of income which can properly be called unearned is income from such property as has been created by the efforts of the dead. In other words, again, at any given period in the case of any given country, all income from property is earned which is due to the efforts of the generation at that time alive.

Hence, the active lifetime of a generation being not less than thirty years, the earned income with which we are here concerned will be income from such property as had been created in the United Kingdom during the thirty years preceding the year 1907. Now, this new property, consisting for the most part of houses and shares in companies, amounted in the year 1907 to at least one-half of the total which we are able to identify as yielding rent or interest. If, then, the total income originating proximately in "possession" was at that time, as we have seen, nearly 400 million, nearly 200 million will have been earned by the efforts of the persons at that time receiving it, and nearly 200 million will have been unearned, or inherited by the living from the dead.

The income of the United Kingdom, in short, at the beginning of the twentieth century, in respect of its sources as they actually were on the one hand, and were popularly supposed to be on the other, is comparable to the income of a doctor, which was known by all his neighbours to be slightly in excess of £2000 a year; the prevalent opinion being that he barely made £400 by his practice, and that £1700 was from property left to

---

ing life denied himself every luxury on principle, in order to provide for his children and the old age of his wife and himself. Yet the interest on the savings of these laborious years is treated as unearned. Attention should be paid to the difference between income inherited and that derived from savings."

him by his father, whereas in reality £1700 was from his
practice, about £200 from property left to him by his
father in the year 1877, and another £200 from property
saved and created out of his own fees in the course of
some thirty years of active professional life.   In other
words, the " enormous " unearned " share," which has
haunted the imagination of men like Mr. Webb and Mill,
was not in reality so much as one-tenth of the total,
being equal at the time in question to threepence a day
per inhabitant of the United Kingdom.

In the foregoing illustration, however, one point is
ignored, and still remains to be considered, with regard
to which an error prevails, even more absurd than those
which have just been noted.   By most agitators it is
assumed that unearned income, whatever its amount
may be, is distributed wholly amongst persons who earn
or produce nothing.   Thus a Socialist Society, of which
Mr. Webb is a leading member, issued in the year 1905
a pamphlet, the writer of which having established to
his own satisfaction that the unearned income of the
United Kingdom amounted to no less than 700 million
pounds, immediately proceeded to observe that here we
have obviously the income of the body called " the Idle
Rich," which body consisted, according to him, of some
700,000 adult males, " not one of whom had ever even
professed to have so much as the shadow of an occupation in the whole course of his life."   If this were true
some singular results would follow.   Nobody who had
inherited a couple of hundreds a year could ever in his
life have done so much as a stroke of useful work.
Nobody who had ever done a stroke of useful work could
possibly be the son of a parent who had not by the time
of his death spent everything he had ever possessed.
The fact is, as everybody in his senses knows, countless
men are in receipt of inherited incomes which are nothing
more than additions to incomes earned by work.   How
these additions are distributed there is no statistical
evidence of a direct kind to show.   But, though we
cannot say how, in detail, the inherited " share " was
distributed, there are, with regard to the effects of its
distribution on total incomes, evidences, some of them
direct, some of them indirect, but generally accepted as

valid, which indicate the facts of the matter clearly
enough in outline. We have indirect evidence as to
certain total incomes in the number of houses of certain
rental values. We have other evidences of a kind more
or less direct as to total incomes up to £500 a year. In
particular we have evidences, absolutely direct and
unambiguous, as to incomes ranging from £3000 upwards.[1] These taken by themselves would be quite
sufficient to show how wildly absurd is the doctrine of
" the enormous unearned share " withheld from the
masses by a fabulously rich minority, or, as a radical
sentimentalist has described them, by " the super-
wealthy with their piled-up aggregations." The income
of any typical modern country—England or the United
Kingdom being taken as the classical example—has been
depicted by socialists and others, from the days of
Marx onwards, as an image with a head of gold, which
head, representing the unearned " share," is swollen to
such vast proportions that the atrophied limbs and body
can scarcely sustain its weight. Thus, a member of the
English Labour Party, addressing the House of Commons, declared that nearly all the wealth which had
been created in England since the beginning of the nineteenth century had gone to a few persons who were
" enormously rich already." The founders of an English
labour-league had issued a Manifesto about twenty years
before, according to the figures given in which, if the
unearned income of the rich had at that time weighed
a pound, the income of the rest of the nation would
hardly have weighed more than three and a half
ounces. As a matter of fact, in the year 1907, if
everybody is taken as one of the fabulously rich
whose income amounts to as much as £5000, the
income of the rich was to that of the rest of the nation,
not in the proportion of a pound to three and a half
ounces, but was barely as much as one ounce to a
pound.

But before we attempt to draw any further moral from

---

[1] These figures as to incomes exceeding £3000 a year were not available for the year 1907; but their then amount can be approximately
reached by reference to the general increases of income which have
taken place since then.

this particular fact, or from the others which have just been indicated, the whole of the figures just given with regard to England or the United Kingdom shall be considered in connection with others, which, besides helping to confirm them, will invest them with a fresh significance.

CHAPTER II

IF the figures just given were figures standing by themselves, they might be open to two criticisms which
would, if true, detract indefinitely from their importance. In the first place, since they are partly based on
methods of indirect computation which cannot claim to
be exact, they cannot, it might be said, be taken as the
basis of any definite argument. In the second place it
might be said that, relating, as they do, to the affairs
of one country only, the facts which they indicate, even
if indicated correctly, are largely local and accidental,
and are for that reason deficient in any general meaning.
If these figures stood by themselves, such criticism would
be plausible. The actual state of the case is, however,
widely different.

The general ideas with regard to the modern distribution of income which underlie the arguments of most
social revolutionaries have been mainly derived from
theorists who either neglected, as Henry George did,
statistical methods altogether, or who flourished when
these methods were at a stage much less advanced than
that which they have reached since the time of Henry
George's death. It is true that, so far as the distribution
of incomes is concerned, much remains to be done in the
way of collecting information—a kind of work which
must mainly be performed by governments; but this
work has in many countries been now advanced sufficiently to render the employment possible of the
method of international comparison. Such is the case
especially with regard to the four great countries in
which wealth-production has increased to the most conspicuous extent—namely, the United Kingdom, France,
Prussia and America. In each of these countries statis-

ticians, using independent methods, have been endeavouring to ascertain with as much correctness as possible what the distribution of incomes in that particular country is. In each case large use has been made of the method of estimates, yet when the general results of these various computations are compared, the main features of distribution in any one of these countries are found to be almost identical with its features in all the rest. If each of these several results is expressed by a curved line, and the four lines are exhibited in a single diagram, the tendency of each is to approach and often to overlap the others.

The most elaborate example of this kind of coincidence is that provided by a comparison between the United Kingdom and America, for which a mass of material will be found in a volume by Dr. W. I. King, already referred to, on *The Wealth and Income of the People of the United States.* It was published in the year 1913, and relates to the year 1910. Let us begin then with re-examining the case of the United Kingdom in the light of the evidences already used or mentioned— namely, the known total income of the country about the year 1907, as shown by the Census of Production, the Income-tax Returns for the same period, and the numbers of houses of various rental values; and let us summarise the results as either directly shown by, or inferable from, them, not with regard to the various sources of income, but with regard to the distribution of incomes taken as so many wholes. And let us first, for purposes of a rough and preliminary comparison, divide these incomes into the five following groups, showing what percentage of the total is formed by the inferable or the known aggregate of each.

The First Group shall consist of incomes of £5000 and upwards.

The Second, of incomes ranging from £3000 to £5000.
The Third, of incomes ranging from £1000 to £3000.
The Fourth, of incomes ranging from £500 to £1000.
The Fifth, of incomes not exceeding £500.

The total income of the United Kingdom having been at the time 2100 million, it appears from the various evidences which have just now been mentioned that the incomes comprised in the First Group formed 6 per cent. of the total; those in the Second, 2 per cent.; [1] those in the Third, 8 per cent.; those in the Fourth, 10 per cent.; and those in the Fifth, 75 per cent.

Let us now turn to Dr. King's Tables for America, in which, with extraordinary elaboration, American incomes are grouped in a like way, the aggregate in each case being reduced to a fraction of the entire income of the country. Decimals being omitted, Dr. King's figures for America, as against those just given for the United Kingdom, are as follows.

The aggregate of incomes comprised in the First Group —namely, those exceeding £5000 a year—is given by Dr. King as 8 per cent., the corresponding figure of the United Kingdom being 6.

The aggregate of incomes in the Second Group— namely, those lying between £3000 and £5000—is given by him as 2 per cent., the corresponding figure for the United Kingdom being the same.

The aggregate of incomes in the Third Group—namely, those lying between £1000 and £3000—is given by him as 6 per cent., the corresponding figure for the United Kingdom being 8.

The aggregate of incomes in the Fourth Group— namely, those lying between £500 and £1000—is given by him as 9 per cent., the corresponding figure for the United Kingdom being 10.

The aggregate of incomes in the Fifth Group—namely, all those that do not exceed £500—is given by him as 75 per cent., the corresponding figure for the United Kingdom being 74.

If we take the first two groups together—namely, those comprising all incomes in excess of £3000—and examine them more minutely, we shall, with the exception of one notable detail, discover other parallelisms no less remarkable than these. The exception relates to the largest incomes of all. If we take the hundred and fifty richest men in America, and compare them with the seventy-five richest men in the United Kingdom (the

[1] The percentages for Groups 1 and 2 are based on the super-tax returns, made subsequently to the year 1907, and giving the actual numbers and total increase of the persons concerned.

two numbers being the same relatively to the different populations), it appears that this group in America had an aggregate income of 75 million pounds, or an average income of half a million per person, whilst its counterpart in the United Kingdom had an aggregate income of 13 million only, the average income per person being roughly 170 thousand. Otherwise, the grouping of incomes in excess of £3000 exhibits in the two cases what is not so much a likeness as an identity.

Thus, if, to vary our method of classification, we take, not the total amount, but the total number of incomes exceeding £3000, the number of those ranging from £3000 to £5000 will in both countries be nearly half of the whole; the number of those ranging from £5000 to £10,000 will in both countries be nearly one-third; the number of those ranging from £10,000 to £20,000 will in both countries be a little more or a little less than a seventh; and the number of those exceeding £20,000 will in both cases be one-hundredth.

The close similarity between the two countries which is shown by figures such as these—figures worked out by absolutely independent inquirers, dealing with absolutely different and differently presented data—forms a strong confirmation of the substantial, though it would be rash to say of the exact, accuracy of each. It may, at any rate, be taken as refuting, beyond the possibility of doubt, the fundamental assumption of all socialist reformers that some " enormous share " of the wealth of the modern world passes, in virtue of the accident of mere " possession " or otherwise, into the hands of the conspicuously rich. It may be taken as showing that even the rich and the moderately rich between them manage to secure no more than a relatively small fraction of it.

But the significance of this similarity does not end here. The fact that out of the productive activity of each of these two populations a scheme of distribution arises which is in its main features nearly, if not absolutely, the same, shows that these results must be determined, not by any local accidents, or by moral conduct peculiar to particular groups of individuals, but by general principles of some kind to which certain human activities, whenever they come into operation, tend naturally and inevitably to conform. The practical meaning, however, of a broad conclusion like this will be very imperfectly represented if we give our minute attention to the larger incomes only, which have their origin in more or less exceptional enterprise. We must examine with the same minuteness the lower incomes also, which mainly, though not wholly, consist of the earnings of wage-paid labour. We must not content ourselves with ascertaining that, if all these be taken in the mass, an overwhelming portion, and a portion the same everywhere, of the total income of any modern country is absorbed by them. We will, therefore, still using Dr. King's figures for America, presently pursue our comparison between that country and the United Kingdom farther. Let us first, however, realise the nature of the main question with which such a comparison will concern itself.

This is a question relating to the universal conditions under which, in any modern country, the incomes, which are mainly the wages, of the masses of the population are received by them, and relating more especially to a conception of the nature of these conditions, which still forms the basis of the revolutionary logic of to-day. The import of this conception, when put into plain words, expresses itself in the theory of wages which Marx, though he did not invent it, was the first thinker to invest with what claimed to be a scientific form. It has the merit of being extremely simple, and may be summarised in a few words. According to this theory, society under modern conditions is divided into two classes—a small employing minority who own all the implements of labour, and a vast majority who own nothing but the labour-power resident in themselves. Such being the case, then, labour is a mere commodity which the labourer sells to the employer; the price paid for it is wages, and is in each case the subject of a bargain. If the two parties met on an equal footing, the price might bear some relation to the value of the labour sold. But the footing on which as an actual fact they do meet is, said Marx, in its very essence unequal. The labourer must sell his labour from week to week, or he will starve. The employer can afford to wait. The labourer, therefore, unless he is prepared to die, is forced to accept a price which bears no relation whatever to the value of what his labour produces, but is measured by the cost of keeping a man just above the level of starvation. This result is, according to Marx, inevitable, not so much because the employer is wicked, wicked though he generally is, as because, from the very nature of a bargain, nobody will give more for anything than the lowest price which the vendor can be induced to take for it. Hence, said Marx, under the existing economic system, wages are everywhere by a kind of universal fatality forced down to a common, and to the lowest possible, level. And this theory, in spite of some modifications, continues to dominate socialist thought to-day. It is, indeed, now admitted by socialist thinkers themselves that the wage-earners since the days of Marx have managed to extract from the employers something in excess of the bare means of subsistence; but wages, they say, still resemble a table-land, the level of which, although it may have risen somewhat, is everywhere raised but slightly above the uniform cost of keeping a human being alive; and this rise, such as it is, they attribute to collective bargaining through unions, which has proved to be of greater efficiency than Marx was able to anticipate.

Now, there is nothing in this account of the matter which is *a priori* impossible. On the contrary, if we take it as a mere description of facts, it is roughly applicable to England at the beginning of the nineteenth century, when the modern industrial system had but partly displaced the old. Only some 5 per cent. of the adult male labourers of the country received at that time as much as 23s. a week. About 8 per cent. received from 18s. to 19s. The average for 87 per cent. was not more than 10s. 6d. Even socialists cannot deny that wages have increased since then; but when they seek to explain this rise by attributing it to democratic action in the form of collective bargaining, they ignore another change more important, as a symptom, than the actual rise itself. Collective bargaining may account for the fact that wages have risen as a whole, but it will not account for the fact that wages have risen unequally. Still less will it account for a certain peculiar change in the manner in which wages of unequal amounts are distributed. In these two latter respects what has actually happened is as follows.

In the first place, an admitted increase in the minimum wage-rate being allowed for, wages as a whole at the beginning of the twentieth century had come to differ from wages at the beginning of the nineteenth in the fact that their range and the minuteness of their graduation from a given minimum upwards were very much greater at the later period than they had been at the earlier. Whereas a diagram of their graduation as they were at the earlier date would have had the contour of a slight and hardly perceptible slope, a diagram of their graduation as they were a century later would have had throughout the contour of an ascending staircase.

In the second place, with regard to the number of persons amongst whom wages of various amounts were distributed, the distribution at the beginning of the nineteenth century was what is called "pyramidal." A century later it had, up to a certain point, come to assume the form of a pyramid upside down. This means that, at the earlier of the two dates the most numerous class of recipients was the class whose wages were lowest, and that as the wages increased the number of the recipients declined; whereas a century later those who received the minimum, which was then (we may say) £40, were very much less numerous than those who received £50, that these again were less numerous than those who received £70, and these yet again less numerous than those who received £90; but that after some such point the pyramidal order reasserted itself, those who received £90 outnumbering those who received as much as £100; whilst as to the salaried class, those who earned more than £1000 were, in respect of their numbers, a mere vanishing quantity.

This, roughly stated, is what has happened in the United Kingdom after a century of bargaining between the employing classes and the employed; but it has not happened in the United Kingdom only. A situation essentially similar has developed itself in America also, and during a much shorter period. Thus, in a table devoted to the earnings of married men, Dr. King divides these into twelve graduated amounts, ranging from a minimum of £50 up to nearly £300; and his figures show that for every 50 men earning no more than £50, there were 300 earning £70, 600 earning £80, 1000 earning £100, and 2700 earning £150. That point having been reached, the same change occurred which occurred in the United Kingdom lower down in the scale. Thus, the number of those whose earnings averaged £170 was only 2100; the earnings of only 1600 reached or approached £200; and the earnings of only 600 reached or approached £300.

To many readers these details may doubtless seem dry enough, but their dryness will vanish when we realise their general import; for the remarkable parallelism which they have here been cited to illustrate between the results of bargaining for wages in these two widely separated countries is virtually a refutation, so far as this question is concerned, of the theory which has been the basis of all revolutionary agitation from the middle of the nineteenth century down to the present time.

This theory has, as we have seen already, its root in the idea of a bargaining process which, since one of the parties to it is in a position to bide his time, whilst the very life of the other depends on his selling his wares— namely, his personal efforts—immediately, enables the former to beat down the price of these wares, no matter what their value, to the minimum which will enable the latter to keep body and soul together. Now, such a situation, let it be said again, is conceivable. The question is, does it, as a general fact, exist? Is it the typical situation which capitalism, after a century of trial, has produced? A mere glance at indubitable facts is enough to show that it is not. No minute insistence on the accuracy of detailed figures is necessary to show that such a situation, if it prevails at all, prevails in relation to a minority of the wage-earners only—a minority the proportions of which we shall very greatly exaggerate if we say that, in the leading capitalist countries of the world it amounts to, or even approaches, one-fifth of the whole. Let us suppose, then, that the wages of as many as one-fifth of the wage-earners are determined, as Marx argues, not by the value of their products, but merely by the naked cost of the minimum of food required by them. The typical question as to wages still remains unanswered. The fact that the employer pays this irreducible minimum to a fifth of his men, but to a fifth of his men only, does but bring into prominence the fact that, in dealing with the vast majority of them, the price which he actually pays is not this minimum at all; it is this minimum plus some amount added to it, which in each case must, according to the psychology of Marx, cost the employing Shylock a twinge of acute pain.

Thus, the question as to wages generally which really requires explanation is not why they tend as a whole in the direction of a common minimum, but why they tend to move, in various degrees, away from it. To say that this result has been due to the pressure of collective bargaining is no answer at all. So far as collective bargaining is concerned, there is an upward pressure all along the line; but in the case of each section of wage-earners the result of this pressure differs. All along the line there is a downward pressure on the part of the employers also. In each case they give way up to a certain point, but they do not give way beyond it. What, then, are the final limits between which, as extremes, the conscious process of bargaining can do no more than reach some mean? These extreme limits are in all cases the same. The lower limit is the smallest possible sum on which a wage-earner can be kept alive. The upper limit is determined no less rigidly by the total product of the business in which the wage-earners play a part.[1] But, these limits being present in all cases alike, how is it that, as the result of individual transactions, the intermediate sums finally agreed on vary, so that out of 1000 men working for the same employer some will get £40 or £50, others £60 or £70, others £80 or a £100, others £150, others £200, and a few very much more?

[1] This is true of the self-directed labourer also. His income must be something between the maximum he could produce if he strained his muscles to the utmost, and the minimum which, produced with more desultory work, would just save him from death.

In the light of the facts and figures which we have just been considering, one thing is evident. However the results of each individual transaction may be affected by the personal temper of those directly concerned in it, they are affected by it to a small extent only. They are mainly determined by certain facts or forces which are altogether external to any cupidity, generosity, any strength or weakness of will, which is peculiar to any one employer or any one body of workmen; and that such is the case is evident for the two following reasons. One of these is the fact that, throughout any one country, the graduations of wages which result from countless individual transactions tend in all like industries to be uniform. The other is the fact that, if two great countries are compared, the details of this graduation are relatively the same in each, even in respect of their most unlikely particulars.

To what, then, is this elaborate graduation, as a fact in itself, and to what is its world-wide but unintended uniformity, due? Here is a question to which there is only one answer. The graduation is due to the fact that industry, as intellectualised by the modern scientific oligarchy, is a process the product of which, to a degree far greater than was the case under simpler systems, depends on the efforts of men who differ widely from one another in their several degrees of efficiency, some of them adding more to the total, some of them adding less, and wages being determined by the particular efficiency of each; whilst the graduation is similar in different and distant countries for the simple reason that Nature, in dealing with different populations, distributes unequal efficiencies in very much the same way.

Even, however, if all this be granted, those who cling to the idea that the wage-earners nevertheless are robbed of some enormous share of the value of their products somehow, may yet as a matter of theory urge the following argument. Wages, it is open to them to say, may be adjusted with perfect accuracy to the value of every wage-earner's personal product in this sense, that, if the work of A is worth double the work of B, B is certain to get for it twice the price that A gets; but that A and B, to a like fractional amount, may each be

defrauded of wages really due to him.   A's work may
be worth £200, and B's work may be worth £100; but
if B, instead of £100 gets £75 only, and if A, instead of
£200, gets only £150, the difference between the larger
of these two sums and the less will be strictly proportionate to the difference between the two values produced, yet each man will be the victim of a similarly
proportionate theft, his receipts falling short of his
product to the extent of one quarter.   The facts of
graduation may no doubt be inconsistent with an indiscriminate robbery of the kind imagined by Marx, but
they are perfectly compatible with the supposition that
wages are everywhere curtailed by a system of embezzle-
ments which, though not indiscriminate, are monstrous.

Now, in this argument, just as in the argument of
Marx that all wages tend downwards to one irreducible
minimum, there is nothing which, as a matter of mere
theory, might not or may not be true.   Here, again, the
question is, Does the theory coincide with actual facts?
And certain facts are ascertainable which will enable us
to reach an answer, not indeed absolutely precise, but
sufficiently so to enable us to establish a broad conclusion.   For if the wage-earning classes as a whole are,
to some enormous extent, really the victims of a theft-
system of the kind described, the stolen portion of their
products is bound to be discoverable somewhere in the
incomes unduly swollen of other people of some sort.
The question is, then, Who can these other people be?
Before we can go further, it is necessary to understand
this.

If to any socialist meeting in Chicago or New York
this question were put as follows, " Who are the great
embezzlers of income produced by, and therefore due
to, the masses of the American people? " there can be
no doubt as to what the instant answer would be.   It
would be, " The factory kings, the railroad kings, the
oil kings, the kings of finance and speculation "—men
whose type would be indicated by shouts of " Vander-
bilt," " Harriman," " Carnegie," " Rockefeller," " Mor-
gan."   If a similar question were put to a socialist
meeting in London, the answer would be substantially
the same, though the names of typical plunderers might

be less easy to find. On either occasion orators would spring from their seats and descant on the outward signs by which such men may be known—their palaces in Grosvenor Square, or Fifth Avenue, the tiaras of their wives, their moors in Scotland, their salmon rivers in Norway, and the luxury of their monstrous yachts. In America and Europe alike the typical embezzler, the typical cause of poverty, who robs the labourer's home of the necessaries, and the middle-class home of the modest embellishments of life, figures in socialist art as a species of bloated ogre, clutching so many sacks, each of them labelled " A million " or " Ten million dollars." That is to say, according to current ideas of him, the typical embezzler, be his country what it may, obviously belongs to that small cluster of persons whose wealth is sufficiently great to be matter of international, or at least national, knowledge, and especially so great as to be worthy of celebration by newspapers.

Now, if ideas of this kind have any justification any-where, they have it in the recent growth of enormous incomes in America; and it may be reasonably con-tended that incomes such as these, which transcend all sane possibilities of the amplest private expenditure, are liable to convert themselves into implements of public and political corruption. But to suppose that they represent any appreciable abstraction from what would be otherwise the income of the nation generally, will, when facts are examined, reveal itself as a pure delusion. The number and aggregate income of the super-millionaires of America, and the number and aggregate income of the class which in the United Kingdom most nearly approaches them, have been given here already. The result of what Mr. Webb would call a " recovery by the people " of the entire income of this class in America would mean, in the language of school-boys, a weekly "tip " of a threepenny-bit for everybody; and a similar " recovery " by the people of the United King-dom would mean for everybody a weekly " tip " of three halfpence.

Let us, however, suppose that the robbery of the poorer classes by the richer is imputed, not to a little cluster of super-millionaires only, but to the semi-millionaires as well—that is to say, everybody whose income was as much as £20,000. The number of this class in America was approximately 3000. It was in the United Kingdom approximately 1500. If we suppose that every one of such persons stole the whole of his income, and the people "recovered" what would vulgarly be called "the lot," the results would be doubtless superior to those we have just considered. The weekly "tip" would in America be raised to tenpence-halfpenny, and in the United Kingdom to fourpence. Or, again, if we find it amusing, we may carry our suppositions further. We may first consider what would happen if the people of the two countries "recovered" all incomes in excess of £5000, and then what would happen if they "recovered" all that exceeded £3000. We should find that the "recovery" meant for the American workman a rise in wage-rates of a penny-farthing in every shilling, and for the British a rise of a penny. But if we wish to deal with the matter seriously, we may pass on at once to a supposition probably wider than the widest to which any temperate socialist in cold blood would commit himself. This is the supposition that every man who receives an income of more than £1000 a year steals as much of it from "the people" as happens to exceed that sum. The supposition is, of course, absurd, but it will nevertheless be interesting to see how it works out. The total of incomes in excess of £1000 formed in both countries 17 per cent. or 18 of the total; but if we suppose that the recipients are severally taken to have come by as much as £1000 honestly, the portion assumed to be stolen will have been in America 11 per cent., and in the United Kingdom it will not have been more than 8. Thus, a "recovery by the people" at the beginning of the twentieth century of all incomes which exceed £1000 per head would have meant for the American workman a rise in wages at the rate of a penny-halfpenny in the shilling, and would have meant for his British comrade a rise of about one farthing less.

It is not necessary to insist on either of these figures as exact. The broad fact which alone concerns us here is this, that even if we estimate the possibilities of

" recovery " at a maximum, the object in view being a more complete adjustment of wages or other payments to the actual product of workers varying in their degrees of efficiency, such a " recovery " would result in no greater change than that which is constantly due to a good business year or a bad one. It would effect no change more noticeable in the existing scheme of distribution than that which would be effected in the configuration of a human being if his measurement round the waist rose from thirty-five inches to thirty-eight or forty. In other words, within a maximum fraction, whether of one-ninth or one-twelfth of the total amount involved, the various producing units under the modern industrial oligarchy tend to receive, in all their various degrees, what their personal work is worth, this fact being shown by the identity of the complex features of the general scheme of distribution which comes into being wherever that system operates.

The facts, however, as thus far stated, are in the main empirical. They are facts which experience and observation show to be the results, natural and unintended, of that principle of industrial oligarchy (commonly described as " capitalism on the great scale ") which, having established itself first in England, became there widely prevalent about the beginning of the nineteenth century, in America about fifty years later, and in Germany after the conclusion of the Franco-Prussian war. Such results being peculiar to the novel system in question, they must obviously have been due to the development of the oligarchic principle somehow; but if we wish to render them intelligible—if we wish to see why these results have shaped themselves as they have done everywhere, and have not shaped themselves otherwise, it is necessary to connect them with the working of the oligarchic principle in detail; and this task can be accomplished in one way only. It can be accomplished only by a comparison more or less precise, not between the affairs of one country and the contemporary affairs of others, but between the affairs of some one typical country as they actually are to-day, and the affairs of that country itself as they were when the new system was beginning to displace the old; but the old, though its days were numbered, was the dominant system still. There is one country, and one country only, in which evidence sufficiently definite for such a comparison can be found. That country is England. Not only are the statistics of production and distribution in England or the United Kingdom voluminous with regard to conditions that prevail to-day, but similar records are extant, curiously minute and comprehensive, of the corresponding conditions as they were more than a hundred years ago. The principal changes which such a comparison reveals, together with their inner significance, shall be reviewed in the following chapter.

CHAPTER III

A CENTURY OF CHANGING DISTRIBUTION

THE income of England in the year 1801 was, according to a number of concurrent evidences,[1] about 180 million pounds, or £20 per head of a population of 9 million. The income of the United Kingdom about the year 1907 was, as we have seen already, about 2100 million, or £47 per head of population of 45 million. Now, if the process of production had itself undergone no change except such as resulted from an increase in the number of persons engaged in it, the simplest arithmetic will show us that, in the year 1907, the income of the United Kingdom would not have been more than 900 million, whereas it actually was 900 million with 1200 million added to it. About an eighth of this increment, however, was derived from British enterprise abroad; and, since no home labour was involved in it, it cannot be attributable to any novel forces acting on the population of the British Islands themselves. The home-produced increment, which here alone concerns us, will have been accordingly about 1050 million. If, then, it be true that the modern increase of wealth is due primarily to the Mind of a novel oligarchy of em-

---

[1] In the year 1801 an income-tax was imposed on all incomes exceeding £60 a year, or 23s. a week. These incomes were classified in the returns according to their total amounts, the sources not being specified, and were divided seriatim into 34 groups. There is also a large mass of evidence relating to agricultural and other earnings below 23s. a week. Mulhall, in summing up the records relating to Poor-relief in England at various periods, gives the income of England (including Wales) in 1801-5 as £180,000,000. His computation was independent of those on which the same sum, as given in the text, are founded. It is necessary in dealing with that period to take England alone, England being the part of the United Kingdom which was first " industrialised," and no sufficient records with regard to Ireland having been then in existence.

ployers, as a force directing the labour by which matter is moved and manipulated, it will follow that, at the present time, more than half of the income of the United Kingdom is produced in a primary sense by a body of persons which, numerically, is so small as to be hardly visible.

The actual meaning, however, of this proposition is not so paradoxical as it seems. What it comes to is that, at the beginning of the twentieth century there was on an average one directing mind, whether that of an individual or two or more partners, for every 500 or 600 labourers, whereas in any comparable undertakings a hundred years before the labourers directed by one Mind would have been, we may say roughly, a couple of hundred only.[1] But the difference between the two periods may be further explained thus. At the beginning of the nineteenth century, about one-third of the productive business of the country was carried on by independent workers or small family groups, and another third by employers on a very small scale—still a numerous class, such as jobbing builders, plumbers, makers of carts, and so forth—who worked as labourers themselves along with their own subordinates. Not more than one-third of the productive business of England had so far passed into the hands of industrial oligarchs, or employers whose individual profits reached or exceeded £1000 a year. In other words, businesses of the modern oligarchic kind—and even these were small as compared with their successors of to-day—produced at the beginning of the nineteenth century 33 per cent. only of the industrial output of England, and the smaller businesses, which were absolutely or relatively democratic, produced, to speak roughly, 67 per cent. A hundred years later the oligarchic businesses were producing 86 per cent. The democratic businesses produced no more than 14 per cent. The latter persisted, and they persist, in various familiar forms such as those

[1] The figures given as to industries at the beginning of the nineteenth century are based on the income-tax assessments for the year 1812, published in the year 1815. The income-tax tables for the year 1801 classify incomes according to their total amounts only, without indicating their source.

which have just been mentioned. Their absolute
number, apparently, has not increased or diminished;
but, relatively to the increased population, it had by
the end of the nineteenth century dwindled to a fifth
of what it had been at the beginning of it.   Their profits,
ranging from £80 a year to £1000, representing an
average of something less than £300, appear to be much
what they were a hundred years ago.   The oligarchic
businesses, on the other hand—namely, those producing
profits of £1000 a year and upwards—have, concurrently
with the relative decline of the others, increased in two
ways.   Each of the employing units has brought within
the circle of his influence a larger number of labourers,
and the average product per employee has been raised
on an average in the ratio of 4 to 10.   Of this fact it will
be sufficient to give two illustrations.   If the oligarchic
businesses of England had remained what they were at
the beginning of the nineteenth century, except for the
fact that they had increased in the same ratio as the
population, their total profits at the beginning of the
twentieth century would not have exceeded 50 million
pounds, the average profit per business being £2500.
Their actual profits, as we have seen, were at that time
300 million, the average profit per business being £10,000.
In the year 1812 there were in England only 1000 businesses which severally produced a profit of more than
£3000.   The total profits of all of them were barely
above 6 million, £6000 being the average profit of each.
Ninety years later, of the thousand largest businesses
the profit of the smallest did not fall short of £50,000;
the aggregate profits of all were 180 million, and the
average profit of each was £180,000.

It is, therefore, in the development of these larger
businesses since the beginning of the nineteenth century
—in the application of single units of brain-power to the
direction of a larger and larger number of labourers—
that we must look for the action of oligarchy as the
cause of increasing wealth.   The case is summed up by
Goethe in the second part of *Faust*, where the secret
of material progress is said to consist in this:

"One Mind suffices for a thousand hands,"

and in the progress of England since the beginning of the nineteenth century this fact is presented to us in a definitely measurable form. At the beginning of the nineteenth century, each of the larger employers, such as they then were, directed on an average about 250 labourers, the total product per employee being about £40. A century later each of the larger employers directed on an average the labour of twice or three times as many, the average product per employee being raised from £40 to £100. As a natural consequence of the increased productive power which industry acquired as the principle of oligarchy developed itself, it has come about in the course of a few generations that about five-sevenths of the business output of England is produced under the direction of the minds of a few men ; and here, when roughly translated into terms of statistical and historical fact, we have the import of the thesis that, at the beginning of the twentieth century, the Mind of the larger employers was the primary producer of an income of some 1050 million pounds, added to an income which would otherwise have been 900 million only.

And now we reach the question to which all these observations have been tending. If the total reward which, in the shape of profits—profits being taken as including all interest on industrial capital—went to Mind as embodied in the persons of the industrial oligarchy and their associates, was, as we have seen, about 300 million pounds, and, if, as we have seen also, these profits would have amounted to no more than 50 million had industrial methods remained what they had been a century before, and had all the subsequent conquests of directing Mind been absent, the question which confronts us is this. Why, if Mind is the producer of a total increment of 1050 million, do the representatives of Mind get only 250 million, or less than a quarter of it, for themselves ? What becomes of the remainder ? The more we reflect on the detailed facts of the situation, the more evident will the pertinence of this question become. For these men, the heads of the larger businesses, are, as socialists put it, " the great national pay-masters." The wages and salaries, which are the incomes of the vast majority of the population, must in the first instance have passed into these men's custody. Why, then, did they pay away, and to whom did they pay away, four-fifths of a certain increment, if their own minds had really produced the whole of it?

To this question there are two principal answers, each of which goes to the roots of the modern industrial system, and without invalidating the thesis that the modern increase of wealth is primarily due to the Mind of the modern industrial oligarchy, modifies its practical import by showing what, in actual life, the operation of such an oligarchy implies.

The first of these answers may be given by means of a simple illustration. Let us suppose that the introduction of the modern locomotive engine was due entirely to the genius of one exceptional man, in the sense that a dozen mechanics by blindly following his directions presented a specimen engine, complete in every detail of its mechanism, to a world which would never have dreamed, if left to its own wisdom, of any means of traction other than a horse or a donkey. But one such specimen engine, however perfect and powerful, would, if it stood alone, be nothing more than a toy, or a wonder for the world to gape at. In order that the world should derive from it any practical benefit, huge works would be necessary at which replicas of this specimen could be turned out by the thousand. Let us, then, suppose further that this same man, the inventor, establishes such works himself, he being his own capitalist, and secures the services, not of twelve but of twelve thousand manual workers, all of whom he engages for the specific purpose of so moving particles of matter from one position to another that finally, like pieces of a puzzle, they shall coalesce into engines devised by his own brain. The operations of Mind, as embodied in the persons of the great employers, could not be exemplified in a more complete form than it would be in the person of an industrial genius such as this.

Now, it might seem that here we should have two factors only—namely, the labour of some thousands of men moving particles of matter on the one hand, and a single mind dictating how and when they should be moved on the other. In actual life, however, the situation would be widely different. Between these two factors there would necessarily be a third connecting them. The most absolute monarch who ever flattered himself by saying " L'etat c'est Moi " could not govern even the paltriest province unless he were surrounded by ministers, each of whom had an army of lesser officials under him; and the same thing holds good in the case of the intellectualised industry of to-day. If Mind, other than the minds of the manual labourers themselves, were represented solely by that of the supreme employer, and if the labourers in executing their thousands of daily tasks had to get their orders direct from him or from nobody, he would not find minutes in the longest of working days for issuing orders to one labourer out of a hundred. For him, the first thing necessary before he could set his business going would be to secure the services of certain principal managers—men who were capable of grasping his main ideas, and were masters of the technical knowledge required for putting them into execution. His next step would be to get together a mixed array of sub-managers, draughtsmen, calculators, clerks and foremen, from the top to the bottom of a long descending scale, until at last the men were reached, who would, under this system of elaborate mental direc-, tion, deal with particles of matter by the use of their hands and muscles.[1]

Now, all these officials, no less than the employer

[1] As a type of the difference between oligarchic businesses as they had come to be at the beginning of the nineteenth century and as they were a hundred years later, we may say with approximate accuracy that for every five or six hundred manual labourers at the earlier period there would have been five employers, each directing a separate business of his own, and employing a staff of 100 or 120 labourers and 3 or 4 mental workers. At the later period, there would have been on an average 1 employer of a higher order, who, superseding the original 5, employed 600 manual labourers and 45 mental subordinates, or 1 mental worker to every 12 manual. The proportions borne to-day by the subordinate mental workers to the manual vary greatly in different businesses, according to the degree and quality of intellectualisation from above. Thus in the construction of ships (*i. e.* hulls) there was, according to the Census of Production (1907) 1 mental subordinate to 29 manual workers. In the construction of marine engines there was 1 to every 9. In the following businesses the proportions were these :— Gas, 1 to 10 ; Chemicals and Bicycles, 1 to 8 ; Clocks and watches 1 to 3.

himself, represent not manual effort, but mental. Hence, when the Mind of a class whose functions are mental only, and involve no formative contact with material substances whatsoever, is spoken of as directing the operation of human hands which, unless they are in contact with such substances, produce nothing at all, this cannot be the Mind of the employing class alone. It must, in practice, include another class as well, whose function it is to see that material substances are handled in accordance with a purpose which the brain of the employer specifies. Hence, if the primary peculiarity of the modern industrial system is the extent to which, under it, the handling of matter is intellectualised by submission to the control of a small employing class, a secondary peculiarity will be the development of this class of mental subordinates. It will, moreover, be natural to expect that, in proportion as the control of the employers increases in range, and grows more and more scientific, these mental subordinates, in respect not alone of their number, but also of their earnings, as an index of their productive value, will increase likewise, and increase to such an extent that even the roughest statistics will exhibit an unambiguous record of it.

And such we shall find to be the case. According to Colquhoun, whose investigations relate to the year 1812, the number of business employees in England, Scotland and Ireland, other than manual labourers, did not amount at that time to more than 70,000, their average earnings being £70 per head. This would mean that in England some ten or twelve years earlier the number of such employees could not have exceeded 60,000,[1] their aggregate earnings being just over 4 million pounds. Had the industrial system undergone no other changes than those resulting from a mere increase of the population, the number of such persons employed in the United Kingdom rather more than a century later would have been 300,000, and their aggregate earnings but just over 20 million pounds. As a matter of fact their number

---

[1] This would allow on the average about three mental workers, besides the employer or the employees, to every business in England which made a profit exceeding £310 a year.

had by that time reached one million;[1] their average earnings had risen from £70 per head to £200, and their aggregate income had risen from 20 to 200 million. This means that out of the total increment ascribable primarily to the Mind of the supreme employers, the employers had to part with 180 million in payment for the services of a new class of mental coadjutors. If this be added to the increment retained by the employers and their financial associates for themselves, the share of the new wealth taken by these two groups of mental workers together will have amounted to 430 million out of a total increment of 1050 million.

Who, then, appropriated the residue?

This residue of the income—more than 600 million— went as an addition to the wages of manual labour. Had manual labour throughout the United Kingdom been paid in the year 1907 at the rates prevailing in England at the beginning of the nineteenth century— and this is precisely what would have been the case had the doctrine of Marx been true—the aggregate income of the labourers at the latter of these two dates would have barely been as much as 400 million pounds. As a matter of fact, the labourers' share of the increment raised this total by 160 per cent.

Now, in one sense the most remarkable feature in this division of the spoils of progress is the share secured by the subordinate mental workers; for, in respect of the increases alike in their number and their earnings, these persons are practically a new class.[2] When, however, the functions of mere Mind as an agent of production are realised, and the great differences in efficiency between some minds and others, the rise of this class and the wide range of its salaries are at once sufficiently intelli-

---

[1] About half this number were subject to income-tax, their average earnings being about £300 a year. The earnings of the other half were below the income-tax level, and averaged £100.

[2] As the result of the investigations of a committee of distinguished economists, it was shown in a paper presented to the British Association at Sheffield that out of a non-assessed income of 1300 million, about 250 million represented (about the year 1907) the earnings of a Lower Middle Class, in which the lower ranks of the Salaried Mental Workers were included.

gible excepting in one particular. If the productive
faculties which the members of this class exercise are
such as to command payments, notably in most, and
in some cases enormously, exceeding those of the highest
manual labour, why were they not in operation a
hundred years ago, and securing, if not the same, yet
proportionately the same rewards ? Are we to suppose
that in the course of a hundred years the percentage of
persons born with such capacities has trebled itself ?
A supposition like this would be absurd. The percentage
of persons in whom capacities such as these were con-
genital was, presumably, no greater at the beginning of
the twentieth century than it had been a century before ;
but what had increased in number and become novel in
kind were the means or opportunities of applying such
faculties to productive purposes. Thus the construction
of a ship like a modern Dreadnought demands and gives
scope for the exercise of high mathematical talents, by
the studious development of which a number of picked
workers earn large rewards to-day ; but talents of this
order would have been useless in the days of Nelson,
and many of the men who helped to construct the
Victory may have had in them the makings of mathematical experts, and yet, hardly conscious themselves
of endowments then so sterile, been obliged to earn their
living by the use of the axe and hammer. In other
words, the intellectualisation of industry, which primarily
has its origin in the Mind of the supreme directorate,
increases the supply of subordinate mental talent in
action by creating opportunities for the use of faculties
which would else be dormant.

The presence, then, of the subordinate mental workers
as a factor in modern industry carries its explanation on
the face of it, and though it considerably modifies the
practical import of the thesis that the modern increase
of wealth is due to the supreme employers, it does not
conflict with that thesis in any fundamental way. But
when we turn from mental effort to manual, and consider
the fact that these same manual labourers have secured
far more of the increment than the two other classes
together, it may seem at first sight that the case is
totally different. It may seem either that the thesis

in question is in itself erroneous, and that the hands and muscles of the self-directed average man do increase in efficiency, which that thesis denies, or else that the employers, according to a scheme of minutely graduated generosity, paid twice as much to each labourer as his labour could possibly produce.

Of the difficulty thus suggested the solution is discoverable in two sets of facts, both of which are of the first importance, but which are in current controversy altogether neglected. One of them is purely economic, the other is moral, political, or, in a general sense, social. The latter will be discussed hereafter. We will here confine ourselves to the former—namely, facts which are purely economic.

In the case of mental capacities, such as an innate talent for mathematics, which a workman is incapable of using if there is no opportunity for their use, but which, if a use is devised for them by the genius of a scientific employer, he at once does his utmost to cultivate, and finds that their industrial value embodies itself in an ample salary—in the case of capacities such as these, two things are equally evident. One is that, apart from the genius of the scientific employer, the potential talents of the employee would be, for practical purposes, as though they did not exist. The other is that, in the same practical sense, such potential talents would be equally non-existent unless the employee developed them by certain extra efforts of his own. If the employer represents the oligarchic principle in industry, and the employee the democratic, the case is similar to that which exists, as we have seen already, in the sphere of political government. Action from above being given, there is not only submission from below, but a positive reaction also. The worker who develops high mathematical powers in response to the demands of an employer who provides him with the opportunity of using them is, when they are actually used by him, and his earnings are thereby increased, a co-creator of the increment out of which his increased earnings come.

And what is true of subordinate mental effort is, with certain qualifications, true of manual effort also. The manual labourers of to-day—or, in other words, the mass of average men—would produce no more than they did a hundred years ago if they were left to the direction of no minds other than their own; for they would have no opportunity of doing, in the way of productive work, anything different from what they did a hundred years ago. But the technical control of their labour by a scientific oligarchy being given, there has not been on the part of masses of the labourers the mere passive response of conformity, or a doing under the guidance of others the same order of work which they had previously been doing under their own. In many respects there have been changes in the character of the work itself, and the labourers have, in accordance with their several natural endowments, been called on to exert themselves in the development of various faculties which were previously unused for the reason that they were not usable.

Of this fact a rudimentary but a very striking illustration is to be found in the first modern event which awoke in the legislators of England a consciousness of industrial change. This, which became notorious very early in the nineteenth century, was the growing employment of children of tender years in factories. A little child at the beginning of the nineteenth century was a creature no stronger or cleverer than its predecessors had been at the time of the Norman Conquest; but certain master minds, by concentrating themselves on the industrial process, had so far simplified a number of manual operations, and had so far substituted non-human force for human, that the feeble hands and the limited intelligence of infants were able to produce daily the value of a loaf of bread, whereas previously they produced, and could have produced, nothing. The infants had played no part in devising the scientific apparatus on which the possible exercise of their productive powers depended. Were the apparatus withdrawn, their small productive powers would at once have been withdrawn also. But the point to be noted is that, the existence of the apparatus being given, the infants in using it were not doing to order something which, like playing a game, they would have done somehow in any case, but were making some extra (and to them arduous) effort, the like of which they never had made before.

And of manual labour generally under the modern industrial system, the same thing holds good, not in all its forms, but in most of them. It is true that, unlike infants, the majority of human adults must in any state of society perform manual labour of some kinds, these kinds being such as are necessary for the bare support of life. These are still essential to production, no matter how elaborate, as may be seen when some piece of super-scientific machinery is transported by a carter in a van to the premises of the final user. The carter who, acting under orders, does this kind of work to-day, does nothing which he could not have done, and would not have had to do on his own account, had he been a mediæval peasant carting his own barley. He differs from his predecessor as a child who reproduces on tracing-paper certain lines which a drawing-master has drawn on a slate beneath it, differs from a child who, with a pencil equally firm, describes on a blank slate figures of its own devising. The sole factor present in the first case and not present in the second is no new positive effort either of mind or body, but a passive act of absolutely easy obedience. The labourers who still perform work of this simple kind to-day cannot be said in any accurate sense to produce more to-day by any faculties resident in themselves than their predecessors did a hundred or even two thousand years ago; and the fact that these men, whose earnings represent the minimum, are twice as well paid as their grandfathers for work precisely similar, is due to causes of a moral or social kind, the discussion of which must be reserved for a later stage of our argument.

The labourers, however, whose work is still of this primitive kind, and who still receive the minimum, what-ever that may be, have sunk under the modern system to a relatively small minority; and the minimum sum secured by these men being given, the fact that the majority in varying degrees earn more is of purely economic origin; and, although it may have a social side also, we are here concerned with it as an economic fact alone. We have seen, then, that the wages generally, a

minimum sum being given, owe all their upward graduations, in so far as these occur, to a corresponding graduation in the efficiencies of the workers earning them.
This holds good under all systems of which wages form
a part. What concerns us here is the fact that, in proportion as, under the modern system of oligarchy, industry has been intellectualised from above, the graduation of the wages, not only of mental, but of manual
work also, has acquired a wider range, and become more
minute in character, than it was when this system of
oligarchy was still in its earliest stages; and if we compare industrial oligarchy as it is to-day with what it was
in England a hundred years ago, the difference between
the two may be briefly expressed thus. Any employer
demanding work from his labourers is like a schoolmaster
setting sums to his class. The sums set by the typical
employers of yesterday were all so simple that most of
the class could do them. The cleverest boys in doing
them used and revealed no more talent than the dullest.
The sums set by the typical employer of to-day, though
certain of them are simple still, are for the most part
in varying degrees difficult. They require for their solution talents which are not only greater than those possessed by all, but which also, before they are usable for
any particular purpose, must be cultivated by deliberate
effort on the part of the possessors themselves, the details
of such effort depending on what the purpose is. This
is what socialists forget when they reason about labour
as a commodity which is bought and sold. They think
of it as a commodity which is always of one grade only,
and if all labour were still of those simplest kinds of
which all human beings must be capable who are capable
of keeping themselves alive, this conception would correspond with fact. It did, we may roughly say, correspond
with fact in England at the beginning of the nineteenth
century in some such sense as this: that, if labour at
that time had been bought by the larger employers, not
from the labourers directly, but through some salesman
representing them at a central office, and if at that time
an employer had asked to be supplied with labour-power
to the extent of a hundred units, most of the units
wanted by him would have been of a low, and a more

or less uniform, efficiency; and that the salesman might
have taken so much for granted unless the intending
customer had made some statement to the contrary.
But to ask him in the same fashion for a hundred units
to-day would be like asking a wine-merchant for a
hundred bottles of wine. An order given in these general
terms would be meaningless. The salesman of to-day,
were it necessary to explain the situation, would say to
the employer, "What qualities of labour do you want?
In former times we supplied three qualities only. Our
chief trade was in the lowest, but we kept them all in
stock. To-day we supply the article, not in three
qualities, but in sixteen. The lowest quality, for which
the demand to-day is small, we keep in stock as we
always did, but the higher qualities have to be made
to order. You must specify in each case what you want
the labourer to do; the labourer, so far as he can, must
make himself capable of doing it, and the extra effort
involved in his self-preparation must, according to
circumstances, be secured by some extra payment."
    What the new accomplishments on the part of the
manual labourers are which the modern oligarchy
demands, and for the use of which it creates opportunities, need not, and cannot, be discussed in detail here.
It will here be sufficient to indicate their general character. By largely substituting for mere muscular effort
the powers of steam and electricity, and thus liberating
the labourer from duties exhausting to mind and body,
the industrial oligarchy has demanded from the labourers
generally, and has thus enabled them to develop, a self-
concentration on tasks in which energy, mainly mental,
plays a part considerably larger than it did in the tasks
which previously were alone open to them. These novel
tasks remain still essentially manual in the sense that
they involve, and are in each case bounded by, a manual
contact on the labourer's part with so much or so many
of certain prescribed substances as can be brought within
the reach of one pair of human arms; but these tasks
have become matters of habituated and alert attention
rather than of mere muscular endurance on the one
hand, or of mere tricks of dexterity, themselves difficult,
on the other. In any case the main fact which concerns

us here is this : that, whatever the new tasks now demanded of the manual labourers may be, they involve
on the whole more self-preparation, and a greater
graduation of efficiencies from an inevitable minimum
upwards, than did the tasks demanded by the employers
a hundred years ago.[1] Since, then, each of these new
efficiencies needs a voluntary effort on the labourers'
part to develop it, and since, in its own degree, each
adds its something to the success of the employer's
projects, the employer is bound to elicit them in the
only way that is practicable—namely, by paying a price
for each proportionate to the excess of its value over
that of the crude effort which is all that the labourer
would have troubled himself to put on the market
otherwise. Such, then, is the primary, though it is not
the entire, explanation of that increase which has, under
the modern industrial oligarchy, taken place in the
earnings of mere manual labour. The primary cause
of this increase has not been the generosity of the
employers, nor the pressure of collective bargaining.
Its primary cause has been the fact that, the action of
the oligarchy being first assumed as an essential, various
new efficiencies—we may call them kinds of super-labour
—in response to the demands of the oligarchy have been
developed by the labourers themselves.

Here, then, in these three productive classes—the
oligarchy of employers whose business is mental direction, the great subordinate staff whose business is mental
direction in obedience to the employers' orders, and the
manual workers through whom Mind is brought into

---

[1] Many persons deny this. Those who do so have mainly in view
kinds of manual work which are of the nature of artistry. And it is
true that the rôle of the artist, as a direct fashioner of goods that come
into the market, has, under the modern system of production, become
relatively less important than it once was. It is, however, not extinct.
It flourishes under limitations of a very obvious kind, with which sentimental democrats least of all people should quarrel. In proportion
as goods are fashioned by the direct labour of artists, each of whom
possesses some special genius, the supply of such goods is necessarily
slow and small. They can, therefore, be acquired by the few only,
and these few are the exceptionally rich ; but unless artists work under
scientific employers who can use their designs as patterns, wealth, as
represented by art-products, can never diffuse itself outside a narrow
circle.

contact with matter, we have the three main agencies, to the interaction of which, not only the increase of wealth is due, but the general features of its distribution also.   We have these classes and their respective functions before us, not as mere abstract quantities, but as localised and concrete facts, the development of which, in the case of one country at all events, is historically and statistically measurable with some rough but sufficient accuracy; and with the aid of such concrete facts we can more or less definitely see how the scheme of distribution, which to-day is substantially the same everywhere, substantially reflects and coincides with the actual dynamics of production.

In the following chapter we will consider these facts again, with reference to the more recent attempts of socialist or democratic thinkers to exhibit some vast change in the present distribution of wealth and circumstance as possible through a fuller operation of the forces of pure democracy.

CHAPTER IV

DISTRIBUTION AS IT IS

LET us sum up briefly the argument of the foregoing chapter with regard to modern production and the process of distribution as contingent on it, in a country which is the classical type of the progressive countries of the world.

In the course of little more than a century the modern industrial system has not only provided occupation and the means of livelihood for a population five times as great as that which could otherwise have maintained itself within the limits of the British Islands, but it also has more than doubled the average product per inhabitant. This result is primarily due to the fact that intellects of a superior order have concentrated their powers on the business of directing manual labour; and, since manual labour was, at the beginning of the twentieth century, not superior, either in muscular force or skill, to what it had been at the beginning of the nineteenth, or indeed to what it had been in ancient Rome or Egypt, the whole of the increment which is new since the beginning of the nineteenth century must, in a primary sense, be the product of Mind alone, as embodied in the persons of those by whom labour is now directed. Such, then, in a primary sense, being the principle of production to which the modern increment is due, it was pointed out that this principle, when translated into actual practice, has resulted in a scheme of distribution which, within something like a tenth of the total, tends so far to accord with the minutiæ of the productive process that what a man or a class receives is a roughly accurate index of what he or it produces. We have seen, however, that, if this measure of individual production be adopted, the practical result differs

174

to a vast degree from anything which our general theory, if taken without qualifications, might reasonably lead us to expect. We have seen that out of an increment of 1050 million pounds the representatives of controlling Mind received as an actual fact something less than a quarter. Hence, if it is true in any sense that Mind produced the whole, it must be true in some other sense that its product was a quarter only, whilst Subordinate Mind and Labour between them produced the rest. If, therefore, our discussion is to have any practical meaning, we must consider more closely how, in any sense that is practical, these two propositions are related to one another, or whether the former, which credits the Mind of the oligarchy with having produced the whole, has in actual life any meaning whatever.

In order to understand this question it is necessary to revert to a discussion which occupied us in a previous chapter, with regard to the nature of practical reasoning generally. It was there pointed out that all practical reasoning is in its nature hypothetical, resolving itself into a statement that, if such and such a particular thing be done, such and such a result will be thereby caused or produced. It was pointed out further that, if such reasoning is to have any immediate import, the action which is the subject of the hypothesis must be of a kind which it is likely or reasonably possible that an individual or a class may, under existing circumstances, elect to perform, having not performed it previously, or, having performed it previously, may elect to perform no longer. Thus, if manual labour, by availing itself of the new opportunities which, as we have seen, have been created for it by the Mind of an industrial oligarchy, can be said to produce more to-day than it did at the beginning of the nineteenth century, or indeed to play any part in the production of the increment whatsoever—especially if it can be said in any serious sense to produce more of the increment than is produced by the Mind of the oligarchy or as much—one condition must first be taken for granted. This condition is that the existing system of production, with an industrial oligarchy at the head of it, is established as a going concern, and that no question of what would happen if the action of the oligarchy were suspended presents itself as relating to possibilities which are near enough to be worth considering; whereas if this condition disappears, the whole situation changes.

Thus, for example, when the Jesuits were a power in Paraguay, they selected certain of the more intelligent natives, and succeeded in teaching them the delicate art of watch-making. By these natives, though experts in arts immemorially their own, such a use of the human hand had never before been dreamed of. In response to the demands, and under the supervision of their instructors, they nevertheless acquired it. Under such conditions the industry so far prospered that the Jesuits are said to have made a considerable profit from the products of it, these being sold in Europe for the benefit of their own Order; and whilst this situation lasted, the craftsmen, who profited also, may be said to have done as much in producing the total output as the men who merely set them their lessons and told them what to do. But when, as subsequently happened, the Jesuits were driven from the country, the native watch-makers, deprived of their guides, were helpless. There was no longer a question of which did most in the making of this new merchandise—the Mind of the directors or the labour of the men directed. There was for the labourers, as soon as they were left to themselves, no merchandise of this new kind at all; and the proposition that the directors had produced the whole of it—a proposition which would otherwise have been true in an abstract, a remote, and a speculative sense only—would then have represented for the natives a highly important and directly experienced fact.

This illustration is taken from a chapter of history very unusual in kind, but it turns on an event the substantial reproduction of which on an incomparably wider scale is not only not impossible if we take it as a practical hypothesis, but is actually the precise event which the theory of pure democracy indicates as the object of all popular endeavour,[1] and which the earlier

[1] A most remarkable illustration of the vital pertinence of the above passage has been provided by the course of the Russian revolution—an event which did not begin, and which was indeed anticipated by

leaders of democratic opinion were urging year by year all labouring men to work for by strategical strikes, by violence, or the capture of governmental power. The event which was to be thus worked for is simply the entire cessation of any kind of influence which is exercised over industrial effort by the knowledge, the intellect or the energy of any purely directive class, and the " emancipation "—such is the agitator's favourite term—of the masses of the workers from all mental guidance other than that which originates in their own minds only. So long as such an event continues to be aimed at by any large section of the workers, or to haunt their minds as an object of ideal endeavour, the proposition that the oligarchy, which such persons have often attempted and may again attempt to destroy, really produces the whole of the new wealth of the world, in the sense that if the oligarchy were paralysed this new

---

nobody, till more than a year after the words in the text were written. The following facts, recorded by the socialist correspondent of an English newspaper at Petrograd (July 1917), speak for themselves. M. Skoboleff, a revolutionary leader himself, declared that the great danger of the revolution was caused by the masses, whose one object was " *to terrorise and compel the dismissal of all controlling persons of any kind*," and manage industry (as Owen and Lane attempted to manage it) by purely democratic committees, which had no power except in so far as they reflected the intelligence and the immediate inclinations of the wage-earners. These committees (as Owen found, and as Lane found) proved absolutely incompetent. In one factory the helplessness of the committee being apparent to all, the experiment was attempted of turning the foremen into so many petty dictators. The foremen proved as helpless as the committee. The workers were accordingly driven to come for guidance to the old management. In a dyeing business in Petrograd the wage-earners had demanded wages so far beyond the value of the total product that there was no revenue out of which to pay them. There was, however, on the premises a large store of chemicals. The wage-earners insisted that these should be sold, and wages paid out of the sum thus obtained. These chemicals were essentials of the industry. Nothing could be done without them. The works accordingly had to close down. The more intelligent revolutionists, like M. Skoboleff, may denounce such insane proceedings " as a direct menace to the gains achieved by the revolution," but they are simply the logical results of the principles of pure democracy—which principles necessarily mean, if they mean anything, " the dismissal of all controlling persons," or, in other words, any oligarchic person who imposes his own will, or the results of his own knowledge, on others.

wealth would presently exist no longer, is not a proposition which is true as a piece of mere abstract theory. It is one which is fraught with a meaning as momentous and as strictly practical as any social politician, or any sane man, can imagine.

Nevertheless, let it be said again, in so far as we take, and have reason to take, the operation of the oligarchy for granted, the practical truth will be that what the oligarchy produces by the process of intellectual direction is by no means the whole of the increment, but merely a small fraction, the larger part being the product of those democratic reactions—reactions both manual and mental which the action of the oligarchy evokes, and alone makes possible, but without which the oligarchy itself would in all industries be crippled, and in many reduced to impotence.

Here, then, in the operations of these three great agencies—in Supreme or Controlling Mind, Subordinate Mind, and Labour, the interaction of which is the essence of the modern productive system, we see the reason why, in all progressive countries, the resulting scheme of distribution, elaborate as its graduations are, is almost indistinguishably the same, and why Controlling Mind should, in spite of its primacy, get out of the total product such a relatively small reward. The reason lies firstly in the fact that the modern productive process depends on the interaction of units who differ greatly in respect of their unitary productive powers; secondly, in the fact that the distribution of the product everywhere tends to adjust itself to what each unit produces; and, thirdly, in the fact that these various powers themselves are everywhere distributed by nature in very much the same proportions. The international similarities of distribution are explicable in no other way. There is, indeed, in all highly civilised countries, such as the United Kingdom and America, about a tenth part of the total annual product which, like a kind of precipitate, goes to its recipients as income from inherited capital; and, even if this fact is ignored, it cannot be pretended, as to the rest, that the adjustment is as yet in individual cases complete. It is enough to say that the adjustments resemble those of coats to individual human figures.

The coats adjust themselves generally to the dimensions of their respective wearers, though in many cases the fit may not be perfect.

Now, if such allowances be made for maladjustments of this kind, the general adjustment of income to the product of individual effort is gradually being admitted by socialist thinkers themselves. It is being admitted by them partly in the way of revised theory, partly in the way of a series of revised statistics. Thus, the "enormous share" stolen from the products of the workers by an absolutely non-productive class was, according to Marx and his immediate followers, something between 80 and 75 per cent. of the total. Twenty or thirty years later, the strike-leaders of Australia had reduced this estimate of the stolen share to 66 per cent. Ten years later, again, the more educated of the English socialists had reduced it to 33, and others, later still, have reduced it to 25.

These changes are reflections, not only of an improved arithmetic, but also of an advance in thought from the crude puerilities of Marx, by which the earlier socialists were dominated, to something more closely resembling the complexities of actual fact. The Marxian ideas of distribution in the modern world were perfectly logical as related to the Marxian theory of production; but, despite the talent displayed by Marx in his exposition of it, his theory of production is, as applied to the modern world, one for which the word "puerile" is the only correct epithet. Modern economic society is, according to that theory, divided into two, and no more than two classes—a mass of employers on the one hand, whose sole activity is theft, and who hardly know the nature of the industries of which, as Mill said, "they are the possessors," and a mass of labourers, exclusively manual, on the other, who are all of the same grade, who all receive or tend to receive the same starvation wages, and who, unaided by any intellect or any imagination but their own, produce all the wealth of the modern world between them.

If such a picture were correct, the Marxian estimate of the stolen or unearned share would doubtless be correct also. It stands or falls, however, with two

definite assumptions : firstly, that the labourers are all
of the same grade, and all receive the same minimum
wage; and, secondly, that neither the employers nor any
intermediate class have anything to do with the operations of labour whatever, whether as masters of science,
as men of enterprise, or as organisers, or in any other
way.   Each of these assumptions has come to be recognised by the later socialists as absurd.   They recognise,
on the one hand, that wages do not all tend to a
minimum, but rise for the most part in varying degrees
above it, the aggregate share of the wage-earners in the
national product being thus indefinitely larger than the
fifth part or the quarter which the logic of Marx
assigned to them.   They recognise, on the other hand,
that the modern employers, as distinct from the mere
investors, are, instead of mere idle " expropriators," the
most active agents in production that have ever been
known to history.   One modern socialist writer, who has
already been quoted here, admits that they owe their
positions to the fact that they are born with certain
peculiar energies of which they are the practical monopolists; that their function consists in the issuing of
technical orders to which the mass must conform in a
spirit of " strict subordination and discipline "; that
these men are producers as truly as the labourers themselves; that a large share of the income of " a complex
industrial state " is produced by them, and that this
share must be regarded as the rent of their special
ability.   Other representative socialists, English, Belgian,
German, Italian and American, have come to admit in
almost the same words that the special abilities of men
who were classed by Marx as idlers "make all the
difference to a business between success and ruin."

   In proportion, then, as socialists have come to perceive on the one hand that wages are greater in the
aggregate than according to Marx they could be, and
on the other that employers produce a large part of the
income which according to Marx they steal, it is obvious
that the socialist estimate of the stolen total has, as
compared with the Marxian, been necessarily reduced
to very modest proportions.   The latest socialist estimates have, as was just now mentioned, reduced it from

80 per cent. of the entire product to 25; and, if we allow for the fact that at any given time about half of the income directly coming from property is from property created by the actual recipients themselves, the income really unearned, according to this computation, will, though somewhat excessive, be not far from the truth.

Nor does this more reasonable view of the actualities of the existing situation lead to a revised conception of unearned income alone. It leads to a revised conception of the causes which mainly determine the distribution of incomes generally. In proportion as socialists have now come to perceive that if, in respect of incomes derived from inherited property (which alone are really unearned), allowance be made to the extent of a tenth or even a twelfth of the total income of·a typical modern nation, the entire remainder is the product of the efforts of living men—in proportion as they have come to perceive further that these efforts, instead of being, as Marx assumed, equal, rise from the bottom to the top in a minutely graduated scale; that distribution is graduated in a manner no less elaborate, and that in different and distant countries this distributive graduation exhibits the same contour or pattern—one thing has, generally if not in exact detail, become as plain to socialists as it must be to other men. It has become plain to them that this uniform graduation of incomes cannot be accounted for on the supposition that millions of workers, all of them equal in efficiency, are robbed of their equal products to systematically unequal degrees, but that primarily and mainly their shares of the total product must, with substantial accuracy, be adjusted to the unequal amounts which their efforts severally produce.

This profound change, however, in the trend of socialist thought has not been due to a development of thought alone. It has been due largely to two kinds of experience. One of these has been the growth since the days of Marx of State-owned or Municipal undertakings, such as railways, gas-works, electric lighting and telephones. The other has been the growth of the great Trusts of America.

According to the implications of earlier socialist argu-

ment, and according to the dream of all the earlier
socialists, as soon as any industry had passed into the
hands of the State, " the people "—that is, the employees—would enjoy, somehow or other, a vague something called " economic freedom "; that they would
divide in equal shares the entire proceeds amongst themselves; that they would settle for themselves, without
any dictation from above, what their several tasks
should be; and the State, as holder of the capital, would
be no more than their banker. Since the days of Marx
every one of these expectations has been falsified. It
has been found that in State-owned industries the
general conditions of employment are in no essential
feature different from those that prevail under private
companies. The same discipline from above, as a
matter, not of choice, but of necessity, reappears in yet
stricter forms. Wages are graduated in substantially
the same way, being adjusted to the value of work with
the same fatal precision. Equality of income and freedom are as far off as ever. All this is admitted by the
serious socialists of to-day. Experience has shown, says
one of them, who once was an ardent Marxian, that a
State-owned industry, such as the Post-Office (which
Marx adduces as a specimen of ideal socialism in action),
is merely private capitalism rehabilitated under a new
name.

Since the days of Marx the world-famous Trusts of
America have, by the facts of experience, been teaching
socialists precisely the same lesson. The growth of these
huge corporations from the closing decade of the nineteenth century onwards, each of which is a combination
of countless businesses into one, has affected the socialist
imagination, and, through it, socialist theory, in a
manner yet more remarkable. It has done so in two
ways. On the one hand, to a degree much greater than
any of the industries which have thus far been owned
and monopolised by the State, these corporations have
shown how efficient as instruments of production groups
of industries may be rendered by uniting them under
one control, and have thus provided socialists with the
spectacle of a feat accomplished which, if only carried
to its full logical consequences, would realise their idea

of what socialism, as a productive scheme, would be. On the other hand, nowhere else has the principle of industrial oligarchy been developed to so extreme an extent. Nowhere else are the graded efficiencies of the mass so conspicuously signalised by a scale of unequal wages. Nowhere else is the contrast greater and more obtrusive between the fortunes of the directed many and those of the directing few on whose constant vigilance the vitality of these mammoth enterprises depends.

This latter aspect of the question modern socialists recognise no less clearly than the former. State-owned industries and Trusts, more especially the latter, represent the productive system which socialism necessarily demands ; and yet these very persons, who lead and reflect the movement of socialist thought to-day, admit that both such systems are, if taken by themselves, utterly subversive of the object at which any kind of socialism aims. " Let us," they say in effect, " organise men in whatever way we please, so long as it will render their corporate industry effective; let us pay them as nearly as possible the full value of their individual work ; and the very features against which the idea of socialism is a protest will reappear as they are under the system existing here and now."

An admission of this kind by the leaders of socialist thought might at first sight seem to be nothing less than a relinquishment of every idea by which socialism has thus far been actuated. Such, however, is not the case. So far as socialism has for its ultimate object a general equality of material conditions or incomes, the admission in question is merely a prelude to the revival of the old promise in a yet more alluring form. What the change in theory is which has made this revival possible may be gathered from the number of new tentative formulæ which have, to speak roughly, since the close of the nineteenth century, crept into the language of socialist thinkers generally. They differ as much in their implications from the theories of a productive monism, which aimed at merging the industrial oligarchy in the mass, and which have already been examined here, as they do from the theory of Marx, in which there is no recognition of the functions of oligarchy at all. These new formulæ have now become so familiar that the following examples of the ways in which they are worded will suffice. " It is a mistake to suppose," says one writer, " that socialism is identified with any one theory of economic production. It relates to something wider than the act of production, and beyond it." " A system of production," says another, " is socialist or non-socialist, not according to the manner in which wealth is produced, but according to the social uses to which it is put afterwards." " Socialism," says another, " does not necessarily mean, and as a matter of fact it cannot mean, that everything is to be done *by* the people. Its sole essential meaning is that everything is to be done *for* the people." Condensed statements such as these, from the nature of the case, are informative in the way of implication only. What, then, when stated in fuller and more precise terms, does the implication mean which emanates like a scent from all of them? What new principle do they indicate, by the practical application of which all the inequalities incident to an oligarchic system of production shall have for their final issue a paradise of democratic equality?

This question was asked with incisive candour, and the modern socialist answer to it was indicted no less clearly, in a sort of manifesto published in the year 1907 by a clerical exponent of socialist thought in America. There are traces in his language of a temper peculiar to churchmen only, but his main argument was wholly independent of religion. It was merely a logical expression of the ruling idea now common to intellectual socialists generally. The democrats of the eighteenth century, and the Marxian socialists of the nineteenth, both, said this writer, made an error, and the same error, at starting; not, indeed, as to the object of the democratic movement, but as to the means required for its accomplishment; and nowhere, so he proceeded, is this fact more clearly shown than in the great Charter of Democracy on which the American Constitution rests. The ideal State was there declared to be one in which each man would be free to do his best for himself by the use of his own faculties, so far as this course was compatible with a like freedom for others. Now, a State thus constituted would work, he said, well enough if it were not 'for one fact, and this fact the fathers of the American Constitution overlooked. They assumed that the faculties of all men were, not perhaps precisely, but at all events very fairly, equal. This, however, he went on to observe, is just what men's faculties are not; and, in respect of no faculties, the use of which is generally necessary, do men differ more conspicuously than in the intellect and energy necessary for the production of wealth. Hence a government which aims merely at providing them with equal opportunities of producing as much as they can, and keeping as much as they produce, is a hotbed of those ultimate inequalities which democracy aims at minimising. The few who are endowed with faculties of one special order—faculties ethically void and often allied with baseness—are left untrammelled to accumulate wealth and power, whilst the many are left unaided in absolute or comparative poverty. Hence the earlier democrats, and more particularly the earlier socialists, though right in their estimate of the evils by which society is at present afflicted, were radically wrong as to their cause. The cause of existing inequalities does not lie in the fact that most men, under the existing system, do not get all that they produce. It lies in the fact that on the whole this is precisely what they do get. They get what is due to them as producers. What justice demands, what democracy demands, what socialism demands, is that they shall get what is due to them, not as producers, but as men.

In other words, according to this argument, a just distribution of material goods and circumstances has nothing to do with what happens within the precincts of production itself. Within those precincts the principle of oligarchy may preponderate. Some men may cast much into the treasury, others relatively little. Justice relates to what happens outside the factory gates, and demands that when the treasury is opened the last shall be as the first, the first no greater than the last. Thus, with one of those touches of nature which make the whole world kin, the writer illustrates

his meaning from what probably was his own experience. He complains of the shameful fact that, under
the existing system, a minister of Christ, if he wants to
build a church, may have to come hat in hand to some
coarse-grained individual whose one and only superiority
is a wholly non-moral, a wholly non-Christian power of
producing the dollars which the Christian desires to
spend. Under a system of socialist or truly democratic
justice, what the Christian now begs as a favour—here
is the writer's conclusion—he would be entitled to
demand as a right.

In this train of reasoning, apart from its clerical
applications, we see what the theory of wealth and distribution is to which socialist and democratic thinkers
are now generally approximating. In this theory they
find what, ever since they detected the fallacy of the
Marxian doctrine that the value of the product of every
worker is equal, they have all been looking for in one
place after another. They find a means by which two
things, seemingly incompatible, may be harmonised,
both of which are essential to socialism in virtually the
same degree; one of them being a system of production
from which oligarchy, subordination and all kinds of
inequality are inseparable; the other being a system of
distribution which shall nevertheless be equal. Nor is
this the only advantage which the new conception of
the socialist principle brings them. By its means their
estimate of " the enormous share recoverable by the
people themselves " is restored to its old proportions,
if not, indeed, swollen beyond them; for what the masses
are promised by a polity which ignores the facts of production is not merely that limited sum which at present
certain persons enjoy in excess of their actual products.
Everybody who produces, and can only produce, a little,
is promised nearly all the products of those who possess
more.

How such a scheme of socialism would work out in
practice is a question which shall be dealt with when we
have seen in greater detail what its operation would be
as anticipated by socialists themselves. Meanwhile, it
will be enough to observe that if the essence of socialism
is to be found in the process of democratic distribution,

and if this is not to be determined by the facts of individual production at all, the entire conception of socialism or a socialist polity, in so far as such a polity is novel, belongs to a domain of life which is not industrial but social; and social democracy, not industrial, is the democratic element which is involved in it.

In order to realise this fact more clearly we will presently consider the modern socialist programme as set forth and expounded by one of the few socialist writers who has won international distinction as a critic of life generally.

BOOK IV

DISTRIBUTION BY DEMOCRATIC SENTIMENT

CHAPTER I

THE SENTIMENTAL PROGRAMME

WHAT is meant or suggested by the term Social Democracy, as distinct from " Political " and " Industrial," is the application of the principle of " one man one unit of influence " to every province of life which is distinguishable from that of technical industry on the one hand, and that of the making and administration of governmental laws on the other. The exclusion of these latter activities will not, indeed, be complete; for if principles purely moral are, as modern socialists contend, to determine amongst other things the distribution of material products, such principles, as we shall see presently, will require laws to enforce them; but a development of these principles into an active and compelling power must, as the writer about to be quoted insists, both precede such laws if they are to be made, and accompany them if they are ever to be effective; and the nature of these principles themselves, as moral or social phenomena, is the matter with which we are first concerned.

The writer in question is Mr. G. B. Shaw, whose peculiar talents, joined with his socialist sympathies, have been made known by his dramas to a wide and international public. These dramas, whatever may be their merits otherwise, display an alertness of thought and logic, a keen observation of character, and an insight into social relationships and the current ideas involved in them, which qualify the author in a very signal degree,

188

not to lead, but to reflect contemporary socialist thought, and to express its essential content in the most coherent, the most logical, and generally in the most favourable form of which it is, from the nature of things, susceptible; and nowhere can a better or more representative exposition of socialism as a scheme of social, to the exclusion of industrial, democracy be found than in an exposition of it which was given by Mr. Shaw as a challenge to adverse criticism, on an occasion designed to secure for it an attention as wide as possible. In order, then, to understand clearly what a socialist polity would be, as advocated, defended and understood by the serious socialists of to-day, Mr. Shaw's exposition of the matter, as given by him on that occasion, shall in substance be reproduced here.[1]

Mr. Shaw begins by saying that the one essential characteristic by which a socialist State, as properly understood, is distinguished from all others has been obscured in the minds of its opponents because they mistake for its essence what is merely one of its incidents. They identify it, he says, with a mere unification of industries, which ought always to be distinguished from socialism by the name of "Industrial Collectivism." If the essence of socialism be, what it really is—namely, an equal distribution of incomes or material circumstance—collectivism, says Mr. Shaw, emphasising the precise illustration which has just now been mentioned, would in itself no more tend to produce this than the great Trusts of America. But socialism begins where industrial collectivism ends. Instead of leaving distribution to be determined by the facts of production, it appears on the stage precisely at the critical moment,

---

[1] Mr Shaw's views, as here given, were expounded by him at great length in a controversy carried on by himself and Mr. Harold Cox in the *Morning Post*. The nature of the occasion led to great diffuseness of statement on his part, and to much dislocation of the logical order of his arguments. Their true logical order is, however, perfectly clear to an attentive reader, and is carefully represented in the text. Some socialists would probably say that Mr. Shaw presses the demand for an absolute equality of incomes too far. But this is a mere matter of detail, and does not affect the representative character of his reasoning; for a virtual or effective equality is demanded by them all alike.

and imparts to collectivism a totally new character by
subjecting the distribution of its products to a force
which has no relation to industrial facts whatever. This
force, he says, which is the soul of socialism, may be
best described as a sentiment, of which the nature and
the genesis are as follows. The sentiment, he says, is
one which will, when fully developed, render the very
idea of unequal incomes intolerable; and although at
present it is doubtless far from general, to suppose that
it will soon become so is no mere idle dream. It has its
roots in ordinary human nature. A sentiment prevails
already amongst all civilised men which demands that
the beggar shall be covered with clothes of some kind,
no less than the plutocrat. Socialism, then, regarded
as a practical project, does not require for its basis
the creation of any sentiment that is new. It merely
requires a development—and this is in rapid progress—
of one which is familiar to all of us, as operative here
and now, and which will, when developed only a little
further, make the spectacle of a poor man as intolerable
as the spectacle of a naked man. Hence, it will no
longer content itself with demanding a coat for everybody. It will insist on filling the pockets of all coats
alike with what Mr. Shaw, in language of almost needless
precision, calls "the quotient of the national income
divided by the number of the population." In short,
the socialist State, as expressing the sentiment in question, will, Mr. Shaw proceeds, say to every one of its
citizens, "We guarantee you a standard income from
the day of your birth to the day of your death, and
whatever else we allow you to do, we will not allow you
to be poor."

We must, however, remember, Mr. Shaw hastens on
to observe, that if a socialist State is to prosper, the
national income out of which all these incomes are to
come must, relatively to the population, be certainly
not less than the incomes of the richer countries of to-
day; and that collectivism, though it may be capable
of producing an ideally adequate maximum, depends
after all for its success on the efforts of individual
workers. Hence, income-producing work must be somehow exacted from everybody; and socialism, if the State

is to save itself from "national bankruptcy," "may not dare to tolerate a single idle person."

How, then, he asks, is the requisite work to be secured? Under the existing system, he says, the problem is self-solving; for, "except in the case of the few who are men of property," a man who will not work is necessarily condemning himself to starve. But if socialism guarantees to him that, whether he work or no, he shall live in equal luxury so long as there is breath in his body, the old stimulus will be gone, and socialism must supply a substitute. And this, says Mr. Shaw, is very easily found. The status of the socialist citizens as income-producing workers must be assimilated to that of soldiers in the Prussian army. They must all be subjected to a quasi-military discipline. The sluggish, the insubordinate and even the truants will, "up to the day of their death," suffer no diminution of income; but the slothful will have a touch of the cane, the insubordinate will have a touch of the dog-whip, and the truants will be treated like military deserters and shot.

Now here, says Mr. Shaw, anticipating an obvious criticism, we have a system of society which at first sight might seem to be one of slavery—a system which recalls the condition of the Children of Israel in Egypt, with the melons and the flesh-pots in front of them and the lash of the taskmaster behind. Of all the apparent difficulties which socialism has to encounter, this, he says, is the most important. It is, however, apparent only. It is based, he says, on two misconceptions, which vanish under the touch of analysis.

The first of these relates to industrial work generally. In order to ensure a diligent and universal performance of it, the socialist State would require certain punitive and coercive powers. Let this be at once granted. But all States—so Mr. Shaw argues—are bound to equip themselves with powers of a like kind, as precautions against theft and murder. This, however, does not mean that the mass of average men are only restrained from larceny, fraud or murder by dread of the policeman's bludgeon, of the cell, or of the hangman's rope.

They obey the law spontaneously, not because they are slaves but because they are free. The State as a punitive, the State as an enslaving power, is felt, in practice, by none but a perverse minority. In the socialist State the case would be just the same. As soon as industrial work was transformed into a legal duty, the majority would perform it freely and as a matter of course, just as they now obey the laws which prohibit murder.

So much for the first of the misconceptions in question. The second, according to Mr. Shaw, is grosser and more unpardonable. It relates, not so much to the amount as to the quality of the work required, and those who give voice to it express themselves in effect thus : " Industrial work is of various kinds and grades, and the vice or absurdity of the socialist system is this : it would pay for all qualities at exactly the same rate." To this objection, says Mr. Shaw, which can only be urged by the " base " or the blindly foolish, the obvious answer is as follows. This objection assumes that work is invariably performed for payment. No fallacy could be more absurd than this. Work in general is usually, and the higher kinds of work are always, performed without thought of a reward which affects to represent their value in terms of money or its equivalents. Indeed, says Mr. Shaw, not only " is the man base who asks to be paid for doing his best for his country, but the man who thinks that such services can be measured in coin is a fool." " The talents which are precious to humanity and build up great States have (so far as coin goes) mostly a minus value. Indeed, those who exercise them are fortunate if they are not persecuted as well as unpaid." Mr. Shaw illustrates his meaning by reference to men like Socrates, Paul, Spinoza, Leibnitz, Newton and others, and he very justly contends that the life-work of such men as these owes all its value to the fact that it was performed spontaneously, and not for the sake of any income or " coin " commensurate with it. Who can doubt, then, he asks, that, in a great socialist polity, which starts with assuring an equal and ample income to everybody, most of the industrial workers, and especially the ablest section of them, will eagerly do their utmost in contributing to the total stock, without any other motive than the desire of " being precious to humanity," and without adjusting their services to the likelihoods of any private gain? In socialism, then, as a scheme of equalised incomes, despite the draconian powers which the State would have in reserve for the purpose of extorting work from a certain debased minority, there is nothing which conflicts with the freedom of any reasonable and decent man.

Mr. Shaw's picture, however, is not yet complete. A brilliant finishing touch still remains to be added to it. Industry, says Mr. Shaw, when organised under one directorate, will run with such perfect smoothness and so slight a waste of effort that the hours of daily work requisite for the production of an adequate national income will probably sink to five, and at all events to not more than six. Thus the socialist State will be a paradise, not only of general affluence, and of the happy freedom which comes when work, in any case necessary, is performed with a willingness which anticipates and outruns compulsion; but it will, as Mr. Shaw depicts it, be a paradise of leisure also. In such a State Humanity will at last come into its own.

Now, the whole of this argument in a certain sense hangs together, and may be taken as representing, in a signally favourable way, the amount of cohesion that exists in socialist thought generally. Moreover, up to a certain point it is not only consistent with itself, but is also in sober relation to fairly definite facts. In the first place it is quite conceivable that, though industrial collectivism in itself would have no tendency to result in an equal distribution of incomes, a sentiment so strongly in favour of such a distribution might develop itself that the forces of law would be utilised with some success to secure it. It is also conceivable that, as happened in the days of Sesostris, arduous labour might be extorted from multitudes by mere compulsion, though all direct connection between work and income were eliminated. Nobody will quarrel with Mr. Shaw's argument thus far. Everybody will agree with him when he admits that, if industry in a socialist State would wholly, or even mainly, have mere compulsion as its basis, socialism would be rightly repudiated ·as a resuscitation of slavery.

But the whole of his argument thus far is simply of the nature of a preamble. His argument proper, as he himself insists, hangs on the thesis that, as a matter of fact, the entire work demanded by the socialist State of the citizens would be, by the vast majority of them, performed of their own free will, coercion for them having practically no existence; and as soon as he crosses the Rubicon, and comes to this crucial point, his reasoning acquires a totally different character. Comparative clearness gives place to a confusion which is doubly grotesque because he does not himself perceive it. It is a confusion arising not so much from an error in his logic as from a confused conception of the things to which his logic is applied. It is a confusion which reflects itself in his use of the ordinary word " work."

" Work " is a word which is, in different connections, used to denote effort of very different kinds; and what is true of one kind may be quite untrue of another. Now, Mr. Shaw's main argument deals with work of one special kind only, which he, with the utmost precision, defines in terms of the object at which it aims—that object being the production of the national income. All men must work, he says, to produce a national income which is adequate, for if they do not the socialist State will be bankrupt. But when he seeks to prove that a work of this particular kind would by most men be performed so freely, and indeed with so much ardour, that not even a threat of external compulsion would be necessary, and appeals to facts as showing that the best and most effective work is and always has been performed for its own sake only, it is evident from his own description of them that the kinds of work which he selects to prove his proposition are totally different from that with which, and with which alone, his main argument has any sort of connection. The kinds of work to which he is here referring are, to take a few of his instances, the kinds of work accomplished by men such as Socrates, Paul and Spinoza; and on these kinds of work he expatiates in the following way. It is evident, he says, that they cannot be due to coercion, for coercion is generally applied, not to stimulate, but to suppress them. It is equally evident that they cannot be performed for the sake of any equivalent in the way of " coin or income "; for they do not produce, and have no relation to, any of the things of which income ultimately consists. Indeed, if financially they have any result at all, this result is, he says, " mostly a minus quantity," and the men who perform them " are fortunate if they are not persecuted as well as unpaid."

If such be the case, then, one thing at least is clear, that however " precious to humanity " these kinds of work may be, they are not work of the kind which produces a national income. They are not the work which, according to Mr. Shaw's definition of it, the socialist State would be bound to exact from everybody unless all the citizens are to die of national bankruptcy; and not only is the man very far from being a fool who thinks that work of this kind can be measured in terms of " coin " or its equivalents, but the man must be a fool who imagines that it can be measured in any other way. Men produce potatoes in order that they may eat potatoes; and the only ground on which the socialist State would have to insist, " under pain of death if need be," that every man for so many hours should do as much of this work as he can, is that there would not otherwise be enough potatoes to eat. Since, then, every average citizen would know that, whether he himself produced much income, or little, or none at all, or even a minus quantity, the total product would be affected to a barely appreciable degree, and that, whatever he did or did not do, his own reward would be the same, is it likely that he would burn with desire to do more work or better than such as would just save him from the lash of the watchful taskmaster?

The absurdity of supposing that he would, sufficiently obvious on the face of it, is emphasised further by the two following facts. The first of these facts—we shall have hereafter to deal with it at greater length—is this: that when socialists argue about incomes, they think of incomes in the abstract, or as though, like water, they were so many homogeneous quantities, which differed only in magnitude as measured in terms of money.

Now, when incomes are so small that they only suffice
to purchase a little more or less of the simplest necessaries of existence, this way of thinking is accurate and
clear enough; for the necessaries of life are few, and in
most cases much the same. But these are precisely the
incomes which socialism aims at abolishing. These
incomes of equal primary poverty it aims at expanding
into incomes of equal affluence. In other words, to a
minimum of bare necessaries it aims at adding a multitude of superfluous and alternative luxuries. Let us
suppose, for example, that all the material commodities,
the enjoyment of which distinguishes affluence from
poverty, are books, and that the actual substance of
each man's affluence is his library. There may be a
thousand libraries representing the same expenditure,
and yet no actual book ranged on the shelves of one
might be a duplicate of any actual book discoverable on
the shelves of another. The shelves of one might be
packed with nothing but Protestant sermons, those of
another with tomes of Jesuit casuistry, those of a third
with novels, or amatory verse, or histories of stage
dancing. Thus no individual citizen, as a worker in the
socialist State, would be asked to be " precious to
humanity " by printing and producing books. Each
would be asked to display an impassioned diligence in
multiplying copies of this or that book in particular.
But any worker might say that, though literature, taken
in the abstract, was wealth in its most precious form,
the particular book in the production of which he was
thus invited to strain himself was not precious but
injurious, or at best utterly futile, and that he would
be much more precious to humanity by idling as much
as he dared, and so diminishing the supply, than he
would be by working his hardest, and so raising it to a
maximum. If a Catholic were asked to multiply books
by Baptists, if a puritan were asked to colour engraved
pictures of ballet-girls, the task imposed on each would
be certain to excite in him, not ardour, but antipathy;
or if the task, as it might be, were to multiply a sentimental novel, it might well excite in any serious man
contempt. Such conscientious objectors might, it is
quite conceivable, do as the State told them, thus bowing

themselves in the House of Rimmon; but, since the socialist State would, *ex hypothesi*, pay them an equally ample sum whether they obeyed orders or no, they certainly would not obey them for any conceivable reason other than a wish to save themselves from the whip of the State slave-driver.

But, quite apart from this fact, there is another which is embedded by socialists themselves in their own prospectus of promises, and which leads to the same conclusion. Foremost amongst the promises which they dangle before the impassioned average worker is the promise that income-producing work will, under socialism, be reduced to something like a vanishing quantity, most of his life being thus left to him as a playground for perfectly free activities whether of mind or body. But if income-producing work really is, as they say, equivalent to " being precious to Humanity," and if a sense of being precious to Humanity is the choicest of all human pleasures, why do the prophets of socialism advertise as a prospective blessing the reduction of these hours of supreme bliss to a minimum? In acting thus they are, on their own principles, like the keeper of a restaurant who, having informed the public that the price of his set dinner included a supply of the finest wine in the world, should add, as a further advantage, that he gave to each of his guests no more than a drop of it. What socialists really feel when they promise a reduction of income-producing work to a minimum is what most men would feel likewise, and what Henry George said bluntly is felt by all men—that if, in the case of the individual, work is rendered unnecessary for securing the means, and the amplest means, of pleasure, it must, for the sake of others, be extorted from each, like the slave's work, as a means of avoiding pain; and the kind of pain to be avoided, as Mr. Shaw himself indicates, could be nothing but that of the whip, either threatened or actually applied.

The uses of the whip, however, under a régime of equalised incomes are by no means yet exhausted. They would not be confined to the workshops of State collectivism. The whip would be needed for purposes which, quick though his mind is, Mr. Shaw has apparently never so much as contemplated. If the hours of slave-labour necessary for producing the statutory national income were, as Mr. Shaw suggests, reduced approximately to five, and if seven should be allowed for sleep, the leisure time of the citizens, during which they might do as they liked, would amount substantially to seven-tenths of their waking life. How, then, do socialists suppose that this life of freedom would be occupied? The question is not an idle one; for here, if anywhere, would be found that spontaneous self-expression of character for which assured and equal incomes can alone provide a basis. According to Mr. Shaw, the State would say to the citizens, " I may rob you of your democratic freedom for five hours a day for the necessary purpose of ensuring that the incomes which you are to enjoy may be produced; but, when once those hours are over, I order and I forbid nothing." But the matter would by no means end here, if a polity of the kind which Mr. Shaw imagines were realised. There are two things, at all events, which, if equalised incomes are really its special and essential feature, a socialist State would have to forbid absolutely. It would, in the first place, have to forbid saving. For if any of the citizens took—as they very easily might do—to saving four-fifths of their own ample allowances, equality of circumstance would not endure for a twelvemonth. The State, therefore, besides seeing that an ample and equal income was punctually got by everybody, would have year by year to see that everybody spent the whole of it. But this is not all. It would have to forbid likewise another thing more important than simple saving. It would have to forbid any citizen in his long hours of leisure to supplement the work performed by him in the State workshops by any further productive work on his own account. Unless this were forbidden, the more practical and energetic of the citizens, when their State work was over, might, instead of being precious to humanity by philosophising after the manner of Spinoza, start businesses for themselves, in which the full fruits of diligent labour or genius would go to individuals as the reward of their own efficiency, and not be frittered away as virtual presents to others who had not the skill or the

will to produce such things for themselves. In this
way an additional income would arise—an income not
common to all, but confined to a special class, all of
whose members would be richer, some incomparably
richer, than the rest.   A socialist State could never
tolerate this.   All supplementary enterprise would have
to be put down at any cost.   A situation would accordingly arise for which Mr. Shaw's logic makes no sort of
provision; but if incomes were to remain equal, it would
have to be met somehow.   The whip which, on his own
admission, would have to be kept somewhere for use in
the collectivist workshops would accordingly have to
perform, not one function only, but three.   Besides
lashing the obstinate or the idle into industry, it would
have to be lashing the conspicuously industrious into
idleness; and when not terrifying the citizens into producing incomes on the one hand, or abstention from
producing them on the other, it would have to be
terrifying these unfortunate persons into spending them.

Such, then, according to Mr. Shaw's account of it,
would the socialist polity be, as intellectual democrats
have now come to conceive it.   But whatever absurdities
this account may involve, they are, let it be said again,
not peculiar to himself.   His account is a vivid and
signally representative exposition of the idea which is
maturing in the minds of the more thoughtful socialists
of to-day—the idea, that is, of socialism as a scheme of
moral or social democracy superimposed on a scheme of
industry the oligarchic character of which, though it
cannot be denied or altered, is for practical purposes
metamorphosed by the final scheme of distribution to
which it will be made subservient.

The value of Mr. Shaw's account of a polity thus constituted lies firstly in the fact that his critical powers have
enabled him to signalise clearly the defects of the old
socialist ideal, and, secondly, in the fact that these same
critical powers have not only enabled but compelled
him, without perceiving it, to exhibit the defects of the
new, which, though different from those of the old,
belong to an order of thought no less remote from the
region of actual life.   The Marxian socialists, indeed,
were in one respect much more reasonable than their

successors. They assumed that the natural sentiment of each man as a worker was what it really is—namely, a sentiment which demanded the full value of his own work for himself; and the demand of the Marxian socialists that all incomes should be equal was merely an incidental result of the theory that no one man in the same number of hours produces more or less wealth than another. This crudely absurd theory the modern socialists have abandoned; but in order to preserve the doctrine that rewards should nevertheless be equal, they have been obliged to replace the original theory by another which is no less absurdly at variance with the character of the average man than the theory of Marx was at variance with the actualities of scientific industry. The Marxian conception of labour as the sole agent in production is not more illusory, as the basis of a socialist system, than the general sentiment in favour of equal distribution by which socialist thought now seeks to replace it. . Such, at least, is the conclusion to which logical analysis leads us. We will now turn from logical analysis to fact, and see, with the aid of certain concrete examples, how far a sentiment in favour of equal distribution has proved to be really operative when put to the test of experiment.

CHAPTER II

SOCIALIST EXPERIMENTS

IF a detached spectator—a tourist from some other planet—were to visit the earth to-day, and give his attention to the socialist or social democratic movement, what would probably strike him as its strangest feature is this, that those who take part in it are willing, on behalf of their principles, to do everything in the way of activity except to show that they are practicable by putting them into experimental practice. He would have heard orators at a thousand Trade Union meetings who proclaimed that all the difficulties of the modern world would be solved if only the labourers were masters of their own capital, and secured for their own class the entire product of their exertions. He might have heard them declaring that "the employers have never done anything for labour which we, the labourers, could not any day do for ourselves." But although—to take, for example, the case of the United Kingdom—the wage-earning classes at the beginning of the twentieth century owned a collective capital of a thousand million pounds, our tourist might have failed to discover that any serious attempts were being made by them to employ this capital themselves under their own corporate direction. If of this capital they would venture but one hundredth part, ten socialist businesses, each with a capital of a million, might, as modest experiments, be set going to-morrow; and if socialism is correct in principle, the success of these could not fail to be such that others would soon follow, till the employers of to-day were eliminated, not by violence but by competition, and all who now work for wages would presently be the employers of themselves. Why, then, our tourist might ask, does nothing of this kind happen? The socialists, he might say, were like the prisoner who, according to the story told by an American humourist, had been locked up for ten years in a cell, " when one day a thought struck him. He opened the window and got out."

But to this fear on their part of testing their principles by experiment there have been many memorable exceptions. Experiments have been made of the precise kind in question, which, curiously few as they are in comparison with what might reasonably have been expected, are quite sufficiently numerous, sufficiently different in some respects, and sufficiently like in others, to constitute a body of evidence astonishingly coherent and illuminating.

Many of them, in respect of their origin, have been British or European; the latest and largest was Australian; but the actual scene of most of them has been naturally in the New World, where land is acquired more easily than in the Old, and where life is less encumbered by old habits and traditions. Records of some eighty have been collected by Macdonald, Noyes and Nordhoff. the Australian experiment being the subject of a volume devoted to itself. They cover a period of a hundred and thirty years, and are separable into two groups— namely, those which were animated by a sentiment having its basis in religion, and those from which the religious motive has been practically, if not formally, excluded. Socialism or social democracy as a scheme founded on a sentiment which demands equality in distribution represents socialist thought, not only in its latest, but in its earliest forms also. As an object of possible endeavour, and also as a subject of ridicule, it was perfectly familiar to the citizens of ancient Athens; and the first and most successful attempt to realise it in the modern world was initiated nearly forty years before the word " socialism " was known.

This experiment, which was the formation of the sect or community of the Shakers, began in the year 1774, and thirty years later another experiment followed it— that is to say, the formation of the sect or community of the Rappites. The animating principle of both these was religion. The foundress of the Shakers was an

English woman, Ann Lee, of humble birth but of very remarkable character, who believed herself to be the recipient of a number of divine revelations, and who, acting under this belief, emigrated from England to America, where she hoped to establish a polity consonant with the mind of Christ. George Rapp, the founder of the Rappites, was a native of Southern Germany, the son of a small farmer. He, like Ann Lee, had from his youth upwards divine revelations of his own; and in the year 1805, accompanied by three hundred disciples, he, like her, set sail for America, with the object of founding a Kingdom of Christ on earth.

But though both these leaders were visionaries, both of them, like St. Theresa, united to religious enthusiasm a singular aptitude for affairs; and their respective schemes, as expressed by them in business terms, may be said to have resulted in almost the same prospectus. The principle of the Shakers was, as Ann Lee put it, " that all the members should have a united interest in all things "; that the Society should be primarily the owner of whatever was produced by individuals, and should then dispense to the individuals whatever each might need; each according to his abilities, whether these were great or small, performing in return such work as the Elders might see proper to assign to him. The principles of the Rappites were embodied in a series of Articles of Association, to which every member had to affix his signature. The first of these Articles constituted a deed of gift on the member's part " of all property whatever possessed by him or her to George Rapp and his heirs or assigns for ever, to be held and administered on behalf of the members generally; and the said George Rapp covenanted on behalf of himself and his successors that they would supply the members severally with all necessaries of life, whether in youth or age, whether in sickness or health, together with such care and consolation as their situations might reasonably demand."

During the next seventy years these two pioneer experiments were followed, in the United States, by nearly eighty others, whilst the great Australian venture, of which mention has just been made, came twenty-five

years later, its actual scene being in Paraguay. Some
of these were religious, most of them essentially secular.
Otherwise, the object proposed was in all cases the same.
It was precisely the object described, as we have seen,
by Mr. Shaw—namely, the production by the community
of an adequate total income, and the distribution of this
amongst the members, not in accordance with what each
produced (which would vary), but in accordance with
a sentiment relating to their equal needs, and now commonly expressed in the formula " Each for all." Between all these experiments there was another point of
likeness also, which exhibits the projectors as men who,
up to a certain point, gauged human nature accurately
in the light of sound common sense. They all of them
proposed to secure the triumph of socialism by means
similar to those which had secured the triumph of the
modern private capitalist. Modern capitalism has
developed itself and spread itself throughout the world,
because wherever it has been tried it has generally been
found to work—to be industrially more efficient than any
other system which had preceded it. Its general success
has consisted in a multiplication of successful units.
The practical socialists, with whom we are now dealing,
proposed to establish socialism through units of success
likewise, but through units of a different kind. Instead
of establishing single successful businesses, what they
aimed at establishing was equally successful communities; and the difference between a business and a community was understood by them to be this: In an
ordinary business the employer and the employed alike
work severally for the benefit of themselves and their
own families. In a socialist community all families
would be one. As matters stand, they argued, within
the limits of the family circle economic advantages are
not divided, but shared. Each home, in short, is a
miniature socialism in itself. In order, therefore, that
socialism might develop into a working system, the first
thing to be done was, according to them, so to extend
the socialism of the family circle that a considerable
number of men, women and children might be welded
together into a family of a larger kind, not by blood
relationship, but by a sentiment of human brotherhood,

and by a consequently " united interest " in the fruits of their collective industry. The idea of all the projectors was to begin with an extended family, comprising from two or three hundred up to fifteen hundred persons; and if one such group were successful, others would be bound to follow. At all events they realised that if an effective socialist sentiment could not extend itself throughout a community of a few hundreds of persons, it would be idle to look for its extension through the world, or even an entire nation.

Let us now consider how these experiments worked, beginning with the religious, which deserve special attention, and of which the two just mentioned are curiously contrasted, but equally instructive types. Of these two, when Nordhoff published his accounts of them, one—namely, the Shakers—had lasted for more than a century; the other—namely, the Rappites—had lasted for seventy years. Both had been constantly prosperous; the Rappites had achieved great riches; and yet each body had, according to its own lights, been faithful to the doctrine of a " united interest in all things." Both may be regarded as triumphs of that precise sentiment which, as Mr. Shaw describes it, " renders the very idea of unequal incomes intolerable." As applied, however, to the details of practical life, they understood this sentiment in very different ways.

The Rappites, though unswerving socialists in respect of their own fraternity, made no pretence of socialism in their dealings with the outside world. Possessing, as they did, considerable funds to start with, they used these in the following ways. In the first place, all rough work within the borders of their own settlement they committed to hired labourers, many of whom were Chinamen, and of whom it was caustically said that " they did as much work in a day as the brethren would do in six." In the second place, they became investors, on an ever-increasing scale, in outside enterprises such as mines, oil-wells and railroads, and were ultimately found to be the principal sleeping partners in a cutlery business, then the largest in the whole of the United States. Their success, in short, was the success of a species of exclusive club, their socialism being a pious eccentricity uniting the members, but uniting the members only, and related to socialism in the wider sense of the word, not as an example, but as a negation of it.

Very different in this respect have been the principles and practice of the Shakers. Continuously successful as they have been in producing an income adequate to their modest wants, they have depended on no labour but their own; and their tasks, assigned to them by the Elders, have been faithfully performed by each in obedience to a sentiment which, identifying each with all, and eliminating every thought of gain for self as sinful, makes the labour of each a sacrifice owed, through all, to God. If a polity like that of the Rappites is comparable to a religious club, a polity like that of the Shakers is comparable to a Franciscan monastery. That such a polity may prosper and be self-supporting, the experiment of the Shakers, like that of the Franciscans, shows; and if this were the whole of the matter, it would show in a very striking way that the principles of modern socialism, as expounded by Mr. Shaw, are practicable. As a matter of fact, however, it shows something else also. The Shakers being rigid celibates, it is obvious that a socialism like theirs, though self-supporting, cannot be self-renewing. Denying marriage to its members, it postulates a world outside in which marriage is prevalent. This fact might conceivably be no more than an accident; but it actually was a consequence and an illustration of a fact much deeper than itself. The Shakers enjoined celibacy, not as an isolated merit, but as one detail of a sacrifice co-extensive with the socialist life, another detail of which, and one of prior importance, was the sacrifice of all desire for private or unequal gain; and the fact that these members were not members by birth, but had to be chosen from postulants reared in the outside world, was a means of demonstrating, as the Shakers themselves attested, how rare those persons are from whom, in their inmost hearts, a true renunciation of the hope of unequal gain is possible. No member was accepted till after a year's novitiate, and before a year was over most of the postulants would depart. Thus a socialism like that of the Shakers is, in its very essence, no less exclusive than a socialism like that of the Rappites, although for a different reason. Just as in the latter case, the magic circle of socialism does not include the average manual labourer, so it does not include in the former the typical or average man. Neither of such schemes is comprehensive in any general sense, or contains in it any promise for the masses of the human race.

The only socialist experiments which can yield a direct moral of any general import are those which appeal to the motives of average men and women, and no more confine their promises to persons of exceptional character than they do to persons of exceptional business intellect. We will, therefore, now turn our attention to the secular experiments comprised in the list just mentioned, and see how their fortunes compare with the signal, if limited, success attainable by those of the religious or quasi-conventual type. Of these secular experiments, something like seventy in number, it would be not only impossible to deal with all, but useless. Most of them came to an end in their third year, or earlier. We will, therefore, confine ourselves to the few which outlived or reached their fifth. Of such experiments there are five—namely, that of the Owenites, or, to give it its full name, The New Harmony Community of Equality; three other communities, extended families, or (as they preferred to call themselves) Phalanxes— namely, the Brook Farm, the Wisconsin, and the North American; and, lastly, most ambitious of all, the experiment called New Australia.

The earliest of these, the New Harmony Community of Equality, was financed and founded in the year 1825 by a prosperous British mill-owner, the celebrated Robert Owen. He was fortunate in finding a site equipped already for his purpose. The Rappites, then in the twentieth year of their existence, had acquired amongst other properties an estate of 30,000 acres, and had built on it a model village which they had christened by the name of Harmony. This estate, having ceased to satisfy their ambitions, was offered for sale as it stood, and Owen became the purchaser, taking possession of it with nearly nine hundred followers. To them, at a meeting held in the old town-hall of the Rappites,

he formally recapitulated the principles of the venture
on which they were now embarking. In language almost
identical with that in which Ann Lee had expressed the
aims of the Shakers, their own aim, he said, was to
extinguish all inequalities " by doing away with divided
money transactions," and " thus uniting all separate
interests into one."   All would have to labour, for such
is the lot of man. Each would naturally labour according to his best abilities, but the products of all alike
would be congregated in a common store; and each, for
no other payment than the labour already performed
by him, would have an equal right to select from the
total stock whatever particular articles he or his might
need. Since, however, some time must elapse before
their own labours could fructify, Owen stocked the
communal store himself with all such things as in his
opinion were necessary, from clothes and flour down to
tea, pickles and pills. Such measures were those of a
mere dictator. They were wholly opposed to the principle which he set out to establish, and as soon as they
were in his opinion complete he refused to exert his personal powers further. He transferred the management
of affairs to the hands of a Preliminary Committee, and
took himself off for nearly a year to England, hoping
to find on his return that the mustard-seed of his socialism was already a thriving tree. What he did find was
something signally different. The Preliminary Committee had indeed given general satisfaction by lavishing
his money on bands and on nightly dances; but their
sole capacities otherwise had proved to be those of
talkers, not of industrial managers. The goods in the
store were dwindling. Industry, in a state of chaos,
gave little promise of replacing them. The Preliminary
Committee was dissolved in feverish haste, and a new
body formed instead of it, called an Executive Council.
This, however, in spite of its grander name, proved no
more competent than its predecessor, and the whole
undertaking would have come to an ignominious end if
the flock of members had not, by their universal request,
compelled their shepherd who had led them into the
wilderness to become once more dictator, and do what
he could to save them. As soon as he resumed his

authority, matters began to mend. The community bore some resemblance to an orderly private business, the head of which, though the profits might not be large, was known to allot the whole of them in equal shares to his workpeople; and the novel prospects which it thus offered to labour became soon so widely known, and proved to be so attractive, that new applications for admission to its ranks multiplied, which, as matters were then arranged, it was not possible to entertain. In order, therefore, to provide for the new influx, the original group was supplemented by three others. The single community thus reappeared as four, each of which, devoting itself to industries of a more or less specialised kind, was, as occasion required, to exchange its own products with those of the other three, in quantities to be measured by paper money, or labour-checks. Owen, who seems not to have perceived, or not to have been disturbed by the fact that the serpent of " divided money transactions " was thus re-entering Eden, was fully convinced that socialism would now become self-acting; and the rôle of dictator was again, and for the third time, renounced by him. The method of management by Executive Councils was resuscitated, and each of the four groups had a separate Council to itself. Hereupon there arose a confusion worse confounded. The question of production was entangled with the question of commerce. The four Councils could manage matters no better than one; and at last a day came when a great general meeting urged on Owen that dictatorship must be forthwith revived. Owen, who refused to accept the supreme office, agreed, by way of compromise, that the Councils should be abolished, each group being managed by a dictator of its own; and of four co-equal dictators he consented to act as one. Things being so settled, there were some signs of improvement, but they were not of long duration. The groups quarrelled with their dictators, the dictators quarrelled with one another, and industry, thus disorganised, was again coming to a standstill. One socialist principle alone retained its vitality. This was the sentiment in favour of equal distribution—a sentiment which expressed itself in getting from the communal stores a great many more commodities than the members of the community produced. This sentiment was one day found to have been so active that there were two commodities only of which the popular consumption did not thus exceed supply. One of the commodities was glue. Terrible to relate, the other commodity was soap. Owen could endure a great deal, but all endurance has limits. Anxious as he had been to divest himself of any dictatorial power in the business of communal management, he was still the legal owner of the whole communal property, and he was now driven to an expedient the success of which was complete. He began to allocate buildings and portions of land to individuals in whom he detected some spirit of enterprise. The effect was as startling as that of an electric shock. Facing the communal hall, there was soon a glitter of goods in the windows of a private grocery. Sign-boards began to show themselves on one building after another, announcing the establishment of various private manufactures. Such being the trend of events, Owen accepted the inevitable. After a struggle of twelve years, during which the constitution of his polity had been six times changed, those of his followers who deserved this he converted into private owners, allowing them to lapse into a cluster of variously prosperous families, each pursuing its own " divided interest," and indistinguishable from the families of the commonplace world around them.

The Brook Farm, the Wisconsin and the North American Phalanxes, and, lastly, New Australia, all ran a course which, in substance though not in detail, resembled that of the Owenites. All began with the same high hopes. All encountered and succumbed to the same fundamental difficulties ; and out of the ashes of each, in greater or less vigour, there re-arose the spirit of private enterprise.

The Brook Farm Phalanx, established in the year 1842, when the failure of the Owenites was a tragedy still recent, would, if for no other reason, be memorable on account of the character of its chief projectors. They were mostly persons of education and culture, the philosophic Emerson being a prominent figure amongst them. Their immediate aim was to found, as they themselves

put it, a sort of secluded college which, whatever might
be its own peculiarities, would show how, on socialist
principles, life might be transformed for all. The first
thing needful for such a pattern community of equally
lived lives was, they said, that it should be self-supporting. It must, therefore, have. its basis in agriculture,
and " the perfume of clover must linger over it, though
it aims beyond the highest star." But work in the
fields, if cordially shared by all, would, they said, soon
require but a fraction of the members' time. All desirable manufactures would almost at once be added to it,
and would " provide the elegancies as well as the comforts of life, together with all means of study, and all
means of beautiful amusement," without an expenditure
of more industrial toil than was just sufficient for imparting a healthy zest to leisure. The members had a capital
large enough for all their initial purposes till their labour
should begin to replace it; and in two years' time they
were able to announce publicly that " every step has
strengthened the faith in which we set out, and the time
has passed when even initiative movements ought to be
prosecuted in silence." Their lands, they said, had
yielded abundant harvests; weavers and other artificers
were installed in a great workshop; and one great wing
of their communal college was finished—a building with
a frontage of a hundred and forty feet. A little more
capital might, they said, be acceptable, and in all in-
vestments, theoretically, there is doubtless a risk of loss;
" but we," they went on, " have now reached a point
where such risk hardly exists. We have before us a
solemn and glorious work—to prepare for the time when
the nations, like one man, shall reorganise their town-
ships on the basis of perfect justice such as ours." Three
years later the college home was in ruins, the college
lands had been sold, and the lately sanguine members—
men, wives and children—were seeking to resume their
places in the world which they had left behind them.

The Wisconsin Phalanx, established but two years
later, was better equipped than the Brook Farm Phalanx
in one way. Most of its members were men more
habituated to manual work, and it lasted a year longer;
but its earlier history, otherwise, was very nearly the

same.   At the end of its second year it, too, published
an account, equally sanguine, of what had been accomplished so far.   " We have had," said the writers, " two
excellent harvests.   To a large steam saw-mill, which
we bought along with the property, we have added a
flour-mill, a smithy, a bootmaker's shop, a laundry and
a general store.   We have, moreover, completed a communal residence, with a façade twice as long as that of
the Brook Farm College."   It was further announced
that their capital in the form of agricultural improvements, buildings and implements of production was
increasing at an annual rate of £4 or £5 per member.
Three more years went by, and no check was admitted.
Indeed, by the end of the fifth year accounts had become
so glowing as to raise a curiosity in many minds that
was not very far from scepticism, and inquiries made
on the spot by an emissary of the *New York Tribune*
brought to light certain details by which popular doubts
were justified.   The official accounts were, he found, so
far accurate that the money capital with which they
began their enterprise had, by conversion into buildings,
goods and improvements, not only not been diminished,
but actually did, as was claimed for it, show an undoubted increase.   It appeared, however, that the
increase had been largely over-computed, and other
revelations were added of a much more important kind.
Despite the length of the great communal residence, the
individual lodgings, he said, were of such a kind that
" few labourers in the Eastern States would tolerate
them."   Still more was the writer astounded by the
wretched and filthy condition in which the rooms were
kept, and also by the manner in which this fact was
explained to him.   The occupants, whose lot had been
painted as one of growing prosperity, told him that " the
struggle for necessaries was such that it left them no
time to be tidy "; and they further confessed that many
of them were driven to supplement the little—namely,
the equal pittance—which the Phalanx was able to allow
them by wage-paid labour for employers on the ordinary
farms around them.   Such being the actualities of their
situation, which underlay the publicly issued accounts
of it, it will not be thought surprising that before another

year was over the Wisconsin Phalanx was dissolved. The communal property was broken up into lots, some of the members acquiring their own freeholds, and what was left of the Phalanx reappeared as a common village.

We now come to the North American Phalanx, which Noyes describes as "the great test experiment on which practical socialism in America was prepared to stake its all." The projectors fully admitted the complete failure of experiments like Brook Farm and Wisconsin, and claimed to have discovered the cause to which this failure was due. The projectors of these, they said, made the initial blunder of so pooling their capital that no account was taken of the amounts of the individual subscriptions. No one subscriber could claim or identify so much of the total as his own. To arrange matters thus, they continued, "is simply to substitute for the individual employer the corporate employer; and the corporate employer is still more irresistible, for the individual worker can have no rights as against him. We," they said, "on the contrary, have stricken the relation of employer and employed from the categories of existence altogether" by arranging that each member shall be the owner of whatever may be the amount subscribed by him; and in virtue of his particular holding he will be able to claim from the communal management as a right, "that work shall be found for him suitable to his own endowment." He will thus be employed, they said, not by the community, but by himself. As a member of the community he will receive in the way of wages an equal share of what the labour of the community produces; but the capital used by the community produces an income also, and this income from capital will, as a supplement to wages, be divided amongst the members, not in equal shares, but in strict proportion to the capital held by each. If the members desire, by saving, to increase their capitals they can do so. The better it will be for them, and the better for the community also. Though this recognition of saving may lead to some inequalities, these will not be serious, since life will be lived in common; and that spur will be provided by it to individual diligence, the want of which has been the secret of all previous failures.

Such, in outline, were the principles of the North American Phalanx, and it so far justified the high hopes entertained of it that of all the secular socialisms attempted in the United States, this community, which lasted for twelve years, was for something like nine years apparently the most successful. The standard wage allotted to current labour seems, indeed, never to have exceeded sixteen shillings a week, but the officials of this community claimed, at the close of its eighth year, that the average capital holding per family of five persons had risen from three hundred and fifty to as much as seven hundred pounds. A better test, however, of its prosperity, as compared with the squalors of Wisconsin, is to be found in the picturesque descriptions given by successive visitors of the manner in which the members lived.

The earliest of these relate to it at the close of its second year; and not till the beginning of the ninth do any of the later descriptions appreciably differ from the first. The communal dwelling, with its hall and its endless rows of bedrooms, was surprising, said all these witnesses, in respect not alone of its size, but of its planning and equipment also. The fittings were severely simple, the floors were without carpets, but cleanliness reigned everywhere. The meals, well served at long tables, were plentiful. The lighting at night was brilliant. The members, in summer at all events, would go to their outdoor work as though it were some healthy game. In the hay-fields they often sang. After supper the younger members danced, the girls in summer wreathing their hair with flowers.

Such, till the community was entering on the ninth year of its existence, were its principal features as viewed by the eyes of strangers. In that year, however, a fresh inquirer arrived who, though met by all outward signs of unabated prosperity, could not get rid of the impression that something was wrong somewhere. When, not content with appearances, he tried to discover on what precise principles the business of the community was managed, and how all this prosperity was maintained, the official to whom he addressed himself would give him no plain answers, but wandered

away into discussions as to why, when tested by experiment, socialism always failed. Another member, a
woman, descanted to him on the same subject. But,
whatever the cause of these ominous symptoms, the
same inquirer, returning a year afterwards, was led to
conclude that it could not have been more than temporary. Several things had happened, and the air was
alive with optimism. A new member had arrived,
bringing with him a large capital. The direct wages
of labour had been raised from fifteen to sixteen shillings
a week; the new member had insisted on building a
house for himself, on having his meals alone, and on
living in his own way. It appeared, moreover, that the
new member's exclusiveness was so far from unpopular
that it merely represented a sentiment which in secret
had long been general, and which had now expressed
itself in action. The original system of communal meals
had been abolished, and the great hall now was a
restaurant, where friends or solitary persons could eat
by themselves, and choose what dishes they pleased.
An interesting light on the sentiment which had thus
revealed itself is thrown by another inquirer about a
year afterwards. Many members, he found, were beginning to admit plainly that, though communal life
was not without its advantages, they could any day
make a very much better living by working directly for
themselves or under a good employer than they could
under a socialist system of so-called self-employment.
A little later these further facts were recorded. Although
the officials of the community had not very long ago
claimed for the members a capital which, through their
various savings, had come to represent an average of
£700 per family, the truth had leaked out at last. Few
of them had in reality managed to save anything, and
those who had saved something had been, for some time
past, investing their money, not in the stock of the
community, but in various outside ventures which
promised securer dividends. The wisdom of these
persons was presently justified by the event. It appeared that from the very beginning that part of the
members' incomes which had been paid to them in
addition to their earnings as interest on their own

capital, had not really been interest, but had come out of the capital itself; and that, though the new subscriber might have eased the situation somewhat, the cash of the Phalanx presently would have dwindled to the last dollar. That such was indeed the case became soon painfully evident. Provisions began to fail. The communal hall remained, with its apparatus of tables, but the tables at supper-time would very often be empty; and the socialist edifice was sensibly tottering to its fall when the final crash was precipitated by a purely extraneous accident. A large communal outhouse was one day destroyed by fire. The damage amounted to barely £2000, or less than what, according to the sanguine officials, had been the capital holding of any three average families; and Horace Greely offered to restore the building himself. But the general opinion of the members was that affairs were hopeless. The end was not long in coming. The North American Phalanx, having lived out its twelfth year, was, in the language of its projectors, " stricken out of the categories of existence," and its lands, like those of its predecessors, were once again submerged by the tides of individual ownership.[1]

Experiments such as these, if each of them stood alone, might be looked on as too narrow in their scope, too much at the mercy of chance causes or accident, to afford a basis for any general conclusions. But the causes which proved fatal to all before twelve years were over were, in all these experiments, the same.

To speak broadly, they may be reduced to two, one of them inhering in the nature of all collective industry, the other inhering in the nature of human beings, with the sole exception of small and essentially select minorities. The first of these causes was a want of ability in

---

[1] As an example of the relative efficiencies of the socialist and capitalist systems, it may be mentioned that one of the religious communities of America, not included in the accounts of Macdonald, Noyes or Nordhoff, came to an end about the year 1906. The members numbered about 200, the annual value of their property, as they themselves utilised it, having been about £40 per member. The short newspaper paragraph in which the incident was recorded wound up with the bald statement that the property had been acquired by a neighbouring millowner, who was erecting on it model dwellings for three thousand workpeople.

industrial direction. The second was a want of any general sentiment sufficiently strong and persistent to ensure that directions, if given, should be accepted with submission on the one hand, and carried out with a diligence punctual and sustained on the other, under a social system the essential object of which was to render the conditions of the worst worker equal to the conditions of the best. But before we discuss this question in any greater detail, there is another experiment which awaits our examination still—the experiment of " New Australia," projected by William Lane.

Lane, by birth an Englishman, had early in life been frenzied by the doctrines of Karl Marx, and had sought a career in Canada as an apostle of the universal strike. The effects of his oratory there, however, being not equal to his expectations, he betook himself to Australia, about the year 1890, in quest of human material more quickly inflammable. What he hoped for he found. Australia was at that time being agitated by a series of strikes so savage, so obstinate, and concerted with such deliberate care, that business was largely paralysed, banks were suspending payment, and the whole industrial structure seemed on the verge of ruin. Lane at last found himself in a thoroughly congenial atmosphere. To the native apostles of the strike-movement he added himself like a second Paul; but even here the trend of events, when he had watched it longer, disappointed him. The employers were, in appearance, being brought rapidly to their knees; but the strikers more rapidly still were reducing themselves to a state of destitution; and the movement threatened to collapse, having only effected this—that wages, which had been rising for the previous forty years, would have sunk back to the level of the year 1850. With a flash of genuine insight Lane adapted himself to the situation. The popular logic of democracy was, he realised, vitiated by one great defect. Labour was accustomed to tell itself that labour was all-powerful, for if the labourers ceased to labour, the employers would have nobody to employ; but a general cessation of labour was, so he saw, impossible, since, before the employers were ruined, the labourers would, if they still stood idle, be dead.   He accordingly began to address the Australian wage-earners thus: "As a method of getting rid of the employers I have," he said in effect, "hitherto preached the strike to you. I was wrong. I am here to show you a more excellent way. Instead of withdrawing our labour in the sense of ceasing to exercise it, the proper course for you and me to pursue is to withdraw our bodily persons, and our active labour along with us, and find some place of our own where we can labour for ourselves only. The employers, with no one to steal from, and nothing left to steal, will die like flies, as they should do; but as for us, who produce all wealth already, whatever we produce we shall keep, instead of getting in wages not more than a third of it."

Lane, who was gifted with remarkable powers of persuasion, was soon the head of a large throng of disciples —men who, drawn from the upper ranks of labour, had been earning, before the strikes, an average annual wage of some £170, and who, if they worked in concert under no other master than themselves would, according to his prospectus, all have uniform incomes of something above £500. In a time incredibly short he had, for the purpose of carrying his ideas into action, founded a Company, the subscriptions to which were beyond his extremest hopes. He was not, however, betrayed into any undue precipitancy. He began with paying certain men of experience to visit the likeliest countries, and discover what available territory would be fittest for the impending enterprise. Such a territory was at last discovered in Paraguay. It was eminently rich in pasture, in cultivable lands, and forests, these last comprising some of the finest timber in the world; it was half as large as an average English county; and, so long as the settlers did their best to develop it, the Paraguayan Government would concede it to them as virtually their own for nothing. This offer was accepted, and so ample were the Company's funds that Lane purchased a vessel which, packed to its utmost capacity, conveyed to the land of promise a first contingent of shareholders, and which would, it was so hoped, be making in the near future constant similar journeys.

The voyage was marked by but two embarrassing

incidents. Some of the immigrants were so affected by
the air of equality that they wished to have their say
as to how the ship should be navigated. It appears
that they were somewhat surprised when ordered to
hold their tongues. But greater friction was caused by
certain of the younger members, not of the same sex,
who developed a propensity to haunt the decks at night,
two by two in joint contemplation of the moon. Lane
may not have regarded romance as the tainted child of
capitalism, nor capitalism as unmasked romance, but,
he being a rigid puritan as well as a professed atheist,
the one shocked him just as much as the other. He
issued an edict that these proceedings must cease, and
battened the young ladies down at the first approach
of twilight. The would-be lovers, however, were more
restive than the would-be navigators, and disputed the
right of an equal to order his equals thus. Lane's
answer was, " This ship is owned by a Company. Companies are governed by the shareholders, and shareholders have votes in proportion to the shares held by
them. I have in my pocket a proxy for every share-
holder we have left behind us, and my votes alone will
outweigh those of the lot of you." To this anti-capitalist
logic the lovers had no answer, and all disagreements
were forgotten in the joys of a safe arrival. The purchase of cattle and implements, and the erection of
temporary dwellings, had all the excitements of a picnic.
These dwellings, constructed of rough woodwork and
mud, were, as the builders observed, less fitted for men
than animals; but everything must have a beginning,
and these were well enough as a makeshift. Meanwhile,
money was so plentiful that one of their early transactions (as happened in the case of the Owenites) was the
purchase of instruments for a band; and as soon as
matters were sufficiently far advanced, the incipient
township was visited by officials of the Paraguayan
Government : there were trumpetings, speeches, a great
unfurling of flags, and the settlement was formally
recognised under the title of " New Australia."

The way to universal wealth, to universal equality,
to true social democracy, to the brotherhood of emanci-
pated man, now seemed to be clear. As the settlers

looked round them at their great herds of cattle, at the
prairies green with pasture, at their forests waiting for
the axe, at the soils promising plenty at the first touch
of the spade, at all their accumulated implements of
cultivation and woodcraft, and even at their simple
shelters which soon would be solid mansions, their
emotions were similar to those of the members of the
Brook Farm Phalanx. They foresaw themselves setting
an example which, at no very distant time, " the workers
of the world " would follow, but first and foremost the
wage-slaves of old Australia, who would presently come
in their thousands, leaving that land of bondage, to
enjoy the freedom and plenty of the New Australian
paradise. In twelve years' time New Australia was a
thing of the past. Most of the members were starving.
Many of them were begging the officials of capitalist
governments to pay their passages back to the home
they had so rashly left. Lane himself disappeared as a
ragged fugitive, and the only members of his company
left in the socialist paradise were a few vigorous men
who acquired lands of their own, and, growing into
capitalists on their own account, became all of them
substantial, and some of them very opulent, farmers.

The precise events which led up to this catastrophe
were partly due to the character of Lane himself, partly
to that of his followers. In him, as in most demagogues,
were united two tempers, and two sets of convictions.
He was no doubt a believer in the natural equality of
men, and in the equal and astonishing affluence which
the masses would secure for themselves, the moment
they escaped from the depredations of a small, dominant
class. At the same time, as not only his conduct but
also his own statements show, the conviction lay deep
in his mind that these, his natural equals, could only
achieve equality by submitting their wills to that of
some one exceptional man—" some better Napoleon,"
it was thus that Lane described him, " with the brain
of a Jay Gould and the heart of Christ." In drawing
this picture, he was undoubtedly drawing what he took
to be a portrait of himself; and, so far as the conception
of his enterprise and its earlier stages are concerned, it
is obvious that, apart from him, there would have been

no such enterprise at all. Indeed, it may be said that on his part some measure of autocracy was inevitable up to the time when the settlers took final possession of their territory, and certain divisions of labour had at once to be made by somebody, for the purposes of running up dwellings, driving their cattle to pasture, and beginning some sort of cultivation. But though the spirit of the autocrat never deserted him to the last, a time came when he was compelled by his avowed principles, and also by a formal agreement of which he was himself the author, to place the control of industry on a purely democratic basis by handing it over to directors chosen by the workers themselves. This step came none too soon; for the spirit of pure democracy, which had twice asserted itself on the ship, had been subsequently exasperated by Lane on two still graver occasions. Lane was a strict teetotaler. He did not believe in God, but he believed that alcohol was the devil. Whilst the mass of his company were making their way to the settlement, he discovered that some of the mothers had brought with them jars of treacle, not for themselves, but for their children, to whom it was extremely soothing. Lane, who declared that treacle had the venom of alcohol lurking in it, gave instant orders that the jars should be snatched from them and thrown away. But the consternation which this act produced was mild in comparison with that produced by another. As soon as the settlement had assumed some semblance of order, Lane issued a formal and general edict forbidding the consumption by anybody of intoxicating liquor of any kind. But, although men's lips might obey him, he could not command their cravings, and at last it came to his knowledge that certain obstinate rebels had been drinking native whisky in taverns beyond the border. Faced by so gross an outrage on the part of his dear equals, Lane at once invoked the aid of the Paraguayan army, and those who had dared to disobey him were expelled from the socialist Eden by the bayonets of alien capital. It is not surprising to learn that a sentiment which had long been smouldering began now to express itself in the observation that Lane was " a changed man." But the spirit of pure democracy had its own triumphs before it. On one occasion, indeed, it had shown its mettle already, when Lane, by a happy accident, was too far off to interfere with it. Before the mass of the immigrants transferred themselves to their new kingdom, a party was dispatched in advance to make some preparation for their arrival. The journey took two days, the pioneers of democracy had to sleep on the way, and accordingly, when night drew on, the question arose as to where they should pitch their tents. No action could be taken till the general will had expressed itself. Hereupon there ensued a general chatter. One man was in favour of one spot, another was in favour of another, and whilst they were still disputing they were startled by drops of rain. These drove them at once to the only decision possible, which was to set up their tents on the nearest ground accessible into which they could drive a tent-peg. Of all the spots they might have chosen it happened to be the most exposed. The rain turned to a deluge, the wind was rising rapidly; their tents were blown down as fast as they set them up; the lamps in their stoves were blown out as fast as they put a match to them; they could not cheer themselves with so much as a cup of tea; and they at last exhibited to the sunrise, after a night under the naked sky, the first practical triumph of the principles of pure democracy.

This event may seem trivial enough in itself, but it is not trivial as a type of what was about to follow during the twelve years that were ahead of them. At a very early stage of the drama, when Lane still acted as autocrat, the different groups of workers, whatever might be the tasks assigned to them, began to complain that their own work was the hardest, the rest being unduly favoured; and when Lane's initial autocracy gave place, as agreed, to a system of industry controlled by " the people themselves," they were fully determined that these wrongs should cease. The workers under the new constitution were directed or superintended by officials of their own choosing; and so complete was the concession made to the principles of pure democracy that if any group of workers was dissatisfied with the man chosen to direct them, a bell might be rung, a popular meeting called, the obnoxious official deposed, and another chosen instead of him. The general result was that, in every group, whenever a director tried to secure from his men work which seemed to them either too hard or too orderly, instant revolt ensued. The tocsin of democracy was sounded, and the director superseded by another, certain sooner or later to suffer the same fate. The only work, indeed, to which they took with spontaneous vigour was that of ringing the bell— a species of exercise in which the boys delighted. But this was not all. Except when united for revolt, the workers respected one another no more than they respected their officials. One of their industries was the cultivation of melons; and so completely was the spirit of " each for all " absent, that they would trample down the fruit raised by the labour of their fellows if they could, by so doing, take a short cut home to their dinners. When they left their work they would constantly lose their tools, as things which, belonging to everybody, anybody might be left to find. They allowed their cattle to deteriorate for want of sufficient attention. Though they did a little dilatory wood-cutting for their own immediate purposes, one man only, whose example was not followed, endeavoured to show what wealth was lying idle in their enormous forests. Even in the matter of their dwellings, the settlers proved so helpless that many of them, when the enterprise ended, were occupying the huts which, when first hastily constructed, had been said by themselves to be fit only for animals.

Nevertheless, these stalwart men, in possession of a most fruitful soil, and a very considerable live-stock, would hardly have been human if, however disorderly their work, they had not for a time provided themselves with the bare necessaries of life. It is true that, under their new conditions, their way of living at its best was poverty as compared with what it had been in the days of what they called their slavery; but for many years they were far removed from want, and even when it approached they were not at first conscious of it. But, meanwhile, the industrial millennium was as far off as ever; and at last, as they waited in vain for it, their efforts, such as they were, began gradually to decline. A

certain number seceded, demanding from Lane repayment
of a portion of their own capital, and new arrivals from
Australia did but in part replace them; but their first
general awakening to the actual facts of the situation
was due to Lane himself, who one day informed them
of the interesting fact that, as matters then stood, the
average value of the total product of each of them was
less than the actual wages of an English agricultural
labourer, and that ruin was directly ahead of them if
they did not at once bestir themselves and do better
than this. So desperate, indeed, did the situation
prove to be that another remedy was needed of more
immediate kind. This was the raising of capital by the
sale of all their cattle, now miserable beasts, to some
capitalist speculator, who gave for them little more
than the bare value of their hides. The community
breathed again, and Lane informed his followers that
all would yet be well if they, who had once been earning
70s. a week, would only do work of the value of as much
as £7 a year. His appeal would, however, have been
fruitless if it had not, from some quarter or another,
called forth a proposal which was accepted as a new
revelation. "Our cattle," it was said, "may have
gone, but our forests still remain. Let us use our capital
as wages, and turn our forests into gold by employing cheap native labour." Whatever Lane may have
thought of this proposal himself, he gave it his sanction
as the sole immediate means of securing the triumph
of pure social democracy; and John Lane, his brother,
was forthwith dispatched to Melbourne with the new
programme in his pocket, to canvass for fresh members,
and also for fresh subscriptions. He succeeded in
obtaining neither. His failure, he explained on his
return, had been due to two causes. One was what he
described as "a slump in Australian socialism"; the
other was the fact that they, whose avowed object was
to escape from the tyranny of employers, were about
to re-establish on their own account the accursed thing
themselves. He had urged on the objectors that the
principles of pure social democracy, and the doctrine
that all men are equal simply because they are men,
were applicable to white men only, and did not apply

to their dealings with men who were black or yellow; but the long and the short of it was that his arguments and his mission had been in vain.

Convinced at last that his enterprise as it now stood was hopeless, William Lane turned round on his followers, and informed them, like a Hebrew prophet, that their ruin was on their own heads; that the life-blood of socialism was a living and sustained enthusiasm—an enthusiasm of each for all, and that this in them was wanting. "As for me," he said, "I can work with enthusiasts only; and amongst you," he proceeded, "though most have been found wanting, there are yet a chosen few who are men after my own heart." These he would take away with him, and he and they together, the majority being abandoned to their fate, would presently build up elsewhere a Kingdom of Heaven for themselves. Of the abandoned majority, most, as has been said already, were shipped back to Australia by the charity of the heartless rich, whilst some remained behind and blossomed into substantial farmers on parts of New Australia which were granted to them as their own property. But the story of Lane and his remnant still remains to be told. It forms the climax of a drama which combined the incidents of an Aristophanic farce with the fatalities of a Sophoclean tragedy.

It was alleged by many that Lane had retreated to a portion of the original settlement which he had long been coveting as the choicest for his own exclusive use. This was wholly untrue. He obtained from the Paraguayan government the concession of a new tract, comparatively small, called Cosmé, and there in the wilderness he and his chosen band began, with unquenched hopes, their work of construction over again. They erected a preliminary hamlet—a cluster of forlorn shanties, adding to these, as the heart of their distributive system, the inevitable common store, stocking it with such simple goods as their funds enabled them to purchase, and leaving each as a part of the " all " to draw from it whatever particular articles were for him or for her necessary. The faith of these persons in the principle of " each for all " was plainly a living force in them up to a certain point. Whilst waiting for the dazzling wealth which they still believed to be imminent, it enabled them to bear with patience conditions of the nudest poverty—food of the scantiest, dwellings that would barely shelter them, clothes that were little better than carefully mended tatters. But even in these elect Lane had occasion to observe that the spirit of private gain was by no means wholly wanting. For example, by the women constant efforts were made to secure from the one poor store better clothing or more of it than could possibly be supplied to all. He was, however, still so satisfied that the true socialist spirit would completely triumph in the end that he presently set out for England, prophesying a quick return with a new contingent of members—crushed victims of capitalism, who were burning to exchange slavery for freedom and impending opulence. Within limits he was as good as his word. He duly returned himself, and there came, visibly enough, some new converts along with him. These, indeed, might have been much more numerous had he only consented to add free love to his programme; but they could not, however numerous, have created on their arrival a greater sensation than they did. The old members were as wretched and as ragged as ever, but the new victims of capital had an air of such signal prosperity that those who were enjoying economic freedom already could at first sight hardly believe them real. The feminine victims, in particular, were such figures of frills and fashion that Lane was soon the spectator of even more enthusiasm than he wanted. Every woman amongst his old adherents was glaring at her new sisters, and was eager, we need not suppose to tear them limb from limb, but at all events to appropriate the best of their boots and blouses. From that moment there was new discord in Eden, and Lane, who had thus far survived discords so grave and many, was unable to compose this. Having admitted that socialism, or pure social democracy, had difficulties to contend with which he had not at first realised, but predicting that, nevertheless, its future triumph was inevitable, he took himself back to a land where capitalism still was rampant, and sought for a private livelihood in the offices of a Melbourne newspaper.

Of all the secularist experiments in socialism, as attempted in the United States, it has already been said briefly, after a survey of the most important of them, that their failure was due to two and the same two causes, both of them inherent in, and peculiar to, the socialist scheme as such.   The proximate cause, it was said, was the want of efficient industrial direction; but the primary cause was the absence of any industrial motive which could, when the motive of preferential gain was eliminated, compel any regular response to industrial orders of any kind.   These experiments show that, if we exclude the whip of the taskmaster, such work as is requisite for the success of a socialist polity can, under a system of equal rewards for all, be elicited only by a passion in each of the workers for some object which is external to all of them in the sense that the work of each affects his individual welfare, whether for better or worse, to a degree so small as to be barely appreciable by himself.   This is precisely the conclusion on which Mr. Shaw insists, and from which, having insisted on it, he attempts in vain to escape; and this is precisely the conclusion of which, amongst the ruin of his own projects, Lane had at last a vision which was clearer even than Mr. Shaw's.   Mr. Shaw calls the requisite passion " a sentiment."   Lane gave it a much more adequate name when he described it as a passion which must not fall short of an " enthusiasm."

Let us now, with the experiment of Lane before us, take the five together, and see how they all unite in teaching the same lesson.

CHAPTER III

WITH regard to these five entirely independent experiments, the most obvious fact to note is that the plot or story of all, as though they were Synoptic Gospels, is in Substance, if not in every detail, the same. In each case we have a group of human beings, nearly all of whom, with the exception of the Brook Farm venturers, were drawn from the upper ranks of wage-paid manual workers. In each case they were led to believe that the average man produces from three to four times as much as the modern employing class, in the way of wages, allots him. In each case they were led to believe that, when once the employer "had been stricken from the categories of existence," and the labourers had access in common to land and capital of their own, their lot would be one of equal and almost fabulous affluence. In each case they left the employer behind them. In each case they were provided with land carefully chosen, and a capital sufficient for starting those basic industries which, having—such was their hope—supplied them at once with comfort, would soon be followed by others productive of universal wealth. And yet, in each case, so far as their socialist lives were concerned, these dreamers of golden dreams ended in helpless beggary. That this could not have been the result, as some persons pretended, of a mere series of errors made in the choice of lands is shown by the fact that in each case, when the socialist community was dissolved, a certain number of the ex-members—those who had any grit in them— restored once more to the world of private motive and property, began on those selfsame lands to make an ordinary peasant's livelihood—some, indeed, to lay the foundations of considerable and enduring fortunes. The industrial paralysis of which, so long as they submitted to a socialist rule, they were the victims, and from which, when that rule was ended, they forthwith recovered, was the visible result of a paralysis of industrial motive, and this it is the avowed object of a socialist polity to produce. It consists of a temporary severing of those nerves or muscles by which the prospect of unequal gain is normally connected with the exercise of unequal effort, and a replacing of such prospective gain by the prospective gratification of a vague and diffused sentiment which, though not wholly fictitious, has no permanent tendency to stimulate those prosaic activities on which a continuous supply of even the necessaries of life depends.

Every chapter in the history of all these experiments shows this. Thus, for example, the Owenites, so far as their lives depended on their own produce, would have died of want except during those periods for which Owen himself consented to wield the powers of an autocrat, which were only his because the undertaking belonged to him, and he could, had he not been obeyed, have done at any moment what at last he did, and brought the entire scheme of equal distribution and " undivided interests " to an end. Whenever he transferred the control of affairs to Councils, obedience to which was a matter of mere socialist sentiment, there was no obedience at all. Industry lapsed into indolence. Consumption outran production, and want once more began.

Of the cultured idealists, who projected the Brook Farm experiment, one, looking back on it, said with regretful candour that its failure was inevitable from the first. Its success, he said, was contingent on the absolute supremacy of a sentiment which has, as a motive to work, no actual existence. In the mere fact of the family, he added, " we have an element so subversive of enthusiasm for general association that, for practical purposes, the two cannot co-exist."

In the case of the Wisconsin Phalanx, socialist sentiment was for a time more operative, but was finally extinguished by the wretchedness of its own results. Indeed, its more active members were in their heart of hearts so little enamoured of equality, as an end in itself, that they sought to increase their incomes by wage-work in the world outside. The North American Phalanx owed its greater longevity—and such, it appears, was the explanation of its own projectors—not to the driving force of a greater desire for equality, but rather to its careful concessions to the spirit of private gain. Moreover, quite apart from the question of the desire for equality as a motive, many of the members, long before its end was imminent, had begun to express their weariness of equality as an experienced thing; and one of their number, with reference both to that body and others, subsequently made public, as the results of close observation, his own diagnosis of equalitarian sentiment generally. What he said may be briefly summarised thus.

The sentiment in favour of equality, if taken in the socialist sense, owes much of its vogue, as the basis of a practical polity, to a certain class of propagandists, to whose temper, as though by instinct, that of the mass is always ready to adjust itself. These men are drawn, he said, from a class which is quite peculiar, " and is always to be found floating on the surface of any complex society—a body of discontented, jealous, indolent spirits, disgusted with our present social system, not because it enchains the masses, but because they cannot render it subservient to their own private ends. This class," he said, " as experience shows, stands ready to mount any new movement that promises ease, abundance and individual freedom; it has entered as an active element into all these socialist ventures; and then, as soon as it becomes evident that the enterprise cannot continue to support men, unless everybody works his hardest, and in strict subservience to orders embodying general principles, these persons raise at once the old cry of tyranny and oppression. Anarchy ensues, and the enterprise goes to pieces."

These words, which were used with reference to the American experiments generally, and to one experiment in particular, would have been still more poignantly applicable had they been used a generation later with reference to the experiment of Lane. What Lane learnt from experience—what the conduct of his followers taught him—was this, that the equalitarian sentiment on which he, taking it at its face value, relied as the driving force of an industry by which all, irrespective of their various individual efficiencies, should be made the possessors of equal and almost fabulous wealth, was, in so far as it existed, a sentiment very different from that which he himself imagined. This sentiment was found by him, when viewed through the prism of experience, to resolve itself into three, all equally incompatible with the achievement of their professed object, one being a secret impatience of the burden of any industry whatever; another being an open impatience of anything like industrial discipline; and the third being a jealous fear on the part of most lest some should, through superior energy, rise to any position which would overshadow their own. Sentiments such as these are not only insufficient to stimulate the production of any such wealth as it is the primary promise of socialism to distribute equally amongst all, but as Lane, like his predecessors, found out to his cost, they render the maintenance of even a tolerable poverty impossible.

And yet, if we take a wider view of the matter—if we take the sentiment which, identifying each with all, will tolerate nothing for self unless all alike share it—and if we consider this sentiment as applied, not to any planned experiments, but to those vicissitudes of life which are intended or planned by nobody, we shall find that it is far from being altogether a dream. We shall find that, on certain occasions, it exerts a force so great as to be clearly measurable by the dynamometer of precise results; and, thus seeing what it *can* do, we shall be better able to sober ourselves by a definite understanding of what it cannot.

That this sentiment may be practically operative in certain religious sects which are in their nature exceptional, and which aim in a material sense at nothing more than the competence which is necessary for a penitential peace, has been pointed out already. But it still remains for us to note that on certain exceptional occasions it is actually operative likewise amongst ordinary men and women, and turns them for a time into socialists

without either their will or knowledge. Of this fact we
have a trenchant example in the conduct of crews, either
rowing to save themselves in the boats of a sinking ship,
or struggling, in the hope of rescue, for food on a barren
island. The objects and ambitions of all are here reduced
to one—that is to say, a bare escape from death. Even
in situations such as these, a preferential care for self
sometimes comes to the surface in singularly brutal
forms; but when the persons concerned are sufficiently
few in number to constitute an undivided flock, all
hedged in by circumstances from which there is no
escape, and each member being a witness of the struggles
and sufferings of the rest, a sympathy of each with all
becomes constantly so acute that each will work for the
others as though their lives were his own, the strongest
in particular being stimulated to supreme exertions by
the spectacle of those who can do little or nothing for
themselves.

But desperate situations of this kind are not only in
fact exceptional. They are the precise conditions which
socialism aims at abolishing; and even though socialist
experiments, with the exception of one detail, have
resulted in conditions which were certainly no less desperate, these have, in case of such experiments themselves, entirely failed to produce that self-identification
of each with the equal welfare of all which in other
emergencies is, as a rule, conspicuous. The reason is
that, when socialism has been attempted in practice,
there has been no hedge of circumstance, as there is on
barren islands, which excludes the persons concerned
from any choice but the choice between selfless enthusiasm and death. The socialist experimenters have had
always a third alternative—namely, that of walking
away, and pursuing their own interest under circumstances of a different kind; and this was the very alternative which they all in the end adopted.

The actual extent and the limits of a selfless enthusiasm for others may be further illustrated by other
examples, which, though less extreme, are of wider range
than these. In no countries is a generally democratic
sentiment supposed to be more active than it is in
America and Australia; and this sentiment includes, we

may safely say, a sympathy with human suffering and a practical desire to alleviate it on the part of multitudes who are not sufferers themselves.   Thus, if Japan were visited by an appalling famine, appeals on behalf of its victims would at once be made to Australian and American sympathies, and to no class of appeal would popular response be larger than it certainly would be to this.   Nevertheless, when in normal times the Japanese have evinced a desire, by working for themselves in either of these two countries, to reach a higher standard of life than they found to be possible at home, American and Australian sentiment, the sentiment of Labour more particularly, has not only failed to welcome them, but has actually insisted on driving them back to conditions which, as measured by American and Australian standards, are poverty.

Such diffused exhibitions of the actual extent and limits of average human sympathy are merely phenomena which, from the Middle Ages onwards, have been recognised by Catholic moralists as part of the order of nature.   The sympathy which, in respect of the distribution of material things, is possible for the average man, and the Christian religion demands of him, is, according to them, divisible into three grades, these being determined by the circumstances of the person or persons by whom the " all," as objects of sympathy, happen to be represented.   Let the " all " be represented by a single person A, and the generalised " each " by a single person B.   If A be moderately prosperous, B, though much richer than he, will owe him nothing but a sentiment of general amity.   If A be in difficulties but not in extreme distress, it will be meritorious on B's part, though not obligatory, to use his wealth in giving him judicious aid. If A's situation would be desperate unless aid were forthcoming, it will then be obligatory on B to give him what aid he can.

To suppose that a sentiment proper to the last of these three cases could be or ought to be raised to the same pitch by the others is, unless we resort to a supposition more ridiculous still, to contemplate a change in human nature which would render peace or happiness impossible for any human being.   For if all men should ever grow sensitive to such an extreme degree that each man bewailed the lot of all other men as miserable whose incomes, though sufficient for life, fell short of his own, even the poorest classes in any rich country like England would be constantly tortured by the thought of countries like Russia and China, the total incomes of which, if divided equally amongst all, would still leave everybody poorer than the least skilled English labourer.

But the matter does not end here. If human sympathy grew so acute as this, it would not concern itself with matters of income only. Other ills would remain independent of wealth or poverty, from the pangs of toothache to those of despised or bereaved love ; and these, diffused amongst all by a sympathetic contagion, would make everybody unable to smile whilst a single human being was weeping. Every bride and bridegroom would have to wear black at the altar for those who at the same hour would inevitably be burying their dead, and the news of one old woman with a toothache in Pekin would cast the gloom of midnight over every home in Europe. This œcumenical misery would be curable on one supposition only, which is merely the logical sequel of the root-supposition of the socialists. This is the supposition that, if sympathy were really so super-sensitive that the wants and sorrows of others produced affliction in each man as though they were really his own, the happiness of others would conversely have a like effect on the miserable. In that case, not only would every bride feel her happiness blighted by the thought of contemporary widows, but every widow would be consoled for the loss of her husband if on her way to his funeral she encountered a wedding-party. Not only would Mrs. Smith be robbed of all satisfaction in the silk of her Sunday gown by the thought that Mrs. Jones, her neighbour, went to church in alpaca, but Mrs. Jones, as her eyes strayed from her hymn-book, would be filled with satisfaction by the spectacle of Mrs. Smith in silk. This last supposition is one in which not even socialists would indulge—Lane, as we have seen, discovered its fallacy for himself—but it is in reality not more absurd than their own.

The truth is that a certain thickness of skin, or a

certain sluggishness of the sympathetic imagination, is necessary for the mass of mankind in order to make life tolerable, just as a certain degree of obtuseness in the matter of hearing is necessary to protect them from sounds that would otherwise drive them mad; and that kind of super-sensitive sympathy which will not be satisfied till all men are not only removed from want, but are equal in wealth also, may indeed haunt men's minds as a sort of ideal protest against certain forms of inequality, but it does not provoke, or even tend to provoke, most men to any attempts at realising an ideal equality which they in their hearts view with repugnance, or at best with complete apathy.

To suppose, however, that a sympathy of each with the lot of all is a sentiment which, except on occasions of rare and extreme danger, has no power whatever over the social lives of men, would be graver error even than that of the socialists, who make its power ridiculous by supposing it to be greater than it is. Without some such sympathy, some quasi-socialist sentiment, demanding and securing equality of conditions in some respects, there could be no such thing as civilisation, or even as a coherent tribe. In every society there is an element of socialism and socialist sentiment. If men have neglected this fact hitherto, they have merely neglected it because they took it for granted. One of the earliest examples of a socialist institution is a street. One of the principal modern examples of a socialist institution is the Post Office. On the other hand, the ultimate process to which both institutions minister is the growth and vitality, not of socialist life but of private. A socialist street exists to give access to private houses. The socialist Post Office performs, in transmitting letters, a like service for all; but the letters themselves are private, indeed most of them are secret products, and minister, with few exceptions, to essentially private interests. That is to say, in each of these two typical cases there are two factors, two principles, two sentiments involved, and the error of all socialists is that, confining their attention to one of these, they imagine that it can operate alone. They reason like builders who proposed to complete a bridge by pulling down one half of its arch, and using the bricks to beautify and extend the other. If they would but realise that the socialist principle in itself, which they take to be something new, is no new principle at all, but is one which (as ministering to, and assuming the action of, another) must always exist in any complex society, and that the sentiment at the back of it, in so far as it corresponds with anything actual, is normally a form of instinctive common sense, they might well be justified by existing social conditions in their attempts to rouse this sentiment into a more alert and more self-conscious activity. For, as has been here observed with reference to political government, though the principles of oligarchy and democracy are both equally necessary, their powers need not be always in precisely the same proportions. As the circumstances of any nation change, it will sometimes happen that for their solution a greater exercise of oligarchic power is necessary, sometimes a greater exercise of democratic, though in no complex society will either be operative alone. Hence, then, if, without regard to their details, the principles and projects of socialism are taken as representing an attempt to secure for the democratic principle a greater influence in some respects than, at present, it actually exerts, there is one strong reason, at all events, for supposing that this attempt indicates the actual existence of social mal-adjustments of some kind, in the cure of which the democratic principle will be a signally active element. The reason which makes this supposition antecedently probable is a fact analogous to one which was cited by Cardinal Newman as a proof in itself of the divine vitality of the Church. This fact was the scandalous character of Popes such as Leo X, in spite of which the Catholic Church survived. The same argument is applicable to the principles and projects of socialism. Whenever these have been reduced to any definite form, they have shown themselves, in one way or another, so inconsistent either with the technical facts of industry or with the actual character of the great masses of mankind—they have, moreover, when tested by experiment, always ended in such farcical failures—that the unabated though vague response which they still continue to excite amongst masses of men everywhere cannot be otherwise than a proof that actual evils exist, against which these principles and projects are a protest and a call for help.

To discover in these principles and projects what the residuum of actual truth may be, and how it may be developed into some practicable scheme calculated to allay the discontent of which socialism is the misleading symptom, is one of the most important tasks to which the practical statesman or the thinker at the present time can address himself. In the following chapters the principle of "each for all," as meaning that, without regard to the facts of individual production, all shall receive equal shares of the produce—the principle summarised by Mr. Shaw as the essence of scientific socialism, and as put by Lane and his predecessors to the test of direct experiment—shall be reviewed with reference to the bald actualities of life; and, absurd as it is when taken in the form with which socialists themselves invest it, we shall find that a something emerges from it which is, not only what Americans would describe as a "plain, practical proposition," but which also accords more closely with the actual sentiments of those who at present, for want of better, take the doctrinaires of socialism as their guides.

BOOK V

THE PHILOSOPHY OF SANE REFORM

CHAPTER I

THE IDEAL MINIMUM WAGE

IN order to extract the truth underlying or latent in the socialist conception of a sentiment which, without regard to the facts of individual production, shall demand and secure equality in the distribution of the total product, it is necessary to realise that in such a conception as this, an absurdity is involved even greater and more radical than any of those to which attention has been called already.

One thing at once is evident, and even socialists admit this, that in very simple communities, consisting mainly of peasants cultivating their own plots, the conception of distribution by sentiment would have no practical meaning. In such a community the differences of wealth are slight. Each man and his household, either by direct consumption or exchange (the latter process being hardly less simple than the former), visibly get the whole of their own product between them; and so long as this is the case distributive justice, as understood by all, will be satisfied. The idea of determining distribution, not by the facts of production, but by moral or social sentiment, acquires an intelligible meaning only when the mass of the workers, ceasing to work in isolation, co-operate in large bands, each of which is directed by the mind of a non-labouring master; and when, owing to the development of mind as a productive agent, the members of the master class, together with their mental subordinates, actually come to produce, quite apart from

238

what they may steal, incomparably more per head of
their small number than what is or could possibly be
produced by any unit of the average mass.   The idea
of determining distribution by the dictates of a general
sentiment which, filling the hearts of all, will demand
and secure equality, necessarily presupposes inequalities
of some conspicuous kind in production, for otherwise
there would be little or nothing for such a general sentiment, as an equalising agent, to do.   How remote from
reality is the supposition that any such sentiment exists
in force sufficient to accomplish the task assigned to it,
we have seen already by reference to a series of test
experiments; but it remains to be pointed out that it is
not only inconsistent with facts, but that the very conception of it is also inconsistent with itself.

If sentiment in any community is to have sufficient
force to render the distribution of unequal products
equal, what is really required, and what socialists unconsciously postulate, is not one sentiment animating
all alike, but two sentiments sharply opposed in kind,
though conducing to the same end, one of which will
animate some of the citizens, whilst the other animates
the rest.   For unless the productive efficiency of all the
citizens is equal, they will from the nature of things be
divisible into two main classes—the men who produce
more than the average, and the men who produce less.
Hence, if by the action of sentiment the distribution of
the products is to be equalised, the sentiment which must
animate the former will be one which impels them to
transfer nearly the whole of their own products to other
people; and the sentiment which must animate the latter
will be one impelling them to the very different, and
perhaps less arduous, task of being " precious to humanity " by demanding this transference as their due.
Socialism, in short, as a scheme for equalising incomes
by the action of two opposite sentiments severally operative in two contrasted classes, would be a topsy-turvy
reproduction of the iniquity which, according to Marx,
is the essence of the existing system.   Under that system,
said Marx, the few live on the efforts of the many.
Under a régime of sentimental socialism, the many would
live mainly on the efforts of the few.   Or, if socialists

should think this statement too crude in its candour, they might express their promises more delicately by describing a socialist polity as one which would secure for the great mass of its citizens indefinitely more than these citizens themselves produce.

It may well be thought by sober and sensible people that the force of folly can go no farther than this. And yet in this very promise, and even in the detailed supposition that some sort of sentiment exists which will in some near future bring about its accomplishment, there lurk certain elements of actuality a sane recognition of which may well lead to far-reaching modifications of the temper and actions of men under the conditions which exist to-day.

In order to see how this is, let us begin by translating the general term " income " into the particular term " wages "; for when socialists talk about equalising, and so raising, incomes, the incomes which they have in view are, as we have just seen, the incomes of the great majority; and under the existing system, in all civilised countries, wages form the incomes and represent the material circumstances of at least four-fifths [1] of the population. Whenever the distribution of material things is discussed—whether in a Papal Encyclical or on the platform of a social congress—the question of wages is that towards which discussion gravitates. Further, though the question of wages may be looked at from many points of view, it is always, by all parties alike, discussed as a question which is primarily a question of quantity, and which, being so, is referable to some idea—or, we may say, to some sentiment—of justice. Socialists may say, if they like, that the wage-earner ought in justice to get, not only the full value of his own product, but more; but they, like everybody else, will maintain that the typical wage-earner should at all events get as much.

Here, then, at all events, is one point of agreement; and this brings us back to the question of how, when a

---

[1] This proportion does not hold good in Russia, Serbia, Bulgaria and certain other countries, in which the modern industrial system is but partially developed, and which are the poorest countries in the Western world.

multitude of wage-earners work, as is the case to-day, in co-operation with one another and also with a common master, we can measure what the individual wage-earner produces in his own person, as distinct from his fellows on the one hand, and from the common master on the other.   Now, although, when men work collectively and the product is collective likewise, we cannot do what we can when they work singly, and identify the product of each by the method of direct observation, it has been shown in an earlier chapter that it is measurable, in principle at all events, by a method no less valid.   What each man virtually produces is so much of the collective product as would cease to be produced if his own efforts were withdrawn, or so much as is added to it if his efforts, previously absent, are added to those of some given number of other men.   This method of measurement has been constantly used in war-time by employers when they have claimed for this or that member of their staffs exemption from military service, on the ground that his withdrawal would cripple the employer's business to this or to that precisely specified extent.   This method is similarly applicable to a measurement of the respective products of different co-operating classes, such as the wage-earners and the employers of a country, each class being taken as a whole.   It has thus been used here in a former chapter, when, in order to estimate roughly the actual product of the modern employers of England, a comparison was made between the product per head of the entire working population as it is at the present time, with what it was when scientific employment had barely outgrown its infancy.   In the case, however, of a class, such as the wage-earners as a whole, it is not generally practicable, as it is in the case of any employee taken singly, to remove them from the influence of the scientific employer altogether, and leave them to show their mettle by producing what they can for themselves.   Such being the case, then, the socialist experiments reviewed in the last chapter have here a peculiar interest quite apart from their consequences.   They show that those who devised them recognised the fundamental validity of this method of measurement themselves, and their experiments were deliberate applications of it in its most difficult and comprehensive form. "Our aim," said the founders of the North American Phalanx, " is, by eliminating the employers altogether, to provide an index of what the masses, as such, produce, and to show that, without aid or guidance from any class external to themselves, they may produce co-operatively all the means of life, and even increase the present rate of production." Lane said the same thing at greater length, and, so far as it went, in a really scientific way. The result of these experiments, as we have seen, was the very opposite of what the projectors anticipated. It showed that when the average worker deprives himself of the aid of a specially able directorate, the total product, instead of being maintained or in-creased, shrinks to a fraction of what it was when the ability of the directorate was operative, this fraction alone being his true personal product. We need not, however, dwell on the details of these experiments longer. What immediately concerns us here is not that they yielded this or that precise result, but that they consti-tute emphatic admissions on the part of socialists them-selves, that out of the collective product of a mass of inter-acting workers it is perfectly possible to identify certain portions or values as the personal product of particular men or classes, and that thus, when we speak of the fraction which, whatever its precise amount, the wage-earner himself produces, we are not speaking of any fanciful quantity, but of one which in actual life is potentially measurable with quite sufficient exactitude.

Let us take, for example, some industrial group con-sisting of 500 wage-earners together with one director, and suppose that the total product is expressible as x plus 40, x being what the wage-earners produce by their own personal faculties, and 40 being the product of the employer, or " the rent of his directive ability," in the sense that it is an increment which comes into being when he directs, and when he ceases to direct disappears. Thus the average product of each wage-earner individually will be x divided by 500, and the individual product of the director will be 40 divided by 1—that is to say, 40.

Now, it is obvious that the system of oligarchy which

the authority of the director represents would never have been developed at all unless some such increment had resulted from it, which went as a gain to somebody. Let us suppose, then, that the whole of it went to the employer himself. In so far as justice demands that each man shall enjoy the whole of whatever product is contingent on his own exertions, the employer in securing the whole of it will be acting with perfect justice. On the other hand, it is equally evident that if, by abusing his position, he appropriates anything more, his action will be grossly unjust; for the " more," which must come from somewhere, can be nothing else than an abstraction from the personal product of the wage-earner. The wage-earner would, in that case, by submitting his technical efforts to the control of another person, however superior to himself, get less for his own consumption than he once got, or might get, by working as his own master. No employer, not even the most grasping, if the matter were plainly put to him, would deny that by such an arrangement every sentiment of justice was outraged.

Here, then, we have at once a standard below which, without injustice, no wages can fall. This standard is the amount which a man now working as a wage-earner could produce for himself, either by working in complete independence, or else as a member of some group of equals, no one of whom exercised any greater authority than the rest. If by working for wages under an employer he gets less than this he is robbed. Let us suppose, however, that the typical wage-earner does not get less than this. Let us suppose that what he gets as a wage-earner is fully equal to anything which he could by his personal powers get for himself otherwise. How would the case stand then? If justice relates to industrial facts only, all pretence that the man was robbed would be gone. His own personal powers, whether exercised under a master or otherwise, would yield him the same return—namely, the whole of what they were capable of producing. Pure industrial justice would have nothing more to say.

This is, however, not the whole of the story. In the first place, even if, in a strictly material sense, the inde-

pendent worker, by being converted into a wage-earner,
lost nothing, he at all events, in a material sense, gains
nothing; and in the second place he would lose something which, though not material, is appreciable none
the less. What he would lose is his independence; and
this is a something which, other things being equal, he
would, to say the least of it, rather have than not. He
would, therefore, through the wage-system, if he found
himself compelled to submit to it, be obviously a net
loser to a very appreciable degree; and the extent of
his loss would be magnified in his own eyes when he saw
that, by this same system, other men were conspicuous
gainers. Without overestimating the moral sympathies
of mankind, we may safely say that the situation of the
wage-earners generally, as represented by a man thus
circumstanced, would be recognised as contrary to
justice, not by those only who suffered from the existing
system, but by those also who personally did nothing
but profit by it; and that, even amongst the latter, a
socialist sentiment would develop itself which demanded
that an injustice of so plain a kind should be rectified.

What, then, if stated definitely, would such a demand
mean? If it were not a demand that the existing system
should be abolished, it could only be a demand that
those persons or classes who, though neither gaining nor
losing otherwise, had through it lost an independence
which they might still conceivably enjoy, should not
merely receive as wages the entire value of their own
personal products—which is what they presumably would
do if they worked as their own masters—but that they
should, when working as wage-earners, receive something
more as well; this extra wage, which would necessarily
come out of the increment produced by the employers
themselves, being of such an amount that the wage-
earners' loss of their independence might be reasonably
taken as counterbalanced by it.

But however evident the justice of such a demand
might be, it is doubtful whether its power would suffice
for the accomplishment of its own object, if abstract or
ideal justice, and nothing more, were at stake. The
truth is that all men have naturally a sentimental inclination towards the Just; but in most men it tends to

remain an inclination and nothing more, if justice, as related to any concrete question, is difficult to define precisely, if the means of achieving it are disputable, or if it appears to threaten any loss to themselves, or is anyhow not closely connected with their own immediate interests. If, however, it be made apparent to them that their own self-interest and the sentiment for justice coincide, the latter, thus liberated from all impending influences, will acquire that practical force which, as Lane found out from experience, pure socialist sentiment when put to the test lacks.

This is signally true of ideal justice to wage-earners in its relation to those persons—namely, the employing classes and their allies—with whose self-interest it may at first sight seem most likely to conflict. To such persons, at all events, whatever it may be to others, the existing industrial system is essentially a source of gain. Their whole fortunes are bound up with it; and, if having paid the wage-earners the full and fair value of what the wage-earners themselves produce, they are invited on sentimental grounds to pay them something more as well, their natural impulses would be, whilst admitting that the invitation had force in it as a counsel of ideal perfection, to set it aside as a counsel too perfect to be practicable. But, if such persons will consider their situation further, they will see that their own interest in the existing industrial system is by no means limited to their gains from it at this or that given moment. They will realise that their interests are no less closely identified with a reasonable assurance that this system shall be secure; and no system can be secure if the majority of those whose activities are essential to its operation, and who in this case are the wage-earners, have something to gain, and nothing to lose, by over-throwing it.

Now, if wages were less, and were known by the wage-earners to be so, than what they could produce inde-pendently by their own unaided powers, the system which entailed this loss on them would, it is needless to say, be the object of their unmixed antagonism. The tasks which it imposed on them they would execute with a sluggish reluctance, in the hope that by thus crippling

it they would bring it altogether to an end; and even if
their wages were fully equal to the value of anything
they could produce independently, the sense of their lost
independence would suffice to engender a temper in
them, perhaps of a less violent but of a no less hostile
kind. What director of labour, if his men were in a
temper like this, could feel secure from one year to
another that his own directive ability would continue
to produce anything? His business, even if it did not
collapse, would be structurally insecure, and would be
always in danger of collapsing. If, then, with this
situation confronting him, he compensates his men for
their sense of lost independence by paying them an extra
wage—a wage which is over and above the industrial
value of their products, and thus removes from their
minds all positive grounds of enmity—he will not only
be doing what his sentiments have already, so we assume,
suggested to him as an act of justice, but he will, as a
business man, have taken a step essential to the security
of his own fortunes, and will enjoy the comfortable sense
of being a just man also.

But although this extra wage—this compensation for
lost independence—might eliminate from the temper of
his employees the element of inevitable enmity, and
indeed do all that abstract justice requires, it would still
be insufficient in the long run for his own practical purpose. It is true that the employees, this extra wage
being granted, would now have no ground for feeling
that the employer and the system represented by him
did them any positive injury, but they would have just
as little ground for feeling that it brought them any
positive good. They might cease for a time to have any
interest in its overthrow, but they would be just as far as
ever from being interested in its permanent maintenance.
Such being the case, in the employer's own private
interest a second supplement would be needed over and
above the value of what the wage-earners themselves
produced; and the reason why it would be needed is
this—that a system whose efficiency and undisturbed
continuance have no better basis than complete indifference on the part of the majority of those concerned in
it, hardly possesses more structural strength than one

whose popular basis is a sentiment of unmixed antagonism. A system which rests on the indifference of the
majority of those concerned in it is, indeed, in equilibrium, but the equilibrium is not stable; and the second
extra wage will be necessary in order to render the condition of the wage-earners, not only equal to the best
which they possibly could compass for themselves, but
so definitely and indubitably superior to it that any
crippling of the system through which such advantages
were secured to them would be recognised and dreaded
by all of them as fraught with calamity for themselves.

Thus of these two wage-sums, each of which is something in excess of the full value of the wage-earner's
personal product—of the product which, apart from the
employer, he would be able to produce by himself—we
may call the first the Wages of Industrial Equilibrium,
and we may call the second the Wages of Industrial
Stability. The latter would constitute for the wage-
earners, taken collectively, a stake in the existing system
analogous to a stake in the country—a stake which,
though smaller in the case of each wage-earner as an
individual, is no less real than that of the great employer,
and which is, if taken collectively, beyond all comparison greater.

Regarded, then, as a general concept, the ideal or
typical wage which mere self-interest would agree with
the sentiment of justice in prescribing would not consist
in practice of three separate portions, but would be
found, when analysed, to be a compound of three elements.[1] The primary element we may call the Wages
of Economic Equivalence, this being prescribed not only
by industrial justice, but also by the self-interest of the

---

[1] An Australian correspondent, writing to a London paper in July
1917 with regard to wages, mentions that Australian wage-courts deal
with the just wage as a composite quantity, in a manner not unlike
that indicated in the text. "The basic wage," he says, "is laid down
as a wage which will enable the average employee to renew his strength
and maintain his home from day to day. The secondary wage is re-
muneration for gifts and qualifications requisite for the performance of
skilled functions." No reference is made, however, to the principle
insisted on in the text, that some ultimate reference must be always
implied to what the wage-earner could produce for himself, if he worked
as his own master.

wage-earners and the employers alike. The second, which is compensation to the wage-earners for their lost sense of independence, is prescribed by the self-interest of both the two parties likewise, and coincides with the demands of sympathetic or human justice. The third, which, when added to the others, converts the whole into a wage sufficient to ensure stability, not only coincides with the suggestions of political or social justice, but is demanded by the ultimate self-interest of the employer who pays it, no less than by the immediate self-interest of the wage-earners to whom it is paid.

Thus from the most fatuous of the doctrines or implications of socialism there emerge, when these are submitted to dispassionate but sympathetic analysis, ideas and principles which in many ways closely resemble them even in their most unlikely particulars, and impart to them a vital meaning by reducing them to a reasonable form, just as a scientific inventor might reduce Swift's dream of a flying island to an aeroplane.

This will become yet more evident when our analysis of wages is concluded. Meanwhile, with regard to mere sentiment as a social or economic force, our analysis as thus far carried will suggest the following question. If the demands of justice in relation to wages coincide with those of self-interest to the extent which has just been indicated, does justice, as a moral or socialist sentiment, practically demand anything which diffused self-interest would not demand without it? And to this question it may be answered that, if it did nothing else, justice, by merely repeating what self-interest dictated, would repeat it in a tone or language which would carry to many minds much deeper conviction; but, if our analysis of wages as a quantitative question were complete, it could hardly be said that, if taken as an independent force, the sentiment of justice plays a larger part than this. Our analysis, however, is as yet so far from complete that it has, if taken as it stands, no definite relation to concrete facts whatever; and when we come to consider it as susceptible of application to these, the independent functions of justice—or we may say if we like of mere socialist sentiment—will be found to exceed anything which our argument has as yet suggested.

The ideal wage, whether as the just wage or the wage of industrial stability, we have thus far treated as a general concept only; but, when we come to translate it into terms of actual life, it will not be a general concept, but some particular thing, which, as we shall see, varies according to particular circumstances, and to which the relation of justice—of moral or socialist justice as distinct from mere self-interest—will be found to vary also.

CHAPTER II

MORALS, WAGES AND SECURITY

No general principle relating to a matter like wages will have any practical value unless we are able in any concrete cases to express its demands in terms of some definite pecuniary amount. Now, in any concrete case— that is to say, in the case of any actual country—the amount of any wage, whether this be just or unjust, which could possibly be made universal, must lie somewhere between two definite limits. The lower limit is a wage-quantity ·sufficient to keep the wage-earner in bare bodily health, and we may call this Wages of Necessity. The upper limit is, in the case of any given country, the average product per head of the occupied population as a whole. Now this latter fact, though no less obvious than the former, makes one thing clear which sentimentalists often forget. The average product per head of different populations differs. It was computed, for example, by statisticians towards the close of the nineteenth century that, if the national incomes of Spain, Austria, Portugal, Italy and Russia had been divided in equal shares amongst their adult populations generally, the income of no individual, whether a wage-earner or anybody else, could in Spain have exceeded eleven shillings a week, in Austria, Portugal and Italy nine shillings or ten, and that it could in Russia not have exceeded seven, whilst in France, England and America the corresponding average would have ranged from twenty-eight to forty. Hence, if a just wage bears any relation whatever to the maximum theoretically possible for all, it cannot be any absolute sum which is due in justice to all workers alike, on the ground that they all of them are workers and human beings. It must be a sum which, in each particular case, is due to them on

the ground that they are citizens of some particular
country, and it will in some countries be twice, three
times, four times, or even five times as great as in others.
But this is not all. The just wage, whatever its amount
may be, will not be different in different countries only.
It will in the same country be different for different men.
For the purpose of momentary illustration the assumption has just been made that, in any given country, all
the wage-earners are, as productive agents, equal. As
a matter of fact, however, their respective products
vary, and the barest industrial justice will, as we have
seen already, demand that their wages shall vary in like
proportions. By no one is this latter proposition endorsed with greater emphasis than it is by the spokesmen
of specially skilled labour, who are often more anxious
to maintain the graduation of wages than they are for
the moment to secure an immediate increase. Thus,
whatever, as expressed in terms of some general average,
the ideally just wage may in any given country be,
justice will mean for some men a larger wage than for
others, and for certain of these others it will necessarily
mean some minimum; and, as will appear when the
matter is considered further, it is with the ideal minimum
that moral or sentimental justice, as diverging from or
transcending self-interest, is mainly, if not exclusively,
concerned.

With regard to the minimum wage, no less than to any
other, mere self-interest will demand that it constitutes
a wage of stability—that besides representing the value
of the personal product of the wage-earner, it carries
with it certain extra advantages, sufficient to ensure his
attachment to the system under which he receives them.
But so far as the employer is actuated by self-interest
only, these extra advantages might, it is quite conceivable, be provided by him in kind, just as well as in
money. They might take the form of so many kegs
of whisky, added every Saturday night to so many
weekly shillings; and so long as the whisky kept the
wage-earner in a good temper, deprived him of any wish
to strike, and did not make him incapable of doing his
work on Monday, the mere self-interest of both parties
would be satisfied. But moral justice, though it might

not demand of the employer any greater expenditure, would arrive at the sum in question, not indeed by wholly, but by largely different methods. Admitting that the ideal minimum must be partly measured by reference to the stability of the industrial system, it would view it in relation to something else as well—a something quite incompatible with a wage which, however ample, was half made up of intoxicants. This something is the life of a human being as a moral end in itself; and it will, as thus considered, include all those faculties and impulses, together with the development and satisfaction of them, by which all men not subnormal are generically distinguished from even the highest of the subhuman animals. It includes man's spiritual or ideally moral impulses, whether these are associated with any definite religion or no. It includes his capacity for the great primary affections, for some acquisition of knowledge, for the exchange of thought, for something at all events in the way of artistic taste, and for ordinary social intercourse. In the eyes, then, of moral justice the minimum wage of stability will represent, not merely the net advantage of one industrial system over another. It will represent the material means by which even the least efficient of men—the men who have no talents but such as are virtually universal—may secure, if they use these reasonably, a life which, as an end in itself, is worthy of human beings.

That such is the case is shown clearly enough when the logic of the problem is expressed in terms of a religious creed, as it has, for example, been expressed by various Catholic thinkers in dealing with the relation of the Church to the industrial conditions of to-day. Thus the two Papal Encyclicals known as " Rerum novarum " and " Graves de Communi " lay it down that in the fixing of wages, though regard must always be had to the industrial possibilities of the time, and an element must always be present of pure business contract, " there must nevertheless always underlie the contract an element of natural justice, anterior to the will of the two parties and superior to it "; and it is further laid down that the object of such " anterior justice " is " to secure that the wages of the worker, even when these are no more than the minimum, shall be such that he will feel himself to be not a mere economic implement, but a man who (in living a life of human relationships) is free to devote himself to the attainment of the final and spiritual good for which we all came into the world."

Here we are again brought back into the regions of prosaic business. The bald question confronts us of how a minimum wage ideally sufficient for these moral and spiritual purposes, and also sufficient for the stability of the industrial system by which it must be itself provided, can be expressed in precise terms of pounds, shillings and pence. What, in other words, is the minimum on which a man can afford to be a man?

Now, for the simple reason which has been pointed out already, that the range of possible wages differs in different countries, the question admits of no general answer. It has, however, been rendered much more difficult than it need be by a class of perverse sentimentalists who, by exaggerating the claims of justice, tend to divest them of all practical meaning. To this error many thinkers are liable whose knowledge and judgment otherwise entitle them to sincere respect; for if we allow ourselves to be guided by mere moral imaginations of what might be, our conceptions of an adequate minimum will have no limits at all. Thus two English economists, writing shortly before or after the close of the nineteenth century, have gravely committed themselves to the assertion that if the whole of the then income of England, including taxes and savings, were equally divided amongst all for the purpose of annual spending, each man's income would provide him with but a meagre instalment of what, for its full development, the nature of man demands. Now what do such statements mean? The only sane meaning which can possibly be read into them is a vague suggestion that the productive powers of the people of England generally should, to an indefinite degree, be somehow or other increased; and if the persons by whom such statements are made were armed with some practical scheme by the adoption of which a result such as this might be accomplished, they might be justified in fomenting discontent with the utmost possibilities of the present as a means

of exciting the masses to some definite action through
which some ampler lot might be possible for them in an
immediate future.   But so long as the persons in question have no such schemes in their pockets, and are quite
unable to indicate anybody else who has one, these
inflated estimates of the minimum to which every man,
as a man, is entitled, can do nothing but manufacture
a general mood or temper which will of necessity, for
nine men out of ten, make any kind of content with
human life impossible.[1]

Such a mood, though many examples of it might be
cited, and though it is sufficiently common to be mischievous, is no doubt, in its more extreme forms, exceptional; but it is not for that reason any the less instructive.[2] It is neither more nor less than the moral and
logical consequence of that sentimentality, mainly of
middle-class origin, which suggests impossible estimates
of what justice demands for all men—estimates which
tend to render, in the judgment of those affected by
them, a maximum wage hardly less inadequate than
a minimum.

The homely truth—and this men naturally realise when

---

[1] Of this mood or temper a very interesting example was provided in
the year 1917, by the language of certain men who figured as the
leaders of strikes amongst the munition workers of Sheffield. Of these
men, who were mostly young engineers, there was one who expressed
the sentiments of himself and his fellows thus : " We are asked," he
said, " to fight for our homes. Our answer is, that we have no homes
to fight for. The best homes of the English workers to-day are in our
opinion no better than dog-kennels," whilst another developed the
sentiments of his colleague thus : " We don't," he said, " want to fight,
and we don't want to work either. The only men I can see as has got
any money don't work at all." These young men were all of them
earning wages far in excess of anything which an equal division of
the entire income of the country could have possibly rendered general
only forty years before ; and yet, despite this fact, they were more
discontented than their fathers, and were discontented in a far more
irrational way.

[2] This very mood, since the words in the text were written, has
spread like a conflagration in Russia, and has been the despair (for the
time at all events) of the more rational of the revolutionary leaders.
The Russian correspondent of a London paper reported an impassioned
appeal of M. Kerensky to the masses, urging them not " to waste their
time in thinking of the best things they could imagine, but to strain
every nerve in securing the best things which it was possible to get."

no germs of artificial suggestion disorder their common sense—is that, if they are ever to be contented with their material circumstances at all, they must adjust their estimates of satisfactory circumstances to facts. Hence, unless the average workers, who naturally earn less than those whose skill is exceptional, are doomed by the nature of things to a life of subhuman misery, there must, in any given country and at any given time, be a certain minimum wage which will lie somewhere between certain definite limits, and which average men, or the workers of least efficiency, will recognise and accept as just, because it is the largest practically possible.

If we suppose, then, that in any given country such a minimum wage has been fixed which at once represents for the recipients a better lot than would be theirs were they left to their own devices, and is also sufficient for the needs of a reasonably human life, the fact of its being so recognised will not mean merely a recognition of it as the largest minimum possible. It will mean that the lot represented by it is, and for the time must be, the normal human lot, with which every man ought to be content, unless by exceptional talent of one sort or another he is able, as an exception, to provide himself with some addition to it. The only question, in short, which the lot of those receiving such a wage will suggest will be, not why these men get so little, but why anybody else gets more.

The minimum lot, however, though the minimum wage is the foundation of it, is, as we shall see presently, not necessarily determinable by the minimum wage alone. Justice and self-interest alike will prescribe certain additions to it which, though closely connected with wages, belong to different categories. Of these we shall speak presently. But, so far as mere wages are concerned, moral or sentimental, as distinct from merely legal, justice, when the minimum has once been fixed, need have nothing more to say. For when we turn from the workers who earn the minimum to those of greater efficiency who, in varying degrees, earn more, there is no necessity here for any renewed insistence on the fact that a certain minimum is due to all workers alike on

the ground that they all are human. The wages here
in question will in any case be more than this, and the
larger sum will include the less. A larger sum will be
claimed by this worker and that, not on the ground that
he is a man, but on the ground that he is a man whose
special productive faculties are, as measured by their
results, definitely greater than the faculties possessed by
others. What this excess amounts to must be settled
by technical evidence relating exclusively to this or to
that case; and all that justice can do which it has not
done already will be to pronounce as to some particular
man that, whatever the excess may come to, the full
value of this shall be included in the wages due to him.
It will thus be seen that, when wages exceed the
minimum, justice divests itself of an element which was,
in fixing the minimum, one of the first importance.
When justice enjoins that the minimum shall not be less
than so much, there is always in any such judgment an
element of hypothetical compassion—compassion for
those whose condition, if they got less, would be pitiable.
But when a minimum which satisfies justice has been
once definitely secured, the element of compassion in
respect of any higher wage disappears. If justice decrees
that the wages of some exceptional man shall be, not the
minimum x, but x plus 5, or 10, or 20, as the case may
be, it does so, not because his condition if he got less
would be pitiable (for x is sufficient to remove him
beyond the reach of pity), but because x plus some extra
quantity happens to be the value of this particular man's
work. Compassion in his case would be, not justice, but
favouritism; and even when in fixing the minimum
justice calls compassion to its aid, it aims at expunging
everything which could possibly form an excuse for the
action of such a sentiment afterwards. To say this is
merely to say what a clear recognition of facts would
turn into a political axiom—namely, that any numerous
class, the co-operation of which is essential to any
industrial system, is a constant cause of industrial
instability and danger if any elements provocative of
reasonable compassion survive in it.

Let us suppose, then, that so far as mere wages are
concerned—the minimum so far being the key to the

whole situation—the demands both of moral justice and industrial stability are satisfied. But even if so much be granted, a satisfactory scale of payments for current labour will not do more than partly cover the case. Account must be taken of three other conditions, the relation of one of which to the minimum wage is so intimate that it ought to be here dealt with as though the two were inseparable, the second and the third being reserved for discussion in a separate chapter.

The nature of this first condition may be briefly explained thus. In order that wages under a system of industrial oligarchy may satisfy the demands of justice and of general stability likewise, they must, let it be said again, include not only the equivalent of anything that the wage-earners could produce by themselves, but certain additions also, so that such wages, as the results of the oligarchic system, will represent for the wage-earners a balance of net advantage. Moreover, of such wages one essential element must be compensation for the independence which the wage-earners under a system of oligarchy lose. If, however, with regard to their broad features, we contrast this oligarchic system with what history exhibits as its democratic alternative, we shall see that what the workers lose by exchanging the latter for the former is not independence only. Let us take, for example, a peasant cultivating his own plot, and compare him with a mechanic working for wages in a factory. The product of the peasant may be worth fifteen shillings a week, the wages of the mechanic may be thirty shillings; and the peasant, in becoming a mechanic, might feel that a doubled income more than made up to him for the privilege, which he had to surrender, of prescribing the details of his own task-work to himself. He will, however, it is constantly urged, have lost by the change, not his technical independence only, but something else as well, for which no mere wages can compensate him, and this something is security. So long as he owned the materials which render production possible—these for the peasant being land—he could always produce something, although it might not be much; whereas if he works for wages, no matter how ample, he may any day be dismissed, and

for some indefinite time may be able to earn nothing.
This contrast is very often exaggerated (for the peasant
is not secure from the danger of bad seasons), but there
is in it nevertheless an important element of truth. The
wage-earners, in losing their ownership of the means and
materials of production, have increased their incomes as
a whole, but the security of the individual income has
been very considerably diminished. The mere fluctuations of business, apart from sickness or accident, may
any day, in the case of any individual, cut off his income
for the time being at its source—an event which is for
the working-owner impossible. The proportion, indeed,
of workers affected by such calamities may, at any given
time, not be actually more than five out of every hundred; but the chance of their occurrence will, in countless wage-earning households, do much to counteract
the contentment resulting from present plenty. It will,
indeed, do more. It will tend to promote amongst considerable masses of a population the peculiar sense or
sentiment which socialists describe as "proletarian."
By this they mean the consciousness of a certain economic insecurity which is not necessarily connected with
inadequate wages, but which results from, and is for the
wage-earner a constant reminder of, the fact that the
materials and implements of his work are not personally
his own, and that his access to them being thus determined by persons other than himself, these persons have
somehow dispossessed him of something which he once
enjoyed. This idea of dispossession, as the socialists
themselves suggest it, is in many respects altogether fallacious. If in any typical country—let us say, for
example, England—we take the wage-earners as they are
to-day on the one hand, and the implements and materials of production as they are to-day on the other, it
is absolutely absurd to say that there ever was a time
when the wage-earners, or the ordinary workers, were
personally in possession of either. The materials of production are represented mainly by Land. The wage-
earners of England and their families number to-day
nearly thirty-five million persons. In the days when
agriculture was the principal occupation of the country,

and when a statutory interest in the soil was most nearly universal, the total population did not exceed four millions.   In what sense can some thirty additional millions regard themselves as dispossessed of a limited geographical area which had never been possessed by a similar body at any time?   What is true of the materials of production is true of the implements also.   The typical implements of to-day, which are vast scientific mechanisms, not only never have been, but by no possibility could have been, possessed by each unit of the mass of labourers using them.   It is true that a thousand weavers might, as equal shareholders, possess the plant of a great mill between them; but this fractional form of possession—this possession by each of a thousandth part of the whole—would not be the kind of possession enjoyed by their great-grandfathers, each of whom, through possession of his own hand-loom, could use his implement of production when and how he pleased. The wage-earners have not been dispossessed of the main implements of production which are in use at the present day, and on the use of which the increase in their own wages depends.   They have not been dispossessed of land on which, in their present numbers, the mass of them could ever have maintained themselves. Nevertheless, development of the very conditions which make large wages possible has been accompanied, so far as the individual wage-earner is concerned, by a certain insecurity which was in the days of small earnings and diffused ownership absent; which socialists, though they grossly exaggerate it, are right in regarding as a very serious evil, and which thoughtful persons of strong conservative sympathies have come to recognise as a serious evil also.

For this evil, in the opinion of all competent thinkers, the remedy must be sought in one or the other of the two following forms—either in some form of insurance against periods of involuntary unemployment, or else in some statutory recognition of what is called the Right to Work.   These two schemes, though they both have the same object, involve or imply different methods of reaching it.   A system of insurance would protect the willing or potential worker against loss of income through loss of immediate opportunity of work by guaranteeing him a livelihood till suitable work was found. A recognition of the Right to Work would involve an obligation on the part of the State or some public body to provide him with work at once of one sort or another, and presumably to pay him a wage proportionate to his highest potential efficiency, whether the work actually found for him were worth such a wage or no. Both these schemes are beset with obvious difficulties.. Any scheme of insurance, if it really had the effect of rendering any man who happened to be out of employment as well off as he would be when doing his normal work, would naturally tend to render unemployment popular, and thus to foment the evils the pains of which it was meant to neutralise. Insurance, however, can, as experience shows, be largely carried out by the persons concerned themselves; and, all of them being interested parties, precautions can be taken by their own general vigilance against any great abuses of the funds which they have themselves subscribed. On the other hand, the Right to Work, as recognised and guaranteed by the State, though much more logical and soundly moral in theory, is, by reason of its greater completeness, beset as a practical scheme by difficulties much more formidable. It is logically and morally sounder because, instead of pensioning idleness, which might very often be voluntary, it aims at providing for all the conditions of continuous industry; but, for reasons already mentioned in the course of an earlier chapter dealing with political government, its logical development would, in most countries at all events, be hampered by limits which no government could remove, or would else depend on conditions which no government could ensure. In countries like Australia or New Zealand, which are but sparsely occupied, the State might conceivably for many generations to come secure the right to work for all possible applicants by grants of virgin land; but in old countries such as England, every acre of whose usable land is occupied and used already, no such course is possible.

If in such countries the State is to provide remunerative work for every one of its citizens who are
unable to find such work for themselves, it can, as Mill
points out, fulfil this obligation on one condition only—
on condition that in some way or other it is empowered
to limit their number. It might, as Mill suggests, conceivably limit their number by legal restraints on
marriage; it might do so by forced emigration. In any
case a limitation would have to be effected somehow.
But quite apart from any difficulties connected with
increasing numbers, the power of the State to guarantee
remunerative work for everybody is limited ultimately
in a way more obvious still. It is contingent, not on
the mere numbers of whatever may be the population
in question, but on the wealth of the population relatively to its numbers also. For work provided by the
State would be work provided only because none other
was forthcoming. It would be a kind of work for which
there was no natural demand; and the payments made
by the State for it would, in an economic sense, be merely
a drain on the wealth of those who were employed normally. If the community as a whole was prosperous,
especially if its wealth were increasing, the cost of State-
paid work might be more than counterbalanced by its
advantages. But if the wealth of any community were
as a whole declining, no system of State-paid work, no
system of insurance against loss by unemployment either,
could avert the doom which would threaten, not the
wage-earners only, but the heads of those enterprises
also out of the gains of which the wages were paid.
States have risen and fallen, such as Carthage, Venice,
Florence, and will rise and fall again. They have risen
through the enterprise of their rulers and the answering
activity of the ruled, whether in war, in industry, or in
trade. They have fallen through the fortunes of war,
through the rise of rival industries, or some gradual
changes in the trade routes of the world. What could
State-paid work, what could any system of insurance
against unemployment do to avert the doom which
would, in cases like these, threaten the wage-earners and
the payers of wages alike? What could they have done

to maintain the vanished argosies of Venice, or to recreate prosperity amongst the ruins of Carthage?

If, however, the general conditions of industrial prosperity be given—namely, an harmonious interaction of oligarchy and democracy on the one hand, and a wage-system having as its basis a just minimum on the other—either of these devices, namely, insurance against unemployment or a statutory right to work, or both taken together, might accomplish, or go far towards accomplishing, the result which is here in question. That result is the provision for every honest and willing worker, not only of a wage which is just in respect of quantity, but also a permanent opportunity of earning it, or else some sort of guarantee that if the opportunity on this or on that occasion is not at once forthcoming, the worker, meanwhile, shall not suffer in consequence. The achievement of such a result, or even the partial achievement of it, would be tantamount, in its effects on the wage-earners, to a re-diffusion of small industrial ownerships. For, in the case of the working owner—the hand-loom weaver, for instance—his earnings being a given quantity, the ownership of the implements used by him is materially advantageous or even perceptible to himself for this reason only, that his right to work or his opportunity of working is established by it. If, then, by working as a wage-earner under the direction of a scientific employer, and by using the implements with which the employer provides him, he not only earns far more than he ever did or could do by working as his own master, but also recovers under another form the permanent opportunity of working which the personal ownership of his loom or of any other implement gave him, the balance of advantages derived by him from his technical status of wage-earner, as compared with those derivable from working as his own master will, in respect of his mere material circumstances, be as great as either moral justice or his own self-interest could demand.

But even if we assume that all these conditions are fulfilled, there are, as has been said, two others, which both justice and self-interest will demand for the wage-earner likewise, if the conditions of industrial stability, so far as he is concerned, are to be complete. One of these is distinct from mere material claims altogether. It relates to the moral esteem due to him, quite apart from his wages, as a member of the wage-earning class. The other, closely connected with moral esteem likewise, relates to the individual wage-earner, not as a type of his class, but as a unit of it who is, if he can, entitled to rise out of it.

CHAPTER III

THE RIGHT TO RESPECT

WE have seen that in estimating the amount of a just minimum wage regard must be had, not to the wage-earner's physical needs only, but also to the decency of his home as distinct from its mere comfort, and to a reasonable gratification of his moral and other human emotions. Such being the case, then, in considering these last, we have thus far had in view two quantities only. One of these is the wage-earner, who is a moral and emotional being as well as a mere worker. The other is some aggregate of material goods or conveniences —such as house-room, chattels, clothing, food and drink, newspapers, books, tobacco, means of amusement—which in the form of wages is offered to him as the reward of his work, the opportunity of working being guaranteed to him at the same time; and if our argument as thus far stated were complete, the wage-earner would, so long as these goods were delivered to him, feel that every debt due to him from the employer or from society had been discharged. If, however, we take men as they are, experience and observation will show us that amongst the wage-earner's natural desires there is one which no mere wages, however just, could satisfy. This is a desire on the wage-earner's part in respect of his dealings with the employer, for what we may call just treatment as distinguished from just payment.

The difference between these two things and the importance of it were illustrated in an interesting way by a letter from a professional agitator which was addressed to, and published in *The Times*, towards the close of the year 1916. It related to a wage dispute—one of extreme bitterness—then in progress in the South Wales coalfield, and professed, in language of a relatively temperate

264

kind, to enlighten the general public as to what were its main causes. The ostensible matter at issue was a matter of wages only. A certain wage was, by a standing agreement, due to the miners under certain trade conditions. The dispute turned on the question of whether or no these contemplated conditions had arisen, and it might in principle have been settled by an auditing of the employers' books. But behind any facts connected directly with wage-rates, there lay, said the writer, one of a much more general kind. This, he said, was the fact that the personal tone or attitude adopted by the employers towards the men had shown for many years such an absence of all " good will " that the men would put no faith in the employers' books if they saw them. Indeed, he continued, to make a long story short, the behaviour of the employers had become so " overbearing "—such was the word in which the essence of their offences was condensed by him—that the men were resolved to put up with it no longer.

Now, whatever the rights or the wrongs of this particular case, the word "overbearing" gives a very sufficient clue to the kind of personal treatment which the wage-earners naturally resent, and it serves, by its implied contrast, as a clue to the kind of treatment which, whether they analyse it or not, they claim naturally as their due.

What, then, as applied to conduct, does the word " overbearing " mean? It is a word in very common use. It, or its equivalents, have been familiar to all men in all ages, and the kind of conduct which it indicates is no invention or monopoly of the industrial employers of to-day. As soon as we begin to analyse it, it will be found that its essential element is an implied denial by one man of some sort of equality in another which the latter believes, and obstinately feels himself to possess ; and a belief or feeling that all men are equal is, in some sense, and always has been, so widely diffused that it cannot, in the case of the wage-earners, be set down as a foible of individual vanity. What, then, we must ask further, is the nature of the equality the existence of which this feeling or belief asserts?

The most logical explanation of its nature is provided

by the supernatural doctrine that every human being possesses an immortal soul, each soul being in God's eyes equally precious, and that all men, even if they cannot explain it, carry about with them a dim consciousness of this. It is logically explicable also, though with a logic less complete, on the assumption that every man possesses a quasi-supernatural conscience, to whose dictates it is the supreme duty of all men equally to conform. But, quite apart from attempts to explain it by religious or mystical theory, a sense of the existence in all men, unless they themselves destroy it, of some moral and equal dignity, is a sense which, as a matter of fact, is, like the sense of self, co-extensive with the human race. It is, for example, expressed in the celebrated line of Terence—*Homo sum: humani nihil a me alienum puto*—which, as St. Augustine says, would always rouse the plaudits of heathen playgoers. It cannot be supposed that these "vain and ignorant persons" (for so St. Augustine called them) had any definite belief in God, the soul, or conscience as the Christian world understands them; but the residual equality, of which they proclaimed their recognition as existing between man and man, was an equality of relationship to something of which conscience is virtually the equivalent, and it will for practical purposes be most clearly described as the equal right of every man to his own self-respect.

The kind of conduct, then, which is commonly called "overbearing" is, in the last analysis, conduct on the part of one man towards another which shows a want of respect for the respect which the other man entertains for himself; and the correctness of this definition, and its signal pertinence to the case of the modern employer and the wage-earner, is curiously illustrated by the fact that in ancient Athens conduct of this precise kind was recognised as a legal offence, even when indulged in by a master towards a slave who was in law his chattel. This offence was technically known as *hubris*—a word denoting conduct which is injurious to the suffering party, not because it inflicts on him any material wrong (of which the modern economic equivalent would be the payment of insufficient wages), but because it is a provocative outrage on his moral estimate of himself. In making such conduct even towards a slave penal, the object of the Athenians was indeed their own self-interest rather than moral justice. Their object was to render the slaves contented, and by so doing to promote public tranquillity; but in making such a provision they bore witness to the fact that a due respect in a superior for the self-respect of the humblest is one of the main conditions on which popular contentment rests. And what the Athenian recognised as true even with regard to slaves, is on purely utilitarian, as distinct from all moral grounds, still more vitally true with regard to the wage-earners of to-day.

There are two main reasons of a purely utilitarian kind why the modern employer should respect the self-respect of the wage-earner. One of these, though its range is no doubt limited, is that in many cases a wage-earner's self-respect is one of the chief qualities for which the employer values him. No employer would assign any position of trust to a man in whose character he knew self-respect to be wanting; and any employer would be blind to his own interests if he did not respect in others the principal quality which rendered them of value to himself. The second reason relates to all employees, whether in positions of trust or no. The main general conditions which every employer desiderates are, firstly, a calculable peace with his workmen in the matter of wages, and, secondly, their best efficiency in the doing of the work prescribed to them; and unless the self-respect of his workmen is respected by him in a reasonable way, he will jeopardise his own chances of securing or conserving either.

The general explanation of this fact may be given in very homely language, and applies to all human relationships, the domestic as well as the industrial. To outrage the self-respect of man, woman, or child is the surest way of putting either him or her into that condition of mind known as " a bad temper." Thus the story is on record of a child—the daughter of a very eminent person—who, having one day been discovered in a state of war with her brother, a year younger, she explained the matter by saying, " John has broken my dignity."

Bad temper is, indeed, the cause of half the private tragedies of the world; and it is so for this reason—that, if it be more than a passing fit of irritation, it generally takes the form of imputing to another person motives and feelings grotesquely different from—and invariably worse than—those by which, in giving offence, that person is really actuated. If a husband, agitated by the assaults of his wife's lap-dog, spills the contents of a cream-jug over the silk of her new tea-gown, she, should she view the act through the medium of bad temper, will declare that it was done deliberately for the mere sake of annoying her. If next day he slips on a mat, and deluges her with the contents of the tea-pot, she will say, and begin to believe, that such conduct is part of a scheme for making her whole life miserable. If she catches him next day in a corner confiding these events to a sister-in-law better looking than herself, she will soon add infidelity to her list of his other crimes, and be watching for evidence on the strength of which to divorce him. So long as such a temper lasted in her, no reconciliation by appeal to facts would be possible, for she would have lost all power of discerning what the actual facts were.

And what is true of individuals is true also of classes. If the wage-earners of the modern world are treated by the employers generally with such a want of personal consideration as to put them into a mood of chronic and diffused resentment, the conduct of the employers otherwise—that is to say, in matters of wages and technical discipline—however fair it may be, will be pre-condemned by them, and construed into an imaginary offence against themselves. It should, therefore, be evident to any intelligent employer that, if what he wishes for is industrial peace and prosperity, he must not regard the debt which he owes the wage-earners as one which can be liquidated by just wages alone, but that he must also, by his personal behaviour towards them, pay a debt of fellow-feeling to a self-respect on their part, of which no men morally honest could, if they would, divest themselves.

In theory, at all events, the matter is thus far plain. Here, however, in practice there arises an obvious difficulty. Since this self-respect of the wage-earners is a sentiment a respectful recognition of which is owed by the employer to all his wage-earners equally, the peculiar quality in themselves by which their self-respect is excited must be a quality which they all possess in substantially the same degree. If any man's own respect for his own particular manhood is held by him to deserve respect from an employer or from anybody else, which could not be accorded indiscriminately to the self-respect of all, he must hold this opinion on the ground that, besides possessing the quality which imparts a dignity to the lives of all human beings alike, he personally possesses others, which exist in some men only. If, moreover, his estimate of his own deserts is to be taken seriously by others, the exceptional qualities which he thus attributes to himself must be qualities which really exist in him, and correspond to his own valuation of them. If they do not—if they exist in his imagination only—his own self-respect will be not self-respect at all, but vanity, or self-consequence, or self-importance; and the conduct of those who ignore, instead of respecting it, will not be " overbearing "; on the contrary, it will be severely kind, or—which is still more to the point—it will in any case be inevitable. A bad fiddler's respect for himself as a man may deserve as much respect as a good fiddler's, but the bad fiddler would be absurdly self-important if he thought that his fiddling deserved the same attention.

The same argument applies to the moral or social debt which, as from one set of human beings to another, is due from the employers to the wage-earners in the way of personal treatment. The kind of respect which is due to them because they are men—and the importance of this debt can hardly be overestimated—is due to them for the one reason, and the one reason only, that it has its basis in certain actual facts, and it is important only in so far as it corresponds to these. Whether as a natural fact or as a supernatural fact, all men, just as truly as they all have a nervous system, have, though it is often subconscious, a certain self-respect which rests on no claims to any special efficiency, which is much more nearly akin to modesty than it is to vanity, which

responds to fair recognition like a horse to a sympathetic
rider, but which is at the same time very easily wounded;
and when it *is* wounded, either by direct affront or by
not being reasonably satisfied, it converts itself into a
spirit which will not be satisfied with anything.

If, then, any harmonious co-operation between the two
classes is to be possible—between the employers and the
employed—between the representatives of the oligarchic
principle on the one hand, and the representatives of the
democratic principle on the other—the former must pay
to the latter, not one debt only, but two. They must
not only pay to the wage-earners a debt which expresses
the technical, the industrial, or the material facts of the
situation. They must pay a second debt also, in the
way of a personal behaviour which expresses a recognition of the moral facts as well; and it is only by thus
discharging the moral claims of the wage-earners in so
far as these rest on facts, that the danger arising from
claims, at once moral and material, which are out of
accord with facts, and which nothing could satisfy, can
be averted.

But as yet we have dealt with one half of the question
only. It remains to be noted that this moral debt must
be mutual. If the behaviour of the employers to the
wage-earners is to be based on, and to express a recognition of actual facts, the behaviour of the wage-earners
to the employers must be based on, and express a recognition of actual facts likewise; and however completely
the behaviour of each class to the other may express the
moral equality which actually exists between them,
certain inequalities will persist, a like recognition of
which will be necessary for the same reason. The technical function of the employer is to give orders, and the
function of the wage-earner is to obey them; and this
inequality is not the result of accident. Any employer
who has built up a great business has done what thousands attempt to do, and what only a few can do. His
success and the maintenance of it are due (as a socialist
writer already quoted admits) to the fact that he is the
" natural monopolist of some special business ability ";
and all such ability, when exercised, is in the last
analysis an application of talents and energies, which are

conspicuous only in a few, to the task of directing and co-ordinating the operations of many, in whom such gifts are absent, or present only in a much smaller degree. If, then, for the purpose of securing co-operative harmony a personal behaviour is due from one party to the other which recognises vital equalities in so far as these exist, this primary element of behaviour must necessarily be combined with a second, by which equally real inequalities will be recognised no less plainly. If men who are unequal in their relations to any practical enterprise mimic a behaviour, and cultivate a mood of mind which imply that they are, in these particular relations equals, they are reducing life to a foolish game of pretence, which will bring them into constant collision with its most fundamental facts; and co-operative harmony will be farther off than ever.

But although the ideal behaviour of each of these classes to the other can be indicated clearly enough as a matter of general principle, it is impossible, even by way of suggestion, to reduce its details to any precise code. Nobody unfamiliar with what goes by the name of " Society " will enable himself to pass muster as a member of it by reading a book on etiquette before he goes out to dinner. The one thing needful, which no such book could teach him, is a certain something which can only come from habit, and from a host of subconscious associations which render his sympathies kin to the sympathies of those around him. Similarly, the personal behaviour accorded by the two great classes, the employers and the wage-earners, to one another must, if it is to answer the purpose of securing so-operative harmony, have at the back of it some feeling or sympathy, which alone gives it its value, which alone can prescribe its details, and for which no calculated conformity to any code could be a substitute. The efficiency of such behaviour depends, not on its forms, but on the spirit of which it is the vehicle; and its spirit will be best understood by considering, as a matter of history, the most familiar manifestations of the overbearing behaviour which is its opposite.

Of overbearing behaviour towards industrial workers the most familiar historical example is to be found in

pre-revolutionary France; but France, in the persons
of its then ruling classes, did but represent a mood
which, in one form on another, is as old as civilisation
itself.   This mood was one of contempt on the part of
the noble, the intellectual, indeed of the cultured classes
generally, for all who worked in pursuit of economic
gain, the latter comprising, not the labourers only, but
with a few exceptions, the employing classes as well.
The employing classes of France were, indeed, the first
persons to be stung by this contempt into any organised
action, and to raise by way of retaliation the battle-cry
of the " Rights of Man."   In France, indeed, and elsewhere in Europe also, this contempt was more than a
matter of mere behaviour.   It was embodied in a social
system which, closing the roads of ambition to all but
nobles and churchmen, was felt by the employers, or
the *bourgeoisie*, as a daily experienced insult.   But, as
later revolutionists have never been weary of saying,
contempt for the workers, as such, was never experienced
in its full force by the masses till the employing classes
of France had climbed into the nobles' places; and contemporary English economists, in dealing with the
labouring masses, had, as the philosophers of a new
system of industry, not only ignored their manhood, but
deprived them of the very name of men, by converting
the labouring man into so much abstract labour.   Now,
for certain theoretical purposes this substitution of
labour for the man who labours is necessary.   In so far
as we are concerned with the process of production only,
the labourers *are* labour.   They are practically nothing
else.   As Marx himself said of them, they are simply so
much Force.   But the formula which presents them in
terms of this abstract quantity came, as a matter of fact,
to be more than a formula, or an instrument of scientific
investigation.   It came to express a certain moral temper
by which, in dealing with their men, the new race of
great employers was permeated.   When writers such as
Ricardo said of some given industry that a " fresh dose
of capital " would be needed in this case, and " a dose
of labour in that," or described the regions ideally fit
for an enterprise as those " in which labour is at once
cheap and abundant," they expressed a conception of

things on the part of the employing classes from which the image of the labourer as a man had actually, for practical purposes, disappeared.

This result may in part, at least, be explained by the fact that in proportion as the number of labourers whose work was directed by a single brain increased, as the business of directing them became more abstruse and complex, and the directions had to reach the labourers through a growing number of intermediaries, the personalities of the labourers became necessarily more remote from the great modern employer than they were from his typical predecessor, who worked by rule of thumb, who could see all his men at a glance, and could talk to each individually in the course of a single morning. But the moral fact remains that the increasing intellectualisation of industry has been accompanied, in the persons of the employers, by a certain defect of vision, which, though leaving their employees visible to them, perhaps more clearly than ever, as technical mechanisms of so many kinds and qualities, has rendered their manhood, as such, a hardly distinguishable shadow. And this general fact has a natural tendency to express itself in the temper, the mood, the behaviour, not only of one of the two parties concerned, but of both. In each case the behaviour in question corresponds to what is meant by " overbearing," in the sense that it implies a disregard of certain essential facts.

In the case of the employers it implies a disregard of that natural self-respect, a want of which would render the employed contemptible. In the case of the employed it implies a disregard of those abilities and functions which the employers must necessarily possess and exercise if they are not to betray their own interests and those of the employed also. Of these two kinds of behaviour, or of these two moods as expressed by behaviour, the first provokes the second. The employers ignore, or tend to ignore, the moral claims of the employed. The employed retort by ignoring the dynamic functions of the employers. So long as this battle of conflicting exaggerations lasts, nothing in the nature of co-operative harmony is possible; and of the two kinds of behaviour which co-operative harmony demands it will be enough to say, if we content ourselves with speaking broadly, that they must represent a certain revulsion from those which now prevail.

Such a statement, however, though sufficiently correct and intelligible in respect of its general suggestions, must, before we can press it closely, be very carefully qualified. The requisite moods or behaviours must not be merely revulsions from those which prevail at present. Mere revulsion from one form of error may easily lead to another perhaps even more unfortunate. The importance of this consideration, and of the dangers which may arise from a neglect of it, especially in relation to the behaviour of the employers towards the employed, are illustrated clearly enough by the suggestions of many reformers who, in the interest of the employers themselves, are inclined to adopt and press, in some even of their most exaggerated forms, the demands of the wage-earners as their own.

It has, for example, been urged with a view to industrial harmony, by persons of conservative temperament, whose enlightened sagacity otherwise calls for sincere respect, that a just personal treatment, as accorded to his staff of wage-earners by the typical employer of to-morrow, will ultimately involve some such arrangements as the following, in which the practicable and the impracticable are curiously mixed together:

(1) A taking of his wage-earners generally into some sort of co-partnership.

(2) A frank and fraternal disclosure to them of the total profits of his business, and of the principles on which these are distributed.

(3) A giving to them a full control of so much of the productive process as can properly be called their own.

(4) A consultation with them on fraternally equal terms as to any new methods or mechanisms which he has himself invented and may think it desirable to introduce.

Suggestions of this kind, as coming from conservative quarters, are valuable for two reasons. In the first place they are witnesses to the importance of mere mood, temper, or behaviour, as conditions of co-operative harmony. In the second place they show how readily, in the case even of thinkers whose aims are essentially temperate, claims and expectations which are, within limits, reasonable, may by the mere impetus of sympathy be carried far beyond them.

Thus, that the wage-earners should, in a way not at present general, be consulted as to matters affecting their own convenience, is not only morally just, but is strictly reasonable also; for as to such matters even the least intelligent wage-earner knows far more than the employer.[1] Further—and here is a point with which presently we shall deal again—it is absolutely essential for the purposes of industrial peace that the wage-earners should somehow be put in possession of evidence which will show them beyond all doubt the normal ratio of wages to the value of the total product. But to claim that the employer should evince his fraternal respect for them by taking them as a body into his counsels with regard to methods, mechanisms, and the new conceptions and new knowledge involved in them, is to claim what in practice is impossible, and what even if imagined in any detail would be absurd. The great industries of to-day depend mostly on principles mechanical, chemical and mathematical, which few minds can follow, fewer still can master, and which cannot be expressed exactly otherwise than in complex formulæ, which to nine men out of ten would be wholly devoid of meaning, and as to the application of which not one man in a thousand could form a judgment of any practical value whatsoever. How could a great ship or a great steel bridge be constructed, how could a new chemical be brought into general use, if before the construction or manufacture began all the intricate problems involved in its design or composition had to be submitted for approval to every man who hammered a rivet, turned a tap, or helped in moving a carboy from one shed to another? How could the thought of Darwin have been ever communicated to the world if, before his works could be

---

[1] The argument in the text was used, in a very temperate way, by Mr. J. R. Clynes, M.P., a Labour Member, in an address delivered at Oxford, August 2, 1917; in which he urged the desirability " of periodical meetings between employers and employed, to deal with matters that affected the workmen's lives."

published, he had had to take the opinion of all and
each of his compositors with regard to the evolution of
species and the Biblical chronology of Ussher? Ideas of
co-partnership which suggest an arrangement like this,
as the natural outcome of true industrial harmony,
would, if definitely formulated, be dismissed as impracticable by the common sense even of those who put
them forward; and, such being the case, they here concern us only for the two following reasons. In the first
place, as put forward by serious and moderate men, they
are—let it be said again—signal illustrations of how
readily, in connection with matters of sentiment,
moderate men, whose motives are beyond suspicion, may
be led into claiming more than they really mean. In
the second place they indicate the wider and more
important conclusion that a body like the wage-earners,
who are average humanity in the mass, would, were their
common sense not disordered by prejudice, be found to
mean less than their present tempers claim. The difficulty in the case of the wage-earners, as matters stand,
is this: that they come to the question of what is morally
due to them with minds inflamed by the suspicion that
the employing classes as a whole, besides underesti-
mating them as men, underpay them as workers also;
and the more extreme and impracticable claims which
their tempers prompt them to make in the matter of
personal treatment are not so much serious expressions
of what they take to be their moral rights as the rhetoric
of revenge for what they take to be a material wrong.
Every wrong or grievance, whether fancied or real,
involves the idea of inequality in one form or another,
and involves also the idea of equality in one form or
another as its remedy. The demand for equality is
therefore a formula which, so long as any masses of men
are all suffering from a sense of material wrong of some
kind, will, in a general way, fit and express the desires,
however various, of all individuals alike, and invest them
all with a character similarly extreme and absolute. But
if once by some adequate reform, or by the mere diffusion
of knowledge, the sense of some common material wrong
is removed, the idea of absolute equality as a something
which is morally desirable for its own sake, will lose its

power to charm. It will, indeed, lose all practical meaning. Thus, if in any country the government, in collusion with the employers, tried the experiment of condemning every wage-earning man to celibacy, every wage-earning man would demand an absolutely equal right to acquire for himself, if he pleased, a single ideal something—that is to say, a wife. But when once this right had been conceded, the wage-earners, fortunately for themselves, would not be all demanding that this wife should be the same woman. They would not even demand that she should in each case be the ideal wife. Each man would put up with the best wife he could get, and instead of telling himself that he had a right to expect perfection, would make the best of her, and be thankful she was no worse. In the same way if, as we have been here assuming, any general sense amongst the wage-earners of a purely material wrong is removed by a scheme of wages based on a just minimum, accompanied by economic security, and known by the wage-earners generally to represent for each the amplest material lot which, regard being had to his own powers, is possible, the estimates formed by them of their moral, as distinct from their material, due will tend to resemble their estimates of what is due to them in the matter of matrimony. Equality as an idea will indeed be present in all of them, but it will be an equality so tempered by, and so subservient to, circumstance that its absolute character will be lost in the different relativities of different men and classes, or chastened by common sense into modifications which will be practically negations, of itself.

Such a conclusion as this with regard to the natural tendencies of mankind when their sentiments are not warped by any sense of material injury is far from representing a mere theoretical likelihood. It is supported by the plainest evidences, which are partly of a general, partly of a specific, kind.

The general evidences may be summarised in a few words. They are comprised in the obvious fact that, if any masses of men really regard equality as a thing desirable in itself, there is no need to struggle for it. Of all forms of happiness it is the one which may be achieved most easily. Of all the agencies by which men may be completely equalised, none are more sure and efficacious than sea-sickness and famine. If, therefore, complete equality is in itself a condition of happiness, twenty bad sailors need only travel together, and the physical misery of each will be turned into moral bliss by watching all his companions being sick into basins round him. If equality is desirable in itself, a whole nation in the course of a week might make itself happy by doing nothing at all; for by the end of a week, if nobody did anything, man, woman and child would be all in the grip of famine. Since, however, none of the professed devotees of equality show the least inclination to achieve it, easy though the feat would be, in what are its purest forms, it is obvious that equality, considered as an end in itself, though thousands may be ready to shout for it, means nothing for anybody.

Such, then, are the general evidences which indicate that even those extremists who, as a mere expression of temper, are accustomed to call for equality in its most absolute and impracticable forms, would, if all material grounds for ill-temper were eliminated, have little tendency, as sober and practical men, to press their demands for equality to any such fantastic degree as would render them seriously out of accord with fact. But amongst the evidences bearing on this question we have still to consider others, which are, as has just been said, of a much more definite character, and which lead to conclusions much more definite likewise, as to what, with regard to equality, men's natural sentiments are. These evidences are closely connected with what has been described already as the second of the two conditions— just personal treatment being one of them—which, besides those identifiable with adequate and secure wages, are demanded by the wage-earners themselves, and should also be recognised by others, as essential to industrial content. The second condition is a recognition of the Right to Rise.

CHAPTER IV

THE RIGHT TO RISE

THE demand on the part of the wage-earners of the modern world for a recognition of the Right to Rise, though it includes by implication a demand for the Right to Work, includes a demand also which is in the latter absent. The idea of the Right to Work is, as Louis Blanc said, merely a concrete rendering of the idea of the right to live. It relates to all men equally, but with special force to the wage-earners, these being the vast majority, and assumes that the faculties of every man, if only he is permitted to use them, are sufficient to maintain him in some sort of decent comfort. The distinctive assumption implied in the idea of the Right to Rise is the additional assumption, made in accordance with obvious fact, that some men possess faculties superior to those of others; that they would, if allowed to develop them and put them to suitable use, be able to achieve positions superior to those achievable by efficiencies lower in kind or less in degree than theirs; and that, whatever the nature or scope of their potential superiorities may be, means should be within their reach of using them to the best advantage, and of thereby raising themselves from some one of the lower ranks of the wage-paid workers to a higher, or else to some post or position outside the ranks of the wage-paid workers altogether. The demand, then, for the Right to Rise is a demand made mainly on behalf of those who belong by birth to the masses of average or inconspicuous men, that any one of them who possesses potential superiorities of any kind shall be enabled, through his use of them, to achieve and securely enjoy a material and social reward justly proportioned to their tested and objective value.

Of all the effective demands which, as history and

experience show, equality really implies, when considered in a concrete form as the goal of democratic action, this demand for the Right to Rise throws the most searching light on what certain of the workings of actual human nature are, as distinct from the vague formulæ which are commonly employed to express, but which result practically in distorting, them. The right in question has here been described as the Right to Rise. This is, however, not the name under which it is generally known. Napoleon called it an " Open Career for Talent." Equality of Opportunity is the name for it which is most familiar.

The demand for Equality of Opportunity was, as a watchword of democracy, formulated first in France, and was originally a protest against the system there and then prevailing, which, as has been said already, shut out all men not of a privileged class from all the higher prizes of station, place and power, and denied even to considerable wealth, as amassed by ignoble persons, that final recognition without which it lost for them half its value. Thus, if taken as a conscious expression of a certain kind of desire, the demand for equality of opportunity was mainly of middle-class rather than popular origin. But events showed, when once a voice had been found for it, that the desire itself was alive in the masses also; and by a rapid and instinctive adoption of this celebrated formula, they no less than the middle-class came to assert the demand for equality of opportunity as their own. Now the rapid growth of a demand relatively so precise as this out of a vaguer, though more direct demand for an unanalysed equality itself, is apt to be taken by extremists as evidence of the vitality of the sentiment which is, according to them, the dynamic principle of democracy in its purest possible form, and through which some entire revolution of existing conditions will be consummated. Such a view of the matter is, however, wholly erroneous. The demand for equality of opportunity may, indeed, wear on the surface of it certain revolutionary aspects; but it is in reality—it is in its very nature—a symptom of moderation, or rather of an unintended conservatism, of which the masses of normal men cannot, if they would, divest themselves.

The very meaning of the word " opportunity "—a word saturated as it is with implications—is enough in itself to show this. For if the ideal demand of pure democracy were realised, and the social conditions of all men made equal by force of law, there would be no such thing as opportunity, equal or unequal, for anybody. To say that opportunity could exist of achieving conditions of any kind, when the conditions of all men whatever they did would be the same, would be like saying of a dozen murderers, condemned and on their way to the gallows, that they all had an opportunity, and an equal opportunity, of being hanged. The desire for equality of opportunity—the desire for the right to rise—in so far as it is really experienced by the morally typical man of all ages and nations, is a desire that everybody (he himself, as included in " everybody," being a prominent figure in his thoughts) shall have an opportunity of achieving by his own talents, if he can, some position or condition which is not equal, but which is, on the contrary, superior, to any position or condition which is achievable by the talents of all. In other words, the very conception and recognition of equality of opportunity as the most important kind of equality which the democratic principle demands, constitute, either by implication or direct assertion, a species of Magna Charta, of which the main articles, clauses or declarations are as follows—

Firstly, whilst all men have as much as a certain average efficiency, a number of men in varying degrees have more;—

Secondly, every man shall have the opportunity of developing his own potential efficiencies, whatever they may be, to the utmost, and applying them to the best advantage;—

Thirdly, the development and application of such efficiencies being given, rewards in justice ought to be, and for practical reasons must be, proportionate in each case to the value of the effects resulting from them;—

Fourthly, whatever position or condition the exceptional efficiencies of any man may have gained for him, this advantage or these advantages shall not be diminished or diluted by any preferential opportunities unfairly granted to competitors of a class other than his own;—

Finally, the equality which in practice the democratic principle demands is not an equality of reward in any absolute sense as between one man and another, but an equality of relation between each man and his work—an equality which can be realised only on the very condition that, in an absolute sense, the amount of the reward varies.

If any one doubts that such is the virtual content of the demands for equal opportunity which are put forward to-day as expressions of the democratic principle, he need but give his attention to the way, or the several ways, in which those who are foremost in invoking that principle as their guide actually do reason when, forgetting more general formulæ, they set themselves to deal with the concrete affairs of life. If we wish to study the actual, as distinct from the apparent principles, of what purports to be extreme democracy, we cannot do better than turn to two bodies of men—the Trade Unionists on the one hand, and the more extreme champions of popular education on the other, and see how they reason about the matters with which they are most immediately concerned.

There are no bodies of men by whom, in a general way, the principles of democratic equality are professed with greater emphasis than they are by the Trade Unionists, especially by such of them as represent the kinds of skill which are the highest and most highly paid. Now, whatever such men may say about equality as a general concept, it is obvious that, when their common sense and their actual feelings, as guided by it, translate this concept into terms of practical life, equality means for them an equality which is not absolute, but is, as has just been said, relative, being absolute only in the sense in which a child's boots might be regarded as absolutely equal to a man's because they fitted with equal exactitude feet of a smaller size. That effort, in respect of its absolute efficiency, varies no less that the size of feet is assumed, and rightly assumed by them, as a fact not open to question; and the essence of their demand is that, regarded as an absolute quantity, reward should vary likewise. The main difficulties—and occasionally they have threatened to prove disastrous—with which the British Government and the nation have, during time of war, been faced in respect of war-work, have been connected with anxieties on the part of the skilled unionists, not so much as to the amount of their wages for the time being, as to the maintenance of their proper graduation, and the chance of the value of their own work suffering from what they called " dilution " through the allotment of work not unlike in kind to competitors not belonging to their own closely guarded body. " Is it just," asked one of their leaders, " can it in our own interest be tolerated, that skill like ours, which is the product of high capacity and an apprenticeship of five long years, should be for a moment treated as though it were on a level with the half-skill which any three men or three women out of four are quite well able to pick up in a week or two ? " [1]   Another spokesman of Labour, arguing in behalf of a certain body of men—men engaged in urgent war-work—by whom a strike for increased wages was threatened at a most critical moment, did not deny that their actual wages were considerable, but urged that, war or no war, the men's first duty alike to themselves and their families was to see that their exceptional position in the ranks of labour was maintained, and to intimidate all who in the future might seek to tamper with it. On another occasion certain of the leaders themselves struck work as against the union on whose behalf they had been conducting a recent strike against the masters. " Is it just," they asked, " that the salaries which the union pays us— salaries barely equal to the stipend of a Church of England curate—should be less instead of more than the wages which, through our own good offices, have been won from the masters for hundreds of mere manual labourers ? "

[1] The above statement was verified by the Report (published early in August 1917), by the Commissioners for Wales, as to the causes of Industrial Unrest. Prominent among these causes, and next to the " antagonism between labour and capital" constantly fomented by extremists, is mentioned " the high wages paid to unskilled men and boys."

Examples of this kind might be multiplied, but those just given are sufficient. Let us now turn from equality as interpreted by labourers and the leaders of labour, to equality as interpreted by democrats in connection with the question of education. "It is in the field of popular education," says a well-known English publicist, who is as to this matter a representative of the extremest democratic school, "that the greatest work of democratic statesmanship is to be accomplished"; and his words reflect the sentiments of the most extreme of the intellectual champions of democratic equality generally. If we want, they argue, to secure for all an equality that is worth the name, we must by education equip all of them equally for the business of life before that business begins. Thus, according to one of them, the immediate object of education is " to train all men born for the best of everything that is human." According to another, it is " to equip all children equally for the full perfection of manhood." " When we define for ourselves," says another, " the immediate object of education, nothing must lurk in our minds of the old idea that ' some vessels ' are naturally ' of honour,' others naturally ' of dishonour.' "

All this is quite in the style of those who dream of equality in its completest imaginable form. But let us now consider how the publicist just mentioned, who has made by adoption all these phrases his own, deals with the question of education when he approaches it as a practical man. In order that education may be an instrument of true democratic equality, the first step to be taken is, he says, to secure adequate teachers; and the adequate teachers being given, their work will mainly consist in " selecting the best minds from among the children of the common people, as though they were diamonds," sifted or washed out of the gravel " of the great national mine," and giving special care to the development, cultural and intellectual, of these. But, so the writer proceeds—and his words have been echoed by a chorus of democratic approbation—teachers of the kind required must be men of peculiar and most uncommon talent; they must, therefore, be paid accordingly; and the great present impediment to true democratic education, in England at all events, is this—that the salaries offered to the teachers, which are often barely equal to the wages of a skilled mechanic, and never equal to the profits of a very moderate business, are wholly insufficient to attract to the teaching profession men of such signal talents as the fit teacher requires. The two things which are essential, then, to a democratic system of education are a staff of highly gifted teachers, secured and retained by the payment of exceedingly ample salaries, and secondly a selection by these persons of specially gifted children, on whom they will bestow a special and preferential care.   The same argument, so far as the children are concerned, was emphasised by an English Archbishop of strong socialist sympathies, when asked on a public occasion for his own definition of what socialism, in its essence, is. The question, he said, might be answered by reference to the case of a boy which had lately come under his observation. The boy, poor and friendless, displayed an alertness of mind of a kind so startling that it could not escape attention; and yet, unless some one should come to his aid by accident, the probable lot in store for him was that of an ordinary labourer, in which all his special gifts would be lost.   The message of socialism to the world might, said the Archbishop, be condensed into six simple words: "Give that poor boy a chance." The Archbishop made no mention of the adequate teachers through whose ministrations the poor boy's chance was to be given him, but we may take these as implied.

Let us now consider the practical arguments of the trade unionists, of the democratic educationists, and sentimental socialists such as the Archbishop, together. We shall see that the assumptions, the aims and the general view of human society underlying them, are in all these cases the same.   In each case, underlying them there is the implied and instinctive recognition that the capacities of men for practical purposes vary.   In each case there is an assertion of the fact that these capacities, as developed and applied, must be rewarded in proportion to the unequal character of their results, partly because a proportional reward is demanded by natural justice, and partly because the higher capacities will not

be developed and will not be applied without it. The
amount of the reward claimed for work of exceptional
value and the value of the work itself may in particular
instances be overestimated; but the principle on which
the claim is based is in strict accordance with the instinctive common sense of man. Even the highly paid
artisans and miners who, in England, Wales and Scotland, scandalised public opinion by striking work in war-
time with a view to increasing their wages by ten or
fifteen per cent., were right in so far as their behaviour
was merely the assertion of the principle that work of
some special efficiency is worth a corresponding price.
The democratic educationists may, and probably do,
absurdly overestimate the amount of sleeping talents
which need but the magic touch of the gifted teacher to
awaken them; but the demand itself that such talents
should, in so far as they really exist, not be rendered
useless for want of the chance which education may give
of using them, is a demand which, if reasonably interpreted, all reasonable men will endorse. Of all these
detailed demands put forward by men who claim the
name of democrats the same thing may be said. They
are perfectly logical. They express what most men
actually think and feel. They may, if reasonably interpreted, be consistent with the soundest sense. But there
is one thing with which they are radically inconsistent,
and that is the vision of pure democratic equality which,
in moments of mere sentiment, the vague formulæ of
democracy pure and simple evoke in the minds of those
accustomed to utter them.

The practical demands of the democratic educationists
show this, not perhaps more clearly, but with greater
emphasis, than those even of the trade unionists. In the
first place, with reference to the children before their
education begins, these apostles of equality start with the
perfectly correct assumption that this juvenile mass will
always contain a few whom the teacher's eye will detect
as congenitally superior to the rest. A natural child-
aristocracy—a caste of intellectual Dauphins—is the first
thing which they postulate; and on this, according to
them, it will be the business of the teachers to lavish

a preferential care. Secondly, they demand in the persons of the teachers themselves another aristocracy or oligarchy separated from the average mass, not by their talents only, but as they specially insist, by a something not yet approached—namely, the magnitude of their emoluments also. Thirdly, as to the children when the process of their education is completed, what do our apostles of equality hope and demand for these? The Archbishop tells us that what socialism demands for them is " a chance." Yes—but a chance of what? It cannot be a chance of getting an average livelihood; for, if socialism demands anything, it demands that an average livelihood shall be, not a chance, but a certainty for all who have the will to work for it. What, according to the Archbishop, socialism demands for the typical " poor boy " whose gifts far exceed the average, must be a chance of achieving a position which exceeds the average likewise, and which is for the mass of boys who have no such gifts impossible. Should there be any doubt as to the matter, one of the democratic educationists, whose language has just been quoted, puts into plain terms what the Archbishop only implies. The ultimate object of a truly democratic education is, he says, in somewhat Hibernian language, to secure for each of the " diamonds " discoverable in the gravel of the great " national mine," " an equal chance of getting to the top of the tree."

We thus see how the very men, whether skilled trade unionists, socialist Archbishops, or professional doctrinaires of ideally democratic education—men who, with the greatest unction in moments of mere sentiment, give voice to the demand for equality in its most absolute and impracticable form—moderate these demands, or rather (we may say) forget them and instinctively invert their character, when they come to adjust their reasoning to the actual affairs of life, and to what in reality are their own normal feelings. The democratic educationist who declaims in moments of mere sentiment against treating any one child as " a vessel of more honour than another," begins his argument, when he speaks as a practical man, with laying it down that the

first task of the teacher is to pick out certain children
like diamonds from the national gravel, and give them
a polish which is possible for such things of honour
alone.

The skilled trade unionists, when they protest against
the " dilution " of their labour, do not demand the
highest wages for " all who are born men." They
demand the highest wages for work of the highest kind,
by which they mean the work to which they themselves
are trained, and of which, so far as is possible, they
desire to retain the monopoly.

In all such demands as these, which merely translate
the demand for equality pure and simple into a demand
for equal opportunity (or, as many trade unionists would
put it, opportunity restricted to themselves), the animating principle, or the assumed basic fact, is not
equality but graduation; and below this fact lies another,
implicitly assumed likewise—namely, the existence of
some average mass, whose capacities and whose wages
represent those normal lots, by their upward distance
from which those ampler lots are measured, which opportunity offers to talents above the average.

The idea, then, of equalised opportunity, and the
various concrete forms in which the demands for opportunity are made, contain in them a great deal more than
at first sight may appear. They are an epitome of what,
with regard to social conditions generally, and their own
relations to these, men of democratic sympathies actually
think and feel as contrasted with the thoughts and feelings suggested to and fomented in them by the doctrines
of absolute equality which are the content of formal
socialism. These doctrines which, as they stand, are
plausible only so long as they remain vague, are adopted
by the mass of socialists or social democrats, not as a
programme but as a protest, or manifesto of rebellion,
against certain general wrongs which are, or which are
supposed by them to be, interwoven with the fabric of
the existing industrial system, the first and foremost
amongst these being one of a purely material kind—
namely, a crude underpayment of wages. The suspected
existence of this one wrong alone is enough to breed

resentment, and in the doctrines of formal socialism resentment finds a voice—a voice which is sonorous and challenging by very reason of their errors and exaggerations. That these doctrines, taken as they stand, reveal themselves as more grotesquely absurd the more clearly they are expressed and the more closely they are analysed, has been shown at length already; but something else has been shown also. It has been shown that, underlying, or disguised by, the absurdity of these doctrines, certain demands and ideas lurk which are sanctioned alike by justice, by sober reason, and by the self-interest of all, equality of opportunity being one of them. Such being the case, then, it has been here contended that, in proportion as the conditions corresponding to such ideas and demands are realised, and any general sense of wrong is thereby allayed, the natural tendency of men will be to acquiesce in the practicable, whilst the impossible demands and hopes, which are the sole distinctive content of formal socialism or of pure social democracy, will evaporate for the simple reason that they no longer even symbolise any intelligible meaning.

Finally, as a proof and illustration of the correctness of this contention, the most widely spread and spontaneous of all the definite demands which have been made by the spirit of democracy in the progressive countries of the world—that is to say, the demand for equalised opportunity, or otherwise for the right to rise—has been analysed. It has been analysed, so as to bring into light all its essential implications; and the results of this analysis are, we shall find, as follows—that the general configuration of society which this demand takes for granted, and the particular conditions on which it insists as just, in a democratic sense, for particular men or classes, correspond substantially with those which have here been set forth in detail as representing such elements of truth, moral justice, practical sagacity, and the self-interest of all classes alike, as are latent in even the most insane hopes, the wild disregard of facts, the intellectual self-contradictions, and the inverted psychology of socialism. The nature of this correspondence shall be presently reviewed in full; but we will first consider more precisely where, as a matter of principle, the essential difference lies between the conditions demanded by the temper and logic of socialism with a view to overthrowing the existing constitution of society, and those which have been here indicated as essential to its undisturbed conservation.

BOOK VI

CHAPTER I

THE PSYCHOLOGY OF SANE REFORM

IF, beginning with its manifestations in the later years of the eighteenth century and the earlier years of the nineteenth, we consider socialism or social democracy firstly as a sentiment having an absolute equality of material conditions as its object, and secondly as a reasoned scheme by which this ideal object may be realised, we shall see that, as a principle and a project, it has passed through three stages, which are broadly distinguishable as follows.

According to the earlier socialists, such as Ann Lee and Owen, the one peculiar element requisite for the realisation of a socialist polity was a general sentiment in favour of equal wealth for all; and it seemed to them that, such a sentiment being given, the process by which wealth was produced would naturally adjust itself to an object in which it was assumed that the producers were all equally interested.

Except in the case of religious sects like the Shakers, this expectation was completely falsified by events; and, considered as the basis of any practical system, socialist thought might have died a natural death if, some forty years after the collapse of Owen's experiments, it had not been reconstructed by Marx on a practically new basis. The change which Marx effected in socialist thought was this. Whereas the earlier socialists had regarded the equalisation of wealth as a feat to be accomplished by the magic of a peculiar sentiment to which the facts of production would adjust themselves, the relative importance of these two factors was by Marx inverted. The equalisation of wealth required, according to him, no sentiment of a peculiar kind at all. Its basis lay in the purely economic fact that wealth is produced by manual labour only, one labourer producing as much wealth as another; and the only kind of sentiment for which there was any occasion was simply the common desire of every man to get and to keep the whole of what he individually produces.

So long as this doctrine as to manual labour prevailed, everything for the socialist mind was invested with a false simplicity. But, as time went on, intellectual socialists themselves began to discern that this so-called " scientific " doctrine was, as Bismarck said of a certain British diplomatist, "nothing more than a lath painted to look like iron." They began to see that in the complex production of to-day the mental workers are agents no less real than the manual; that the former are in many cases incomparably more productive than the latter, and that if distribution is to be based on the mere facts of production, a régime of equalised incomes will be farther off than ever. They have, therefore, in respect of the two main elements of the case, had to restore these to what was their original order, sentiment as the equalising element being put once more in the first place, and the mere facts of production being relegated to the second, as subservient to it.

This third stage of socialist thought may, in Tennyson's language, be described as " a riper first." It is riper in two senses : firstly, in the sense that socialist thought in this third stage includes a far more scientific conception of the nature of modern production, with all its complex inequalities in respect of powers and functions; and, secondly, in the sense that it involves a more complex conception of the task which socialist sentiment must perform as an instrument of equal distribution—a task which must comprise, not the act of distribution only, but also that of providing some overwhelming incentive to all those complex submissions and complex inequalities of effort, without which there would be nothing, or very little, to distribute. But with whatever care this conception may be developed, it remains a mere conception, a mere figment of the imagination still. Indeed, its very development, whether implied or explicit, into fuller logical form, has but rendered more plain than before how remote it is from any sentiment which is actually operative amongst men.

Now, one illustration of this remoteness has been pointed out already—namely, the fact that this imaginary sentiment, if it is to do the work required of it, must be in reality not one sentiment but two, each being the opposite of the other, so that some men will be animated by a passion for producing more than they get, whilst some will be animated by a passion for getting more than they produce. But in the whole conception of a sentiment which, as a stimulus to individual work, has for its object an equality of rewards for its own sake, an error is involved far deeper than any which comes to the surface in the form of such a paradox as this. It is an error which goes to the very roots of the whole psychological process by which the feelings and actions of the individual are normally brought into contact with the affairs of his fellow-men. It amounts, indeed, to neither more nor less than a farcical turning of this process upside down.

When socialists conceive as possible a sentiment which shall so affect the industrial workers of a community that the happiness of each is identified with a purely objective fact—namely, the material equality of all—they do not, indeed, maintain that the individual will forget his own interests altogether, or regard them with complete indifference; but they do maintain or assume that the equal conditions of all will be the primary object habitually present in his mind, his own welfare being a miniature image of these, which is reflected in his consciousness of the fact that the " all " will include himself as a thousandth or a millionth part of it. If such were really the nature of the psychological process by which the self-interest of the individual as a productive agent is brought into relationship with the material welfare of others, the process would not be peculiar to this special relationship only. It would be a type of the process which was normal in the case of all relationships through which the interest of the individual in his own affairs is associated by him with an

interest in the affairs of others, no matter what the
nature of these affairs may be. A man who was liable
to sea-sickness would, when embarking on a voyage, be
primarily occupied by an anxiety that none of the
passengers should be sea-sick—a mass of vague persons
altogether unknown to him—and would surprise himself
by discovering that he, as one of the crowd, hoped to
escape sea-sickness amongst them. A mother's love for
her daughter would be the result of the following psychological syllogism : I love all daughters. My Jemima is
a daughter. Therefore I love Jemima. To suppose, as
is supposed by the later logic of socialism, that self-
interest is deduced in this way from a prior interest in
others, is like supposing that the flame of a lamp in a
lighted room is a miniature condensation of the light
diffused over the illuminated walls, instead of the light
on the walls being an enlarged reflection of the flame.
A mother does not desire the welfare of her own daughter
because she first desires the welfare of daughters generally. She desires the welfare of daughters generally
because her sympathies have been previously quickened
by solicitude for the welfare of her own. Like the
ripples on the surface of a pond, which circle outwards
from the spot at which a stone has struck it, the inclusive
emotions and interests circle outwards from the centre
of self or family, becoming fainter and less precise in
proportion as they become more and more comprehensive. If any one doubts this fact, he may very easily
find ocular proof of it. Let him watch the faces of a
crowd which, drawn together by the news of some great
shipwreck, is searching the lists of those who have been
saved or lost. What each member of the crowd will be
looking for, in obedience to an eternal instinct, is the
name of parent, wife, husband, child or lover ; and if
the person in question is named amongst those surviving,
the expression of the searcher changes from one of
agonised tension to one of supreme relief. A shadow
of sadness may overcast it, as a sign of sympathy with
the bereaved, but this sympathy will be a secondary,
not a primary, fact. It will be a surviving emanation
from the pangs of personal anxiety which a few moments
ago had been undergone by self.

In the same way, with regard to material welfare or income, a man's solicitude for self is not a miniature deduction from an antecedent solicitude for the equal welfare of all. A solicitude for the welfare of all, so far as regards income, is an enlargement partly rational, partly emotional also, of an antecedent solicitude for his own. The enlargement is rational because in no community are the material conditions of any one unit isolated. It is emotional because a certain good will towards his fellow-citizens generally, a compassion for extreme distress, and a preferential affection for his own chosen associates are for each unit essential to those pleasures of social intercourse, without which life would have few, if any, pleasures at all. But an interest of this kind in the affairs or incomes of others has nothing to do with any quasi-religious belief—for this is what the sentiment which socialists postulate comes to—that nobody can be happy, let his income be what it may, unless everybody else has an income of precisely the same amount. If a man, in view of what he takes to be his own needs and abilities, should judge that six hundred a year was a proper income for himself, he might well wish that everybody was rich enough to escape privation; but his judgment as to his own income will not even tend to enlarge itself into a passionate conviction that nobody should earn either less or more. It would certainly not stimulate him—and this is the important point—to strain himself in producing a thousand pounds instead of a bare six hundred, merely for the sake of securing a certain objective symmetry by handing over four hundred pounds to a neighbour who was earning a substantial income of two hundred pounds already.

The simple fact is that, except in the case of persons of a quasi-monastic temperament who regard equality as a sort of religious discipline, equality as such, and for its own sake, is a thing desired by nobody; and if we ask why, as an ideal object of endeavour, equality appeals so readily to the imagination of multitudes, the answer is this: that it is, by those who desire it, not desired for its own sake at all, but is desired because, in the mind of this man or of that, it happens to be associated with one or other of certain incidental results,

which are generically different from itself. Let us suppose, for example, that ten shipwrecked men are waiting
for rescue which will take many days to reach them,
their sole provisions, meanwhile, being bread which is
just sufficient to keep life in their bodies until the rescue
comes. Such men will no doubt insist that the bread
shall be allotted to all in absolutely equal proportions,
but they will not do so because they all wish for equality.
They will do so because, by accident, equality is for the
time identified with escape from death. Apart from
exceptional and extreme cases like this, an equalisation
of incomes would, if the forces of production were not
generally crippled by it, have two incidental results,
each of which two would appeal to men of a very
common type. One of these results would appeal to
the man temperamentally idle, by ensuring that the
worst work was as well paid as the best. The other
would appeal to the man temperamentally jealous, by
making him feel secure that, whatever he got himself,
no detested superior would affront him by getting more.

As to these incidental results of artificial equality, it
might to many people seem enough to observe that the
sentiments of idleness and jealousy hardly make up
between them that passion for equality as such, which
the logic of socialism postulates as the great motive to
labour, and which it also presents to the world as the
apotheosis of brotherly love; but this obvious criticism
does but touch the surface, not the root, of the matter.
The fundamental fact which requires to be noted is as
follows.

Though a system of equalised incomes might minister,
through its incidental results, to the self-interest of any
idle man or any jealous man individually, it would be
absolutely hostile to the self-interest even of the idle or
the jealous as classes. It may be to the self-interest
of A, as a man temperamentally idle, that all incomes
should be equal, because such a system as this would
secure for him the maximum reward, though his own
contribution to the total were little or next to nothing,
as in that case it would be. But it would not be to
A's self-interest that a system of equality should prevail
which would have the same effect on the several con-

tributions of B, C and D; for if work were generally reduced to a minimum quantity like his own, there would soon be next to nothing either for himself or for anybody else. The socialist polity would, as Mr. Shaw admits, die of corporate bankruptcy, which, in the case of all socialist experiments, other than the quasi-monastic, is precisely the thing it has done. Hence, since general equality must be a general system or nothing, it is not to the self-interest even of the idle that general equality should exist; and there can, even amongst the idle, be no such thing as a corporate sentiment in favour of it.

The same observation applies to the equalisation of incomes as a scheme whose incidental results would be gratifying to the temperamentally jealous. Any jealous man, taken singly, might well be pleased with a system which would prevent super-competent men from getting, through their exceptional talents, an income larger than his own; but jealous men, as a body, would not be pleased with a system which, affecting all alike, would prevent super-competent men from producing more than the minimum they were likely to get; and would thus reduce to a minimum the equal shares assignable to the jealous men themselves.

The socialist supposition that a scheme of equalised incomes, unless incomes stand for beggary, can be brought about by a sentiment in favour of equality for its own sake is a mere psychological mare's nest. It is an absurdity of a double kind. In the first place, equality for its own sake, as an object of practical endeavour, is a thing of no interest to anybody. In the second place, though the most obvious of the immediately incidental results of it might be gratifying to each idle and each jealous man individually who looked upon these as embodied in himself alone, they would be fatal to the expectations of each man the moment they were embodied in all. In a word, to repeat what has been said in a previous chapter, equality of reward irrespective of unequal work, whilst promising that the many, no matter how little they were able to produce, or were willing to produce, for themselves, should all be financed into affluence out of the products of the super-competent few, would deprive the few of every conceivable motive which could prompt them to produce the fund from which the affluence of the many was to be drawn.

Such, then, being the radical errors which, due to an inverted psychology, render all the social conditions promised and projected by formal socialism absurd, let us now go back to those conditions which have here been set forth at length as conditions which, demanded alike by common sense and justice, the absurdities of socialism indicate even in the very act of obscuring them.

Of such conditions the first—and it is for practical purposes the basis of all the others—is one which relates to wages, these being considered in respect, not of their absolute amount which will differ in different cases, but of the elements of which, in every case, the ideal wage is composed. The essential feature of the ideal wage— the wage demanded alike by common sense and by justice—is, it has been said, this : that it represents a value in excess of the value of the personal product of the wage-earner, the excess being provided out of the product the production of which is contingent on the directive ability of the employer. Now this contention is, in a certain sense, identical with the socialist promise that, under a system of socialism, the many shall live very largely on the efforts of the super-competent few, which promise has been here held up to ridicule as the crowning absurdity of the whole socialist programme. Why, then, is the ideal wage, as here described, rational, if the ideal income, as it figures in the socialist programme, is absurd ?

The answer is that, whereas the socialist programme disregards or annihilates those motives of self-interest by which all productive work in the actual world is animated, the ideal wage, which has here been described as rational, appeals to such motives in a way which is at once the most precise and the most comprehensive possible. By substituting for a maximum income assignable to all alike a minimum wage assignable to the workers of least efficiency, and by making this minimum contingent on honest work, a guarantee is provided that the workers of least efficiency shall persistently do their best, whatever that best may be. By including in this minimum a large—possibly the larger—part of it, an element produced by the efforts, not of the wage-earner himself, but of the employer whose mind directs him, the stability of the system is secured of which the directing employers are the head. The fact that, according to the scheme here set forth as rational, all work (that of the employers included) which exceeds in value the work of the wage-earners of least efficiency, shall, whatever the excess may be, receive rewards which exceed the minimum wage proportionally, will constitute a stimulus to every higher efficiency, as measured by its results, from the minimum standard upwards.

Finally, as to the surrender which the greater, and especially the greatest, producers would have to make of a portion of their own products for the purpose of raising both the minimum and every wage to a total greater than anything which the wage-earner could produce himself, this surrender, though absurd as it figures in the programme of formal socialism, is, as a part of the programme here described as rational, not an absurdity, but a sound business transaction. As it figures in the socialist programme, it is absurd for the simple reason that it would, if viewed from the standpoint of those who would have to make it, be surrender without a motive, and would, if enforced by law, ensure that the things surrendered should never be produced again. It would give every man an interest in the utmost efficiency of others, but would, at the same time, deprive every man of the smallest interest in his own. The kind of surrender here described as rational is rational because, as made by the great employers, whilst still leaving them with fortunes (not, indeed, equal, but proportional to the magnitude of their own products), it would yield them a *quid pro quo*—something for themselves no less important—namely, the stability and solidarity of the system on which their own fortunes depend. In other words, whilst the promises and postulates of formal socialism are absurdities, the conditions which, though closely resembling these, are here described as rational, are rational because they rest on a totally different basis. The method by which they are reached is one which, instead of deducing the material interests of the

individual from some fantastic vision of the united
interests of all, deduces a reasonable conception of the
united interests of all from its true psychological source
—namely, the self-interest of the individual.

Here, then, we have the main material conditions
which, as the essentials of a sound and practicable polity,
socialism discredits by investing them with impracticable
forms, and placing them in impossible settings, but which
reason and sober justice at the present day demand. In
addition, moreover, to these material conditions, reason
and sober justice demand, as we have seen, certain moral
conditions also. One of these relates to the status of the
wage-earner as a man, the other to his status as a man
who, possessing or believing himself to be the possessor
of talents beyond the ordinary, demands the right to
rise. These latter conditions are more than rational
renderings of a something which, however obscurely, the
logic of socialism suggests. They are conditions which
the logic of socialism, if it means anything at all, positively and definitely excludes, thereby denying, little as
socialists recognise this, two of the main demands which
are really instinctive in the masses to whose passions
formal socialism addresses itself.

That such is the case with regard to the right to rise
is obvious.

It is less obviously, but no less truly, the case with
regard to that moral recognition which, it has here been
insisted, is due to the wage-earner as a man. Such a
recognition, it has been said, is, in the last analysis, a
recognition of each man's life—even that of the com-
monest labourer—with all its affections and all its possibilities of pleasure, as an end in itself, like a statue
complete on its own pedestal.[1] But this is precisely
what the logic of socialism denies. It assumes, as we
have seen already, that the sole direct object of the
endeavours of the human unit is not to promote his own
welfare, bodily or spiritual, in any way, but is solely to
aid in the production of an aggregate of material equali-

[1] Professor F. Nitti calls attention to the dictum of Hegel which, he
says, the German Socialists adopt as the basis of their social senti-
mentalism : " *Man is beyond all doubt an end in himself, and should,
as such, be respected, not with regard to the State.*"

ties which are essentially external to himself, and merely include his own lot by accident, as an insignificant and barely distinguishable part of them.

That such is the case will be shown in greater detail hereafter, when we shall have occasion to analyse the curiously confused ideas which are associated by popular thought with one common name, "The State." For the moment it is enough to note that the moral conditions here described as rational include, as integral parts of a possible order of things, conditions which, coinciding with the instinctive desires of mankind, the logic of socialism rules out of existence.

Let us now consider the various conditions, mental and moral, together, which have been here set forth as representing whatever is vital and practicable either in the concepts of formal socialism, or in those popular desires which formal socialism ignores; and let us consider how far these conditions, if fulfilled, would be calculated to allay that widely diffused unrest of which the promises of formal socialism may, despite their absurdities, be seriously taken as a symptom, or a vaguely tentative symbol.

In considering this matter, we must begin by once more noting that the conditions in question are here set forth as reasonable because they have as their basis two general facts, one of which is now admitted by all serious socialists themselves, whilst the other is attested by the demands of the democratic spirit whenever men, and the wage-earners more especially, express them in terms of what the masses really feel.

The first of these facts—that admitted by modern socialists themselves, or by those, at all events, who claim to be serious thinkers—is that efficient production —the kind of production which they postulate as the basis of their ideal polity—involves the interaction of workers of whom a few are productive to a degree incomparably greater than others, whilst the various degrees of productivity between the highest and the lowest are numerous. The second fact is this. Whatever socialists may foolishly say to the contrary, the natural and real demand of workers of all classes, more especially the skilled wage-earners, is that men shall get and keep, and be protected in getting and keeping, a wage or reward in proportion to what they produce. We may, therefore, assume as given, and not open to dispute, the general fact that, in any satisfactory polity, the scheme of distribution will be not equal but graduated, and that some men consequently will, in an absolute sense, have a larger interest in the total product than others. Hence, the crucial problem is how to adjust these interests so that all parties may feel that relatively, if not absolutely, their various interests are equal, that all their interests rise and fall together, and their various lots in life may, from the simplest upwards, be severally the best which the nature of things makes possible.

Such being the desired end, the conditions here set forth as the practicable means of securing it may be restated as follows.

First comes a minimum wage for the workers of least efficiency, far in excess of anything which, as a body of self-directed equals, the recipients could produce for themselves, this condition being taken as carrying with it an assured continuity of the work on which the earning of the wage depends.

Secondly, for all whose efficiency exceeds the minimum comes a wage which exceeds the minimum wage in exactly the same proportion; this condition being taken as carrying with it a provision for exceptional talent of encouragement to develop, and adequate opportunities of applying, itself.

Thirdly comes a respect on the part of the employing class for the wage-earner, not merely as an industrial implement, but as a man—a being whose life has an absolute value in itself, and is therefore a type of the values in which all human effort and human existence culminate.

If, then, we assume that these conditions are realised, is there any reason for doubting that, as a matter of theory at all events, the masses of mankind, even those whose present "unrest" is most conspicuous, would accept these conditions with contentment, in the sense that, as practical men, they could not, if asked to do so, formulate or devise better?

As a matter of theory, we may say that these conditions would fulfil, if established, everything within the limits of the possible which the victims of contemporary "unrest" are endeavouring to visualise in their dreams; but the meaning of the qualifying phrase, "as a matter of theory," is this. The conditions here in question have been contrasted with the ideals of formal socialism, not because the former are susceptible of more complete fulfilment than the latter (for few ideals, if any, can ever be fulfilled completely), but because the more nearly the ideal conditions here in question are approached, the more nearly do the actual conditions achieved coincide with the actual facts of human motive and the varieties of human capacity, whereas the more nearly we approach a realisation of the ideals of socialism, the farther should we leave actual facts behind us, and the more completely would the whole structure collapse. The true ideal of a carriage-wheel is, for instance, a circle. No actual carriage-wheel is a circle absolutely perfect, but the more nearly it is circular the better will it perform its purpose. On the other hand, if we start with assuming—and such a procedure would be comparable to that of the socialists—that the form of the ideal wheel is not circular but oval, the more nearly we realised such an ideal as this, the more impossible, for practical purposes, would our actual wheels become.

With regard, however, to the social conditions which are here described as consonant, in idea or principle, with the concrete facts of life, the question still remains of how near an approach to these conditions is feasible. The idea of a piston and a cylinder was as perfect in the mind of Watt when he made his earliest steam-engines as it ever has been in the mind of any engineer since; but the earlier engines of Watt were very imperfect implements, owing to the extreme difficulty encountered by himself and his workmen in adjusting one of these parts with sufficient accuracy to the other. In the social ideals with which we are here concerned, is there any similar difficulty which would render impossible an approach to them sufficiently near to produce the content and harmony which would otherwise be their natural consequences? And the answer to this question is as follows. Whilst none of these conditions are capable of being realised completely, they are all capable of being realised to a degree quite sufficient to change the popular mood from one of unrest and of protest against the established order generally to one in which a reasonable content shall be at least the prevailing element; but even this consummation is beset by certain difficulties, which, in order to overcome or remove them, must be clearly faced and recognised.

These difficulties are of two kinds—those which are primarily objective, material, or economic, and those which are primarily subjective or moral. They are so far distinct from one another that each must be considered separately.

CHAPTER II

OBJECTIVE DIFFICULTIES

THE objective difficulties just mentioned are all exemplified in connection with the minimum wage, and, although they are not confined to it, it is in connection with the minimum wage that they are exemplified most clearly.

The first and most obvious of such difficulties is this. The whole scheme of wages which, having as its basis or starting-point a satisfactory minimum, has here been represented as calculated to produce content, must, it has been said, carry one condition along with it. Every wage must, from the minimum upwards, be contingent on the exercise, by such persons as claim it, of the best efficiencies they possess; and for indolence, for carelessness, or for want of prompt obedience there must always lurk in the background some curtailment of the wage which would otherwise be the worker's due. By workers of special skill this species of penalty need not be felt as any serious hardship. They might, indeed, find occasionally that the pleasures of partial idleness were well worth some loss in money. But for the average worker, who would normally earn the minimum, any such loss through indolence would, if frequent, be a very much graver matter. It would soon mean substantial inconvenience, then galling privation; and only a renewal of diligence would at last save him from destitution. This possibility of destitution is one of the primary conditions against which Mr. Shaw informs us that the sentiment of socialism protests. One of the favourite themes, indeed, of all socialist orators is the fact, which they describe as terrible, that for the great mass of the workers of the modern world nothing but a week's wages stands between them and famine. In a general sense this may be true enough; but it is not true of the

305 .

wage-earners, or of the modern world only. In a general
sense it is true of the whole human race. It always has
been true, and to the end of time it will be. A small
minority of men in highly civilised countries may enjoy
what is called "an independence" by having created
for themselves in the past, or else by having inherited
from their fathers, certain permanent things the use of
which assists the productive efforts of others, and for
which use those who use them pay a certain price to the
owners. But such owners are exceptions; and if all
their possessions were distributed amongst the working
mass, the plight of the mass would in this respect be
just what it was before. All the capital of the world
might be divided in equal shares amongst everybody;
but if the human race at large did no work for a week,
everybody at the end of a week would be either dead or
dying. The capital of the world may be compared to
so many million spades, and the masses of mankind to
cultivators. If one man owned all the spades, and let
them out to the cultivators at a shilling a year for each,
this one man, without working, might have a colossal
income of many million pounds; but if the spade of
every cultivator suddenly became his own, every cultivator would, if he were not prepared to starve, have to
go on with his digging just as he did before. No individual would join his fellows in working unless want
or pain of some sort lay in wait for him if he failed to
do so. Thus no minimum wage, however ample its
amount, could prevent men from being miserable who
were not willing to work for it. Even socialists themselves, as Mr. Shaw bears witness, admit that this is
true in principle, and can only propose to mend matters
by visiting wilful idleness, not with want, but with the
whip. No conceivable constitution, political, economic
or social, could ensure content for everybody; but by
making the material conditions of a healthy life accessible to every plain man who is honestly willing to work
for them, the material bases of content would be provided for an overwhelming majority, and nobody in his
senses could demand or hope for more.

So much, then, for the first material difficulty which
would stand in the way of rendering our ideal conditions

complete. The second arises in connection, not with the perversities of men temperamentally idle, but with an assured provision of suitable work for the industrious. This provision, which means an assured continuity of wages, is a matter no less important than that which assures their quantity; for if quantity means the enjoyment of superfluous plenty in the present, continuity means freedom from something even more fatal to happiness than a lessening of present plenty—that is to say, anxiety as regards the future.

Now, as has been said already, could such a provision of continuous work be complete, it would be equal to a re-diffusion of industrial property generally. A peasant, let us say, who by cultivating his own plot has been making an income of £30 a year, sells his plot to some scientific farmer, and by working under his direction earns, let us say, an annual wage of £60. His income, whilst it lasts, is doubled, but he is no longer, as he once was, master of the means of earning it. He is no longer master of the means of earning any income at all. But if he had the right of earning such a doubled income continuously in one way or another, even though this particular farmer should some day have to dismiss him, he would be no less secure of access to the means of an undiminished livelihood than he was when the plot which he once cultivated was his own. If a skilled engineer, earning £3 a week in a factory, had a similar right to exercise his skill somewhere and get for it the same payment, though this particular factory was compelled to close its doors, his position would be as secure as it would have been if, as a village blacksmith, he were earning half that sum by blowing his own bellows under the shade of his own chestnut tree. Indeed, if we assume that, at any given time, all the wage-workers in a great manufacturing country are provided by the employers with work which is paid for in proportion to its full value, and if we suppose, further, that this state of things is permanent, security would be self-established. There would be no need to guarantee it.

The possibilities of insecurity, apart from those due to sickness, can arise only from one or other of two things—either that the population increases whilst the opportunities of work remain stationary, or that whilst the population is stationary the demand for work declines. In either case the result would be unemployment, unless certain businesses already prosperous could be multiplied, or businesses which were naturally declining could be artificially kept alive, or new businesses created of kinds unknown before by which the declining businesses might be replaced.

Now let it be said again that in countries sparsely occupied, and sufficiently rich in cultivable lands and pasture (such, for example, as New Zealand, with an area equal to that of England and Scotland, and a population equal to that of Glasgow), the first of these feats—namely, a multiplication of businesses already prosperous—would be easy. Every new family could, as the population increased, be provided with a new farm, and thus enabled to supply itself with the primary needs of life. But in any country which is already so thickly peopled that its inhabitants need more food— more bread, more meat, more milk—than all their acres can yield them in response to their utmost labour, certain of the inhabitants are already dependent for their very lives on the manufacture of goods exclusively designed for export. That is to say, every crust of bread they eat is the product of other nations, and it comes to them only in return for certain products of their own—such as coal, dyed fabrics, lace trimmings, machinery—which the food-producing nations want, but cannot, or cannot as yet, produce so well for themselves. If, then, the foreign demand for the manufactures of such a country declines, this will mean that the goods which it manufactures for export are failing to satisfy the desires of the food-producing countries any longer. The continued production of them would be so much labour lost; and if, for the benefit of those who have hitherto lived by producing them, new industries are to be created by which they may live still, the goods which these industries produce must be goods of a novel character, devised by inventive genius, not to supply the wants of the home consumer, but to stimulate or captivate afresh the alienated appetite of the foreign, so that the latter may be willing to give food in return for them.

By many foolish sentimentalists this fact and its consequences are altogether forgotten. Such persons are accustomed to argue that no country, equipped with the modern mechanisms of production, need necessarily suffer from any lack of employment so long as one cottage remained in it for labour to improve and amplify, or one poor man who would be the better for a new suit of Sunday clothes. But this argument ignores the entire crux of the situation. In any country which cannot, by means of its own agriculture, provide food, let us say, for more than a half of its population, the primary meaning of unemployment due to a decline in exports is, for the unemployed, this, that no employment, as matters stand, is open to them, the prosecution of which will procure for them imported food. Such food is the first necessity; for mere employment, as such, is nothing more than a name if it does not, before all things else, enable the employed to eat. If thousands of English workers had hitherto made their living by producing cloth of some special tint for America, and getting bread and meat in return for it, and if the Americans come to want this cloth no longer because they could get a cloth which they liked better from Germany, how would the English unemployed be profited should some socialist sage tell them that, instead of working to get food from America, they might make any number of things, which were not food, for themselves? To such a consoler men in·this plight would answer, "We ask you for beef, and you tell us to enlarge our kitchens. We ask you for bread, for tea; and what you offer is a double supply of trousers."

However a state such as that of England was organised—whether production was controlled, as now, by many private employers, or, as socialists propose, by the directors of a great national trust, the crucial difficulty would in this case be the same. The directors would have to devise, by an exercise of the constructive imagination, a variety of new commodities, together with the machinery for making them, which commodities would so titillate the fancy of food-producing workers in America or elsewhere that they would, for the sake of securing them, be willing to send food to England which English workers could not produce at home.

Here we have a task which, in England or in any country whose home-grown foodstuffs cannot keep pace with the population, might any day prove impossible; and no scheme of insurance—no contrivance for providing continuous work for all—could, under all circumstances, render its achievement certain. Thus, except in such countries as have within their own borders reserves of agricultural land which are still waiting to be developed as the needs of the population demand, assured continuity of work for wage-earners of all capacities can at best be only partial. But this is true, not of the wage-earners only; it is true of the employers also. No particular business or class of businesses, however great, or however flourishing to-day, could by any system of insurance be rendered secure in perpetuity. Unemployment and ruin, so far as their present occupations are concerned, would always be possible for masters and men alike. Of all occupations, the most indestructible is agriculture, which can never perish so long as mankind endures. It may, however, dwindle in this or in that locality; and of other businesses even the greatest may be locally, or even universally, destroyed. What system of insurance could have secured perennial prosperity for the owners of stage coaches when once the railway had begun to outdo the road? What system of insurance could possibly perpetuate the fortunes of the Standard Oil Trust when, as will probably happen before the end of the twentieth century, not a well in all America has a drop of petrol left in it? But beyond the inherent insecurity of individual businesses there always lies an insecurity of a more comprehensive kind. This is the insecurity of the corporate fortunes of States. What system of insurance could have rendered the trade perpetual which enriched Venice and Florence when the Doges wedded the Adriatic, and the Pitti Palace was the home of a private citizen?

Complete security, then, either for wages or profits,

or even security from the effects of all recurring vicissitudes, is no less impossible for the individual wage-earner than it is for the individual employer. It is no less impossible for the employer than it is for the State or nation, and a recognition of this fact is very necessary as an antidote to a certain childish idea with which sentimentalists are apt to besot themselves. Thus a writer, in many ways remarkable for sound judgment, has observed, with regard to England, that "we (the English) have given, it may be, too much thought to wealth—that we should, on the whole, be happier and better men if we had less wealth, and more open air and elbow-room; but we have," he proceeds, "got the wealth. Here it is as a fact, and our business is to make the best use we can of it." Persons who use such language as this are living in a land of dreams. To their eyes the wealth of a country like modern England resembles a marble column, which will stand up erect for ever when once placed on its pedestal. What it really resembles is a column of water forced into the air by the action of complex and unresting mechanisms— mechanisms which a careless or hostile blow might dislocate, and any dislocation of which would cause the column to collapse. All modern wealth, in short, in proportion as it is great is essentially artificial and precarious. This must never be forgotten. So long, however, as in any given country such wealth lasts—so long as it exhibits no serious symptoms of a decline likely to be permanent, or of any permanent failure to keep pace with the population, and so long as it is subject only to local and temporary fluctuations—assurance for the wage-earners that opportunities of work shall be continuous is a condition which, unlike the fantastic ideals of socialism, is capable of being practically approached to the advantage of all parties, and the disadvantage of none. It is capable of being approached in the large, if limited, sense, that wages might, by some system of insurance, be rendered not less secure than the profits of the employers, if the employers are taken as a whole, and more secure than the profits of any one employer individually.

If we start, then, with a scheme of wages which are,

from the minimum upwards, largely in excess of anything which the wage-earners could produce for themselves by their own faculties only, we may go on to say
that assured opportunities of earning them, and a consequent security of livelihood for the household of every
willing worker, are conditions susceptible of being established, if not with absolute completeness, yet at all
events with a completeness sufficient, so far as material
things are concerned, to render the wage-earner's lot,
under a system of industrial oligarchy, incomparably
ampler, and at the same time more secure, than it could
be under any other. Further, if to these material conditions we add the provision of opportunities for exceptional talent to develop itself and achieve for its
possessors rewards in the way of wages and status which
are commensurate with its proved value; and, finally,
if we add to this a recognition of the life of each man as
a moral end in itself, and deserving of respect and sympathetic consideration accordingly, we may say of such
conditions that the natural tendency of the great majority of men would, if no difficulty exists which has not
yet been taken into account, be to accept them with
instinctive acquiescence, not as perfect, yet, at all
events, as the best possible.

A difficulty, however, does exist, or rather two difficulties, both of them purely mental, by which, if not
removed, the development of such acquiescence, natural
otherwise, would be impeded. We will now go on to
consider what these difficulties are.

CHAPTER III

MANY of the bitterest resentments of which human beings are conscious have their origin in ideas, not in facts as known to them by direct experience; and the primary cause of that discontent or unrest so widely prevalent amongst the wage-earners of the modern world is essentially an idea, which agitators, since the days of Marx, have made it their business to disseminate. This is the idea that wages, whatever their amount may be, never represent in full the value of the work which the wage-earner has himself performed. Thus, whether his wages be absolutely large or small, he is taught to feel that he is being cheated, even though he may not feel that he is being starved. So long as a fixed idea of this kind possesses him, no conditions will content him with which the employer is associated. However advantageous otherwise such conditions may seem to be, he will look on them as so many devices for distracting his attention from the thefts of which he is the constant victim. If, however, wages should be such that, universally and beyond dispute, they represent not less than the worth of his work, but more, all ground for pre-condemning his conditions generally would be gone; and if only one other condition were added, he would be in a position to appraise them fairly in accordance with their true value. The other condition is that, not only his wages shall be worth more than his own work, but that this fact shall be also clearly known by himself; and the question is, How shall he be made to know it?

Here is one difficulty, but it does not stand alone. Let us suppose that this is surmounted. Let us suppose the typical wage-earner to be fully convinced that, as a matter of objective fact, his own wage (we will say the recognised minimum) is actually greater than the value of what he himself produces, that it is the largest wage which, for a man like himself, is practicable, and that he would not gain, but would lose, by any revolutionary change. It is, however, one thing for a man to accept a principle as such, and quite another to be satisfied with its particular application to himself. A man, for example, arriving late at a restaurant, may accept, without actual protest, the best bit of fish that is left; but if, having dreamed of salmon, he has to put up with a sprat, he might not be the better inclined to think the sprat delicious by learning that there was on the premises no other fish but an eel. With regard to any given wage, and a minimum wage especially, men of a certain temper might find themselves in the same predicament. They might know such a wage to be the largest that was for themselves possible, and yet, if it failed to provide them with as much as their imaginations demanded, this knowledge, instead of allaying their discontent, might embitter it.

Now, an impracticable mood of this kind, known by its victims to be impracticable, might, if things were left to take their natural course, remain a disease peculiar to a naturally morbid few; but amongst the very conditions which have here been specified as essential to a sane content is one by which this disease might be artificially propagated. The condition here in question is the provision of special opportunities, firstly for the educational development, and subsequently for the practical exercise of exceptional talent, wherever such talent may exist—a provision which would not only recognise the claims of ambitious passion, but would also tend to act as a standing means of inflaming it. The very idea of equal opportunity— every argument advanced in support of it—is an appeal to the spirit, not of content, but of discontent. It does not, indeed, involve the suggestion that a given minimum wage, or any given wage in excess of it, is otherwise than sufficient for a large number of people. On the contrary, a minimum with which large classes must content themselves is practically its first assumption. The idea of equalised opportunity is an idea which makes its appeal, not to any class as a whole, but to each of the units who compose the class; and beginning with those who at any time happen to earn the minimum, what it says to each in a quasi-whisper is this: " The minimum represents a lot which ought to content the great mass of your fellows; but, in this way or in that, your efficiency is appreciably greater than theirs. The lot which contents them ought not to content *you!* and your one object should be, by hook or by crook, to escape from it.''

Now, so far as men are concerned who, ambitious of ampler fortunes than those which were theirs at starting, actually possess the abilities by which these ampler fortunes can be created, the individual ambitions which it is the object of equalised opportunity to inflame are forces of triple utility. They bring content through their results to the ablest of the citizens themselves. They promote general content by demonstrating to the citizens generally that all effective effort is sure of its due reward; and, finally, such ambitions are so many contributions to the forces—industrial, military or intellectual—on which the wealth, the security and the civilisation of any complex modern State depend.

But ambition, when unaccompanied by commensurate powers of achievement, is a malady fatal to the peace of the ambitious men themselves, and injurious to the society of which they form a part. If the son of a ploughman should possess a potential genius which would, if developed, and applied by him as a great director of agriculture, enable the soil of his country to double its yield of corn, to encourage in a man like this the hope of exchanging his father's cottage for a palace would be not only to satisfy the desires of the man himself; it would be, at the same time, to confer on his country a benefit which no private fortune, however large, could repay. But to encourage similar hopes in the sons of all ploughmen indiscriminately would merely cause them to look down with contempt on a lot which they could not better, which they would else have accepted as natural, and which must; moreover, be always the lot of a considerable portion of mankind. The indiscriminate stimulation of ambition, in the case of nine

men out of ten, would be to blight their lives with a
purely artificial disappointment, and to stigmatise with
the sign of failure half the necessary occupations of the
world.

If, then, we assume a system of wages to be established which, regard being had to the total product of a
nation, and to the inequalities of the productive units,
represents for the wage-earners generally the amplest
material conditions which are for them, in their several
degrees, possible, these material conditions must, if they
are to produce content, be accompanied by two others,
which are non-material or subjective. One is a certain
knowledge on the part of the wage-earners generally
with regard to the facts and forces which the industrial
system embodies, and on which the extent and limits
of its productive power depends. The other is a moral
adjustment by the wage-earners, whether as groups or
as individuals, of their several desires or expectations
to the best lot which is possible in each particular case.
And here we come to the question of how these two
essentially subjective conditions—namely, a knowledge
of certain objective facts, and an adjustment of expectations to circumstances—are to be secured.

The general answer to this question is obvious. They
must be secured, if they can be secured at all, by certain
processes of education; and these will be of two kinds.
One process will be that of imparting knowledge, which
is very largely statistical, whilst all of it relates to
matters of a kind more or less precise. The other,
which may seem more difficult because it is more vague,
may be described as a training of the imagination.

Of these two educational processes, let us consider the
process of instruction as to definite facts first.

The general character of the facts with which such
instruction would concern itself may be indicated by
a few examples.

The first question which the typical wage-earner will
be inclined to ask is this: "By what primary conditions
is the wage which I earn, or am likely to earn, limited?"
If we suppose this question to have been put by a citizen
of the United Kingdom at the beginning of the twentieth
century, the facts which would have to be imparted to

him as the basis of a rational answer would, before all others, be these : The total product, or income, of the United Kingdom at the time, together with the income per inhabitant which this total represents. Then, for purposes of comparison, would come similar facts relating to other countries, and to the United Kingdom itself at other periods of a more or less recent past. A knowledge of such outstanding facts would put him in a position to appreciate one which he would readily recognise as bearing on his own situation. This is the fact that, at the beginning of the twentieth century, the actual average wage of the workers of the United Kingdom was incomparably greater than that which in many European countries, and even in the United Kingdom itself a couple of generations earlier, could have fallen to the lot of any body had the total income of such countries been divided equally amongst all.

A knowledge of facts like these would enable him to appreciate another—namely, that so many workers of average capacity being given, their possibilities of material welfare vary in accordance with conditions which are altogether external to themselves. He would recognise this fact as one which demands explanation; and his mind would be open to an understanding of what these conditions are—such, for example, as the application, more or less comprehensive, of the exceptional talents of the few to the task of directing the co-operative efforts of the many.

Further, in the case of such countries as the United Kingdom, the United States and Prussia, the statistical records of which are sufficiently exact for the purpose, definite information might be given him as to index facts such as the following :—the total of the wages and salaries of the workers employed by masters, the earnings of independent workers like small shopkeepers and professional men on the one hand, and of the larger employers and of the rich generally on the other.[1]   And

---

[1] The super-tax returns for the United Kingdom now give precise information as to the number and aggregate amount of all groups of incomes exceeding £3000. Many of the absurd ideas current with regard to the rich would be reduced to sobriety by the dissemination of definite knowledge as to these details.

to such outstanding facts there might, as occasion required, be added others which have constantly been subjects of wild discussion—for example, the amounts of income which are severally represented by land-rent taken as a whole, by the annual increment in the rental value of building-sites, and the quasi-rent received by the owners of coal and minerals.

It may be thought that any popular education with regard to facts like these would fail to be effective for the two following reasons. One is the likelihood that the facts, however presented, would be denounced by many as inaccurate, or at least as unfairly selected with the object of suggesting conclusions desired by some one party. The other reason is that, as a part of any possible curriculum, an exposition of these facts would, for most teachers, be difficult, and would therefore have little influence on the tempers and opinions of the taught.

But there is ample evidence to show that neither of these objections is valid.

In the first place, as to the facts themselves, there is a very considerable number of them, and these of the first importance, which, though not popularly known, are recorded almost as accurately as the distance from New York to Liverpool. Such, for example, are the incomes of certain great countries; the number of persons commonly called "the rich"; and the ratio of the aggregate income of such persons to the whole. Such, also, are the fractions of the whole which are represented by land-rent, by "unearned increment," and by royalties paid to owners in respect of minerals such as iron ore and coal. Facts such as these, attested by direct records, not by conjectures or estimates, would, if generally known, constitute so many sign-posts, by which popular thought and expectation would be warned off from the regions of fantastic guess-work, and guided at least in a more or less right direction. Nor need such facts be too complex or numerous for an intelligent teacher to communicate, or an average pupil to understand. They need not be more complex or numerous than the salient facts of geography which are taught, and found generally intelligible in any national school. They would enlighten a man's conception of the social possibilities of his life very much as the outlines shown on a geographical chart enlighten his conceptions of his own place on the globe.

If any one doubts whether a correct popular education with regard to facts like these would tend to exert an influence such as that which is here predicted, his doubts may be set at rest by the demonstrative evidence of history. He need merely consider the influence which, with a contrary object, has constantly been, and is constantly being exerted, by education, incorrect and distorted, but otherwise of the same order. The earliest Manifesto of the socialist party in England began with the words, "Educate, Educate, Educate," and then went on to explain that the great and primary fact which a socialist education would have to bring home to the people was the fact that the manual labourers—the sole and only begetters of all the wealth of the country— received only "three-thirteenths" of what they themselves produced. Socialists, indeed, from the days of Marx onwards—herein exhibiting the soundest practical sense—have recognised statistical education as the most potent means of appealing to the passions which they desire to rouse.

Let us take two signal examples. Of all the intellectual leaders of the modern socialist movement, two men—a German Jew and a Californian—stand out from the rest in respect of their powers of exposition, and of the world-wide influence they have exercised over the tempers and the imagination of multitudes. One of these is Marx himself, the other is Henry George; and, apart from the merits of their exposition, which was the mere vehicle or instrument of their teaching, the teaching of each was influential for the sole and simple reason that it culminated in a passionate insistence on an alleged statistical fact. The alleged fact was this, that, in every progressive country, the classes who produce all wealth are robbed of four-fifths or three-fourths of their products by a class absolutely idle, and that consequently the producers ought by rights to get from three to four times as much as they actually get now. The Marxian doctrine in this respect has been here examined already, and even by serious socialists his statistical arithmetic is now denounced as preposterous. The Georgian argument, though leading to a like conclusion, differed from that of Marx in one important particular. According to Marx, the robbers who reduced the masses to beggary were the owners of industrial capital. According to George, the capitalists were extremely respectable persons. The real criminals were the landlords, who robbed, not only the productive wage-earners, but the no less productive owners of industrial capital along with them. This conclusion was deduced by George from an assumption which was, according to him, of universal validity, that in proportion as the income of any country increases, the rent of crude land, as distinct from the rent of improvements, forms an ever-increasing fraction of the total, eating up "the earnings of capital as well as the wages of labour," until nothing is left for the majority but a residue just sufficient for the bare support of life. Now if anything in the world is capable of being proved by evidence, one such thing as this :—that the basic assumption on which the whole fabric of George's reasoning rests is altogether a delusion. In Great Britain, for example, which George cited as the classical illustration of its truth, land-rent has, as the national income increased, been a relatively dwindling, not an increasing, fraction of it. At the beginning of the nineteenth century it was 14 per cent. of the total. A century later it was barely as much as 4 per cent. The Georgian proposition that in all progressive countries 75 or 80 per cent. of the entire national product is stolen from the nation by a small group of landlords is no more true than the Marxian proposition that a similar fraction is stolen by a small group of capitalists.

Emanating, as they do, from the two most important thinkers who have moulded revolutionary thought in the course of the nineteenth century, it is amusing to note, with regard to these two propositions, not only that both of them are contradicted by definitely ascertainable facts, but also that each proposition is a vehement contradiction of the other. The point, however, which mainly concerns us here is that Marx and George alike exercised a profound and disturbing influence on the judgment and temper of multitudes, and that they did so by a process of education, the practical object and the practical effect of which was to create a popular belief in the actuality of an alleged statistical fact, the alleged fact being in each case a preposterous falsehood.

To these signal illustrations it may be interesting to add two others, on a smaller scale, but essentially the same in kind.   George's doctrine that land-rent in every progressive country necessarily eats up most of any growing national income, and that thus, in Great Britain especially, the only rich people are the peers and the country squires, has never been practically accepted even by any radical government; but many years after his death the British Government accepted two minor doctrines implied in it, and won, by so doing, the frantic applause of all its most extreme supporters.   One of these minor doctrines related, not to land-rent as a whole, but to the annual increase of the rent of the sites of urban buildings.   The other related to the income, derived in the form of royalties, from minerals, and more particularly coal, which was described by an eloquent statesman as the basic capital of the country.   On both these kinds of income—on royalties and on "unearned increment"— the government determined to levy a special duty; and both these kinds of income were presented to the public imagination as quantities so enormous that visions were rife everywhere of the almost illimitable revenue which a tax on them would extract from the rich for betterment of the population generally.   Both these kinds of income proved, in reality, to be quantities so minute that the duty imposed on them was hardly worth the trouble of collecting.[1]

[1] If any one year be taken between the years 1900 and 1915, the portion of it which consisted of the unearned increment of site-values was between one three-hundredth and one four-hundredth part of it. So much might have been easily discovered beforehand, by collating the returns of the Commissioners of Inland Revenue with other kindred evidences.   The over-estimate of the total of mineral royalties was much more pardonable.   The then Chancellor of the Exchequer was right in describing the coal-deposits of Great Britain as its main capital asset; and the fact that royalties (or the profits) on this capital are only a few millions is due to the fact, not at once apparent, that coal-deposits differ from other property, such as the surface of the land, in this way.   If so many acres of land are let for a house and garden, the occupant enjoys

The curious ebullitions of popular temper and expectation which these essays in sensational finance excited were due altogether to what was virtually a process of education—an education wildly fallacious—as to two statistical facts—namely, the actual amounts of the two kinds of income in question. If with regard to either of these two cases the statistical facts involved had been matters of general, and more or less accurate, knowledge, the fiscal policy of the government might have roused public attention, and elicited many sober, perhaps many sound, judgments; but it would not have roused, as it did, storms of popular passion which, so long as they lasted, made sound judgment impossible.

If, then, a false education with regard to statistical facts can produce an effect so profound on the popular temper in one way, a correct education will, we may safely assume, produce an effect no less profound, in another. Finally, since experience has shown that a deliberate and effective system of inaccurate education is practicable, it stands to reason that a system of accurate education relating to the same order of facts is no mere academic dream, but is what would be called in America a " practical proposition " likewise.[1] It would not involve—for this would be indeed impracticable—the general inculcation of any one economic theory. To imagine such a system as this would be no less absurd than to imagine a national system of education in politics, which would inculcate blind adherence to one particular politician. The kind of education here indicated—and it is only a

---

the entire value of the land—its convenience of situation and its amenity —at once. But of the coal deposits of the country, so much only can be enjoyed from year to year as is brought to the surface ; and the larger part of it will not have been usable capital for generations.

[1] A scheme of education, precisely similar in kind to that above indicated (though relating not to economic conditions generally, but to economic conditions amongst others, as bearing on the question of war) has, since the above passage was written, been actually projected in America by President Wilson, who—it was so announced in June 1917 —" was considering the appointment of a special board, not only for the dissemination of ordinary news, but for bringing home to the people at large by a series of lectures . . . . and also by exhaustive summaries, what their vital interests, material and otherwise, in the conflict are."

part of education, if the word "education" be used in its wider sense—would bear the same relation to particular economic theories that geography bears to schemes of international policy. It would deal only with facts of a certain order, these being mainly, though not wholly, statistical; and it would leave the individual, with such facts in view, to judge of social conditions and social possibilities for himself. It would, however, if it did no more than this, create an atmosphere in which outrageous expectations and outrageous judgments would die. More particularly it would create in the earner of a just minimum wage, who belongs to any one of the richer countries of the world, a sufficiently correct idea of the advantages which he gained as a participator in the intellectualised industry of his own country to-day. It would liberate him from the belief or suspicion, which at present is the parent of unrest, that, instead of being a gainer by the existing system, he is a loser. It would enable him to recognise for himself, with his eyes open, his lot under that system as the best which was for the time possible; and, so far as knowledge and common sense are concerned, we shall have the warrant of all history for saying that the wage-earners of the modern world, from the earners of the minimum upwards, would tend to accept with content, were their judgments not otherwise disturbed, such conditions as, lying within the limits of recognised possibilities, were the best.

Such would be the case if men's judgments were not otherwise disturbed; but, whilst knowledge and common sense might tend to produce content with the best conditions, and more particularly with the amplest minimum, definitely known to be possible, the imagination, as a disturbing influence, has still to be reckoned with. A natural tendency to content, as the joint result of knowledge and common sense, being given, the mood of mind which the imagination, if improperly trained, and imaginative ambition, if indiscriminately stimulated, would naturally tend to foment, might not, indeed, disturb the conviction that the existing order of things was the best order possible, and that any revolutionary change could only be a change for the worse; but what it would do is this: it would always be prompting multitudes to resent the best as bad. It would be a mood resembling that which was tersely expressed by the distinguished but irritable scholar, Porson, when he spilled, by an untoward gesture, the contents of his ink-pot over the pages of a Greek play. This ornament of learning, having for some moments sought in vain for something on which he might vent his rage, finally astonished a friend by ejaculating, "Damn the nature of things." A society would hardly be in a condition of corporate harmony and content if any considerable section of it, whilst accepting their respective lots as unalterable parts of the nature of things, were all the while in a mood of imaginative rebellion against them; and much of the social unrest which prevails in the modern world is due, not to the fact that the conditions of the persons afflicted by it are insufficient in themselves as the material apparatus of happiness, but to the fact that the imagination of such persons, artificially inflamed or not reasonably disciplined, makes the good seem despicable by obtruding on them, as the standard of goodness, some visionary and impracticable better.

Now, to train the imagination in such a way as to adjust its suggestions to limiting facts of life may seem, at first sight, a much more difficult task than that of training mere judgment by making the facts known. Indeed, a universal adjustment of imaginative desire to facts is beyond the power of any education to accomplish. There will always be people in the world who can never produce the wealth or secure the social estimation which they obstinately imagine to be their due. But an imaginative content with facts, which is at once approximately general and sufficient for the happiness of those who have it in their hearts to be happy, is a result so far from impossible that it would, in most cases, tend to occur naturally if a false education were not at work to prevent it. That is to say, a proper training of the imagination, especially with regard to the conditions represented by the minimum wage, would have for its object, not the creation of any mood that was artificial, but the healthy development of one to which most men naturally incline.

With this object in view, such a training of the imagination would resolve itself into two parts, one of which would relate to the material circumstance of life, the other to its moral, emotional and intellectual interests.

To begin with the former, there is a certain tendency in most men, with regard to their material circumstances, to cherish an ideal somewhat more ample than any which they stand much chance of realising; and if their ideal is not taken too seriously, or if it does not exceed the possible in any very great degree, it does little or nothing to interfere with a spirit of reasonable content. But certain forces at work in the modern world express themselves in a scheme of deliberate and emphatic teaching which aims at developing this tendency to a degree so extreme and unnatural that multitudes are led to adopt, as the standard of a satisfactory life, a life equipped with appliances which, from the nature of things, are possible for a few men only, and thus to regard all lives from which such appliances are absent as lives unnaturally blighted, or deprived of adjuncts which human nature requires.

As an example of the mood resulting from this falsification of values, mention may be made of an expert who, when called on to give evidence in a law-suit relating to the cost of repainting a yacht of six hundred tons, described himself as "one of those unfortunate persons whose business is to build great yachts, not as one of the fortunate persons who own them." Now, it may fairly be said of a man who is a good sailor that, if he owns a yacht of six hundred tons he is fortunate; but if everybody who does not own one is to be looked on as unfortunate, the whole of the human race is unfortunate except a little cluster of persons whose names are comprised in a page or two of *The Yachting Calendar*, and who might dine together at the same table in the local Assembly Rooms of any small provincial town.

Another example, less extreme than this, may be cited from a book in which the author, a semi-socialist radical, living himself on large official emoluments, described the typical dwellings of the skilled artisans of England. He did not deny that their houses, situated for the most part in the outskirts of manufacturing centres, are, so far as they go, substantial, well-planned and sufficient for a decent and comfortable life; but, with a sigh of condescending pity, he described their dimensions as "tiny." Now, as compared with Buckingham Palace or Blenheim, most houses are tiny; and the houses here in question are no doubt tiny as compared with the author's own. But should one of these houses be turned into steel and wood, and placed on the upper deck of a great Atlantic liner, it would at once assume the proportions of an enormous family suite, and a rich American traveller would pay eight hundred pounds as the price of enjoying its amplitude for the inside of a week. House-space which, if none ampler were possible, would be looked on as a luxury by the most exacting of plutocrats, must, unless the popular imagination is disordered by artificial suggestion, be not "tiny," but ample, for the majority of the human race. The only sane standard, by reference to which the typical dwelling sufficient for the normal man can be measured, is not any type of dwelling which is possible for this or for that minority whose efficiencies are, to some marked degree, exceptional; but the best type of dwelling which is possible for any numerous and necessary class whose efficiencies, to speak broadly, do not exceed the average. This is a fact which most men naturally tend to recognise; and the mental disease which, by suggesting as a standard of sufficiency conditions which must always be at least relatively rare, renders the best conditions susceptible of common achievement despicable, is largely due to a deliberate campaign of education, which aims at training the imagination, not rightly, but wrongly.

This kind of mal-education (as observers in various countries and at various times have noted) is due mainly to the pathological activities, not of the masses, but of certain peculiar sections of the middle class; and that such is the case may be seen by reference to a very interesting agitation, in which, though middle-class activities were very largely concerned in it, this particular kind of mal-education was absent. This was the agitation which, beginning about the year 1880, was directed against the landlords of the mountainous parts of Scotland. The charge against the landlords was that,

for the purpose of increasing their rent-rolls, they had
evicted their tenants wholesale—their tenants who were
also their clansmen—and had converted entire counties
into playgrounds for rich sportsmen. Few agitations
have ever been based on arguments in which elements
of undoubted truth were seasoned with wilder falsehoods; but there was one fact—and this, even if somewhat exaggerated, was indisputable—which the agitators,
most of them Scotchmen, put before all others, as
familiar to them from their own experience. This was
the fact that the men who had been driven from their
homes had been one of the happiest, the healthiest and
the most contented peasantries in the world. And yet
what sort of homes were these in which so much content
sheltered itself? Compared even with those of the
poorest peasants of England, they were not only "tiny,"
but rude to an extreme degree. They were cabins whose
chimneys were mere holes in the thatch; the occupants
lived mainly on oatmeal and potatoes; and yet not
only was their lot one to which they were passionately
attached themselves, but, despite its primitive simplicity, it was proclaimed by a succession of agitators
to have been one so worthy of men as moral and social
beings that few crimes could be greater than those which
had put an end to it. Here, then, in the persons both
of the Highland peasantry themselves, and of the agitators closely connected with them who spoke with such
vehemence on their behalf, we have examples of the
mental process on which, certain material circumstances
being given, men's content with such circumstances
tends naturally to depend. It is a process consisting
of certain uses of the imagination which with most men
are instinctive, and which cause them to identify the
conditions of a satisfactory life with the best, even if
these be simple, which life with its affections and
memories has rendered to them familiar, and which the
circle of possibilities encloses within its horizon line. It
is an imaginative process the precise reverse of that by
which middle-class apostles of discontent would stimulate men to despise houses as "tiny" which have four
times as many rooms in them as the houses for which
the Highland peasantry, when compelled to leave them,

wept, and which agitators themselves belauded as homes of ideal happiness.   So far, then, as material things are concerned — and by material things is here meant primarily what is the key to the whole situation, namely, the material things purchasable by a just minimum wage for the workers of least efficiency—such training of the imagination as would be necessary to promote content with these, would be necessary, not for the purpose of creating in men any mood that is new, or over-strained, or artificial, but simply for the purpose of restoring them, as sober and sensible beings, to a mood of mind which is, to most men, natural.

But in concerning itself merely with material circumstances as such—that is to say, with such things as can be measured and bought by wages—an educational training of the imagination as a means to general content will, if it goes no further, have done but half its work. The more important half remains, and this will consist in fixing the imaginative attention and interest on those affections, passions, faiths, social excitements, recreations and other self-fruitions, which are to material circumstances what drink is to the cup that holds it, and without which a goblet of the costliest crystal in a palace would be as useless to a thirsty man as an earthenware mug in the kitchen of a "tiny" cottage.

In any case, a certain minimum of material circumstances must be given. This, in any country which is enriched by the forces of industrial oligarchy, must, let it be said again, be a minimum which fulfils, or is associated with the following primary requirements. It must represent a material lot which is not only free from physical want and, so far as may be, from the fear of it, but is also much ampler, so far as amplitude can be bought by wages, than any which the wage-earners could secure if they worked as their own masters. It must, moreover, be one which all exceptional workers shall have the means of amplifying in accordance with what their work is worth; and with these conditions must be associated a diffusion amongst the wage-earners generally of such elementary knowledge with regard to statistical facts, and the manual and mental forces on which efficient production depends, as will enable them to estimate accurately their own situation for themselves.

Should such conditions be established—and they are conditions which would subserve all interests and at the same time antagonise none—whatever is valuable and practicable in the ideals of formal socialism—ideals in themselves impossible and self-destructive—would be secured; and the causes of "industrial unrest," in so far as they are capable of being expressed in any definite terms, would be removed. We shall have an established order to which, with all its graduations of circumstance, common sense would resign itself. But if the imagination is to complete what common sense has begun, and convert resignation into an acceptance which deserves to be called content, it must not concern itself with economic circumstances alone. The interplay of oligarchic and democratic forces to which the magnitude and graduated distribution of modern wealth are due is but one manifestation of a process which is much more comprehensive; and if the imagination is really to grasp its full significance, the imagination must be trained to grasp it as part of a larger whole. When this process has been considered in all its various forms, what we shall find is this—that, as means to a certain complex end, the oligarchic principle permeates every domain of life, but that the final end itself which these oligarchic means subserve is, in its very essence, democratic—that it is a life-process in which genuine democracy at last comes into its own.

Of what, then, does this life-process consist?

BOOK VII

DEMOCRACY AND THE FINAL LIFE-PROCESS

CHAPTER I

THE MATERIAL DATA OF CONTENT

ALL life implies the will to live. This in itself can hardly be called rational, for all living things, even the lowest, possess it. If a kitten and a philosopher are thrown into deep water, both will struggle to save themselves in substantially the same way. But in man the will to live is, under normal circumstances, rational in the sense that the enjoyment of life is consciously distinguished alike from the bare fact, and from the material means, simple or elaborate, of its maintenance. The poorest peasant who can by his constant labour just provide food and firewood for himself and a single child, would, if the child died, miss it; and, looking at its empty chair, he would find that life, no matter how hard, had held for him something more than the act of laborious living. A celebrated English statesman, wealthy and highly placed, found, when his character had been blighted by the breath of malignant slander, that of all the luxuries in his bedroom one alone was of service to him, and this was the razor which he drew across his own throat.

However simple, then, or however elaborate the material appliances or adjuncts of men's lives may be, the human satisfaction to which they minister consists of a something which, in one way or another, men themselves add to them out of their own natures: and, if two words are taken so as to cover all that is implied in them, this something may be described as *social intercourse*.

It is for the sake of social intercourse that men are,

as Aristotle says of them, "gregarious or political animals." Their instinct is to live in clusters of more or less adjacent families, each family maintaining itself by applying its own industry to some particular portion of a limited geographical area. Men experience in so living the need of conformity to certain common customs; customs mature into a system of definite laws and government; and as soon as any one cluster, on coming into contact with another, arms itself, for the protection of its territory, as a single military force, the cluster becomes what is commonly called a State. But neither the military system nor the legal system nor the industrial system is an end in itself. These, taken together, are merely the shell of the nut. Social intercourse is the kernel—social intercourse or, in other words, all those affections, activities and experiences which constitute the drama of private or individual life which directly minister to its amenities, or which otherwise raise its character. The end of all political government is to regularise these. The end of all armed force is to protect them, or possibly to provide them with an ampler field for their exercise. A State which had no lovers in it would not be worth fighting for; but a State might be worth fighting for although there were no fighters in it, if the lack of fighters was due—and such for many years was the case of the United States —to geographical conditions which rendered fighters superfluous.

Social intercourse is, however, not self-supporting any more than it is self-regulating or self-protecting. It must have, as its immediate basis, an industrial system which provides it with its material appliances. It depends, therefore, for its existence and security on three processes external to itself, which are these: industrial production, political government, and the process, actual or potential, of offensive or defensive war.

Now the process of war, even amongst the simplest tribes, has always been in a large measure oligarchic. In modern warfare, which becomes ever more and more a matter of industrial as well as of military genius, the oligarchic element becomes more and more pronounced.

Political government, and industry in times of peace— both of them processes of almost pure democracy so long as States are primitively small and men primitively poor —become more and more oligarchic as States increase in size, and poverty is metamorphosed into wealth such as that of the modern world. In other words, if we consider men as agents capable of affecting the external conditions of life and of social intercourse, as distinguished from life and from social intercourse themselves, the majority of the citizens in any modern country will not only be undistinguished and obscure (as everybody must be whose talents are not exceptional); they will also be persons who in some sense are subordinates. On the other hand, the units of the minority, from the specially skilled labourers up to the higher directorates, will necessarily be persons of some sort of distinction, and in the material appliances of their lives these graduations of function and of personal efficiency will be reflected. The minimum may increase with the increase of the total produce, but between the minimum of individual circumstance and the maximum the difference, instead of decreasing, may tend to become greater. In other words, if we consider men merely as agents maintaining and amplifying, according to their several capacities, the material appliances of life, the spectacular signs of oligarchy will be more clearly apparent than the spectacular signs of democracy. But if, instead of considering men as agents whose function is to affect the external conditions of life, we consider them as participators in the social intercourse itself to which external conditions minister, the case will be reversed. The actualities of democracy will obliterate, if not the signs, yet at all events the actualities of oligarchy.

This proposition to many may no doubt seem a paradox. They may urge that, so long as absolute differences in external conditions exist, it is precisely in social intercourse that the special results of an oligarchy most sharply obtrude themselves. But persons who argue thus confuse actualities with abstractions. By a certain subconscious juggling with the ambiguous word "Society," which may mean either the State as a means, or social intercourse as an end, they come to regard the latter as a power coextensive with the former, so that social intercourse, taking place within the limits of a great nation, is, according to their conception of it, one undivided process in which all classes participate. Now if, with regard to any great and complex community, this conception of social intercourse really coincided with fact—if the members of all classes, in taking their daily pleasure, were jostled together in a kind of collective outing, the differences between class and class would, it is quite true, be not expunged but accentuated. The result would be aggressions of undesired familiarities or repulsions of them, rather than anything in the way of promiscuous concord. But in no community larger than that of a small village—in no great country of any kind—does social intercourse take such a form as this. For each individual it begins with his own family circle, and thence extends itself gradually to a larger circle of acquaintances, lovers, friends, and habitual or casual associates; and for each individual this larger but narrowly limited circle comprises the actors with whom, and with a view to whose esteem, affection or applause, that drama is played by him for the sake of which industrial oligarchies and political oligarchies exist. For each individual the number of such fellow actors, or the content of what is for him society, is thus strictly limited for the very simple reason that, except in a public capacity, no one human being can be known as a personality or a personage to more than a number, comparatively small, of others. Hence, so far as social intercourse is concerned, any large community, such as a great nation, automatically divides itself into a vast number of small ones. These sub-communities, consisting of kindred, friends, and acquaintances, will differ in respect of the number of units comprised in each. We may, however, say roughly that the number of persons with whom, on an average, each man lives on terms of familiar intercourse will not be more than some two hundred and fifty. Each of such communities, as a part of the body politic, will resemble a complex cell having a private social life, more or less separate, of its own; and a great national community, such as that of France or the United Kingdom, will, so far as social

intercourse is concerned, be an aggregate of some two
hundred thousand cells or sub-communities such as
these, though the national life, industrial, political and
military, which protects and subserves the interests of
each social cell, is one.

By what, then, is the composition of each of these
social cells determined? It is determined partly by
family ties and familiarities, partly by continued pro-
pinquity and the physical possibilities of more or less
frequent companionship, partly by similarities of wealth
and the habits of life dependent on it, and largely, also,
by similarities of taste and of moral temperament.
Thus, if we take " society " in the aristocratic sense of
the word, as a small group of persons distinguished by
wealth, rank or lineage, there is a constant tendency
amongst its members, despite these similarities, to
separate into what are called " sets," such as an ultra-
fashionable set, an intellectual set, a racing set, and so
on. But, whatever may be its principle of cohesion, the
members of each sub-community are, for purposes of
social intercourse, equals.[1] Their intercourse is an
exhibition of what they are, not of what they do or have
done. It is an interplay of lateral varieties, not a
parade of vertical inequalities. A statesman, when in
society he is talking to a charming woman, desires to
exhibit himself not as a statesman, but as a man. A
woman famous for her exploits in the world of County
Councils would far rather be taken in society as a woman
of personal charm than as a walking index to her own
Minutes on Education. An artisan obscure in a factory
may, in his social life, be the hero of a woman's affections. Anybody in social life may become unique for
somebody. Within the limits, then, of each of those
countless sub-communities beyond which no social intercourse of an intimate kind is possible, social intercourse
is democratic in this fundamental sense, that each unit
taking part in the process is a unit of free and equal
influence in respect of the object which each unit has in

[1] Thus Louis XV, when he played the part of private host in the
country, placed his guests at dinner, on the first day of the visit,
according to their technical rank, but afterwards according to royal
and other personal preferences.

view—that object being to make the best he can of his own personal character either as a husband, a father, a lover, a wit, a conversationalist, a boon companion, or a man of respected judgment.

But this process of social intercourse is democratic, not only in the sense that the units of each sub-community who play a part in it act as equals in respect of the process itself. It is democratic in the sense that the units, taken collectively, also constitute a democracy the force of which is external. We shall find that the units, in using, as the material basis of their lives, those industrial activities to which, in any rich country, the principle of oligarchy is essential, not only make use of the services which the industrial oligarchy offers them, but also determine ultimately what the nature of these services shall be. Nor does this hold good of the industrial oligarchy only. It holds good of other services also, which are no less essential than industry to civilised social intercourse, which are likewise oligarchic in origin, likewise democratic in result, and to which reference, except by implication, has, in our present argument, not yet been made. These are the processes, intellectual, æsthetic and moral, the results of which are familiar to us as knowledge, philosophy, science, art, religion. Each of these results which, as elements of civilisation, are no less important than an ample minimum wage, has everywhere a history from which the action of oligarchy is inseparable; and yet, as an element of civilisation, each is what it is—and is what it is only—through the action of forces which are, in their essence, democratic.

Let us consider first the influence of the democratic principle, as embodied in social intercourse, on the industrial oligarchy which, in a civilised modern country, provides it with the larger part of the material adjuncts of its existence.

A rudimentary illustration of this influence may be found in the relation of social intercourse to architecture. Social intercourse always begins with the family. It does so because human beings are all of them born and reared in essentially the same way; and the spontaneous unity of the family everywhere finds expression in the separate house or hut, which primitively is a single room. As social civilisation advances—as comforts and decencies are added to bare necessaries—the spontaneous habits of the family find expression in the house, larger and more elaborate, which has two rooms or several. That is to say, in proportion as the productive powers of the architect or the builder increase, the democracy of social intercourse exercises a more elaborate control over the final uses to which these powers shall be put. Wealth, as embodied in a house, becomes a commodity of a more elaborate kind.

Here is a fact which most thinkers wholly fail to recognise. They fail to recognise that as, under the influence of an industrial oligarchy, the volume of wealth increases, wealth, taken as a whole, undergoes in one respect a fundamental change in character. To this imperfection of thought attention has been called already, in connection with Mr. Shaw's exposition of what, in respect of the distribution of wealth, ideal socialism or social democracy means. The ideal object of socialism is, he says, to secure for all an absolute equality in respect of material circumstances, which equality, as measurable by "coin" or some other medium of exchange, will be for each individual "the quotient of the national income divided by the number of the population." That is to say, he, and those who reason like him, think of the income of a nation as though it were a sort of homogeneous fluid such as water, any one gallon of which would be throughout of the same substance as any other. And in the case of a country so primitively poor that the entire income of the inhabitants was but just sufficient to keep them all alive, such a conception would be no doubt correct. It is, however, correct in the case of such a country only.

Even in a country whose condition is one of primitive poverty, income, as measured by money, is a mere sign or abstraction. Its substance is a certain quantity of certain specified goods; and all incomes the substance of which does not consist solely of irreducible necessaries, are divisible into two elements—necessary goods and superfluous goods. Now in any given country or climate, the goods which are necessary for a life just above the level of crude physical hardship are practically constant in respect both of kind and quantity. Hence, in proportion as industry becomes more and more productive, and the income per head of the total population increases, the substance of the increment consists wholly of goods which are, to a greater or less degree, superfluous. The element which consists of necessaries, though it cannot from the nature of things suffer any diminution absolutely, is always decreasing relatively, and the element which consists of superfluities is always becoming a larger fraction of the total. Thus, if we take for example the average income per head of the population of England, firstly as it was at the beginning of the nineteenth century, and secondly as it was at the beginning of the twentieth, we may say, with very fair accuracy, that superfluities at the later date made up at least four-fifths of it, and at the earlier not more than a quarter.

Now the enormous increase in income which, typified by the case of England, has taken place since the beginning of the nineteenth century, and which is primarily due to the forces of industrial oligarchy, does not necessarily mean the production of better goods, for the products of the self-directed craftsman are in some respects still unequalled. The most obvious function of the oligarchy has been to increase their number; but it has, in increasing their number, performed another function also, which, though less obvious, is morally of far greater importance. Besides increasing the number or the volume of the products, it has, to an indefinite extent, diversified them. Thus, to take, for example, such ornaments as are used to decorate chimneypieces— let us say china figures of Nelson—it has not only multiplied china Nelsons and cheapened them, thus putting them within the reach of an increasing number of people. It has supplemented the Nelsons by a hundred other figures of human or other creatures—such as bishops, nymphs, missionaries, milkmaids, cows, kittens—which are offered to the taste of the purchasing public as alternatives, and from which each purchaser will make his own selection.

Thus the two elements of which a typical income in

any rich country is composed differ not only in the fact
that the one consists of necessaries which represent men's
needs, and the other of superfluities which represent
men's tastes, but also in the further fact that, whereas
the goods which satisfy men's needs are not only constant in quantity, but constant in kind also, the things
which gratify their tastes are, if considered generally,
never the same from one ten years to another, and are,
if considered particularly, never the same in the case of
any two individuals.

Apart from certain durable things like houses, the real
income of a nation in any given year is comprised in the
goods of all kinds and descriptions offered for sale in all
the shops of the country; and the actual substance of
each individual income will consist of such of these goods
as each person, or each head of a household, brings
home for use in the course of a year's shopping. Let us
suppose, for example, that the necessaries and superfluities, which form the real income of a nation for some
particular year, are represented by four groups of commodities displayed on a shop's counter. Each of these
groups, let us say, is made up of ten units, and the
price of every unit is, let us say, five shillings. The first
group consists of bread, and represents all necessaries.
The three others, representing all superfluities, consist
respectively of ten lengths of green silk ribbon, ten
boxes of chocolates, and ten books—copies of the works
of Shakespeare. Here we have forty units which, at
five shillings apiece, represent a money value of ten
pounds in all. And now let us suppose that ten women,
representing the nation, each with a pound in her pocket,
which ten pounds represent the national income of the
year, enter the shop for the purpose of converting this
money-income into real income or goods. Each begins
with converting five shillings of her pound into bread.
She then converts three similar sums respectively into a
length of green silk ribbon, a box of chocolates, and a
copy of the works of Shakespeare. When these transactions have been accomplished, the conversion of money
into real income will be complete; and the two will
coincide in the very practical sense that every one of
these women will get, in return for every five shillings

spent by her, goods which minister equally to her own Needs and Tastes.

Such will have been the case in the particular year supposed by us. But now let us vary the supposition. Let us suppose that ten years later all these conditions repeat themselves, one alone excepted. Let us suppose that four groups of precisely similar goods are at the same counter offered at the same old prices, and that the same ten women with the same sums of money in their pockets enter the shop for the purpose of converting their money incomes into real incomes as before; but let us suppose further that their Tastes, though not their Needs, have in the interval changed. The women will begin as before with buying up all the necessaries—that is to say, the bread. Money income and real income will still so far coincide; but as soon as they turn to the superfluities, the sort of thing which will happen will be this. On asking for ribbons, they will say, "What we want are blue, or red, or rose de Barri, or orange"; and since none but green are to be had, they will turn away in disdain from them. When they come to the chocolates, they will treat them in the same way, declaring their palates to be so delicate that any sweetmeat but sugared violets nauseates them. When they come to the works of Shakespeare, they will say, "What we want is Ibsen. We would none of us have a volume of Shakespeare's works as a gift." Each of these women accordingly will go home with her bread, and with nothing else but fifteen useless shillings—useless for the simple reason that nothing she wants can be anyhow got in exchange for them. Money income, and the prices of all the articles offered, will be just the same as they were ten years ago; but the real income of these ten women as a whole will have sunk in the proportion of ten pounds to fifty shillings, and the real income of each will have sunk in the proportion of twenty shillings to five.

Now, should such a situation as this arise in actual life, the great object of the producers of these useless superfluities would be to see that such a situation never arose again. If we take the producers to be represented by one man—a "universal provider"—who is the oligarchic head of a single manufacturing business, he would set himself with the utmost vigilance to discover from moment to moment what the changing and diversified tastes of the purchasing public are. It is true that before a taste developed itself for any particular superfluity—a new kind of wall-paper, a new ribbon, a new sweetmeat, or a new anything—he might have to produce samples of each article first, so as to judge of the number of persons to whose Taste each article will appeal; but it will depend on these persons themselves whether, or amongst what number of them, a taste for this article or that is really elicited or no. Thus, whilst the actual process of producing the income of any rich nation, such an income consisting mainly of superfluities, is one in which the democratic principle is subservient to the oligarchic, the process of determining from year to year what the actual substance of this income shall be is one in which the oligarchic principle is essentially subservient to the democratic; and the extent to which democracy, in this final stage of industrial process, is supreme, can be best appreciated by re-considering the necessary limitations to which it is subject when applied to political questions other than such as are primitively and crudely simple.

Even thinkers like Mill and Rousseau admit that there is one obvious reason why, in any complex State, complete political democracy, or government in accordance with the will of each, is impossible. From their point of view this does not consist in the fact, which has been elucidated in the present work, that masses of average men, unless they are guided by the few, have as to complex questions no common will at all. It consists in the fact that of any large population the judgments of one section, however completely they may be unified, are always likely or liable to differ from those of the remainder, so that government by democracy must always mean in practice, not government by all, but government by the larger number, even though, as may any day happen, the larger exceeds the less by a single voter only, and nearly half the population be governed not *by* its will but against it. If this argument be translated in terms of the foregoing illustrations—if we think of voters as customers, and of political measures relating to questions fiscal, electoral, international, and so forth, as commodities which the government has to manufacture and sell, any government, however democratic, will be a manufacturer who, of all the measures which might be devised and supplied as alternative solutions of any one of such questions as these, can supply his customers simultaneously with one, and with one only. If a hundred of his customers demand of him, and get, Free Trade, he cannot simultaneously supply Protection to ninety-nine. He cannot simultaneously be selling a declaration of war against some foreign Power to one man and a treaty of peace with the same Power to another, or manhood suffrage at one counter, and bi-sexual suffrage at the next. In short, any number of customers which is less than half the whole will have to put up with measures which they one and all detest, or will rather have to swallow them as though they were so much medicine.

But when we turn from democracy as applied to political government to democracy as determining the composition of the real national income, all these difficulties disappear. If forty women are asking for blue ribbons at a draper's, and three little groups of twenty are asking respectively for yellow, green or magenta, each woman, let her tastes be what they may, can be satisfied in the same five minutes. That is to say, the units of a nation, as considered in the act of converting its money income, or its potential income, into real income for the purpose of direct enjoyment, is a democracy in two senses : firstly in the sense that, as a court of final power, it imposes its orders collectively on the entire oligarchy of production; and secondly in the sense that each of its units individually is, for this particular purpose, a unit of equal influence, obtaining goods which correspond to his or to her own will, but not influencing or being influenced by the wills of any other persons.

This fact that each money income, except in so far as it consists of a few absolute necessaries, consists of goods selected from an indefinite number of alternative superfluities, means a great deal more than at first sight may appear. It means that out of a multitude of incomes—

such, for example, as a fixed minimum wage, which are
as money incomes of exactly the same amount—no two,
when converted into real income, will be the same. As
representing in a material sense the conditions of social
intercourse, they will within wide limits be more ample
or less ample—will, according to any reasonable standard,
represent plenty or poverty—according to the character
of each individual recipient.

Vivid illustrations of this fact were given incidentally
by several English journalists who, during the course of
certain coal-strikes in the year 1916, were deputed to
visit various colliery districts with a view to ascertaining
the causes of "industrial unrest" amongst the miners.
Of these districts a feature which attracted the attention
of all the inquirers equally was the curious difference, in
the way of aspect, upkeep and furniture, between the
houses of men or families known to be earning substantially the same wages. Of the numerous cases cited
the following will suffice as types. One of these homes
was on one occasion the scene of such absolute destitution that the mother of the family had appealed to an
opulent lady in the neighbourhood for a few shillings
to buy bread for herself and her starving children. The
cause of the destitution was this. The husband—a man
who had been earning seventy shillings a week—had
converted a quarter of his money income into a high-
power motor-bicycle, his first exploit on which had been
to run into a cart, injure the horse and driver, wreck the
bicycle, and kill himself into the bargain. His family
might have lived for several months in plenty on an
income which, by his own acts, he had converted into
a broken toy. Another house, incredibly bare and dirty,
was the home of a man and his two sons. Their joint
money-income exceeded three hundred pounds a year.
Four-fifths of their real income consisted of port wine—
the strongest and most expensive they could get. Of
this fluid, between every Saturday morning and every
Sunday night, they managed to consume eighteen bottles
amongst them, with nothing to show for it on Monday
but the headaches it had left behind. A third house,
which, though much less squalid than this, was in no
way superior to that of an agricultural labourer, was the

home of a family whose money-income was larger still. Of what, then, did the bulk of its real income consist? From a very dingy ceiling much of it hung in the form of expensive hams. Part of it, on a broken dish, took the form of an incredibly huge beefsteak. A part of it, yet more striking, was a pile of hot-house peaches, at two shillings apiece, on the middle of a bare deal table. From a slatternly fourth house, which seemed to be in danger of collapsing, a large real income emerged on the person of a dazzling female—an income consisting of silken skirts and stockings, laces, high-heeled shoes, a sprinkling of promiscuous jewellery, and a hat of elaborate plumage surmounting a powdered face. At a fifth house, not far distant and not unlike in structure, the inquirer was greeted on a scrupulously whitened doorstep by a woman who looked the embodiment of everything clean and healthy. The glow of her hearth within was reflected on cheerful walls, on her dresser with its spotless plates, and on dustless chairs and tables. Beyond the general living-room the housewife displayed to her visitor an inner world of wonders—of carpets and sofas, of ornaments under glass shades, a gramophone, a piano, and a number of memorial cards on which family affection had lavished the costliest and most appropriate frames. Everything exhaled a spirit, not merely of content and comfort, but of self-gratulation also. "I think," said the woman, "I may give myself the pleasure of boasting that there is not a floor in this house off which you might not eat your dinner."

Now, the money-income of this woman and her family, with their spotless house and their crowd of simple comforts, was less than that of the three semi-destitute drunkards; but who would not say that, in even a mere material sense, their real income was beyond comparison greater? A family with a money-income of only £200, if this is converted into healthy and well-served food, decent clothes and a house replete with comfort, is incomparably richer than a family whose money-income is £300, if all but £50 of it is converted into intoxicating drink, which is swallowed in a dirty hovel by men in rags and tatters, and which, instead of inspiring social intercourse, kills it.

The moral of this fact, and of these illustrations of it, is as follows. In any rich modern country, let a definite sum be given—a certain minimum wage—which is the standard money-income for so many thousand people, and of which, by every recipient, a fifth part must be realised in the form of irreducible necessaries, whilst four-fifths will be a selection from a multitude of alternative superfluities. Such a money-income being given, the real income represented by it, as measured by the needs of a reasonable social life, will, within wide limits, vary according to the character of the individuals by whom this selection is made. A thousand money-incomes, let us say of £200 a year, will indeed be equal in one sense, but in one sense only. They will represent a right on the part of each recipient to the results of so much technical effort—the directive ability of the few and the manual labour of the many; but it is the choice of the recipient himself which determines how, in his own case, these forces shall be employed—whether the industrial oligarchy and all the complex apparatus, mechanical and human, controlled by it, shall provide him with a real income consisting of enough alcoholic drink or too much; with a clean house or a dirty one; with a comfortable ingle-nook or with peaches out of season at two shillings apiece—or whether, as the Vicar of Wakefield might have put it, it shall consist of a gross of green spectacles, or a horse which would drag a plough, and carry his daughters, like "ladies of quality," to church.

Thus, even in the case of a standard minimum wage, which would, if fulfilling the conditions here described as rational, be mainly composed of superfluities selected by the recipient himself from an indefinite number of alternatives, the recipient, though wanting in the abilities by which the money-amount might be amplified, would, within wide limits, be able to determine its real amount, or (if we prefer the expression) to determine its kind or quality. His potential income is largely determined by the forces of industrial oligarchy. His actual income is determined by the forces of democracy expressing themselves in his own person, not through his economic efficiency, but through his own moral tastes.

"The style is the man," a celebrated critic has said with regard to literature. "The real income is the man," may be said with equal truth, so far as social intercourse, and all that social intercourse implies, owe their qualities to the material conditions earned by him.

But, as the basis of human welfare, real income, or an aggregate of material goods, does not stand alone. In recognising real income as measurable in terms of quality, we are appealing to some assumed standard which is not in itself material. It is to be found in certain qualities of the mind, the disposition, or the spirit, which would make the social intercourse of some men very different from that of others, even though material conditions were in every detail identical. A dinner party of twenty Hottentots dressed up as Englishmen, and provided by an English vicar with his cook and his vicarage for the occasion, would differ considerably, in its quality as an exhibition of social intercourse, from a dinner party given next day by the vicar himself to twenty weekly communicants, the pick of his own parishioners.

On what, then, in the case of civilised men and women, will the moral and mental quality of their social intercourse depend?

CHAPTER II

THE MENTAL DATA OF CULTURE

To every social gathering, whether in a tavern, a cottage, a palace or on a village green, to every private interview between friends or lovers, each man or woman brings some hoard of ideas, judgments, interests, secret experiences, or some outlook on life generally, these making up what is commonly called "the heart," out of the fulness of which the mouth speaks. These elements are innumerable, but, classified broadly, they are divisible into three groups : those belonging to the life of knowledge and intellectual reflection, those belonging to the life of emotional or æsthetic appreciation, and those belonging to the life of religion—the word "religion" being taken in its widest sense, so as to include any moral idealisms in which men may seek refuge as substitutes for definite religious creeds. These elements affect not only the process of social intercourse itself, but also the tastes and the acts of choice which determine what, in the form of real income, shall be the character of its material appliances. With regard, then, to these elements of life which are not in themselves material, but which ultimately determine the character of those activities and experiences for the sake of which all political systems and industrial systems exist, let us consider how far, and in what sense, each of these is democratic, or, in other words, is determined by the free use of the faculties of each average unit, and how far (if at all) its origin is oligarchic, or contingent on the influence of an exceptional few. What we shall find is this, that just as in any wealthy country, the bulk of whose wealth consists of endless alternative superfluities, oligarchy in production is essential to selective democracy in consumption, so the action of oligarchy is essential to the inner life of the spirit, but essential to it as a means only, this inner life itself being determined by the democratic principle even more completely than the character of a man's real income.

Let us take the life of knowledge and intellectual reflection first. All democratic thinkers who aspire to be considered seriously acclaim the life of knowledge—of knowledge desired for its own sake—as the choicest birthright of humanity. Knowledge, as thus understood, is mainly of three kinds—historical, philosophical and scientific, and its value is that it endows men with an enlarged vision of existence. Now this is not a kind of knowledge which a man can acquire for himself from his own daily experience, or from watching and imitating things that are done by others, as a shrewd boy may acquire judgment of character, or as children acquire the powers of speech and walking. 'It must, during his earlier years at all events, be imparted to him by teachers, through a deliberate process of education; and the taught are the many, the teachers are necessarily the few. It is true, indeed, that, despite this fact, education in its earlier stages, just like primitive industry, may be fairly described as democratic; for although the teachers are necessarily a small minority, the simpler kinds of knowledge, such as reading and writing, may not only be acquired by anybody, but might also be taught by anybody who made it his trade to teach them. This, however, ceases to be true as the scope of education widens, partly because the things to be taught become very much more numerous, and peculiar gifts for assimilating them must be present in the teacher himself, and partly because the task of conveying them in an intelligible form to the pupils is one for which gifts are requisite of a kind more peculiar still. By no one, as we have seen already, is this fact insisted on with greater vehemence than it is by the extremest advocates of democratic education themselves. In order, then, that the masses may have access to the higher life of knowledge, there must, even democrats admit, be an oligarchy of professional teachers.

But this is not all. The professional teachers, however considerable their abilities, are themselves dependent on an oligarchy higher than their own—on the

supreme thinkers and the supreme discoverers—such as
Plato, Aristotle, Columbus, Bacon, Galileo, Darwin—
whom Nietzsche calls "the shining suns of Humanity,"
and without whom the professional teacher would still
be teaching the geography of Homer, the astronomy of
the Ptolemies, and the ethnography of Martianus Capella.
But the principle is the same in any case. The intellectual elevation of the many is contingent on the activity
of a certain superior few.

Of those elements of social intercourse which belong
to the life of emotional or æsthetic appreciation, the
same thing is true in a no less obvious way. There
are elements of æsthetic appreciation even in the
primitive savage; but the instruments of such appreciation in all its higher forms have always been a
small company of great individual artists. Any professional teacher may interpret art to his pupils, but
he cannot be his own Phidias, his own Wagner or
Shakespeare.

Of those elements of social intercourse which belong
to the life of religion, the same thing is true likewise.
There are few races, if any, no matter how primitive, in
which the crude elements of religion are not diffused and
indigenous, and so far democratic; but even amongst
peoples such as the aboriginal tribes of Australia, any
religion which binds men together has for its nucleus
some kind of oligarchic priesthood, by whom its rites,
rules and doctrines are performed, enforced or perpetuated; whilst as to the higher religions, such as the
Buddhistic, the Christian and the Islamite, which dif-
ferentiate civilised men from the blood-stained savages
of Dahomey, each is inseparably connected with the
person of a single founder.

Thus in each of the three lives—that of knowledge, that
of æsthetic appreciation and that of religion—on which
the quality of social intercourse in a civilised country
depends, the activities of the few play a part of such
supreme importance that were their activities absent the
mass of the citizens, whatever their material wealth,
would be unlettered, superstitious and half-brutal bar-
barians, as many newly enriched men on the outskirts
of civilisation actually are to-day.

This is one side of the case, but it has another as well.

Considered as instruments of civilisation, the great men in the spheres of knowledge, art and religion accomplish nothing by what they accomplish in their own persons. The historian, the man of science, the philosopher, might have all history, all the philosophies, all the sciences in his head; the poet or the artist might produce great poems or pictures, which he secretly read or contemplated in his own study or studio; the man of spiritual genius might spend every hour of his life in secret union with God; but these distinguished persons, if they kept their achievements to themselves, would be candles hidden under bushels. Mankind at large would remain in unbroken night. What they do accomplish, what they have accomplished, as an oligarchy, is to be looked for, not in themselves, but in the effects produced by their agency on the natures and the lives of others. The man of knowledge habitually estimates the value of his own discoveries by the extent to which, through books or through oral teaching, he is able to make multitudes comprehend and accept them. The poet and the painter regard their arts as successful in proportion as, by poem or picture, their own visions and emotions, their own perceptions of beauty, of joy or sadness, are awakened in the hearts of others, and there become conscious of themselves. But it is in the life of religion that the relation of the few to the many shows its nature in this respect most clearly.

A great preacher, with an intellect and a zeal like Paul's, is, let us say, addressing some vast congregation, which comprises men of all sorts and conditions. The preacher is an exceptional man, or crowds would not flock to listen to him; but his one aim is to appeal equally to all—to touch some part of the inmost nature of each which the wise man shares with the fool, the humblest peasant with the prince, and not to galvanise this into any artificial life, but merely to rouse from sleep something which is alive already. Apart from what the masses bring to the religious teacher, there would be no practical meaning in what the teacher brings to the masses. If there were not in man some sense of distress which the Christian religion has interpreted as a sense of sin, the Christian religion could never have come into existence, for no one would have been able to conjecture what the Christian message meant. The Sermon on the Mount, in that case, might just as well have been a pious soliloquy. The stones would have cried out in answer to it sooner than human beings. Let us assume that the Christian religion was revealed by God Himself, through the manhood of Christ, and an oligarchy of chosen interpreters; but Christianity, as a living religion for mankind, is nothing more than such elements of the divine message as the masses of mankind assimilate, selecting them democratically in accordance with their own free proclivities, just as income in the form of coloured ribbons is real income only in so far as their several varieties are selected and worn by women, as becoming to their own complexions.

This comparison of religion to shopping may perhaps by some persons be reprehended as unduly flippant. It is no more flippant than one with which we are all familiar—the comparison of the Holy Spirit to yeast hidden in a meal-barrel. In each case—in that of shopping and that of vital religious belief—there is a presentation by the few to the many of things, material or spiritual, which the many could not have presented to themselves, but which, when once presented to them by others—by the great scientific manufacturer or the great religious teacher—the many, according to their several capacities, make their own by free acts of assimilation. In the life of artistic caste and emotional refinement generally, the process is essentially the same. It is the same in the life of knowledge. In the most rudimentary education administered to young children in any national school, there are elements to-day of philosophies, of synthetic thought and of discoveries to which, if it had not been for the specially gifted few, mankind would still be strangers.

The three non-material life-processes—those of Knowledge, Emotional Refinement and Religion—have their analogues in the processes, wholly or mainly material, of Industrial Production, Political Government and War. But the part played by the oligarchic principle, though analogous, is not the same in all. The six main processes in question are divisible into two kinds, one of which we may call the subservient processes, the other the processes of fruition. The latter consist of those—namely, the intellectual, the æsthetic and the religious—which determine the character of civilised social intercourse. The former consist of war, government and industry, which, except in so far as they subserve social intercourse, mean nothing; and though the principles of oligarchy and democracy are essential to both alike, the principle of oligarchy is in the subservient processes predominant, whilst in the ultimate processes of fruition it loses itself in its own results, and gives place to what, in its essentials, is a process of pure democracy. The religious oligarch, when he has preached his gospel to millions, lives in the democracy of his converts. Similarly, the average wage-worker engaged in the manufacture of chemicals is subject to the oligarchic employer through whose intellect labour results in ribbons of a hundred colours; but his wife knows, as nobody else can know, which of these colours she herself prefers; and she, with a democracy of similar wives, by freely choosing this kind of ribbon or that, gives orders to the industrial oligarch, the master of chemical knowledge, which determine in the long run which dyes shall be produced, or the quantity which shall be produced of each. It is, in short, in the process of social intercourse, whether this exhibits itself in the conversion, by individual character, of money income into real income, or in the free assimilation of moral and religious teaching, that the true and only field of democratic freedom and self-fruition in a civilised society will be found; and the fundamental truth as to the relation between the two principles, the democratic and the oligarchic, may be summed up in saying that *only through oligarchy does civilised democracy know itself.*

But, however true this may be, one thing must never be forgotten. From the point of view of the great masses of mankind the principle of oligarchy is justified only by the fact that through its action an ampler field of self-fruition and choice is offered to the masses themselves, both in material matters and non-material, than is possible in those simple societies where the influence

of the few is absent.   Whatever the few may add to the
possible things of civilisation, the many must, according
to their several talents, share them; and amongst the
additions which the many will thus share with the few,
material things stand practically, if not logically, first.
In respect of these, the debt of the few to the many is
represented primarily by a just minimum wage, of which
the main attribute must be that it shall, as explained
already, represent conditions unquestionably ampler
than any which the recipients could secure by their own
unaided efforts.   In what the average workers could
secure by their unaided efforts only, and without submission to the orders of any minds superior to their
own, we have the standard by ultimate reference to
which their conditions under a system of wage-work and
industrial oligarchy must be measured; and if these
latter conditions—the conditions represented by wages—
are adjusted in the manner here set forth as rational,
and are taken together with those non-material adjuncts
which have been here set forth as possible and rational
likewise, then so far as reason has any effect on the
emotions, however strongly they may be tinctured with
the sentiment of democratic freedom, however strongly
they may be inflamed with desire for material plenty,
such conditions are calculated to elicit the emotion of
content.   If they fail to elicit it, the failure will be due,
not to reason, but to some other affections of the mind,
which have here been already glanced at, and which
shall now, with the aid of certain fresh illustrations, be
re-examined.

CHAPTER III

THE MOOD OF VAGUE REBELLION

EVERY human being, whether he be wise or foolish, a moderate man or an extremist, must, consciously or subconsciously, have in his mind some vision of the external conditions and opportunities which would content him, or at least leave him nothing to grumble at, as the setting of his own life-drama. Further, this vision of circumstances and of the life-drama to which they are subservient must in every case include the assumption, conscious or sub-conscious, that they lie within the limits of the possible. If a man, in his own opinion, is endowed with talents which distinguish him from the great mass of his fellows, these circumstances, in the way of income, of position or otherwise, will not be confined within any fixable limits. They may represent an income of many thousands or tens of thousands a year. But if he does not and cannot persuade himself that his talents exceed the average, the circumstances or income which would content him must be such as would have to content the majority of his fellows likewise; and the maximum which is possible at any given time for multitudes has limits of a fixed and very definite kind. In any case the circumstances which would bring content to himself must be measured by, if they do not coincide with, the amplest minimum which would have to suffice for most.

The case, however, of men who are, or believe themselves to be, exceptional, who believe great prizes in the way of income or position to be their due, and are willing to make their lives a hazardous adventure in quest of them, must, with its successes or failures, be left to settle itself. Their private satisfactions or disappointments will have, as subjective phenomena, no more interest of a general kind than their love-affairs. The problem of how to secure content with the existing system, social, political and industrial, relates to those (let us say four-fifths of the population) whose faculties fail to win for them, or to give them any promise of winning, conditions and positions which, even when they exceed the average, and are ample for purposes of comfort and a rational life, not only fall short of riches, but are lacking in the outward insignia of what many people call mediocrity. The units of this majority might, as has been said already, recognise clearly, though grudgingly, as a mere matter of reason, that their lots, if adjusted in the manner here described, were the best which the nature of things makes possible, in the sense that no radical revolution could alter them otherwise than for the worse; but reason, as matters stand, would fail to impose complete acquiescence on their emotions. Their emotions would be still rebellious. Unrest would still survive all the possible appliances of rest.

In what part of men's nature, then, does this difficulty, as matters stand, reside? It resides not in any belief or opinion which sane reason can endorse, or which any reasonable man would venture to state categorically either to himself or others. It resides in a mood or temper which, in the way of obstinate though but half-recognised implications, retains what reason has altogether rejected; and we shall find, when they are analysed, that all these implications are summed up in those formulæ of pure democracy with an examination of which the present work began. These familiar formulæ—such as "one man one vote," or "one man one unit of influence in virtue of his manhood alone "— are, it was there shown, applicable with substantial accuracy, to the affairs of small, simple, isolated and primitively poor communities; but, as applied to those of the great, complex, interconnected and opulent nations of to-day, they are not loose ways of expressing what is substantially true; they are precise ways of expressing what is essentially false. These formulæ are correct as applied to primitively simple communities because in such communities both industrial conditions and governmental are the result of the co-operation of equals—of human faculties reduced to their lowest common denominator. They are false as applied to complex and opulent communities because in such communities both industrial conditions and governmental are essentially the result of the co-operation of unequals. These formulæ are false, not because they assert democratic principle, but because they deny, or suggest a denial of the oligarchic.

Of the insidious action of the Mood which holds this fallacy in solution, and which is constantly pitted against the reason of those who harbour it, a most remarkable illustration was given by a well-known publicist, who enjoys a deserved reputation, not only as a powerful writer, but in many ways as a temperate thinker also. In the course of the spring of the year 1917, with reference to the real meaning of the struggle between the Germanic Powers and their opponents, he declared in a journal controlled by him that "the struggle, in which almost the whole of the world is locked, is a struggle between two principles—between the principle of democracy on the one hand, and the principle of authority on the other." In this instinctive substitution of the word "authority" for another in more common use— that is to say, "autocracy," in the sense of military despotism, we have a startling illustration of what was, at all events, the momentary triumph of mere Mood over reason. It was a triumph which will justify us in amending the writer's statement, and saying, in a sense much wider and deeper than his own, that "the struggle in which almost the whole of the world is locked is a struggle between the irrational mood which insists on proclaiming the supremacy of democracy simple and unalloyed, and the sober reason which, without ignoring democracy, proclaims the principle of oligarchy as its constant and necessary counterpart." Indeed the reality of this struggle was exhibited on that very occasion by the writer himself; for the same series of Comments which contained his implied attack on "authority" contained, in an adjacent paragraph, an impassioned demand for its exercise—a demand that one entire department of British activities in war-time should be placed under the absolute control of a small body of experts.

If the fallacious implications latent in the formulæ of pure democracy can so overcloud the vision and so vitiate the mood of a mind naturally sagacious, we shall find little to wonder at in the domination, not always active but always ready to become so, of this same mood over the natural common sense of masses unaccustomed to synthetic thinking. It has been pointed out already that, under the modern industrial system, the wage-workers, when dealing with their various sectional interests, exhibit themselves generally as the last people in the world to believe in any general equality, whether of skill or payment; and this is specially true of those whose skill and whose wages are the highest (such, for example, as the metal-workers), and whose unions are most highly organised. On ordinary occasions, such as those of particular wage disputes, each section is preoccupied with the interests of its own members. Exceptional skill is vigilantly jealous of semi-skill. It demands and clings to exceptional rates of wages with as much tenacity as any employer to his profits, or any investor to his dividends; and in principle the representatives of exceptional skill are right. They are right in demanding for it the full excess of its value over that of the ordinary labour of which all human beings are capable, and which is all that large multitudes can, or are required to, exercise. We may even concede that they are right in endeavouring by various methods—by limitation of apprenticeship or otherwise—to convert its competitive value into the value of an artificial monopoly. But whenever any question arises with regard to more general principles—to principles affecting the constitution of the industrial system as a whole—it is precisely men like these who, in alliance with discontented adventurers, mainly of middle-class origin, are foremost in shouting the formulæ of democracy pure and simple, and deluding others, and probably deluding themselves, with visions of a world in which all rewards are equal, and skill, semi-skill and no-skill feast at a common table.

The condition or mood of mind which renders such self-contradictions possible is not susceptible of any rational explanation, for it does not arise from reason. It is a combination of the demand that everybody, in respect both of income and of influence—of influence both political and industrial—shall have at least an equal chance of "getting to the top of the tree," with a demand that the tree shall have no top at all. In particular, so far as the leaders of discontent are concerned—namely, the most successful of the manual wage-workers and the least successful of the middle class —it is a demand on the part of each (as Professor Michels shows by his quotations from the Italian Syndicalist Labriola) that his own position shall be superior to that of the masses of other people, but that the position of no minority shall be in any way superior to his own.

How, then, shall this irrational mood be rationalised —this mood which demands, and at the same time denies, equality, and which, so long as it lasts, renders all content amongst all but a few impossible? It can be rationalised, and brought into accordance with fact, in two ways only. One of these ways is that of persistent appeals to the reason which, however obscured, is present even in the persons themselves whom this mood mainly affects, and through their reason to their imagination. The other way, and the costlier way, is by the teaching of the results which must ensue if this irrational mood is carried to its logical consequences.

The way of appeal to reason, although it may be long and tedious, is of far more promise than at first sight may appear; for reason itself, amongst the present apostles of discontent, leads, as we have seen, already to the very conclusions against which the mood of discontent protests. Socialists, indeed, in defending this mood, which protests against inequalities whereas sober reason asserts them, are compelled to call indirect reasoning, or reasoning by suggestion, to their aid. Certain of their logical feats, which are somewhat of this character, have been reviewed in an earlier chapter— such, for example, as the doctrines that all men are born equal, differences of efficiency being due to differences of position only, or that all forms of effort are equal which in any way whatever are necessary. But in their direct forms, as parts of a formal theory of economics, these democratic crudities are now virtually obsolete, and have been superseded by two ideas or philosophies, more comprehensive in kind, which are connected with

pure democracy by general inference rather than by
direct inculcation, which are peculiarly adapted to captivate a quasi-scientific attention, and which socialist
thinkers parade with all the airs of calm scientific profundity. One of these ideas or philosophies expresses
itself in a certain conception of the State; the other
expresses itself in a certain interpretation of history.
One is derived mainly from the speculations of modern
sociologists, notably of Herbert Spencer. The other is
a resuscitation of the historical, as distinct from the
strictly economic and discarded, doctrines of Marx.

In all socialist thought some conception is implicit of
the activities of the State as contrasted with those of the
individual. Under the influence of what passed muster
as the "scientific" theories of Marx, such a conception
became precise and prominent; and in all formal socialist
projects, from the days of Marx onwards, the State has
figured as a number of public officials who, as overseers
of the national industry and trustees of the national
capital, should take the place of the private capitalists
and employers; and, however democratic the means to
which they owed their power, they would constitute a
class distinct from the great mass of the population.
This conception of the State, though still a necessary
element of socialist thought to-day, has been gradually
supplemented by another, which now exists side by side
with it, and according to which the State, instead of
being a class apart, is a single and indivisible body, the
Marxian State being only one of his organs, whilst the
units, those of the official class included, are but so many
cells of one and the same organism. In a State, as thus
conceived, each cell differs from the rest, as a minute
particle of this organ or of that; but all subserve equally
the corporate life of the whole; and, as one of the philosophers of the English Labour Party puts it, except in
relation to "this organic oneness," no cell has "an
individual end, or any true life of its own."

Here we have, as Bacon would have called them, the
"idols" of pure democracy, such as equality of function,
sentimental solidarity and so forth, reconstructed out of
new materials, or offered to observation from a new
point of view, with the object of inculcating by sugges-

tion, and perpetuating in the form of a mood, the very fallacies which, when expressed in detail, the reason and even the emotions of socialists themselves repudiate.

In the first place it may be observed that, in representing each human unit as a cell of some organic body or animal to whose unitary life and prosperity all cells are equally necessary, socialists are provoking a comparison which is singularly unfortunate for themselves. The cells of a physical organism, such as that of a human being, are by no means all equally essential to its life, or even to its general health. A man may lose the cells which make up (let us say) his thumb or his whiskers, and be otherwise hale and hearty till he dies at the age of ninety. He may lose the cells of his tonsils or cæcus appendix, and be all the better for losing them; but if certain of his brain-cells were lost, he would lose reason or memory. Were others lost, he would die. The analogy between cells and citizens breaks down under the first touch of analysis, in respect at least of the equalitarian moral which democrats seek to draw from it.

This matter is, however, of minor importance as compared with two others, the first of which is as follows.

One of the main demands which the spirit of socialism, as a moral principle, makes is, as we have seen already, a recognition of the moral value of the individual life as such. "It demands," says a socialist writer in an outburst of solemn emphasis, "that every human life, however weak and externally ineffectual, shall be reverenced and treated as a something unspeakably precious in itself." But this is precisely what the theory of the individual as nothing more than a cell in the body of a State-animal, whose corporate life is the sole true life, denies. To regard the individual as a cell which is valuable only according to its effects on a body exterior to itself, is merely to rehabilitate the mood, rightly denounced by socialists, which has caused many employers to regard the individual labourer, not as a human being, but simply as so much labour, his sole value being what his labour produces, such as a wall, a corkscrew, or a drain, and his microscopic humanity being an ash of negligible refuse.

But the modern attempt to exhibit pure democracy as finding its full embodiment in the unitary social organism is vitiated by another absurdity which, including this as a consequence, is even more profound. The analogy between a State and a single living organism has been set forth by no thinker more emphatically than by Herbert Spencer, or with greater elaboration of detail. He maintains that these two phenomena are not merely analogous, but in a literal sense identical. He says, for example, that in a complex modern society the nerves of the human organism (or, as he calls them, the "internuncial" tissues) reproduce themselves in the form of telegraph wires. Indeed to many of his followers, who are otherwise in substantial agreement with him, he appears, when he argues thus, to have pushed his case too far. At all events, the identity of the State with a unitary animal organism is, even if he does not exaggerate it, presented by Spencer in the completest form possible; and it is mainly from him and his followers that the modern socialist philosophy of the organic State is derived. But Spencer, having exhausted his ingenuity in illustrating the minute likeness of a State to an animal organism, at once goes on to insist that, even if they are identical otherwise, there is between the two one insuperable and fundamental difference. A Society or a State, he says, is an animal which, unlike all others, has not, and never can have, any "common sensorium." Its collective activities may be unitary, but it has no unitary consciousness. Whatever consciousness it possesses is distributed throughout the body in millions of isolated units, and only as conceived and experienced by each of these units separately can the State have for human beings any object or any meaning whatsoever. The individual citizen does not value the State directly as an objective fact, or on account of what it is for others. He values it indirectly and derivatively because other men, as units, reflect themselves in his own experience, and because the prosperity of other men in the mass is connected more or less with his own. The contention, then, that each man's life is equally valuable because each conduces equally to the life of the same State may suggest such an equality by a trick of ambiguous language, but has in reality no meaning at all.

If, however, we revert to the fact, which was emphasised in the preceding chapter, that the fruition of life through the State consists of the intercourse of the individual with a limited circle of kindred, friends and companions, the comparison of the State to an actual human organism will yield us, at all events, one instructive analogy. We may say that, on a rough average, social intercourse, in the case of each individual, is limited to a sub-community of perhaps two hundred persons. Thus, in a country like the United Kingdom these sub-communities would be not far short in number of two hundred thousand; and if we liken the population as a whole to a single national organism, we may liken each sub-community, not to a simple, but to a large composite cell, having within it a social life of its own. Now every actual organism, such as a human being, begins in the uterus as a cell compounded of two elements—the female and the fertilising male. This, multiplied by fission, develops into an adhesive cluster, each unit of which, though attached to all its neighbours, lives for a time a life which is exclusively its own, like a man whose house is next-door to that of a total stranger. A moment arrives, however, when this state of things changes. The separate life of each separate cell survives, but signs appear of some one life common to all of them by which they are at last absorbed. The unified life thenceforth is the only life remaining; and it is as a unitary consciousness that the embryo, no longer embryonic, is at last born into the world. If, then, we compare a State to an animal organism which is embryonic and not yet complete, we shall find between the former and the latter a real resemblance which, when both are complete, vanishes. The cells of social intercourse, being all affected by conditions, political and industrial, which are more or less common to all of them, are so far like the cells of the embryo in one of its earlier stages. There is a common life in both cases; there is a common consciousness in neither. But these multiple units of consciousness in the animal organism disappear, being merged in one; whereas the cells of social intercourse, so far as conscious experience is concerned, always remain separate. The development in the direction of unity is arrested—it goes no farther; and, closely connected though these cells of intercourse are, the fruition of such intercourse exists so far only as it is reflected in each of those globules of individual consciousness of which every larger cell of social intercourse is composed.

For all purposes, then, of socialist or democratic argument the relation of the State to an organism is one, not of identity, but of violent and fundamental contrast; and the socialist attempt to suggest, by appeal to such partial analogies as doubtless exist between them, that the process of advanced civilisation is due to the co-operation of equals has been here briefly examined, because it is a signal illustration of the intellectual bankruptcy of those who seek to inculcate by suggestion ideas which they themselves repudiate when translated into definite terms either of action or direct analysis.

Of this intellectual bankruptcy an illustration no less remarkable is the socialist attempt to suggest the same conclusion, and maintain the socialist mood, by an appeal to what is paraded as a scientific interpretation of history. Of the invocation of history as a witness to the essentially democratic character of all social progress, and to the fact that oligarchy has been merely a disastrous accident, the protagonist, as has been said, was Marx; and, amongst the more thoughtful socialists, the historical part of his teaching alone survives intact. There are, indeed, for all thinkers, the elements in it of a fundamental truth, which by the earlier economists of capitalism was altogether neglected. The substance of this teaching is as follows. The history of all nations depends on the conditions under which material wealth is produced. The actual agent of production is always manual labour. The product of all labourers is practically of equal value. Thus the actual producers are always a pure democracy; but history shows that, in one way or another, they have always hitherto been subjected to some oligarchy, which appropriates the results of production but plays no part in the process. The oligarchs first were slave-owners, they then were feudal superiors; the feudal superiors have been superseded by the capitalist employers of to-day; and the business of history is to trace out in detail how one of these oligarchies gave place to another, whilst the actual productive process, in respect of its democratic character, always remained the same. In particular, said Marx, the great business of history is to demonstrate how, why, and when the modern capitalist system followed and supplanted feudalism.

What, then, he asks, have been the historical causes to which the capitalist system of the modern world is due? According to Marx, these must be sought for in England, where the modern capitalist system first made its appearance. The chief of these were, he said, the Wars of the Roses, which caused the dissolution of many great feudal households; the distribution by Henry VIII of vast monastic properties, thereby creating a virtually new plutocracy; and, further, a growing demand for English wool in Europe, which caused an immense conversion of arable land into sheep-walks, so that countless ploughmen and cultivators were turned adrift on the world to look for some new employment. Here, said Marx, we have the beginnings of that division of society into a landless multitude on the one hand, and a small group of plutocrats enriched by accident on the other; and out of this division, which began in the sixteenth century, that system of capitalism on the great scale has arisen, which reached maturity in England three centuries later.

Now let us grant that, considered as an isolated chapter of history, this account of the genesis of modern capitalism is correct. But in view of the ultimate facts, at an explanation of which Marx aimed in elaborating it, its scope is limited in a way which renders it wholly valueless. If a coroner's jury were inquiring into the death of a particular man, and a family doctor who had known him all his life were able to show that it was due to certain causes such as habits of excess, or some tropical fever which had so undermined his constitution that a slight chill had been fatal to him which a sound man would have hardly noticed, the doctor would have told the jury all that they wished to know. He would have explained *a* death, but he would not have explained death. In the same way the historical argument of Marx may do much to explain the rise of one oligarchy in particular, but it does nothing to explain why oligarchy, in one form or another, should be the invariable concomitant of advancing civilisations generally, the capitalist oligarchy of England being only one example of it. If the capitalist oligarchy of England were a fact which stood by itself, every detail of its special antecedents would be of universal import, just as the most trivial incidents which led to the death of one man would be of universal import if only one man died; but, if a kind of event, such as the rise of oligarchies, is general, the more we confine ourselves to conditions which are peculiar to any single case, the more do we lose sight of the elements which are fundamental and common to all.

Even Marx himself saw, and indeed drew attention to the fact that, considered merely as a manifestation of oligarchy, the capitalism of modern England had its analogues there and everywhere in the industrial systems which had preceded it—namely, slavery in the ancient world, and the statutory system of feudal labour-dues in the mediæval. Society, under each of these systems, culminated in the persons of a guiding and ruling few. Nevertheless, with this fact before him he so fixed his mind on the differences by which these three systems were distinguished from one another that he failed to note or appreciate the significance of their persistent likeness; and his failure in this respect was embodied in his famous summary, to which, in its general sense, socialists still cling, of what the world-process of industrial evolution has been, is, and in the future is bound to be. Just as the slave-system was inevitably transformed into feudalism, and just as feudalism was inevitably transformed into capitalism, so, he said, by a process essentially similar, will capitalist oligarchy be transformed into the industrial democracy of socialism.

It seems never to have occurred to him, when he prophesies the advent of this final stage, how completely all analogy between it and the three others evaporates, his whole prediction being merely one vast *non sequitur*. When stripped of its accessories, his argument comes to this : that, because in all civilisations hitherto the principle of oligarchy, however it may have disappeared in one form, has always reappeared in another, we have ample evidence for concluding that it will in the future not reappear at all. If the modern capitalist system had been not only cradled in England, but if, having there matured itself, it had been confined to England also, the Marxian account of its origin in insular events which developed themselves during the course of the sixteenth century might pass muster as plausible. But this same system has subsequently risen into life *de novo* in countries such as America, between whose history and that of England there is otherwise no resemblance. What has the evolution of a wage-earning class in America to do with any evolution of landless men in England which was due to the Wars of the Roses, or the growth of sheep-farms in certain English counties at the expense of tillage four hundred years ago ? What has the rise of an enterprise like the Standard Oil Trust to do with any private fortunes which the favour of Henry VIII assigned to a few individuals out of the plunder of the English monasteries ? If, a few rich men being given, the existence of landless masses is at once necessary and sufficient to explain the rise of capitalism, why has America witnessed the rise of capitalism at all ? For nobody in America need have wanted a substantial farm who had the energy and the disposition to till it.

The more closely we consider what the history of the past has been, the more clearly does the imperfection of the historical theory of Marx, which is still adopted by democratic thinkers, reveal itself. From age to age, in this region or that, societies, unknown to each other, have formed themselves out of human units which have come together like drifted grains of sand. They have gradually risen into civilised States or nations, eminent for wealth and power, for learning and for the arts of life. They have risen, flourished and declined, and out of the dust of their dissolution others have been formed anew. In Phœnicia, Crete, Egypt, Assyria, Carthage,

Rome, Moorish Spain, and the northern swamps of the Adriatic, this same drama has been enacted; and not only in places such as these—not in the Old World only. It was enacting itself in the New World also, as the Spaniards saw to their astonishment when they first set eyes on men who till then had been as strange to Europe as the inhabitants of another planet; and wherever wealth, learning, art and national power have developed themselves, from the lands of the Incas and Aztecs to Tyre, Babylon and Chicago, some special position, wholly disproportionate to their number, has always been present in the persons of a ruling or leading few. Every individual event has its own local and, we may say, its accidental setting; but when an event, always the same in its one essential characteristic, is found to repeat itself in countries whose conditions and histories are various and divergent otherwise in every imaginable way, it obviously cannot be due to any one sequence of local or historical accidents—especially when the event is one so unlikely on the face of it as the adverse possession by a few men of a force indefinitely greater than the cumulative force of millions.

Nothing is more calculated to suggest this conclusion to common sense than the rhetoric which even educated socialists are accustomed to direct against the ruling few in general. From age to age, it is said, they have lived on the plunder of the masses, having first reduced them to subjection. Thus one writer accuses them of having "seized" the railways and locomotives of England. Another declares that they have always "seized on knowledge," and robbed the masses of education. Now to make such statements as these, of which there are endless variants, is like saying that Marx seized on the ownership of his own works, or that a painter stole from the masses the ownership of his own pictures. If such things are owned by comparatively few persons, the primary reason is that it is the intellect and enterprise of the few which has caused them to come into existence—locomotives, books, great pictures, all the higher kinds of knowledge, and so forth.

But let us put the matter on a broader footing than this. Let us take, for example, the statements that the

few in every civilised country have reduced the masses
to subjection, and, by robbing them of the higher knowledge, have made their subjection permanent. If such
statements purport to be even rhetorically true, the
kinds of question which they at once provoke are as
follows : If all men are naturally equal, how has so
prodigious a feat as the constant subjection of so many
thousands of men been brought about and perpetuated
by puny little groups of ten ? And, even if rhetorically
there were some truth in the statement that ten men,
masters of knowledge, withheld their higher knowledge
from the thousand, why, if all men are equal, do the
members of this overwhelming majority not acquire
such knowledge for themselves ? If the subjection of
the many by the few, through a monopoly of knowledge
or otherwise, were an event which had occurred once
only, or only on very rare and fortuitously-like occasions,
such an event might be reasonably ascribed to accident.
But since it is an event which, as socialists are constantly
declaring, has enacted and re-enacted itself everywhere
in all the civilisations of the past, however remote from
one another in circumstances, time and place, it must
obviously have been due to some fact which is not
accidental, but universal; and this can be none other
than the fact that out of every thousand, or every million
of human beings a small minority bring with them into
the world faculties of will, intellect, constructive imagination and leadership which are, in their various ways,
more powerful for constructive purposes than those of
ordinary men.

Of such exceptional faculties those which happen to be
predominant are not always the same. They have
sometimes been mainly military, sometimes political,
sometimes commercial or industrial, sometimes intellectual or artistic. In large and highly civilised States
the faculties which distinguish the few, and which give
them their oligarchic power, comprise all these varieties
simultaneously, so that the national oligarchy is several
oligarchies in one. But in every case the principle on
which progress and the conservation of its fruits depend
is embodied in the persons of a few. Whenever any
oligarchy has existed for any length of time, it will, as

an active body, appear to be larger than it is, and the foundations of its power will be obscured, because the active members of it, owing to family ties, will be surrounded by an accretion of persons who belong to it by accident only.   But, from one generation to another, these adventitious members drop off and disappear; and actual oligarchic power, to use the words of Mill, "always *is in*, or is always *passing into* the hands of men" whose faculties, as applied to some practical purpose, are by overt experience marked out as superior to those of the general mass.

This fact, indeed, is constantly admitted even by socialists, though by childish abuses of language they endeavour to hide its consequences.   One of their stock assertions is this, that the few in all ages and places have acquired exceptional wealth and power "by reason of their superior cunning."   An English semi-socialist, inventing a word for the occasion, has said that their wealth and power are due merely to a superior "pushfulness."   If anybody likes to say that the telephone, the turbine engine, the aeroplane, and progress in the manufacture of chemicals are due to superior "cunning," he is free to do so; but in that case "cunning" is merely another word for genius.   If anybody likes to say that the few have achieved such results merely by superior "pushfulness," he is free to do so, but in that case "pushfulness" is merely another word for wholly exceptional energy.   Changes in words effect no change in things; and even socialists, when they use such language, virtually admit the fact, which cannot be ultimately suppressed, that oligarchy represents the power of exceptional energy and genius, and that, though these may be the results of accident in respect of the pre-natal processes by which natural superiorities are determined, they are not accidents in respect of those post-natal processes which make up the history of nations in their progress towards civilisation and wealth from primitive poverty and barbarism.

Thus the Marxian theory of history, the one object of which is to exhibit the oligarchic principle as an accident of civilisation, as in no sense a necessary cause of it, and as thus susceptible of elimination in the future by force or other arbitrary action, the general wealth of nations being totally unaffected by the change—this theory of history, to which socialists still cling as a means of keeping, by suggestion, the socialist mood alive, suppresses the one cause which alone makes progress intelligible.

If, however, the connection which Marx was foremost in establishing between historical oligarchies and the democratic element in production, together with its social consequences, be taken for what it is, as not accidental but essential, the Marxian theory otherwise will conduct us to a vital fact which socialists use it to obscure, and which other and clearer thinkers too often fail to realise.   History shows us, according to Marx and his followers, that in all stages of civilisation the fortunes of the few have been, and still are, due to a process of pure plunder, disguised as military conquest, or as legal systems such as slavery, which ultimately rest on non-industrial force.   By whatever name they may have been called, these fortunes have always consisted of abstractions accomplished by the few from some revenue due wholly to the efforts of the many, so that, as the few grow richer, the many grow inevitably poorer in exactly the same proportion.   Such, according to Marx and his followers, has always been the case in the past; and under the modern capitalist system—so these persons proceed—this immemorial process of abstraction has, owing to adventitious circumstances, reached, or is reaching, its climax.

Now in this version of history a process is depicted which in the past has actually taken place, and which in some countries and businesses may actually take place to-day; but, under the modern system, it is so far from reaching its climax that it has given way to another of a radically opposite character.   Largely, though by no means wholly, under the slave-systems of the ancient world, production, as we have seen already, was democratic in the sense that its technical details were determined by the slaves themselves, whilst the typical oligarch, who held such details in disdain, took everything that the slaves produced, over and above what was necessary for their own consumption.   The manorial lord of the Middle Ages lived on the product of men whose feudal dues were paid to him by a democratic cultivation of his lands—a process in which, personally, he played no part whatever. Under both these systems the personal enrichment of the few resulted mainly from an increase in the number of persons by whose independent efforts this or that rich man profited. In ancient Rome, at the time when private fortunes were greatest, these, as Friedlander has shown, were largely derived from the plunder of conquered provinces. Many great fortunes in Spain were once derived similarly from the plunder of South America. In France, under the old régime, new men rose into prominence whose wealth was so conspicuous that the noblest of the old noblesse did whatever they could to make it their own by marriage. These new men were the farmers of the taxes. They produced nothing themselves. Their wealth was made up of abstractions pure and simple. All these methods of personal enrichment were alike in the fact that, though they may have resulted in the increase of individual fortunes, they were accompanied by no increase in the products which, relatively to its numbers, were available for distribution amongst the population taken as a whole. It is in relation to this fact that the modern capitalist system—the system of industrial oligarchy in the only true sense of that term—differs in such a degree as to constitute a difference in kind from the systems that went before it. Wherever that system has become mature and dominant—more particularly in the United Kingdom, the United States and in Germany—there has not only been a multiplication of large individual fortunes, but also an increase, to a degree never before paralleled, in the product per head of the several populations generally. Hence, since the increment in question is primarily due, as we have seen, not to any intensification of labour, or to any new faculties acquired by labouring hands, but to the directive knowledge and intellect of employers of a new type, the large individual fortunes which are distinctive of the modern world come out of additions which have been made to the general wealth by such men themselves, not out of abstractions from any general wealth which the mass of the population produces and would continue to produce in any case. It does not necessarily follow that, this increment being given, the masses will derive from it any benefit whatsoever. The super-capable few might conceivably appropriate the whole of it, and might even steal part of the product of the masses into the bargain. But, unless this increment was produced and maintained somehow, the masses could look forward to no increment at all. On the one hand, then, the submission of the many to the few is the first condition which renders its production possible, and, on the other hand, unless they participate in it, the many will have no motive for submitting.

Hence, as has here been shown, the foundation-stone of social stability, and the key to any general progress, is a participation by the many in advantages which they could not themselves produce. If this result, which can be reached by the co-operation of unequals only, and which aims at equalities which are relative but not absolute, is achieved in the manner here set forth as rational, it should not be difficult by an unremitting exposure of the fallacies (such as the socialist conception of the State and the socialist interpretation of history) which are used for the purpose of keeping the socialist mood alive, so to educate the masses that this result shall be accepted by them in a mood, not of sullen resignation, but of temperate and intelligent acquiescence.

The root of the difficulty lies, let it be said once more, in the general idea suggested by the formula of pure democracy—the idea that the life-process of rich and civilised, like that of poor and primitive, societies, rests on the co-operation, not of unequals, but of equals, and that some absolute equality, or an approach to it, is consequently the general condition to which rational society will approximate. This idea gives rise to what may be called the disease of impossible expectations, which are mischievous in proportion as they are vague. The formula which conveys it is a sort of pocket poison, those who admit it into their systems being affected by it as by the bite of a tarantula, so that all their sober judgments, all their natural sagacities are not, indeed, destroyed, but sunk by it below the level of consciousness. It is hard to believe that for this mood of unreason, of which Zola in his novel, *Germinal*, has given a vivid description, a persistent appeal to reason will not be in time an antidote; but if mere education fails to effect a cure, a method which was mentioned at the close of the preceding chapter remains. This is the teaching of experience to those by whom reason is neglected.

CHAPTER IV

OBJECT LESSONS OF TO-DAY

LET us suppose it to be granted by all clear and serious thinkers that the higher achievements of civilisation, whether in the way of wealth or culture, are not, indeed, the work of the superior few exclusively, but are contingent on the activities of the few as influencing those, which must always be pre-assumed, of the many. But, even if this be granted, the question still remains of what the basis ultimately is on which the influence of the few over the activities of the many rests. Now, so far as mental, moral and religious civilisation is concerned, the influence of the few depends on the voluntary assimilation by the many of what the few teach. It depends on what is called *influence* as something distinct from external force or authority. But in the social processes which have here been called "subservient"—namely, political government, military action, and industry—the power of the few must necessarily have some external force at the back of it, which imparts to influence the character of dictatorial orders. Hence with regard to these subservient processes there arises the immemorial question of what the force or sanction is which renders such orders operative.

To this question the great majority of thinkers, including the most conservative—we may say, indeed, all thinkers who have ceased to believe in the divine right of kings—would answer that the force in question resides ultimately in the people. Thus, when the principle of absolute monarchy still held undisputed sway in Europe, a school of Catholic theologians, who had no thought of overthrowing it, proclaimed this doctrine as axiomatic, and asked, with supreme self-confidence, "If the force which is the essence of authority does not come ultimately from the people, from what possible source can it come ? " Now, if we regard this argument as meaning that monarchs govern, not in virtue of a quasi-sacramental power which heaven bestows directly on the heads of particular families, but that they govern with the divine sanction so long, and only so long, as their peoples are thereby benefited, this way of stating the case may be accepted as correct and rational. But if it be taken in the more general sense that the will of the people, if unanimous, can, by mere force of numbers, determine government in whatever manner it pleases, and that a monarchy or an oligarchy in itself, as distinct from the people, has no power at all, the argument, seemingly axiomatic, expresses a pure delusion.

In what, then, does its error consist ? As opposed to the physical force of a monarch, or even of an oligarchy, the physical force of the people arrayed in their millions is overwhelming. It may seem, therefore, at first sight a self-evident truth that the millions, if they object to any order issued by the one or the few, can, if they are substantially unanimous, issue for themselves whatever orders they please, and compel the official power, whether a king or otherwise, to execute them. Thus it is constantly said to-day, not by socialists only, that the people are sovereign in the sense that their power has ultimately no limit at all. How and why is this supposed power illusory ? How does the illusion arise ?

It arises for the following reason, that persons who argue thus have in their minds a picture of the people as engaged in one species of corporate action only —that is to say, in action the object of which is to obstruct or to destroy. Now if we limit our view of the power of unanimous numbers to powers of this negative kind, it is quite conceivable that, any positive government being given, the people could, were they all so minded, destroy it. But a nation cannot live by obstruction or destruction only. It can indulge itself in these processes for not more than brief and rarely recurring moments. Unless it is to die of anarchy, cold and famine, its normal life-process must be one of continuous production and construction; and as soon as any nation returns from destructive activities to constructive, the unlimited powers which are claimed for the mere force of numbers, as arrayed against authority external to themselves, disappear. The first thing which the masses of a people must do, when they are hoarse with proclaiming their freedom to do whatever they like, is to cringe to an authority which enforces on them the continuous production of food, and dictates the primary terms on which alone food can be produced. This authority is based on two things, against which a million wills are as powerless as the will of one, the first being the needs and the structure of the human body, the second being the constitution of Nature, and in particular of the earth's surface. The primary business which is thus imposed on men, and from which there can never be more than brief intervals of cessation, is that of following the plough in good weather or bad, or bending over the spade or sickle. No popular will could abolish the business of agriculture, or radically change its character; and if the power of the people is thus limited in respect of the production of necessaries, it is limited no less stringently, though in part for a different reason, in respect of the production of superfluities. In proportion as nations experience the comforts and luxuries of civilisation, the things—things such as these—on which their keenest desires are concentrated, are things the production and multiplication of which are possible only through the action of a knowledge and intellect which achieves an effective force in the persons of a few men only; and it is only on condition that the people obey these few that such superfluities can be either produced at all, or produced in sufficient volume to satisfy the appetites of the multitudes who are all clamouring for a share of them.

Thus, whatever the powers may be by which masses of human beings are compelled to perform productive work, these powers are not primary, but derivative. So far as the production of necessaries is concerned, these powers represent a pressure put upon men by Nature—by Nature which, with various degrees of severity according to soil and climate, flogs them into labour of some simple and orderly sort, as the sole alternative to death. So far as the production of superfluities is concerned, these powers represent the monopolist possession by a few of that rare directive capacity, obedience to which by the many alone renders an abundance of such superfluities possible, and which compels the many, as the price of obtaining them, to obey. The authority, in short, of industrial oligarchy has its basis in the simple fact that, unless the many submit to it, they extinguish every chance of gaining what they are determined not to lose. The same argument applies to political government and war. The power of governmental oligarchy, whether in war or peace, has its basis in the fact that, unless the many submit to it, even the simplest industries are paralysed, the higher are made impossible, and the wealth, the welfare, the freedom, the lives of all, will be at the mercy of any foreign aggressor whose armies, vitalised by obedience, put them to flight, or make them sane by enslaving them.

The authority of the few, which thus has its real basis in the permanent needs of the many, differs as much from the power imputed to the people in virtue of their mere overwhelming numbers as it differs from any power which has been ever imputed to kings as derived by them from a quasi-sacrament which Heaven administers only to the heads of elect families. The heads of governments may, so far as their formal character in concerned, be Emperors, Kings, republican Presidents, or little groups of Ministers; but the ultimate source of their power, as contrasted with the power of the many, is the fact that they possess amongst them certain more or less rare capacities, the exercise of which by somebody is essential to the many themselves, if they wish in the first place to be kept alive, in the second place to be kept in comfort, and in the third place to be kept secure from the attacks of other nations, whether their attacks are in the way of competitive industry or of war.

In this fact lies the meaning of what has here been said already, to the effect that, if reason should prove insufficient to bring home a certain lesson to the masses, there is another schoolmaster always lying in wait for them, who will teach it to them with rods of iron, this schoolmaster being experience. The lesson to be taught is this, that every civilisation, in respect of wealth, government and self-defence, is due to the co-operation of unequals—of the few who lead and give orders, and of the many who follow and obey; that this fact reflects itself in the general configuration of society; and that in proportion as the masses of any country neglect it, they will, as a whole or sporadically, lose what they have in their efforts to seize more.

Of this fact, which has here been elucidated in detail, various illustrations have been given in the body of the present work. It is, however, now possible, owing to a series of unparalleled circumstances, to supplement these by others of a yet more mordant kind. The present work was begun some months before any immediate war with Germany was regarded as a likely event by most men, or by anybody as an event that was inevitable. This book was, in substance, virtually complete by the end of the year 1916. Since that time two great events have happened, which have given the world a surprise unequalled in history. One of these is the participation of America in a war primarily European. The other, more sensational, and yet more widely instructive, is the outbreak of the Russian Revolution, and certain of its outstanding incidents. As detailed corroborations of the arguments which follow each other in the preceding pages, the author, had he given rein to invention, could have invented none more striking. Whatever the ultimate outcome of the Russian revolution may be, the more important events which have marked its opening will remain for all time as demonstrations of what the principles are on which anything in the nature of civilisation rests, and of the ludicrous ruin which ensues when, or for as long as, these principles are violated. It has therefore been thought well to substitute, at the present juncture, a brief reference to certain of the events in question for a more general summary of the arguments to which this volume has been devoted.

On the outbreak of the Russian revolution a prominent London journal, with very judicious promptitude, secured as its Petrograd correspondent a writer who was a professed socialist, but who was not afraid of proclaiming that socialism, as a practicable system, must find its basis in reason and common sense before invoking the impulses of mere imagination and sentiment. Such

being the case, one of the first and most important facts
recorded by him was, as has been mentioned in a brief
footnote already, that revolution in Russia had converted
itself almost immediately into what, so long as it lasted,
was hopeless ruin for everybody—that is to say, into
"a rebellion *against all controlling persons*."

Now this means, when put into plainer language, precisely what has been argued in the course of the present
work.   It means that in any great country pure democracy is impossible, or that democracy is impossible
unless the principle of oligarchy is its concomitant; and
that Russia should be the country in which, on the
admission of even a candid socialist, such a conclusion
has been first demonstrated by a vast national experiment, is all the more remarkable for the following broad
reasons.

Pure democracy, at all events in economic production,
is, as has here been urged, not impossible in itself.   On
the contrary, it is historically the system of primitive
or sub-primitive poverty.   It is a system founded on
the agriculture of self-directed peasant families.   Their
labour produces little, but is sufficient for their bare
support.   Now of all great countries, civilised or in contact with civilisation, Russia is the one in which the
self-directed agriculture of peasants forms incomparably
the largest element; and of all such countries it is, relatively to its population, the poorest.   According to the
values and prices preceding the war and the revolution,
an equal division amongst everybody of the entire
income of Russia would have yielded to each adult less
than half the wages of the poorest English labourer;
and of a total population of 180 millions, the self-
directed peasant cultivators represented at least nine-
tenths.[1]   Since, therefore, a peasant population, so long
as it continues to exist, must at least be capable of
producing, by its own self-directed efforts, enough to

---

[1] Webb's analysis (Dictionary of Statistics) of the Bulletin of the
United States Labour Bureau, Washington, 1908.   The agricultural
workers who worked for wages were about 7 per cent. of the cultivators
taken as a whole.   Factory and railway workers, miners, dockers, and
industrialists generally, formed only about one-thirtieth of the entire
employed population.

maintain its life according to its own standards of living, it might seem that the Russian masses were so far secure in a merely economic sense that their condition under pure democracy could not, except for the better, differ from what it was already. And yet, even in Russia, democracy or socialism, as a rebellion against "all controlling persons," has caused discord, calamity and death even amongst the peasants themselves.

Of this fact the socialist correspondent, to whom reference has just been made, gives the following illustrations. Socialism, he says, as preached to the Russian peasantry, has been identified both by the teachers and the taught with desires and expectations which are wholly incapable of fulfilment, and which, moreover, directly contradict themselves. The peasants have been taught to expect an era of indefinite enrichment by the acquisition of new lands—the property of individuals or of the State—which are to be seized by them at their own discretion under a system of momentary communism, this system to be followed forthwith by a system of private ownership which will re-establish in their own favour every right which they are themselves violating. Thus, with a curiously correct, and yet curiously suicidal logic, the first ambition of each of them has been in many places "to peg out" for himself as many acres as he could, no regard being had to his own powers of tilling them, and then either to till them by hired labour or sell them—proceedings which have often ended in battles between neighbours, each of whom was determined that the best plot should be his own. Thus the peasants of one village, says the writer here referred to, "were busy in distributing the estate of a local landowner, when a free fight ensued from which hardly a man in the neighbourhood issued without wounds, and in which fifteen were killed." In another case, according to the same authority, a body of revolutionaries, having seized a large estate, appointed men to work it for them "at three or four times the usual wages. They began with paying these wages out of the cash discovered in the estate office. When this fund was exhausted, they continued the payments in question by selling the trees and cattle; and when this source of revenue had run dry likewise (the estate being no longer capable of yielding anything), they actually applied to the expropriated landlord for a cheque to pay the wages of men now employed as their own servants." In yet another case a generous proprietor gave the wife of an absent soldier leave to take grass from a small plot. The local agrarian council suggested that he should do the same with his whole property, but the president intervened with the stipulation that the peasants should only take land on condition that they worked it themselves. A peasant, who had already taken a large slice, calculated on selling many loads of hay to the government, and, finding himself barred from exploiting labour to work it, gave up that particular slice, and, appropriating the plot given to the soldier's wife, sold the hay which the poor woman had raised on it.

Incidents such as these illustrate, not merely the economic chaos to which even the simplest of all possible industries may be reduced by a practical application of the principle of pure democracy. They illustrate also the absence from the natural human character of anything approaching that sentiment of "each for all," on the supremacy of which the more scientific socialists of to-day have been driven to base their hopes of equal conditions and positions as the result of efforts admitted by themselves to be unequal. In accordance with what has been said in a previous chapter as to average men generally, the idea of equality appeals to the Russian peasant, like a match applied to tinder, so long as equality is a mere vague idea; but it does not appeal to him even then for its own sake. It appeals to him so long as it is a symbol of some indefinite change which comprises, as one of its incidents, some indefinite advantage for himself, and which, when its consequences are complete, will leave him in the possession of advantages greater than those of others. Thus, jealous of the high money-wages known to have been claimed and secured by the wage-earners in various factories—munition works in particular—the Russian peasants have been actually burying loaves sooner than supply them to the government for the benefit, so they put it, "of those idle fellows in Petrograd."

The factory workers, so says the same writer, have outdone the peasants by follies of a similar, but more elaborate, kind. As mentioned already in certain brief footnotes, they have demanded that the heads of complex and scientific businesses should transfer the management to committees of elected workmen, who proved so incapable of grasping the most rudimentary facts on which a scientific or any other business depends, that they sold, in order to augment their immediate wages, whatever raw materials happened to be stored on the premises, and thus deprived themselves of the means of earning any wages whatever. In certain cases the wage-earners have demanded that the employers, under pain of death, let conditions be what they may, should keep their businesses going, and pay whatever wages the wage-earners happen to demand. Thus, the writer here quoted mentions a group of eighteen engineering companies, the gross profits of which were less than eight million pounds, whilst the total wages demanded came to nearly twenty-two million. But even this demand was modest when compared with another—a demand in one business for wages which bore to the total value of the product a proportion of not less than two hundred to fifteen.

It is not surprising that, in view of facts like these, one of the revolutionary leaders declared that "Russia was on the eve of a financial and economic crash"; that "never since railways began has transport been reduced to such disorder and anarchy"; and that, unless matters should mend, "winter would find the country in the grip of a colossal famine."

Similar observations have again and again been made by the socialist writer here quoted himself, and by prominent members of the revolutionary party also, with regard to the collapse of all civil order, and to local rebellions (as at Cronstadt) against any central authority; whilst all these events have, with a dramatic fatality, culminated in one which needs no rhetoric to emphasise it—namely, the total collapse of the army wherever, or in so far as, principles accepted as those of pure democracy have prevailed. Well may the socialist writer here quoted say, "It is the irony of

fate that the most socialistic government ever formed
should find its greatest dangers in these nihilistic (or
purely destructive) activities; and that unless the
Russian government can quickly destroy *them*, they will
quickly destroy government, and destroy Russia along
with it."

To what causes, then, in the opinion of this candid
critic, are these fatal results ultimately or fundamentally
attributable? They are, he says, if we take them generally, due to the fact that "our Russian friends," as he
calls them, "have found, rather late in life, some socialist
lumber, which has now been discarded by Western democratic nations, and imagine that they have discovered
brand-new scientific truths, never used before. It will
be useful," he proceeds, "to shatter their flattering
faith, and bring them out of the clouds, to a firmer
earth, and to contact with grim realities." And of what,
then, let us ask once more, do these "clouds" of thought
consist, which "Western democratic nations have discarded as so much lumber"? This writer, in words
which have been quoted already, puts the matter very
succinctly when he says that these "clouds" consist of
the fatal idea which identifies freedom and prosperity
with the extirpation or elimination of "all controlling
persons."

Now if such observations made by a professed socialist
are taken together and analysed, it will be found that
their substance coincides in a very remarkable way with
the arguments which, from the beginning to the end of
it, have been elucidated in the present work, the coincidence amounting in some cases to an equivalence even
of phrase. For example, it has here been said that the
practical effect of the formulæ of pure democracy is to
popularise a mood of mind which may be best described
as "a disease of impossible expectations." Further,
the dementing effect of these formulæ have been here
described as comparable to those of the bite of a
tarantula. The socialist writer whose criticisms we have
just been quoting, declares that the disastrous first-fruits
of revolution in Russia "are the results of the general
upheaval of an immature population, ignorant of economics, and vaguely expectant of an immediate mil-

lennium." In short, the general mood prevalent
amongst the Russian masses—for he, too, recognises the
distinction between a mood and precise thought—was
described by him as resembling the effects of the bite
of a mad dog—in other words, as resembling, not
tarantulation, but "hydrophobia." If between the
main argument elucidated in the present work and the
arguments of a professed socialist there is, as to certain
fundamentals, a resemblance so close as this, there must
be certain elements of agreement between the principles
of the saner socialism and the principles of scientific as
distinct from mere party conservatism.

This will be still more obvious if we consider how the
argument of the writer here in question proceeds.
Having described and analysed the various events and
causes which were threatening to make the Russian
revolution hopeless, he proceeds to ask by what possible
means a situation so desperate could be retrieved; and
he answers that, in his own opinion, and in the opinion
of all Russians who had not lost their sanity, the cause
of democratic revolution could be saved by one means
only—this means being a dictatorship entrusted to the
proper hands. Further, as the one man in Russia, whose
strength of character and whose principles would fit him
for the supreme office, he did not hesitate to name
M. Kerensky; and what the principles were, on a fearless
vindication of which the success of democracy in Russia
for the time being depended, he proclaimed in no uncertain language. We can, he says, best grasp them by
remembering how in the summer of the year 1917
M. Kerensky deliberately ignored the assumed authority
of the so-called Workmen's and Soldiers' Delegates,
when he ordered, as an absolute autocrat, "the beginning of the June offensive"; how he threatened death
to all who should, by disobeying his mandates, prove
themselves, by disobeying him, "traitors to the red flag
of revolution"; and how he declared that, "for the
purpose of checking military retreat, and putting an end
to economic disorder," he would, were commands insufficient, have recourse to the methods of "blood and
iron."

Here, indeed, is a case which might, to the mere cynic,

well suggest the question, "Quis tulerit Gracchos de sedi-
tione querentes?" But the merely cynical mood will, in
a case like this, not carry us far. When men who, as
dreamers or agitators, have been clamouring for pure
democracy, find themselves transformed by action into
oligarchs or imperious autocrats, to denounce them as
renegades is not only an unjust, it is also a ludicrously
shallow, criticism. If blame attaches to them at all,
they are blamable, not because they have renounced their
old opinions, but because they ever entertained and
promulgated them. The act of renouncing them may be
an act of the highest courage; but this courage, unfor-
tunately, is not seldom accompanied by what may fairly,
though regretfully, be called a certain continuation of
cowardice. Such persons, whilst in action renouncing
their earlier principles, permit themselves to pretend,
by a gross abuse of language, that these principles are
still their own; or at all events they do their best to
hide that essential difference between their old opinions
and their new, which they recognise as dividing the principles of military collapse, civil chaos and economic
famine, from those of any possible civilisation, of any
rational freedom, of any effective industry, or secure
material welfare. They endeavour to hide this difference
by continued appeals to what they call "the red flag of
revolution"; though by every constructive act they are,
happily for their country, violating every distinctive
hope with which, in the popular mind, the "red flag"
is associated. They are in this way constantly fomenting, in the form of a vague mood, hopes which, as thinking men, they have themselves renounced as illusory,
and which, as men of action, they have made it their
task to extirpate.

M. Kerensky calls in passionate but vague tones on the
nation "to come down from the clouds," and fix their
minds on the possible instead of besotting themselves
with dreams of what is only imaginable. If he would
but teach them in what precise respects a possible programme differs from those impossible hopes which many
of his own associates have spent their lives in inflaming,
he would be accomplishing an act of statesmanship
as great as any recorded in the annals of the human

race. It would perhaps also be one of the most difficult; but it might, for the following reason, prove less difficult than it seems. The principal difficulty with which M. Kerensky and his supporters have had to contend in the task of re-establishing order is, according to their own estimate of it, and that of the English socialist who has here been freely quoted, the spirit of pure democracy which, already abroad in Russia, is determined not to submit itself to any guidance but its own. Here, however, the champions of order, and their English critic also, in spite of his sober shrewdness, appear, from facts which the latter himself records, to have gauged very imperfectly the actual nature of the situation.

In the present work the fact has been constantly emphasised that, except as to questions which are either primitively simple, restricted in their scope, or conceived so vaguely that no definite meaning is attached to them, no purely democratic will has ever any real existence, what professes to be a popular will being merely so many reverberations of what various small groups have, by their superior energy, suggested to various sections of the many. It has further been pointed out that this fundamental fact is apt to escape notice because oligarchs and oligarchies are traditionally identified with men of wealth, of distinguished birth, of culture, of commanding knowledge, and a high sobriety of intellect. This idea, it has been shown, is altogether a delusion. Men may be oligarchs, however obscure in origin, however unbalanced in intellect, provided only that they have in them an energy and a gift of speech which exceed to any great, or indeed to any appreciable, degree the persuasive powers and energies of most of the men around them. Almost every popular manifestation of discontent and disorder, in so far as it assumes any definite form, is due to such men as these; and the history of all revolutions begins as the history of a swarm of rival oligarchs, most of them squalid, none of them capable of any permanent leadership, each of them (either singly or allied with a small group of associates) endeavouring to destroy some other group or individual, and each of them pretending, by some trick of successful or unsuccessful ventriloquism, that his own voice is really

that of the people. Such is the way in which popular
revolutions begin, and two forces always combine to end
them. One of these is the experience of the people
themselves, who learn that of all evils anarchy is the
most intolerable. The other is the will of some one
man which, associated with that of strong and loyal
supporters, reduces the petty oligarchs masquerading as
democrats to a nullity, and succeeds in restoring to a
nation the order and security without which no tolerable
life is possible.

Now in what precise manner the Russian revolution
may end itself it is idle as yet to speculate; but with
regard to the initial events of it we are in a position to
say this: that the truth of the above analysis has never
been illustrated more clearly than it has, in the case of
Russia, been already illustrated by these. Thus, the
socialist correspondent, to whose evidence we will once
more return, points out that the sub-rebellion of Cronstadt—a rebellion against a rebellion—was the work, not
of "the people," as the word is commonly understood,
but of a middle-class adventurer of some scientific attain-
ments, who had never done a stroke of manual work in
his life. Again, amongst the earlier examples of rebellion
which was purely industrial, he mentions a case in which
an attempt was made at conciliation by inducing the employers to confer with ten deputies representing manual
labour. When the deputies made their appearance, they
were found to comprise two labourers only, the remainder
being middle-class men, agitators pure and simple, who
had no connection with the industries then in question
whatever. According to the same writer and others,
when independence was claimed for certain of the
southern provinces, this was the work of men who neither
had, nor pretended to have, so much as the shadow of
any popular election at the back of them. The body
which pretended to be the voice of all the workmen and
soldiers of all the Russias together consisted at first of
some 1500 persons, or one out of every 6000 of those for
whom they affected to speak. This mob being found
unmanageable, its numbers were reduced to 500, then to
five-and-twenty, and then to no more than five, these
five persons demanding recognition and obedience as the

mouthpiece of 90 millions.[1] According to trustworthy information, said *The Times* of September 13, 1917, the body of extremists whose ambition is to dominate the country "is a self-constituted organisation of idealists, theorists, anarchists, syndicalists, who are largely of the international Jew type, and who have very few workmen and very few soldiers amongst them."

If the men of strong will and practical aptitude for affairs—M. Kerensky may be taken as an example of them—through whose dictatorship alone, in the opinion even of reasonable socialists, Russia may be saved from ruin, or from the virtual dictatorship of Germany, would but realise that the foes of their own household are not the forces of pure democracy as such, but of the forces of democracy reduced to rival implements of ruin by a conflict of bastard oligarchies, a supreme directorate, whether called by name of a dictatorship or no, might recognise in these last a collection of disunited enemies who are less formidable than they seem.

The lesson, however, which is here indicated, though Russia has been teaching it to the world with unexpected and unequalled emphasis, has not been taught by the example of Russia only. History has been teaching it by example in America and Great Britain also.

The history of the formation, under President Wilson, of a will to war in America is a history less sensational, but no less profoundly significant, than the history of the dissolution in Russia of anything like a will, general and practicable of any kind, into a multitude of wills constantly shifting and conflicting—wills either too indefinite to afford guidance to anybody, or serving, in so far as they were definite, merely as guides to ruin—wills which, professing to be democratic, represent nothing more than the dreams of oligarchic visionaries, or the oligarchic ambitions and vanities of criminal or semi-criminal adventurers. In both countries the oligarchic element has been active; but its triumph in America has been constructive, the greater oligarchy of construction having extirpated or crippled the lesser oligarchies of

---

[1] These five professed representatives of the pure will of the people must not be confounded with the five quasi-dictators, with M. Kerensky at their head, who formed subsequently the official government.

disruption. In Russia, at all events for a time, the latter have done nothing but reduce the former to impotence.

Contemporary attempts at socialist rule in Great Britain have shown themselves to be, as from the nature of things they must have been, not democratic phenomena—that is to say, exhibitions of the spontaneous will of the many, but partly as the will of the many manipulated with changing and uncertain results by a few; partly as the will of a few men who, bitterly hostile to one another, have acted, planned and plotted, without any direct reference to the opinions of the many at all.

Anything like an attack on individuals has, in the present work, been, so far as possible, avoided, the aim of the writer being to establish general principles, which always remain the same, however their manifestations vary; but it will not be improper or inappropriate to allude to certain events, the mere mention of which will recall the names of certain individuals to the reader. The professors of pure democracy in Great Britain and elsewhere have constantly, and with perfect justice, declared that, if pure democracy is ever to be a realised fact, the deliberations and plans of the executive must always be public property, anything "secret," as the Russian Council of Soldiers and Workmen put it, being always and everywhere the hall-mark or brand of oligarchy. Such being undoubtedly the case, attention may be briefly called to a series of incidents which occurred in connection with the proposed presence of members of the English Labour Party at a Socialist Conference in Sweden. In the first place, these incidents turned largely on the personalities of particular men— a situation which would have been wholly impossible if the many all thought alike, for in that case any one man would be equal to any other. Events proved, however, that the many, if they had, when left to themselves, any will as to the matter at all, had a will which was never the same from one week to another. In view of these instabilities, the representatives of pure democracy, in order to make it as real and pure as possible, summoned a conference which was held behind closed doors, not a syllable of the proceedings being allowed to reach the millions of adult persons whose will was being manu-

factured within. It might be difficult to imagine any
more complete proof of how distinct is the process of
will-making from the raw popular material out of which
alone any general will can be made, if this secret conference had not been followed by a second, to which
newspaper reporters were admitted, and at which the
most prominent speaker, whose policy had been publicly
repudiated by the very masses to whom he had made
appeal, is reported to have exclaimed to his opponents,
"with a mixture of defiance and mystery," "*Your* committee and *my* executive may have done things before
many hours are over which will make you reconsider
your position." This speaker, who had once held Cabinet
rank, may, in his reasoning, his will and his policy, have
been wrong, or perfectly right. The sole fact with which
we are here concerned is that his will was, on his own
admission, an element essentially distinct from that of
the democratic masses, which, whilst professing to reflect
it, it was in reality his ambition—we may say, if we like,
his conscientious ambition—to dictate.

This confusion, however, of the oligarchic element—an
element inseparable from all complex social action—with
pure democracy, which is an element no less inseparable,
is not confined to extremists. By temperate men, men
of acute insight, men illustrious as the beneficial wielders
of oligarchic power—men illustrious as statesmen, men of
business, as political thinkers, or otherwise—this confusion is constantly disseminated in the form of vague
suggestions, though every one of such men, were he
catechised, would repudiate it as a monstrous error.
This feat of suggestion is accomplished by their almost
unabated use of the formula of pure democracy, without
even the hint of an explanation which might bring this
into harmony with the limited meaning which they
must, in their own minds, attribute to it. Democracy
is a word which may be conveniently and correctly employed to designate the constitution of any complex
State, if by all parties concerned it is understood to mean
simply a state in which the democratic principle is
powerful within certain limits; in which it is provided
with legal means of expressing itself; and which is thus
contrasted with States in which no such means exist.

But if the word is so used as to carry with it the suggestion that in political government, and in human affairs
generally, merely popular power—that is, a power in
respect of which all units are equal—is or can be
supreme in any great State whatever, and that it ought
to be supreme in all, every time the word is so used
by men of light and leading, such men are helping to
diffuse, stimulate and perpetuate a mood which, in proportion as it is generally cherished, tends to render their
own activities difficult, or at best only half successful.
They render it difficult in political government, they
render it difficult in industry, and, as events in Russia
have demonstrated, they render it impossible in war.

Let us take the chorus of official utterances which, in
Great Britain and America, have emanated from sober
and weighty statesmen, Conservative and Liberal alike,
and have been echoed and cheered by multitudes, to the
effect that the great object of the anti-Germanic nations
is to establish democracy everywhere, and utterly to
destroy autocracy. If the word "autocracy" has any
general meaning at all—if it means more than abuses of
autocracy in this country or in that—it means any kind
of power in the way of sagacity and intellect which the
many do not share with the few, or which gives to the
few any power which is out of proportion to their relatively negligible number, the essence of autocracy is oligarchy of one kind or another. Let us, then, in a spirit
of all respect for him—and the greater our respect for
him, the more pertinent will our argument *ad hominem*
be—consider in particular the case of President Wilson.
No statesman, by the exercise of his personal gifts, has
influenced the will of any great nation more conspicuously than he, in respect of a will to war, has influenced
the will of the population of the United States. What,
then, if accurately analysed, has the nature of his influence been? Has it been no more than it ought to
have been according to the philosophers of the French
Revolution, who declared that democracy "had no need
of chemists," and that no one citizen—even if called a
king—should count for more than one will out of so many
tens of millions? Has nothing been done by him and his
chief associates in the government, in the Press, in the

conduct of scientific industry, that could not, and would not, have been done by an equal number of units picked up by chance in the streets of New York, or of San Francisco? With equal pertinence, the same question might be asked of the leading statesmen of Great Britain, amongst whom "the cause of democracy" has been a no less frequent watchword. And in every case, if they answered it accurately, the answer of such men—let us say President Wilson, Mr. Lloyd George, or Mr. Bonar Law—would be the same. The American President and the British Prime Minister may both be sincere democrats, if the word "democrat" is used in a certain limited sense; but they are obviously, at the back of their minds, sincere oligarchs also, for the personal power which they devote their lives to exercising would not be power at all unless it were of the nature of oligarchy—unless it consisted in an exercise, by certain exceptional units, of faculties not possessed in an equal degree by all. Mr. Bonar Law, by implication, admitted this fact with great wealth of detail in his statements (published in June, 1917) as to *Business Brains, and the Men who are Winning the War.* He dwelt on the unparalleled success of the British Government in securing the aid of some hundred of the greatest employers and industrial organisers of the country, mentioning as an example one who alone, by his rare abilities, was saving the country as much as a million pounds a week; and Mr. Wilson, if he spoke for America, could give similar evidence.

If such men are, then, aware—if they show by their own actions—that the case stands really thus : that in great and complex States the principle of oligarchy plays a part no less essential than that of democracy—why do they continue to use and emphatically insist on a formula by which the principle of oligarchy is denied, or (what is the same thing) altogether suppressed? Would any such procedure be tolerable in chemistry, in medicine, in the manufacture of explosives, or the construction of an aeroplane—a procedure which consisted in laying such exclusive emphasis on one necessary factor that another, equally necessary, was not only ignored, but actually relegated by implication to the category of things rejected as superfluous, or definitely condemned as noxious?

The real solution of the difficulty lies in a full recognition of the fact to an exhibition of which, under all its aspects, the present volume has been devoted, that democracy and oligarchy are principles not mutually exclusive, but that in any great and complex State the one is the complement of the other. The formula of pure democracy has, for purposes of agitation, the great advantage of being simple, and easily reduced to a few telling words; but in proportion to its simplicity it is false and its effects fatal, for the necessary elements of civilisation are not simple, but complex. A true formula cannot, therefore, from the nature of things, be presented to the masses in the guise of an equally effective aphorism; but an approach to such an aphorism may be made by repeating what has here been said already, that in any great and civilised State *Democracy only knows itself through the co-operation of oligarchy*, or that the many can prosper only through the participation in benefits which, in the way alike of material comfort, opportunity, culture and social freedom, would be possible for no one unless the many submitted themselves to the influence or authority of the super-capable few.

INDEX